THE OFFICIAL® PRICE GUIDE TO

NATIVE AMERICAN ART

Dawn E. Reno

HOUSE OF COLLECTIBLES
Random House Reference, New York

© 2003 Dawn E. Reno

Published by House of Collectibles, a division of Random House Reference, New York, and simultaneously in Canada by Random House of Canada Limited, Toronto.

 House of Collectibles is a registered trademark and the colophon is a trademark of Random House, Inc.

www.houseofcollectibles.com

Printed in the United States of America

Design and composition by North Market Street Graphics

ISBN 0-609-80966-0

10 9 8 7 6 5 4 3 2 1

First Edition

For my dad, Donald E. Brander

IT WILL HAPPEN

The small bird will be at peace
The piñon where it feeds will rest
The wind blowing will move them
The air will breathe again
The house made of dawn will be safe
The people will be unafraid
The people who sing the Earth
The rainbow will shelter them.

—Carol Snyder Halberstadt

Table of Contents

Acknowledgements

With thanks to my contributors, without whom this book could not have been completed, and to Carol Snyder Halberstadt, the co-founder and co-ordinator of Black Mesa Enterprises for Life and Land, a nonprofit enterprise of the Dine' (Navajo) of Black Mesa, Arizona. They are working to better the economic and social conditions of the Black Mesa Dine' through preservation of traditional lifeways based on sheepherding and the sale of their products—primarily wool and weavings.

Contributors

My heartfelt gratitude to the contributors below, who offered their time, expertise, and photographs:

Arizona Tribal Collectors, Tim and Christine Walsh, Phoenix, AZ, (888) 769-9190, www.tribalcollectors.com.

Bearcloud Gallery, Rod Bearcloud Berry, P.O. Box 1011, Sedona, AZ 86339, (520) 282-4940, www.bearcloudgallery.com.

Black Eagle, P.O. Box 621, Copperopolis, CA 95228, (209) 785-5259, www.warriorart.com.

Black Tusk Gallery, Britt Germann, 4359 Main Street, Suite 101, Whistler, BC, Canada V0N 1B4, (877) 905-5540, www.blacktusk.ca.

Bockley Gallery, Todd Bockley, Minneapolis, MN, (612) 377-4260, todd@bockleygallery.com, www.bockleygallery.com.

Cristof's, Pam Nicosin and Buzz Trevathan, 420 Old Santa Fe Trail, Santa Fe, NM 87501, (505) 988-9881, www.cristofs.com.

Eastern Cherokee, Southern Iroq, and United Tribes of South Carolina, P.O. Box 7062, Columbia, SC 29202.

The Eastern Cowboys, Jay and Edith Sadow, 4235 N. 86th Place, Scottsdale, AZ 85251, www.easterncowboys.com.

Heard Museum, Phoenix, AZ.

Rosemary Hill, Niagara Arts & Cultural Center, Studio Room 216, Niagara Falls, NY 14304.

Alyssa Hinton, Carrboro, NC, www.AlyssaHinton.com.

Joseph R. "Jojo" Jojola, P.O. Box A, White Sands Missile Range, NM 88002, (505) 678-4371, www.whitesandsproductions.com.

King Galleries, Charles King, 7100 Main Street, Suite 1, Scottsdale, AZ 85251, (800) 394-1843, www.kinggalleries.com.

Native American Collections, Inc., Jill Giller, 338 Eudora Street, Denver, CO 80220, (303) 321-1071, www.nativepots.com.

Native Online, Todd Baker, www.nativeonline.com.

Sunwest Silver Co., Inc., 324 Lomas Boulevard NW, Albuquerque, NM 87102, (800) 771-3781, www.sunwestsilver.com.

Joanne Swanson, P.O. Box 53027, Koyuk, AK 99753-0027.

Tribal Expressions, Rob and Jeri Brooke, 7 South Dunton Avenue, Arlington Heights, IL 60005, (847) 590-5390, www.tribalexpressions. com.

Tribe Azure Jewelry and Art Gallery, Nicci Henry, 3966 E 26th, Tucson, AZ 85711, (520) 750-1063, www.tribeazure.com.

Turquoise Tortoise Gallery, 431 Highway 179, Sedona, AZ 86336, (520) 282-2262, www.turqtortsedona.com.

Connie Watts, Port Alberni, BC, Canada V9Y 7L7, chimsstudios@ shaw.ca.

White Buffalo Productions and Products MC, Brent and Jana Taylor, 510 Oakwood Lane, Paradise, CA 95969, (530) 877-3700, www.whitebuffaloprod.com.

Introduction

During the past couple of decades, the number of Native American artists I have met and worked with on previous books has tripled. What amazes me is that the more people I meet, the more artists come to my attention. This is a rich and rewarding field to be involved in. The artists included in this volume are incredibly talented but often spend their lifetimes without receiving proper recognition for their artistic gifts. Hopefully, books like this one will bring these artists to the forefront of American art and provide them with a venue in which to promote their work. These are the first artists of our country and thus should be viewed as the most important since they represent all that North America was. They are the past, the present, and the future. Their quiet dignity and incredible genius always astound me.

The various media with which these artists work is as different as the art they produce. Some create artistic pieces that belie the traditional Native American styles, while others create works that speak to the larger international community or to the one solitary voice with which they speak through their art. Whatever the case, the innovative manner they utilize to produce their work comes from the heart. There is no other group of people who have been the genesis for such a large and varied body of art.

An incredible network of mentoring and teaching goes on within the soul of the Native American art world. Families learn the techniques of pottery making or rug weaving from grandparents, aunts, cousins, or siblings. They teach each other how to make jewelry, how to craft silver items, how to tan hides, and how to bead baskets. Without this network, most of the artistic works within these pages would not exist. The families represented here are the heart of the Native American art world.

The galleries, festivals, shows, and museums that represent Native American artists often fight an uphill battle. Most amateur collectors have absolutely no idea of the time and effort it takes to make one small rug or a pottery bowl. The prices or values put on pieces created by Native artists often result in their getting paid mere pennies per hour for their work.

Galleries wage a continuing war in their effort to pay the artists what they deserve for their work, while getting the market to bear the weight of that artistic value. Most of the artists have no other way of making a living other than to create necklaces, baskets, rugs, or pottery. It is heartbreaking to hear stories of pots that broke during firing after a potter had spent many hours getting the piece ready for that final stage. I must commend those who represent these artists for the heroic work they are doing in getting the artists themselves recognized and respected.

As always, I must thank the vast number of people who have cooperated with me in my efforts to put together a volume such as this. I am grateful for the contributors and their e-mails, packages of photos, personal phone calls, and hospitality when I visited them. For this particular book, I must offer an additional note of thanks to the Heard Museum for opening their doors and library to me during the time I was in Phoenix. Their hospitality and excellent files on many of the artists covered here were invaluable. To my old and new friends—gallery owners, artists, and museum curators—my gratitude knows no bounds. You folks have become friends, and this mere note of thanks hardly seems to be enough.

Though I am sure that there are artists of note who have been left out of this volume, it is not because they should not be included, but rather because time, space, or lack of information stopped me. If any of my readers know of artists who should be included in the next volume, I invite you to contact me via my publisher. If I left out anyone of import, I offer my sincere apologies. However, there are more than 1,000 artists here, and my hope is that everyone reading this volume will find the information they desire.

THE OFFICIAL® PRICE GUIDE TO

NATIVE AMERICAN ART

CHAPTER 1

Art

There is a commonly held belief that most Native American artists concentrate on subject matter indicative of their culture, and though some of them do, there are many whose work is not instantly recognizable as "Indian." Those artists who produce nontraditional work would be the first to tell you that an artist is an artist is an artist, no matter their tribal affiliation. Keeping that in mind, one should celebrate the work created by the artists whose biographies are listed in this chapter because they are *artists*, not strictly because they are Native American.

When compiling a text about art, one commonly attempts to explain the contemporary by pointing to the past. However, to record a history of Native American art and to explain the myriad influences on the artists working in each tribe would be as difficult as recording the separate histories of the hundreds of tribes inhabiting North America at any given point in time. Little is known of the early artists themselves or of their work, thus we have been robbed of historical information that is commonly known about artists from other cultures. It is important to remember that art produced by Native Americans prior to the advent of the white man is just as significant as that created by Native American artists since that time. However, since there are no records of those early artists themselves, they are not included here.

Though certain schools and mentors definitely had an influence on many of the artists working during the past century, few records were kept of Native American artists (of Native Americans, period) before that time. Birth and death records of indigenous peoples are few and far between before the beginning of the 20th century, and even today we find contemporary artists whose birth dates are not recorded. Not until collectors started putting a value on the work created by Native Americans were the artistic endeavors of tribal artists considered collectible, and when that happened, European standards of information began being imposed: birth dates were recorded and tribal affiliations noted. We are not stating that birth dates were recorded *only* to note artistic achievements, but that researchers and museums deemed that information to be of some importance when learning about Native art. To the Native American artist, facts such as birth dates, death dates, and tribal affiliation weren't important; only the meaning of the artwork itself was considered to be of cultural value.

That point made, it is also important to note that, if not for the tourist trade, Native American art might still be confined to everyday objects and personal adornment. Only after tribes were confined to reservations did Native American families begin creating works of art that would be passed on to others. Many of the artists in this volume are members of a family tradition that stretches back centuries. Mothers who made pottery taught daughters; fathers who carved totem poles passed on the skill to sons; jewelry-making uncles brought nieces and nephews under their wings; grandmothers who made baskets shared their skills with generations after them. Would this tradition be a reality if those items never made it to galleries and shops? Without a doubt. Would the items created be similar to what is on the market today? Perhaps not, simply because originally the items were not created to be simply admired and enjoyed but to be utilized in daily life.

Early examples of Native American art adorned cave walls, tents, horses, pots, baskets, and everyday objects. Formal art was the work of European and Asian artists, not of the American Indian. American Indian artists did not paint simply to produce pretty pictures. Instead, they told stories through their art, relaying family histories, recording tales of battle, or providing directions to another location. Their work incorporated symbols that were used to deliver a clear, definitive meaning. Even the color of the design was important and could change the meaning of the symbol. For example, a pipe tomahawk represented a peaceful council, but if painted red, could denote a war council.

Meanings of particular symbols can also vary depending on the tribe from which a piece originates. A symbol such as a triangle or a semicircle with straight lines descending from the base represents a rain cloud and rain to one of the Pueblo tribes, but it can denote a mountain with streams to a Plains Indian, or a bear (or bear claw) to other tribes.

The Southwest tribes use many different, distinctive designs, as do the Pacific Coast, Northwest Coast, and Plains tribes. Southwestern Indians decorate pottery, rugs, sandpaintings, and Kachinas with their symbols, while Northwest Coast tribes use them on house poles, boxes, rattles, clothing, and carvings, and the Plains Indians use them on hides, blankets, and clothing.

The following list includes some of the symbols used in Native American art and might help collectors to understand the meanings in the paintings or drawings they accumulate.

arrow = protection
arrowhead = alertness
bear tracks = good omen
big mountain = abundance
bird = carefree
butterfly = beauty
cactus = sign of the desert
deer tracks = abundance of game
enclosure = surrounded
Hopi cloud = prayer for snow
horse = journey
lasso = captivity
lightning (backward "z" shape) = swiftness
lightning snake (frontward double "w" shape) = swiftness
rain clouds = good prospects
raindrops = food
rattlesnake jaw = strength
running water = no thirst
squash blossom = fertility
summer bird = prayer for warmth
sun symbol = happiness
thunderbird = bearer of happiness
thunderbird tracks = bright prospects
watchful eye = caution

Though an artist's work is often the result of a group effort (i.e., through the support of family, friends, and tribe), quite a few Native American artists also have had the help of a mentor, in the form of either another artist or a teacher. There have been many notable mentors/sponsors throughout the years, and several schools are noted for producing quite a few talented artists.

Native art has been influenced by such people as Olaf Nordmark, a muralist who taught a cross section of Native American artists; Frederick Dockstader, a former director of the Museum of the American Indian in

New York City and the holder of a large collection of some of the finest Native art; and Dorothy Dunn, a white woman who founded the first department of painting at the Santa Fe Indian School in 1932. The school was an early and important Indian school, and Dunn taught in the classical European style, instructing her students to paint without using any shadows. The Institute of American Indian Arts in Santa Fe has produced many contemporary artists and boasts a stellar group of instructors, all of whom have made their names in the art world.

During the pioneering days of the Southwest, W. H. Simpson, an advertising man, used art to lure travelers to exotic Santa Fe and Taos. Indians learned to do murals and to enlarge their work to poster size. Because of the availability of work and the encouragement given, artists built colonies in the area, and those establishments flourished and gave us a rich tapestry of works.

Since the early part of the 20th century, Native American artists have been far less restricted by cultural barriers and have begun breaking with tradition to use new media and materials not usually associated with Indian artwork. As mentioned before, these artists want to be known simply as artists, not necessarily as Native American artists—not because of a social stigma but because an artist should be able to reach across cultural barriers.

Not until Jeanne Snodgrass's documentation of Indian artists in 1968 were biographies of Native artists available in a single compilation. Snodgrass, the former curator of American Indian art at the Philbrook Art Center, gathered her information from exhibits and competitions held by the center since its first exhibit in 1946. Though other directories have been available through the years, none has attempted to collect the biographies and divide them into the different types of art that the Native artists produced through the past couple of centuries. This volume will do so in a manner believed to be efficient and complete.

The Artists

JIMMY ABEITA

Navajo (1948–) New Mexico
Painter

EDUCATION: American Academy of the Arts, Chicago.
AWARDS: Abeita's many awards include the Grand Prize at the Gallup Intertribal Ceremonials (New Mexico) and Tanner's All-Indian Invitational (Scottsdale, Arizona). Winner and featured artist of the Totah Festival, an

annual American Indian Art Festival at Farmington, New Mexico, September 2–4, 1995.

REPRESENTATION: Sunwest Silver, Albuquerque, New Mexico; Sunshine Studios, Santa Fe, New Mexico.

ABOUT THE ARTIST: In 1976 a book called *The American Indians of Abeita: "His People"* was published about this artist. The author, Joseph Stacey, called Abeita a "genius" and stated that Abeita's work was "executed to the superlative degree of Indian, Navajo, Western and American art standards." Born in Crownpoint, New Mexico, Abeita now lives in the Southwest with his wife and four children.

NARCISSO PLATERO ABEYTA
(a.k.a. Ha So De, Narciso Abeyta, "Ascending")

Navajo (1918–) Canoncito, New Mexico
Artist—various media

EDUCATION: Studied with Dorothy Dunn at the Santa Fe Indian School (1939); Somerset Academy School (1940); B.F.A., University of New Mexico (1953).

AWARDS: Fourteen, including the ITIC Grand Award.

REPRESENTATION: Kiva Gallery, Gallup, New Mexico.

ABOUT THE ARTIST: His work has been published by Tanner (1957) and in books such as *Art in America* and has been exhibited in shows such as the San Francisco World's Fair (1939–40), and his works are held at the University of Oklahoma, the Museum of New Mexico, and the Arizona State Museum. Though he follows the conventions set forth by the Santa Fe Indian School, he is considered an innovative painter.

TONY ABEYTA

Navajo (1965–) Gallup, New Mexico
Painter, printmaker

EDUCATION: Haystack Mountain School of Crafts, Deer Isle, Maine (1985); A.F.A., Institute of American Indian Arts, Santa Fe, New Mexico (1986); Lacoste, Ecole Des Beaux Arts, France (1986–87); Studio Arts Center International, Florence, Italy (1987); B.F.A., Maryland Institute College of Art, Baltimore (1988); Master Study Program, Santa Fe Institute of Fine Arts (1988); Post Baccalaureate Program, Art Institute of Chicago (1989).

AWARDS: Eight Navajo Nation Tribal scholarships (1984–89); Association of American Indian Affairs, New York, scholarship (1985); Oklahoma for Indian Opportunity, first and grand prizes (1986); Institute of American

"Dieties" by Tony Abeyta. Mixed Media, 50" × 72", $15,000. Courtesy of Turquoise Tortoise Gallery, Sedona, Az; www.turqtsesedona.com

"Spirits Together" by Tony Abeyta. Mixed Media. 70" × 50". $10,500. Courtesy of Turquoise Tortoise Gallery, Sedona, Az; www.turqtsesedona.com

Indian Arts, T. C. Cannon Memorial Award (1986); Maryland Institute College of Art scholarship (1988); Ford Foundation Minority scholarship (1990); SWAIA, Santa Fe Indian Market, awards in painting, graphics, and mixed media.

REPRESENTATION: Glenn Green Galleries, Santa Fe, New Mexico; John Cacciola Galleries, New York; Turquoise Tortoise, Sedona, Arizona; Adobe Gallery, Albuquerque, New Mexico; Abeyta Studios, Venice, Italy, and Santa Fe.

ABOUT THE ARTIST: Abeyta has experimented with sand and uses it in his paintings, working in a three-dimensional style. His style covers a wide range, from working with black and white to primary colors. Utilizing many different media, such as charcoal, oil, sand, copper, and printmaking, he has depicted strong images of Navajo deities; he incorporated those techniques when he painted a cover of *Indian Market* magazine (1992).

NADEMA AGARD

Sioux/Cherokee/Powatan
Artist

EDUCATION: B.S., art education, New York University; master's degree, art and education, Columbia University, concentrations on painting and drawing.

AWARDS: Smithsonian Institution Fellowship Award, Washington, D.C.; National Endowment for the Arts Fellowship, Washington, D.C.; and Scholar in Residence, Phelps Stokes Institute, New York.

ABOUT THE ARTIST: Agard has taught art through the New York Board of Education, as well as the American Indian community. She is multitalented, having illustrated a children's book, lectured, counseled, and taught. Because she is also multilingual, she travels around the world, participating in various summer study programs and exhibiting her work.

JOSÉ VICENTE AGUILAR

San Ildefonso (1924–) San Ildefonso Pueblo, New Mexico
Artist—watercolors

EDUCATION: Otis Institute, California; University of New Mexico; Los Angeles Trade Technical Junior College; Los Angeles County Art Institute (1954); Los Angeles Art Center School (1958–59).

ABOUT THE ARTIST: At first, this artist followed the traditional Native

American style of painting, but he experimented with different abstract techniques in his career. He has painted koshares, the clowns of ceremonial activities, as well as other subjects.

GEORGE A. AHGUPUK

Eskimo (1911–2001) Shishmaref, Seward Peninsula, Alaska
Artist—pen and ink on reindeer skin

EDUCATION: Self-taught artist.

REPRESENTATION: University of Alaska Museum Shop, Fairbanks; Alaska State Museum Show, Juneau.

ABOUT THE ARTIST: Though he had no formal training, Ahgupuk was one of the first Eskimos to achieve notoriety as a fine arts artist. Under the guidance of illustrator Rockwell Kent, Ahgupuk joined the American Artist group and exhibited with them (1937). He became so popular that his work was often copied outright. He referred to his work as "Bering Sea pictures."

PEGIE AHVAKANA

Suquamish; Washington
Ceramist, painter

EDUCATION: Institute of American Indian Arts, Santa Fe, New Mexico; Ray Vogue School of Chicago; Chicago Circle University.

REPRESENTATION: Via Gambaro Gallery, Washington, D.C.

ABOUT THE ARTIST: Ahvakana has worked as a ceramics instructor and commercial artist. Her ceramics incorporate her vision of what her Native American roots mean. Her works are held by numerous private and public collections, and she has exhibited all over the United States.

NORMAN AKERS

Osage/Pawnee (1958–)
Painter

EDUCATION: B.F.A., Kansas City Art Institute (1982); Certificate of Museum Training, Institute of American Indian Arts (1983); M.F.A., University of Illinois (1991).

AWARDS: First place, Scottsdale Indian Arts and Crafts Exhibition (1987); third place, SWAIA Indian Market (1988); Graduate Fellowship Award, University of Illinois (1988–89).

REPRESENTATION: Jan Cicero Gallery, Chicago, Illinois.

ABOUT THE ARTIST: Akers has exhibited his abstract, surreal paintings all over the country and has quite a few shows and exhibits to his credit.

GAIL ALBANY
(a.k.a. Picking Leaves)

Mohawk (1949–) Caughnawaga, Quebec, Canada
Painter

EDUCATION: Mostly self-taught; took a pottery course at Manitou Community College.

ABOUT THE ARTIST: Albany paints on leather, and her themes are usually Native American in nature. She also writes poetry.

ALVIN ELI AMASON

Aleut (1948–) Alaska
Artist—mixed media

EDUCATION: B.A., art, Central Washington University, Ellensburg, Washington (1973); M.A., painting, Central Washington University, Ellensburg (1974); M.F.A., multimedia, Arizona State University, Tempe (1976); fellowship, Alaska State Council on the Arts (1979).

REPRESENTATION: Decker/Morris Gallery, Anchorage, Alaska; Stonington Gallery, Anchorage, Alaska and Seattle, Washington.

ABOUT THE ARTIST: Amason's work is abstract, dramatic, and vivid. A widely respected teacher, his experience as an Indian is reflected in the way he passes on his education to others.

CLARA ARCHILTA

Kiowa/Apache/Tonkawa (1912–) Tonkawa, Oklahoma
Artist

EDUCATION: Self-taught artist.

AWARDS: Two First Awards, Indian Art Exhibition, Anadarko, Oklahoma, as well as many others.

ABOUT THE ARTIST: Archilta began painting in 1957 and has exhibited in many group showings in the Southwest.

PITSEOLAK ASHOONA

Inuit (1904–83) near Cape Dorset, Canada
Artist—mixed media

EDUCATION: Self-taught.

REPRESENTATION: Ashoona's work has been represented in many exhibits and is held in museums all over Canada and the United States.

ABOUT THE ARTIST: Ashoona began to draw in midlife. She recreated the world that today's Inuits have nearly forgotten, telling of the shamans, the tribal legends, and the stories her father had told her of the old days. She produced more than 7,000 drawings in her 20+-year career.

ALICE ASMAR
(a.k.a. Kha-ye-povi)

Santa Clara (1929–) Santa Clara Pueblo, New Mexico
Artist—all media (colored ink a specialty)

EDUCATION: B.A., Lewis and Clark College, Portland, Oregon; M.F.A., University of Washington.

REPRESENTATION: Her mural of Los Angeles, painted in acrylic on concrete, is at the Metro Medical Mall. Collections containing her work range from the Smithsonian to the National Museum in Bulgaria.

ABOUT THE ARTIST: Asmar paints Indians because she sees them "as America's real ecologists." Solo shows of her work have been held at the Gallerie de Fondation des Etas-Unis, Paris, in New York, in Italy, at the Minnesota Museum of Art, and with the Western Association of Art Museums.

GILBERT ATENCIO
(a.k.a. Wah Peen, "Mountain of the Sacred Wind")

San Ildefonso/Spanish/Navajo (1930–95) Greeley, Colorado
Artist—various media

EDUCATION: Santa Fe Indian School (1947).

AWARDS: Two years after graduating, Atencio had already won 17 competitions. He continued to win many awards after that time.

REPRESENTATION: Adobe Gallery, Albuquerque, New Mexico.

ABOUT THE ARTIST: Atencio came from an artistic family (his aunt was Maria Martinez and his mother was Isabel Montoya) and used traditional Pueblo ceremonial figures in his work. In the 1950s his work was realistic, but in the 1960s he became interested in abstract representations of dance figures, pottery, and other symbols of Pueblo life.

JAMES AUCHIAH
(a.k.a. Tse-koy-ate, "Big Bow")

Kiowa (1906–75) Meers, Oklahoma
Artist—opaque watercolors

EDUCATION: Special training in art, University of Oklahoma, Norman (1947).

AWARDS: Certificate of Appreciation, Indian Arts and Crafts Board/U.S. Department of Interior (1966).

ABOUT THE ARTIST: Auchiah was associated with the original "Five Kiowa Artists." He did murals for the St. Patrick's Mission School, the U.S. Department of the Interior, and the Oklahoma Historical Society in the 1920s–30s and painted in the Oklahoma style.

SONJA K. AYRES

AWARDS: Best of Division (graphics) at the 1994 Five Civilized Tribes Competitive Show at Muskogee, Oklahoma; first place, traditional beadwork, Chickasaw Nation.

TODD BAKER

Squamish (1965–) North Vancouver, British Columbia, Canada
Drawer, Graphic Artist, Illustrator.

EDUCATION: Several years of postsecondary education. Self-taught and mentored by Bill Reid.

AWARDS: Commissioned to create "Love Doves" for the Peace Federation of Canada and a variation of those doves for the Teachers' Federation of British Columbia.

REPRESENTATION: Native Online, Todd Baker, www.nativeonline.com.

ABOUT THE ARTIST: The grandson of great leader and speaker Chief Khot-la-cha (Chief Simon Baker), Baker started drawing at the age of 13, then

Thunderbird design silkscreen by Todd Baker. Photo by Martin Ortmayr. Courtesy Todd Baker.

started creating limited editions in 1983 when artist-carver Bill Reid critiqued Baker's first piece. He has worked in the fashion world and began school in Los Angeles and New York. As a fashion designer, he worked for Donna Karan and the Gap. He lived and worked in Europe and New York for nine years, then returned home to work with his Northwest Coast graphics.

MARJORIE BARNES

Mohawk (1957–) Hogansburg, New York
Painter, photographer, ceramist

EDUCATION: Took art classes at the Salmon River Central School; fine arts major at City College of New York (1975–77) and St. Lawrence University (1977–79).

ABOUT THE ARTIST: Barnes uses Iroquois symbols in her work and gets some of her inspiration from traditional Iroquois stories. She paints in an abstract style, with clean lines and blocks of color. She teaches art, has done illustrations, and is known as a photographer and sculptor as well.

RICK E. BARTOW

Yurok (1946–) South Beach, Oregon
Artist; sculptor—mixed media

EDUCATION: B.A., Western Oregon State College, Monmouth (1969).

AWARDS: Bartow's many awards and commissions include being part of the Washington State Arts Commission's "Who We Are: Autobiographies in Art" (1991); as well as fellowships from the Brandywine Visiting Artist Fellowship, Philadelphia, Pennsylvania, and the Oregon Arts Commission Fellowship in Visual Arts.

REPRESENTATION: Jamison/Thomas Gallery, Portland, Oregon; Stonington Gallery, Anchorage, Alaska and Seattle, Washington.

ABOUT THE ARTIST: Bartow lives on land that belonged to his Yurok father. He travels widely to meet other Native peoples. Influenced by Northwest Coast masks and carvings, Bartow's contemporary sculptures are often taken for the traditional ones carved many years ago. His paintings and drawings have been part of many exhibits, both solo and group, including some held at the Jamison/Thomas Gallery and at galleries in Japan, Germany, and the United States. Collections of his work are held by the Portland Art Museum, the Heard Museum, and the Metropolitan Arts Commission in Portland, Oregon, to name a few.

JOSEPH BEAUVAIS
(a.k.a. Kanawarenton)

Mohawk (1922–mid-1970s)
Painter, framer

EDUCATION: Self-taught.

ABOUT THE ARTIST: After an accident that left Beauvais paralyzed, he recovered and eventually set up a studio for himself so that he could paint. He taught himself the art by reading and listening to art critics.

FRED BEAVER
(a.k.a. Eka Le Ne, "Brown Head")

Creek/Seminole (1911–76) Eufala, Oklahoma
Artist—watercolors

EDUCATION: Bacone Junior College, Oklahoma; Haskell Indian Institute, Kansas.

REPRESENTATION: Nineteen one-man shows. Work is held in numerous public and private collections including the Stephen Foster Memorial in White Springs, Florida; the Hotel Lawtonka in Ardmore, Oklahoma; the Philbrook Art Center in Tulsa, Oklahoma; and the Heard Museum in Phoenix.

ABOUT THE ARTIST: The son of Willie Beaver and Annie Johnson, Fred grew up in Eufala, Oklahoma, and graduated from the high school there. He went to college, then took the position of clerk and interpreter under the Five Civilized Tribes Agency for the Bureau of Indian Affairs. In 1942 he began serving three years in Europe in the U.S. Air Corps and continued his career in the Corps until 1960. During that period he also taught art and voice in Italy. Beaver spent his life speaking for his people and showing their history through his art. His paintings show the Seminole and Creek peoples before the Great Seminole War and the Trail of Tears. In 1970 he said, "I wanted to change the non-Indian's image of my people." Beaver's trademark was his utilization of monochromatic color.

ROBERT BECENTI

Navajo; Crown Pointe, New Mexico
Artist—acrylics

ABOUT THE ARTIST: Known as a realistic painter of Navajo life in the Red Rocks area of New Mexico. Uses bright colors in his acrylic-on-canvas paintings.

CLIFFORD BECK

Navajo (1946–95)
Artist

ABOUT THE ARTIST: Beck often created pastel portraits and sometimes used the old Anasazi symbols in his paintings.

LARRY BECK

Yup'ik (1938–) Seattle, Washington
Sculptor—mixed media; painter

EDUCATION: B.F.A., sculpture, and M.F.A., painting, University of Washington, Seattle.

ABOUT THE ARTIST: As with many other Native artists, Beck's inspiration comes from the stories he knows of his ancestors. He especially is influenced by Yup'ik masks. His materials are often recycled, "found" objects.

MARY (THOMPSON) BECKMAN

(a.k.a. Jostwi)

Onondaga; Nedrow, New York
Painter, beadworker, jeweler, native clothing designer

EDUCATION: Took painting classes at Roosevelt School in Syracuse, as well as at the Cayuga Museum.

ABOUT THE ARTIST: Beckman's work has been exhibited throughout New York. She also teaches and writes. Her paintings are landscapes, still lifes, wildlife, and, sometimes, portraits.

ARTHUR C. BEGAY

Navajo (1931–) Newcomb, New Mexico
Artist

EDUCATION: 1950s fellowship with Norman Rockwell.
REPRESENTATION: Sunshine Studios, Sante Fe, New Mexico.

HARRISON BEGAY

(a.k.a. Warrior Who Walked Up to His Enemy/Haskay Yah Ne Yah)

Navajo (1917–) White Cone, Arizona
Painter, illustrator, printmaker, muralist, potter

EDUCATION: The Santa Fe Indian School (1939) under Dorothy Dunn (The

Studio); architecture, Black Mountain (1940–41); attended Phoenix Junior College (1941).

AWARDS: His work has won many awards and has been exhibited in such shows as the First Annual American Indian Art Exhibition in 1964 at Wayne State University, the Museum of Modern Art in New York, and the Philbrook Art Center. He has also won a special commendation from the French government for his contributions to the arts.

REPRESENTATION: Amerind Foundation Museum Shop, Dragoon, Arizona; Kiva Gallery, Gallup, New Mexico.

ABOUT THE ARTIST: Begay likes to paint scenes from the traditional Navajo past, as well as today's events. Internationally known, Begay's work has had a great influence on other Navajo artists, and he is the best-known Navajo artist of the Southwest movement. His works have been published by Frederick Dockstader (director of the Museum of the American Indian, 1961) and in a number of other publications.

DENNIS BELINDO
(a.k.a. Aun-So-Te, "Foot")

Kiowa/Navajo (1938–) Phoenix, Arizona
Artist

EDUCATION: Studied art at Bacone College, Northeastern State College, and the University of Oklahoma.

AWARDS: Has won many awards throughout the Southwest.

ABOUT THE ARTIST: Belindo, a law student who turned to art and eventually became professor of art at the University of California at Berkeley, has exhibited in group and one-man shows throughout the United States.

ROD BEARCLOUD BERRY

Osage (1950–) Amarillo, Texas

EDUCATION: Studied art at Amarillo College, Texas State Institute, and the University of Maryland in England.

REPRESENTATION: Bearcloud Gallery, Sedona, Arizona.

ABOUT THE ARTIST: Bearcloud works in several media. Originally a painter, he speaks of his art as arriving "from the visions that come to me through the sacred pipe and other ceremonies, in the way of my people." He now works in bronze, clay, and acrylic, especially loving acrylic because it has more light. His paintings often have hidden images in them, speaking beyond landscape and into the spirit. He also makes his own frames, letting the mats expand the boundaries of the painting.

Shaman #2 by Frank Big Bear, 2000, 22" × 21.75", prisma color pencil on paper.

FRANK BIG BEAR

Ojibway (1953–) White Earth Reservation, Minnesota
Painter, muralist.

EDUCATION: Studied with George Morrison, University of Minnesota Studio Arts (1973).

AWARDS: Selected grants: Bush Foundation Fellowship (1986, 1998).

REPRESENTATION: Bockley Gallery, Minneapolis, Minnesota.

ABOUT THE ARTIST: Big Bear has done many solo exhibits, and his work is held in numerous collections and museums throughout the United States. One of the special projects he's done was a mural painted in 1994–98, called "Dream Catcher Love Song," for P.S. 75, Mayda Cortiella School, Brooklyn, New York, under the New York Percent for the Art Program.

Untitled Frank Big Bear, 2000, 13.75" × 9.75", prisma color pencil on paper. Courtesy Bockley Galleries, Minneapolis, MN.

WOODY BIG BOW
(a.k.a. Tse-Koy-Ate, "Big Bow")

Kiowa (1914–) Carnegie, Oklahoma
Artist

EDUCATION: University of Oklahoma.

ABOUT THE ARTIST: Big Bow has shown his work throughout the United States and has painted murals for the RCA Building in New York, as well as others.

ARCHIE BLACKOWL
(a.k.a. Mis Ta Moo To Va, "Flying Hawk")

Cheyenne (1912–67) Weatherford, Oklahoma
Artist—many media; illustrator; muralist

EDUCATION: The Seger Indian School; the Chilocco Indian School; studied under Olaf Nordmark, a muralist, at the Indian Art Center in Fort Sill, Oklahoma; studied watercolor at the University of Kansas; studied art at the Art Institute of Chicago, the Rockefeller Art Center, and the Washington D.C. School of Fine Arts.

AWARDS: Numerous, including awards at Santa Fe Indian Market and many national awards.

REPRESENTATION: Blue Deer Gallery, Dallas, Texas.

ABOUT THE ARTIST: Blackowl painted murals for quite a few institutions, portraits of public officials, and illustrations for the Georgia Agricultural Extension Service and was author-illustrator of *Charts for Visual Instruction*. Various publications printed his work. He has held exhibits throughout the United States at galleries and museums, such as the Agra Gallery in Washington, D.C., the Oklahoma Art Center, and various colleges and universities, and his work is held in collections throughout the United States. Made a chief of the Cheyenne Sun Dance clan in 1945, Blackowl resigned from his duties for financial reasons. After that time, he continued to paint the Cheyenne rituals and traditions.

ALEX BOMBERRY

Lower Cayuga (1953–) Caledona, Ontario, Canada
Artist—acrylics, pen and ink, pencil, watercolors

EDUCATION: Took some art classes in high school, as well as summer classes with the Manitou Art Foundation.

ABOUT THE ARTIST: Bomberry's paintings are stylized, photolike portraits of Native Americans. He gives them all titles and has exhibited his work in Canadian exhibits. Bomberry is also interested in photography and filmmaking.

FRANCIS BLACKBEAR BOSIN
(a.k.a. Tsate Kongia, Sate-Kon-Gia, "Blackbear")

Kiowa/Comanche (1921–80) near Anadarko, Oklahoma
Artist—watercolors, gouache on illustration board

EDUCATION: Self-taught. Saint Patrick's Mission School.

AWARDS: More than 30, including Fellow, International Institute of Arts and Letters, Kreuzlingen, Switzerland (1956); Certificate of Appreciation, Indian Arts and Crafts Board, U.S. Department of Interior (1966); and Waite Phillips Trophy for Outstanding Contributions to American Indian Art, Philbrook Art Center, Tulsa, Oklahoma (1967).

ABOUT THE ARTIST: Bosin's art reflected his feelings about what this country would have been like if Columbus hadn't discovered it in 1492. He painted the spiritual, tribal history and myths of Native American life. He was the first generation after his tribe had been "conquered" and put on reservations, and thus felt a moral obligation to paint his people in the same type of manner the storytellers of the tribe used to tell their history. He first came to recognition when *National Geographic* featured his painting "Prairie Fire." Owner and operator of the Great Plains Studio and Gallery in Wichita, Kansas, Bosin exhibited his work in group, as well as one-man, shows throughout the United States and abroad.

FILBERT BOWANNIE
Zuni
Artist—watercolors

REPRESENTATION: Sunshine Studio, Sante Fe, New Mexico.

ABOUT THE ARTIST: Bowannie specializes in detailed watercolors of Zuni tribal ceremonies.

PARKER BOYIDDLE, JR.
Wichita/Delaware/Chickasaw/Kiowa (1948–) Oklahoma
Artist—oils

EDUCATION: Classen High School, Oklahoma City (1965); art scholarship at the Oklahoma Science and Art Foundation.

AWARDS: First place, sculpture, Santa Fe Indian Market (2000).

REPRESENTATION: Sunwest Silver, Inc., Albuquerque, New Mexico.

ABOUT THE ARTIST: His work has been exhibited at Riverside Museum in New York. He's one of three artists who contributed to murals at the Kiowa Tribal Museum in Carnegie, Oklahoma.

LYNDA (HAYFIELD) BRANT

Mohawk (1954–) Kingston, Ontario, Canada
Artist—oils, watercolors, pastels, pencil, pen and ink

EDUCATION: Art major at the Ontario College of Arts.

ABOUT THE ARTIST: Continuously learning, Brant has added photography, beadwork, and pottery to her list of arts. She often sketches from life, then paints the scene later. She has exhibited her work at the Mohawk Fall Fair.

LOUIS BROWN

Navajo (d. 1990)
Artist—tempera

REPRESENTATION: Sunshine Studio, Sante Fe, New Mexico.

ABOUT THE ARTIST: Brown is known for his 1970s–80s paintings of night dances in tempera. His works received little recognition before his death.

CLIFFORD BRYCELEA

Navajo
Painter

EDUCATION: Fort Lewis College, Durango, Colorado (1975).

AWARDS: Brycelea has won many awards, among them three gold medals from the American Indian Cowboy Artists Society, and Indian Arts and Crafts Association 1987 Artist of the Year.

Acrylic painting, Clifford Brycelea, Courtesy of Tribal Expressions, American Indian Art Gallery, Arlington Heights, IL.
www.tribalexpressions.com.

REPRESENTATION: Tribal Expressions, Arlington Heights, Illinois

ABOUT THE ARTIST: If Brycelea paints a sacred ceremonial scene or object, he "say[s] a prayer and sprinkle[s] corn pollen." Though he is Navajo, he paints scenes from all different tribes and is a student of Native American life.

LES BUCKTOOTH

Onondaga (1957–) Nedrow, New York
Illustrator—pen and ink, pencil, chalk, acrylics

EDUCATION: Self-taught.

AWARDS: Among Bucktooth's awards are ribbons from the New York State Fair, a Gold Key Award, and many others.

ABOUT THE ARTIST: Bucktooth likes to do traditional as well as modern drawings. He is especially drawn to nature and animals. He can also string lacrosse sticks and works with beads, leather, and wood.

BENJAMIN FRANKLIN BUFFALO

(a.k.a. Bennie Franklin Buffalo, "Going South")

Cheyenne (1948–) Clinton, Oklahoma
Artist—acrylics

EDUCATION: Studied painting at the San Francisco Art Institute, California.

ABOUT THE ARTIST: Buffalo's style has gotten away from the traditional style and is now focused on an almost-photographic realism, portraying his people as they are today.

STAR WALLOWING BULL

Chippewa (1973–) White Earth Reservation, Minnesota
Painter

Painting, "Distant . . . " by Star Wallowing Bull. Courtesy Bockley Galleries, Minneapolis, MN.

Painting, "Shame-n" by Star
Wallowing Bull. Courtesy Bockley
Galleries, Minneapolis, MN.

EDUCATION: Self-taught.

AWARDS: Smithsonian National Museum of the American Indian, Native
Artist Fellowship (2001).

REPRESENTATION: Bockley Gallery, Minneapolis, Minnesota.

ABOUT THE ARTIST: Star Wallowing Bull's use of color is innovative and
surprising. He creates contemporary paintings with Native American
themes. In the past couple of years, he has been quite active in solo, as well
as group, exhibits, and his work is held in several museums.

DIANE M. BURNS

Anishinabe/Chemehuevi (1957–)
Painter

EDUCATION: Institute of American Indian Arts, Santa Fe, New Mexico
(1974); Barnard College, Columbia University, New York.

AWARDS: Received the Manuel J. Lujan Congressional Medal of Merit for
academic and artistic excellence while at the Institute of American Indian
Arts.

ABOUT THE ARTIST: Burns has exhibited her paintings all over the United
States, including the 1974 Minnesota Governor's Invitational and the 1979
American Indian Community House Gallery Invitational, as well as the
National American Indian Women's Art Show in 1980. Burns is also a
poet and has published several collections.

JEROME GILBERT BUSHYHEAD

(a.k.a. Coyote Walks By)

Cheyenne (1929–April 15, 2000) Calumet, Oklahoma
Artist—tempera on illustration board and other media

EDUCATION: Studied art at Centenary College, Shreveport, Louisiana.

ABOUT THE ARTIST: Bushyhead painted in the traditional Indian style,
often depicting his people as they were in the past. He identified with the

Native American hunter-warrior and avoided gimmicky "Southwestern style" painting. In the mid-1970s, he went to battle for the right of Native Americans to use feathers in their work and won.

TOM WAYNE CANNON
(a.k.a. T. C. Cannon, Pai Doung U Day, "One Who Stands in the Sun")

Caddo/Kiowa (1946–78) Lawton, Oklahoma
Artist—oil on canvas, acrylic on canvas

EDUCATION: Studied under Fritz Scholder at the American Indian Art in Santa Fe, New Mexico (1964–66); studied painting at the San Francisco Art Institute (1966), as well as at the College of Santa Fe, New Mexico (1969–70) and Central State University, Edmond, Oklahoma (1970).

AWARDS: Governor's Trophy at Scottsdale National Indian Art Exhibition (1966), as well as many other awards.

REPRESENTATION: Broschofsky Galleries, Ketchum, Idaho; 21st Century Fox Fine Art, Santa Fe, New Mexico; Wheelwright Museum of the American Indian/Case Trading Post, Arizona.

ABOUT THE ARTIST: This artist used abstract expressionism and pop art to depict the two levels on which the modern Native American lives—one, set in the white world; the second, their native Indian world. Cannon worked as a mainstream modern artist and was often compared to Fritz Scholder.

POP CHALEE
(a.k.a. Marena Lujan, Marina Lujan Hopkins, "Blue Flower")

Taos/East Indian (1908–93) Castle Dale, Utah
Artist

EDUCATION: Tutored by Dorothy Dunn, Santa Fe Indian School (1930s).

ABOUT THE ARTIST: Chalee's style, a light, surrealistic fantasy world, shows the influence of both cultures in which she was raised (her mother was from India). Her work usually is filled with forest creatures who are stylized and delicate (what has since been called the "Bambi" style of painting). She exhibited all over the world and was considered a major influence for female Native American artists.

JEFFREY CHAPMAN
Ojibway (1958–)
Painter, carver, sculptor

EDUCATION: Minneapolis Community College (1977–78); B.F.A., Minneapolis College of Art and Design (1984).

AWARDS: Many, including first and second place for both watercolor painting and graphics at the Annual Minnesota Ojibway Art Expo.

REPRESENTATION: Jan Cicero Gallery, Chicago, Illinois.

ABOUT THE ARTIST: Chapman has exhibited his work in both solo and group shows throughout the Midwest, has been commissioned to create works for the Science Museum of Minnesota, and is active in his community. He is also known as a flute carver and has held many demonstrations of that talent.

CHARGING THUNDER FAMILY

Author's note: This contemporary artist family includes several working artists: Earl Charging Thunder, Alma Charging Thunder, Faye Charging Thunder, Agnes Charging Thunder, Kathy Charging Thunder, Pauline Charging Thunder, and Nora Brings Him Back.

Lakota (various birth dates)

ABOUT THE ARTISTS: The Charging Thunder Family's genealogy extends into other artistic families as well. One of the reasons this book and exhibits held at the Heritage Center, Inc., groups this family together as artists is because they learn from each other, work together, and depend on each other in their daily lives, as well as their artistic lives. For further information on each additional artist, contact the Heritage Center, Inc., in South Dakota (see address in galleries' listings).

FLORENCE NUPOK CHAUNCEY
(a.k.a. Malewotkuk)

Eskimo (1906–71) Village of Gambell, St. Lawrence Island, Alaska
Artist—pen and ink on seal skin

EDUCATION: Self-taught artist.

ABOUT THE ARTIST: Chauncey drew scenes of her people, the walrus, and other animals around her and earned the title Grandma Moses of the Bering Sea. She was chosen as one of 32 Eskimo artists accepted into the Designer-Craftsman Training Project in 1964. The only woman in the project, she completed the program in 1965 and produced work in pen and ink, watercolor, pencil, and crayon. She began producing commercial artwork on paper and plastic items in the later 1960s, often under the auspices of Bering Sea Originals. Her work is held by the University of Alaska in Fairbanks, the Philbrook Art Center, the National Museum of the American Indian, and other museums throughout the country. She died in 1971 after a lengthy illness.

ROBERT CHEE

Navajo (1938–71) Billemont, Arizona
Artist—watercolors, pencil

EDUCATION: Attended school in Billemont, Arizona. Studied under Allen Houser (Apache).

ABOUT THE ARTIST: Chee's works have been published by such magazines as *New Mexico Magazine* and the *Inter-Tribal Indian Ceremonial Annual Magazine*. His work has been exhibited in the Museum of New Mexico and the Philbrook Art Center. Public collections of his work are held by the Museum of New Mexico, the Philbrook Art Center, the Bureau of Indian Affairs, as well as many others.

LESLIE CLAUS

Mohawk (1909–) Tyendinaga Reserve, Ontario, Canada
Painter, sculptor, photographer

EDUCATION: During his career, Claus has worked with many well-known artists in Canada.

AWARDS: Claus has participated in juried shows since 1968.

ABOUT THE ARTIST: An active schoolteacher, Claus always worked to perfect his skills. Much of his early work is pencil, pen and ink, or oil, but he began working in watercolors during the late 1970s and has also taken pottery and leatherworking classes. Claus has been active in Native American art and cultural programs and was a member of the Board of Governors of the Woodland Indian Cultural Education Centre. He retired from teaching in 1974.

FARRELL COCKRUM

Blackfoot; northern Montana
Painter, sculptor—mixed media

EDUCATION: Institute of American Indian Arts, Santa Fe, New Mexico (1984).

REPRESENTATION: Sunwest Silver, Albuquerque, New Mexico; Soaring Eagle Gallery, Inc.

ABOUT THE ARTIST: Cockrum grew up on the Blackfoot reservation in Browning, Montana, and showed an early interest in art. He attempts to introduce the world to his people via his contemporary art and works in several different media, inspired by his dreams and beliefs in the Creator.

GREY COHOE

Navajo (1944–) New Mexico
Artist—oils, acrylics

ABOUT THE ARTIST: Cohoe's work often addresses the gap between the white world and the Indian, with biting sarcasm and portents of evil.

DON CONKLIN

Seneca (1957–) Irving, New York
Painter—acrylics, pen and ink, block printing

EDUCATION: Art major SUNY at Fredonia, New York.
AWARDS: Conklin has garnered several honors for his work.
ABOUT THE ARTIST: Conklin works mostly with acrylics or pen and ink. He enjoys drawing landscapes and wildlife. He has also done some sculpture and silversmithing.

DOLORES PURDY CORCORAN

Caddo; Binger, Oklahoma
Painter—oils, watercolors

AWARDS: Three honorable mentions, Lawrence Indian Arts Show, Kansas.
REPRESENTATION: Southwest and More, Lawrence, Kansas.
ABOUT THE ARTIST: As a child, Corcoran and her family moved frequently. Now that she's an adult, she has settled in Kansas, has worked with several different media, and is starting to garner some local art awards.

RAY P. CORNELIUS

Oneida (1955–) Southwold, Ontario, Canada
Artist—drawings, soapstone carvings

EDUCATION: Largely self-taught, though he has taken classes at Laurier Secondary School in London.
AWARDS: Cornelius's awards for his work include several first prizes for drawings at the Oneida Fall Fair.
ABOUT THE ARTIST: Cornelius's medium of choice is pencil or pen and ink. Though most of his subjects are Native American in nature, he sometimes draws cartoons or comic book characters. He also works in soapstone, carving figures and faces.

BILL CROUSE
(a.k.a. Gahatageyat)

Seneca (1963–) Salamanca, New York
Painter—acrylics, oils, watercolors, pencil, pen and ink, charcoal, pastels, wood; wood-carver

EDUCATION: Mostly self-taught, although he has taken some classes in wood-carving.

ABOUT THE ARTIST: Crouse sketches portraits and Iroquois games and dances; he also does some wood-carving. In addition to his art, he writes poetry and has been dancing and singing all his life, an avid believer in longhouse customs. As a member of the Hawk clan, he acts as a representative of Faith at the Allegany reservation. Crouse's work as a dancer and singer with the Seneca Dance Group has garnered him national recognition, and he was part of a PBS program on Native American dance and dancers.

WOODROW WILSON CRUMBO
(a.k.a. Woody Crumbo)

Creek/Potawatomi (1912–89) Lexington, Oklahoma
Artist—oils, watercolors, drawing, murals

EDUCATION: Studied under Susie Peters, muralist Olaf Nordmark, watercolorist Clayton Henri Staples, and artist O. B. Jacobson. Attended Chilocoo Indian School; American Indian Institute, Wichita, Kansas; Wichita University (1933–36); University of Oklahoma; Wichita State University. Director of art for Bacone College in Muskogee, Oklahoma.

AWARDS: Many honors, including the Julius Rosenwald Fellowship. Inducted into the Oklahoma Hall of Fame in 1978.

REPRESENTATION: Philbrook Museum of Art Shop, Tulsa, Oklahoma; Eagles Roost Gallery, Colorado Springs, Colorado.

ABOUT THE ARTIST: His first painting, "Deer and Birds," was given to the Philbrook Art Center in 1939. In 1944 Crumbo convinced the Philbrook to sponsor the first national Indian art show. Crumbo, the artist-in-residence at the Gilcrease Museum, assembled an American Indian and Western art collection in 1945 and also served as the assistant director of the El Paso Museum of Art (1962–68). Exhibitions of his work have been held nationally and internationally. Collections are held by the Philbrook Art Center, the Gilcrease Institute, the Southeast Museum of the North American Indian, and many others. Crumbo is considered a major influence on other Native American painting, especially in the Southwest.

RICHARD GLAZER DANAY
(a.k.a. Ric Danay)

Mohawk (1942–) Coney Island, New York
Artist—various media

EDUCATION: B.A., California State University, Northridge; M.F.A., University of California at Davis.

ABOUT THE ARTIST: Danay's three-dimensional works are sexy, dry, ironic, humorous, sarcastic, and biting. One can safely say each of the works would have a different interpretation depending upon who was doing the interpreting. He often creates art in response to a historical event or theme.

NEIL DAVID

Hopi
Artist—various media

EDUCATION: Largely self-taught, but has learned some techniques from family members.

REPRESENTATION: Sunshine Studio, Sante Fe, New Mexico.

ABOUT THE ARTIST: David is best known as a Hopi Kachina carver, but he does some paintings of Kachinas and koshares as well.

DAVID DAWANGYUMPTEWA

Hopi (1957–)
Painter—gouache, watercolors

AWARDS: Solo exhibitions at the Southwest Museum in Los Angeles and the Wheelwright Museum of the American Indian, Santa Fe, New Mexico. Honors and awards at the Heard Museum Indian Fair, the Santa Fe Indian Market, and numerous other competitions.

ABOUT THE ARTIST: Dawangyumptewa paints in the abstract style and uses a lot of symbolism in his work. He frequently uses water as a staple in his painting, a reflection of his membership in the Water clan.

FRANK DAY

Maidu (1902–76) Berry Creek, California
Artist—oil on canvas

EDUCATION: Self-taught.

ABOUT THE ARTIST: Day's father taught him the old ways of his people, and Day felt an obligation to pass on his knowledge to the younger generation in his art. He was part of a revitalization movement among California Native American artists in the 1960s.

PATRICK DESJARLAIT
(a.k.a. Nagawbo, "Boy of the Woods")

Ojibway/Chippewa (1921–73) Red Lakes Reservation, Minnesota
Artist—watercolors

EDUCATION: Pipestone Indian Training School, Pipestone, Minnesota; Phoenix Junior College, Arizona.

ABOUT THE ARTIST: Though discouraged from speaking in his native language or learning anything about the history, traditions or culture of his people, DesJarlait rebelled and began to learn about his heritage anyway—using all he learned about the culture and traditions of the Chippewa people in his stylized paintings. His work is often reflective of Mexican muralists work and has touches of cubism, and it is held in several Minnesotan museums.

CECIL DICK
(a.k.a. Dagadahga, "Standing Alone")

Cherokee (1915–) Rose, Oklahoma
Artist—watercolors, tempera

EDUCATION: Educated in government boarding schools; studied painting at Santa Fe Indian School (The Studio) under Dorothy Dunn and at Bacone Junior College under Woody Crumbo.

AWARDS: Sequoyah Medal, highest medal conferred by the Cherokee Nation (1983).

ABOUT THE ARTIST: Dick is an authority on Cherokee myth and language. He paints highly active, competitive scenes of Cherokee life and legend, frequently including horses in his work. He uses brightly colored paints in his work. The Studio strongly influenced his work and gave it a monumental quality.

DUANE DISHTA
Zuni
Artist—acrylics

REPRESENTATION: Sunshine Studio, Sante Fe, New Mexico.

ABOUT THE ARTIST: Dishta paints Zuni ceremonial portraits, dancers, and Kachinas. His work was included in Barton Wright's *Kachinas of the Sun*.

BILL DIXON

Navajo (1950–) Winslow, Arizona
Painter—rock art

EDUCATION: Self-taught.
REPRESENTATION: Sunwest Silver Inc., Albuquerque, New Mexico.
ABOUT THE ARTIST: This artist does work similar to the ancient petroglyphs. He has sold paintings as well as stone art and is currently working
on his "own style."

TOM "TWO ARROWS" DORSEY
(a.k.a. Ga Hes Ka, "Two Arrows")

Onondaga (1920–) Onondaga Reservation, New York
Artist—watercolors; potter; jeweler; weaver

EDUCATION: Self-taught.
ABOUT THE ARTIST: Dorsey is a member of the Falseface Society and
Onondaga Wolf clan. He is known worldwide as an expert on Native
American design and legend, often using Woodlands symbols in his work.

ALTA DOXTADOR

Cayuga (1909–) Caledonia, Ontario, Canada
Painter—oils

EDUCATION: Mostly self-taught.
ABOUT THE ARTIST: Doxtador's paintings were of nature scenes or birds.
She was the granddaughter of Jim Beaver, the earliest acknowledged Iro-
quois painter.

TENNYSON ECKIWAUDAH
(a.k.a. Yutsuwuna, "Able to Stand Up Again")

Comanche (1912–) Anadarko, Oklahoma
Artist—oil on canvas

EDUCATION: Largely self-taught, Eckiwaudah also studied illustration
through a correspondence course.
AWARDS: His many awards include those won at the Indian Art Exhibition
in Anadarko, Oklahoma (1961–62), and the All American Indian Days,
Sheridan, Wyoming (1966), as well as others.
ABOUT THE ARTIST: Eckiwaudah was commissioned to design paintings for
several Native American tribal groups and is widely known for his spiritual
paintings. He is often inspired by the rites of the Native American Church.

KEN EDWARDS
(a.k.a. Ken Rainbow Cougar)

Colville Confederated Tribes (1956–) Greenville, South Carolina
Painter—pen and ink, watercolors

EDUCATION: Institute of American Indian Arts (high school and college), Santa Fe, New Mexico; Haskell Indian Junior College, Lawrence, Kansas.

AWARDS: First place, painting, Hunter Mountain Eagle Indian Festival, Hunter, New York (1994); third place, painting, Aspen Celebration for the American Indian, Aspen, Colorado (1994); second place, painting, Milwaukee Indian Summer Festival, Milwaukee, Wisconsin (1994); as well as many others.

REPRESENTATION: Micah Gallery, Calgary, Alberta, Canada; EarthStar, Klamath Falls, Oregon; Black Wolf Art Gallery, Lake Worth, Florida; The Mill Gallery, Seneca, South Carolina.

ABOUT THE ARTIST: Edwards not only paints but travels around the country lecturing about Native American topics, bringing his storytelling talents to schools, fairs, festivals, and markets. His paintings have been sold all over the United States and Canada, and one of his creations was used on a T-shirt sold at the Santa Fe Powwow.

MARSHALL ELLIS

Oneida (1959–) Oneida, Wisconsin
Painter, silversmith, potter

EDUCATION: Institute of American Indian Arts (1975–77); College of Art Design, New Mexico (1978).

AWARDS: Ellis has received many awards, including the Award of Merit for Outstanding Achievement, Exhibition Techniques and Curatorial Functions, Institute of American Indian Arts (1977).

ABOUT THE ARTIST: Ellis paints nature and what it means to him, although he occasionally will paint Indian scenes, too. In addition to painting, Marshall works with silver and knows how to repair. He's also done some pots.

SAM ENGLISH

Turtle Mountain Chippewa
Painter—watercolors

AWARDS: Best of Division, painting, Red Earth Awards Ceremony (1994).

REPRESENTATION: Long Ago & Far Away Gallery, Manchester Center, Vermont.

ABOUT THE ARTIST: His bold watercolors of contemporary Native Americans have brought English much deserved attention. One such painting, entitled "Them Two, the First Americans," depicts an Indian man and his wife, both wrapped in one American flag. The figures are elongated, their faces raised to the sky. English's paintings are often made into prints. He lives in Albuquerque and has a studio in Old Town there.

L. DAVID EVENINGTHUNDER

Shoshone; Shoshone-Bannock Reservation, Fort Hall, Idaho
Artist—mixed media, pen and ink, air brush, chalk pastels, scratch art

EDUCATION: B.A., Sam Houston State University, Huntsville, Texas; Lee College, Baytown, Texas, AAGS, AST, AA; Electronics Technician Certificate, Lee College, Baytown, Texas (1986).

AWARDS: Many first place awards in juried art shows, as well as other honors, including Best of Show, Memphis Annual Juried Art Show (1998).

REPRESENTATION: ArtNatAm www.artnatam.com.

ABOUT THE ARTIST: Though orphaned and taken from his people at a young age, Eveningthunder still credits the spirituality of his father and grandfather (both medicine men) for the work he does today. His art "pays tribute to contemporary Indian dancers who are keeping our traditions alive."

JOHN FADDEN
(a.k.a. Kahionhes)

Mohawk (1938–) Onchiota, New York
Painter, wood- and stone-carver

EDUCATION: B.F.A., Rochester Institute of Technology.

AWARDS: Fadden's many awards include the United Teachers Journalism Award, many awards for his illustrations, and Best Original Cartoon from New York state's *NY Teacher*.

ABOUT THE ARTIST: Fadden has illustrated many books, articles, and films. His work was first published when he was 13, and one of his sketches was used for a poster for the Six Nations Indian Museum, with which he is closely associated. At first he wanted to be a commercial illustrator, but when he began taking education courses, he realized he liked teaching.

MITCH FARMER

Onondaga (1957–79)
Painter, carver, silk-screener

EDUCATION: Self-taught.

ABOUT THE ARTIST: Farmer worked as layout and graphic artist for *Akwe-sasne Notes* from 1977 to 1978. He designed a special silk-screen T-shirt to commemorate the Longest Walk, did deerskin wall hangings, and made pipes and water drums.

PHYLLIS FAST

Athabascan (1946–) Anchorage, Alaska
Painter—watercolors

EDUCATION: Ph.D., anthropology, Harvard University, Cambridge, Massachusetts.

ABOUT THE ARTIST: Fast's work incorporates dream symbols and Native American glyphs, as well as rising thematically from the search for one-self.

JOE FEDDERSON

Colville Federated Tribes (early 1960s–)
Painter, printmaker, graphic artist, photographer

EDUCATION: Wenatchee Valley College (1979); B.F.A., University of Wisconsin (1983); M.F.A., University of Wisconsin (1989).

REPRESENTATION: Jan Cicero Gallery, Chicago, Illinois.

ABOUT THE ARTIST: Fedderson has exhibited his work in solo and group shows throughout the country. He is a versatile artist who is adept at computer graphics, as well as traditional art.

PHYLLIS FIFE

Creek (1948–) Alabama
Artist—acrylics

EDUCATION: B.F.A., University of Oklahoma (1973).

ABOUT THE ARTIST: Fife comes from a long line of artists and educators. Her work is a reflection of her subconscious. She blurs the images in her work so viewers cannot be sure whether they are looking at a traditional Indian scene or a portrayal of Fife's feelings about how the world of her Indian heritage affects her and those around her.

LANCE FINK

(a.k.a. Po-Gesh)

Coyote Clan Mono; Sierra Nevada Mountains
Artist—pen and ink

ABOUT THE ARTIST: Fink has worked as a cowboy, construction worker, and tree topper. He gets most of his ideas by traveling to powwows.

HARRY FONSECA

Maidu/Portuguese/Hawaiian (1946–) Sacramento, California
Artist—mixed media

EDUCATION: Influenced by the art community of the University of California at Davis.

REPRESENTATION: Suzanne Brown Galleries, Scottsdale, Arizona; Jerome Evans Gallery, Lake Tahoe, Nevada; Rena Haveson Gallery, Pittsburgh, Pennsylvania.

ABOUT THE ARTIST: Fonseca paints Maidu dances and legends, but he is best known for his coyote series of paintings. Each coyote is painted from a different perspective, depicting contemporary ways to follow the Native American into the 20th century. In *Shared Visions*, Fonseca was quoted as saying, "I believe my Coyote paintings to be the most contemporary statements I have painted in regard to traditional beliefs and contemporary reality." His series of paintings on the California Gold Rush have been shown at the Oakland Museum of California.

W. B. FRANKLIN

Navajo; Ganado, Arizona
Painter—acrylic on linen and other media

REPRESENTATION: Raven Dancer Gallery.

ABOUT THE ARTIST: Franklin works spiritual figures and symbols into paintings that resemble everyday items (e.g., Navajo rug with abstract images). His paintings are abstract and utilize complex symbolism.

ADELIDO GARCIA

Cochiti (ca. 1910–70)
Artist

EDUCATION: Dorothy Dunn school.
REPRESENTATION: Sunshine Studio, New Mexico.

ABOUT THE ARTIST: Garcia painted in the style of the Dorothy Dunn school (ca. 1940). Not much is known about the artist.

GASTON GASPÉ

Mohawk (1933–) Oka, Quebec, Canada
Graphic artist, photographer, painter

EDUCATION: Attended Montreal College (1947–53); received his B.F.A. in design from the Fine Arts School of Montreal (1959–63) and a Pedagogie Artistique degree (1963–66).

ABOUT THE ARTIST: Gaspé has taught school and exhibited his work; he also does some photography. He has spent most of his time passing on his knowledge to children.

KLYNN CLOUD DANCER GEAR

Haudosaunee
Painter, carver, beadworker

EDUCATION: Degree in illustration, Rochester Institute of Technology.

AWARDS: Many, including a contract to place the Monacan historical site for a children's museum.

ABOUT THE ARTIST: Wife and mother to Monacan Nation people, she produces noncommercial work that is "heavily lined with cultural symbolism," in the artist's words. She produces two- and three-dimensional work ranging from paintings to carvings, beadwork, regalia, cradleboard, and other types of art. She lives a reformed-traditional lifestyle with her fam-

Painting, "Eagle Dancer." Klynn Cloud Dancer Gear. Courtesy of Tribe Azure Jewelry and Art, Tucson, AZ.

Painting, "Red Bucket III." Klynn Cloud Dancer Gear. Courtesy of Tribe Azure Jewelry and Art, Tucson, AZ.

ily, all of whom are powwow dancers and members of the Muddy Creek drummers and dance group.

GEORGE GEIONETY
(a.k.a. Bei-Koi-Gei, "Water Bag to Travel")

Kiowa (1913–) Lawton, Oklahoma
Artist—watercolor on illustration board

EDUCATION: Learned from his grandfather Haungooah (Silverhorn), who was a well known Kiowa artist at the turn of the century.
AWARDS: Has exhibited in group and one-man shows.
ABOUT THE ARTIST: Geionety paints in the traditional manner, showing his ancestors and the way they lived.

JACK TO'BAAHE GENE

Navajo (1953–) Winslow, Arizona
Painter, sandpainter

EDUCATION: Mostly self-taught, Gene has also received grants from the French/Navajo Intercultural Art Exchange, the Southwestern Association on Indian Affairs, and the Arizona Commission on the Arts, which assisted in his study of art.
AWARDS: Among this artist's many awards are a Best of Division/Fine Arts from the Southwest Museum in 1993, a Best of Show from the Heard Museum Indian Fair in 1993, and a First and Second Place/Pastel Paintings from the 1992 Santa Fe Indian Market.
REPRESENTATION: To'Baahe Fine Art, Winslow, Arizona.
ABOUT THE ARTIST: This artist states that he is "a traditional Navajo cultural painter depicting my experiences of the rawness of the natural being

as contained within contemporary society." He uses sand and pastel paints in his paintings, trying to "go beyond the two-dimensional surface to express the soul of the image."

JOHN GEORGE-MATHEWS

Ojibway/Chippewa (1963–) Sarnia, Ontario, Canada
Painter, muralist

EDUCATION: Self-taught independent freelance artist.

ABOUT THE ARTIST: George-Mathews does fine art on commission or contract, whether it be a mural for an office building or a T-shirt design. In his own words, the artist states, "As an artist I strive to induce shock, surprise, joy, fear, starkness, and shivers down the viewers' spine."

RICK GLAZER-DANAY

Mohawk/White (1942–) Coney Island, New York
Painter

EDUCATION: B.A., fine arts, California State University, Northridge; M.A., fine arts, California State; M.F.A., University of California at Davis.

AWARDS: Many, from exhibiting all over the United States. His work is held in many permanent, as well as private, collections, including the Philbrook Museum and the Department of the Interior.

ABOUT THE ARTIST: Glazer-Danay stated in August 1992, on the occasion of his 50th birthday, that he would "sell [his] creations no more forever." A controversial artist whose work was once called "soft porn," Glazer-Danay has created pop culture work, satire, and political commentary paintings. He has also taught American Indian history at the University of California at Riverside, taught at the University of Wisconsin at Green Bay (1980–85), and taught art at the California State University at Long Beach (1985–91).

HENRY GOBIN

Skohomish (1941–) Washington
Artist—watercolors

EDUCATION: Gobin has experimented with many of the "schools of Indian painting." He studied at the pre-Institute Santa Fe Boarding School, then studied the Northwest Coast cultures.

ABOUT THE ARTIST: His style could be called surrealistic, although it does incorporate some of the Northwest Coast symbols and stylized masks.

STEPHEN GONYEA

Onondaga (1946–) Alexandria, Virginia
Artist—acrylics, pen and ink, pencil

EDUCATION: Gonyea did postgraduate work at the Institute of American Indian Arts (1964–66) and received a B.F.A. with Honors (illustration major) at the Art Center College of Design, Los Angeles.

ABOUT THE ARTIST: Gonyea's work has been exhibited extensively. He has also acted as a freelance illustrator and has had work in magazines such as *American Artist*.

DAVID A. GORDON

Seneca (1948–) Irving, New York
Painter, sculptor, ceramist, potter

EDUCATION: Gordon's parents and art teachers influenced him. He also took silversmithing classes at the United South Eastern Tribes Indian Center.

ABOUT THE ARTIST: Gordon's work has been exhibited by the Institute of American Indian Arts throughout the Southwest. He continues to learn new skills while working to improve his painting.

HARLEY GORDON
(a.k.a. Gah-En-Teh)

Seneca (1922–) Tonawanda Reservation, Basom, New York
Artist—sketches; wood-carver

EDUCATION: Self-taught.

ABOUT THE ARTIST: Harley's sketches are usually of people he knows, animals, or local activities. He also carves spoons, ladles, and paddles.

R. C. GORMAN

Navajo (1932–) Chinle, Arizona
Artist—oils, pastels, other media; sculptor—bronze

EDUCATION: His father, painter Carl Nelson Gorman, inspired R. C. to paint. He also attended Mexico City College, studying art, and was Carlos Merida's pupil. In addition, he attended Guam Territorial College, Marianas Islands; California State University, San Francisco; and Arizona State College, Tempe.

REPRESENTATION: Joan Cawley Gallery, Scottsdale, Arizona; Allard's Gallery, Fresno, California; Georgetown Gallery of Art, Washington,

D.C.; Fields and Rosen Fine Arts, Inc., Jupiter, Florida; Santa Fe Trails Gallery of Southwestern Art, Sarasota, Florida; Donna Rose Galleries/Art Brokerage, Inc., Ketchum, Idaho; Freeport Art Museum and Cultural Center, Freeport, Illinois; R. Michelson Galleries, Amherst, Massachusetts; J. Todd Galleries, Wellesley, Massachusetts; Saper Galleries, East Lansing, Michigan; John A. Boler, Indian and Western Art, Minneapolis, Minnesota; Gomes Gallery Inc., St. Louis, Missouri; The New Riverside Gallery, Red Bank, New Jersey; Roswell Museum and Art Center, Roswell, New Mexico; 21st Century Fox Fine Art, Santa Fe, New Mexico; Wheelwright Museum of the American Indian, Santa Fe; Grycner Studio/Gallery Taos, Taos, New Mexico; Navajo Gallery, Taos; C & L Fine Arts, Inc., Bohemia, New York; Studio 53, New York; Fields and Rosen Fine Arts, Inc., Southampton, New York; Landing Gallery of Woodbury, Inc., Woodbury, New York; Argus Fine Arts, Eugene, Oregon; JRS Fine Art, Providence, Rhode Island; El Taller Gallery, Austin, Texas; Gallery Mack NW, Seattle, Washington; Santa Fe Gallery, Madison, Wisconsin.

ABOUT THE ARTIST: One of the best-known contemporary Native American artists, Gorman has a sensuous style and is known for his large canvases, which have given him a commercial success that reaches far beyond the circle of those who collect strictly Native American art. Posters and lithographs of his Navajo women are sold almost everywhere. Gorman has also written books such as *R.C. Gorman: The Radiance of My People* (1992).

JOHN GUTHRIE

Cherokee
Artist

AWARDS: Many national awards for his work.

ABOUT THE ARTIST: Guthrie's whole family is into the arts. He is represented by galleries, and his work is held in private collections throughout the United States.

ENOCH KELLY HANEY

Seminole/Creek (September 12, 1940–) Seminole, Oklahoma
Artist—acrylics, watercolors, monotype, lithographs, tempera

EDUCATION: A.A. from Bacone College and B.A. in fine arts from Oklahoma City University on a Rockefeller Foundation Scholarship for art.

AWARDS: Master Artist of the Five Civilized Tribes (1975); Governor's Art

Award/Oklahoma, Oklahoma City University Distinguished Alumni Award, honorary Doctor of Laws degree from Oklahoma City University (1994) and inducted into the Bacone Junior College Hall of Fame; Honored One, Red Earth Festival; Indian of the Year, American Indian Exposition.

REPRESENTATION: Kelly Haney Art Gallery, Shawnee, Oklahoma.

ABOUT THE ARTIST: Haney's work is faithful to his heritage, with every detail painstakingly painted and accurate. In addition to being a versatile artist, Haney has served three terms in the Oklahoma House of Representatives and has served in the Oklahoma State Senate.

HELEN HARDIN
(a.k.a. Tsa-sah-wee-eh, "Little Standing Spruce")

Santa Clara (1943–84) Santa Clara Pueblo, New Mexico
Artist—oils

EDUCATION: At the University of New Mexico, Hardin studied art history and anthropology, later winning a painting scholarship to a special school for Indians at the University of Arizona.

AWARDS: Won her first art contest at the age of six. After showing her work in South America, she won major awards in this country and was one of the Southwest's leading artists.

REPRESENTATION: Silver Sun/Helen Hardin Estate, Santa Fe, New Mexico; Inee Yang Slaughter, Santa Fe.

ABOUT THE ARTIST: Hardin was Pablita Velarde's daughter. Influenced by Joe Herrera, Hardin's style was more modern and abstract than traditional Indian painting and often integrated the designs of the potters of Acoma and Mimbres. Her first art show, in Bogota, Colombia, was almost a sellout. Her work, by her own admission, was definitely not traditional or classic. During the 1970s she developed a series of Kachina paintings, then went on to her "Women" series.

MARGUERITE LEE HARING

Seneca (1944–) Irving, New York
Painter, graphic artist, ceramist

EDUCATION: A.A., Bacone College, Muskogee, Oklahoma (1963–65); B.S., art education, Rosary Hill College (1967–70); Master's degree, art education, SUNY College at Buffalo.

AWARDS: Has won many honors, including being part of an exhibit at the Museum of the American Indian.

ABOUT THE ARTIST: Haring was influenced by Richard West while at Bacone. She does abstract, modern work but also does pieces that deal with Indian culture. She has exhibited at art shows, but most of her work is for herself and family.

MARCELLE SHARRON AHTONE HARJO
(a.k.a. Sain-Tah-Oodie, "Killed with a Blunted Arrow")

Kiowa; Oklahoma
Artist—acrylic on canvas

EDUCATION: Bacone College, Muskogee, Oklahoma (1963–65); Northeastern State College, Tahlequah, Oklahoma (1965); Colorado Woman's College, Denver (1965).

AWARDS: Miss Indian America XII (1966). Exhibited in group and one-man shows in Oklahoma.

ABOUT THE ARTIST: Harjo works in an abstract style, painting scenes of Indian life in an almost geometric fashion.

KAREN YXOMME LYNCH HARLEY

Saponi Tribe; Halifax and Warren Counties, North Carolina
Artist—oil, egg tempera, watercolors, pencil, charcoal, pen and ink, gourds, clay

ABOUT THE ARTIST: Harley's work has received national and international recognition for the way she creates emotional images of Native American life. Her work is featured in two children's books. Harley is a member of many organizations, such as Women Artists of the West and North Carolina Native American Artists.

JAMES HAVARD

Choctaw/Chippewa (1937–) Galveston, Texas
Artist—oils, acrylics

EDUCATION: Philadelphia Academy of Fine Arts, Philadelphia, Pennsylvania (1965); B.S., Sam Houston State College, Huntsville, Texas (1959).

REPRESENTATION: Robert Kidd Gallery, Birmingham, Michigan; Channing, Santa Fe, New Mexico; Allene La Pides Gallery, Santa Fe; Naravisa Press, Santa Fe.

ABOUT THE ARTIST: Havard's style is abstract and often difficult to interpret. His work is totally nontraditional and often reminiscent of trompe l'oeil.

HACHIVI EDGAR HEAP OF BIRDS

Cheyenne/Arapaho (1954–) Wichita, Kansas
Artist

EDUCATION: California College of Arts and Crafts, Oakland, California (1975); B.F.A., University of Kansas (1976); M.F.A., Tyler School of Art, Temple University (1979); graduate work in painting, Royal College of Art, London (1977).

AWARDS: Heap of Birds has received numerous awards and commissions for his work, including "Building Minnesota," a work installed at the Walker Art Center, Minneapolis, from March 10 to August 20, 1990. He also received the National Art Award from the Tiffany Foundation (1989).

REPRESENTATION: Jan Cicero Gallery, Chicago; Cleveland Institute of Art Reinberger Galleries, Ohio; University of North Texas University Art Gallery and Cora Stafford Gallery, Denton, Texas.

ABOUT THE ARTIST: Heap of Birds lectures on art throughout North America and Europe, curates exhibits of art, teaches at the University of Oklahoma, and exhibits his own work in group and solo shows. He has painted commuter buses, park and freeway signs, as well as the normal canvas. He believes that it is important to unify language and image in his pieces.

SUE ELLEN HERNE

(a.k.a. Kwa Ne Ra Ta Ieni)

Mohawk (1960–) Hogansburg, New York
Painter—oils, oil pastels, charcoal

EDUCATION: Trained at the Institute of American Indian Arts (1977–78); majored in painting at the Rhode Island School of Design.

AWARDS: First prize, painting, New York State Fair (1976).

ABOUT THE ARTIST: Herne's work is nonrepresentational, somewhat abstract, and not necessarily concerned with Iroquois tradition or style. The Mohawks often work in the Iroquois tradition. She has exhibited at the New York State Fair and other fairs or exhibitions.

JOE H. HERRERA

(a.k.a. See Ru, "Blue Bird")

Cochiti (1923–) Cochiti Pueblo, New Mexico
Artist—watercolors, casein

EDUCATION: Studied the basics with his mother, Tonita Pena, one of the first Rio Grande painters. Later studied with Dorothy Dunn (Santa Fe

Studio), received a B.A. in art (1953) and an M.A. in art education (1963), both from the University of New Mexico. Raymond Jonson at the university taught Herrera about cubist techniques.

ABOUT THE ARTIST: Herrera is one of the first Native American artists to win acclaim for his abstract imagery. He has acted as mentor to other artists who want to create art that is considered mainstream. He had exhibited his work all over the country, but stopped painting in 1958.

VELINO SHIJE HERRERA
(a.k.a. Velino Shije, Ma Pe Wi, or Oriole)
Zia (1902–73) Zia Pueblo, New Mexico
Artist, illustrator

EDUCATION: Studied in Santa Fe with E. Hewett.

ABOUT THE ARTIST: Herrera was commissioned to do murals for the Albuquerque Indian School and others; illustrated books during the 1940s; and had his work published in magazines such as *School Arts*, *American Magazine of Art*, and *Arizona Highways*, as well as in books such as *Compton's Pictured Encyclopedia*. He was also commissioned to do work for the Amon Carter Museum, the American Museum of Natural History, the Corcoran Gallery, the Denver Art Museum, and the Museum of New Mexico. Exhibits of his work were held at the Heard Museum in Phoenix, Arizona, at various tribal ceremonials, at the Museum of New Mexico, and at the Southwest Museum and are included in private and public collections. Herrera's art career ended when he was injured for life in a car accident in the 1950s.

VALJEAN MCCARTHY HESSING
Choctaw (1934–) Tulsa, Oklahoma
Artist—watercolors

EDUCATION: Summer program at Philbrook Museum (on scholarship at 11 years of age); studied art in college at Mary Hardin-Baylor College, Texas, and Tulsa University, Oklahoma.

ABOUT THE ARTIST: Hessing is known as a master painter of horses, and she also weaves narratives or stories through her paintings. Her art reflects the confusion and disillusionment through which her people suffered when on the Trail of Tears. A painting with that subject was part of an exhibit sponsored by the Cherokee Historical Center in Tahlequah, Oklahoma.

BOBBY HILL
(a.k.a. Pau-Tain-Dae, "Whitebuffalo")

Kiowa (1933–) Lawton, Oklahoma
Artist—watercolors

EDUCATION: Self-taught.
AWARDS: Grand Award, Indian Art Exhibition, Anadarko, Oklahoma (1968), as well as many others.
ABOUT THE ARTIST: Hill began painting in 1953, then worked at several jobs, including as a commercial artist for several Oklahoma City television stations and as scenic artist for ABC. His realistic and highly detailed work has been shown throughout the United States.

DONALD HILL

Cayuga/Tuscarora/Mohawk (1959–) Lewiston, New York
Painter—pen and ink, acrylics; carver; ceramist—steatite, clay

EDUCATION: Hill is mostly self-taught, though he has taken art courses at SUNY Buffalo.
ABOUT THE ARTIST: Hill exhibits his work and experiments with different media. He explores his heritage and puts what he learns into his work.

JOAN HILL
(a.k.a. Chea-se-quah, "Redbird")

Creek/Cherokee (1930–) Muskogee, Oklahoma
Artist—watercolors, tempera, other media

EDUCATION: Muskogee Junior College, Oklahoma; B.A., Northeastern University, Oklahoma; studied with W. Richard West, Bacone Junior College, Oklahoma.
AWARDS: During her career she has won more than 200 awards, including 10 Grand Awards and 4 special trophies.
ABOUT THE ARTIST: Hill was one of the first female Native American artists to become successful. Her work bridged the gap between traditional and contemporary Native American painting. A well-known artist, she has paintings and drawings in many permanent museum and college collections, including the United States Department of the Interior, Washington, D.C.; the Philbrook Art Center, Tulsa, Oklahoma; the Heard Museum, Phoenix, Arizona; and the Museum of the American Indian, New York City. Her work is also held in private collections throughout the world.

RICK HILL

Tuscarora (1950–) near Buffalo, New York
Painter, writer, photographer

EDUCATION: Studied with Walker Evans and Robert Frank, Art Institute of Chicago (1968); master's degree in American studies from the State University of New York in Buffalo.

AWARDS: Hill's career has brought him many honors and awards.

ABOUT THE ARTIST: Currently acting as museum director at the Institute of American Indian Arts, Hill has held many jobs throughout his diverse career. He worked for the New York State Historical Society as a photographer of Indian artists, worked in various museums in and around Buffalo, New York, coordinated the development of the new Institute of American Indian Arts museum in Santa Fe, New Mexico, and will be working at the National Museum of the American Indian, scheduled to open in the late 1990s. He also curates many shows, and his own work is held in a number of public and private collections throughout the world.

RON HILL

Oneida (1956–)
Painter, sculptor, silverworker

EDUCATION: Art major, Institute of American Indian Arts (1973–74).

ABOUT THE ARTIST: Hill has been sketching since a young boy, has worked with a variety of other media, and has exhibited his work at annual shows.

TOM HILL

Seneca (1943–) Oshweken, Ontario, Canada
Artist—oils, acrylics, pen and ink, plastic, wood products

EDUCATION: Majored in Fine Arts, Medical Illustration, and Advertising at Ontario College of Arts (1963–67).

AWARDS: Hill has been recognized throughout Ontario for his murals and paintings.

ABOUT THE ARTIST: As a young boy, Hill was encouraged by his uncle Reg Hill's dedication to art. Hill has been using his talents as an artist to promote Native American art and has been involved with the Six Nations Arts Council. His paintings and drawings sometimes express his feelings about the political situations within his community.

ALYSSA HINTON

Katenauaga Band of Tuscarora and Osage (1962–) Philadelphia, Pennsylvania
Artist

EDUCATION: B.F.A., Tyler School of Art, Philadelphia, Pennsylvania; studied in France and China.

AWARDS: Recipient of many awards and fellowships, including 1990 Mid-
Atlantic/NEA Regional Painting Fellowship.

ABOUT THE ARTIST: Hinton works with mixed media, creating intricate
photo-collage narratives that explore her Native American roots. She says
that her work is "inspired by questions and experiences relating to my
tribal identity and personal spiritual awareness. As memories and visions
emerge in my consciousness, the process of creating becomes a vehicle for
ancestral awakening and reconnection. My recent collage images commu-
nicate a universal message of transformation and rebirth." She has exhibited in solo and group shows throughout the country.

Artist Alyssa Hinton. Courtesy of Alyssa Hinton.

"The Heart of the Nation/Refugees #2" by Alyssa Hinton. Mixed media photo collage (32 pieces) with map pieces and colored pencil. 13" × 11". Courtesy of Alyssa Hinton.

"Island Hopping" by Alyssa Hinton. Digital photo/mixed media collage with original watercolor. 12" × 12". Courtesy of Alyssa Hinton.

"Homeward" by Alyssa Hinton.
Mixed media photo collage (37
pieces) with oil pastel drawing.
7" × 7". Courtesy of Alyssa Hinton.

JACK HOKEAH

Kiowa (1902–73) Kiowa Reservation in western Oklahoma
Artist—watercolors, tempera, oils

EDUCATION: University of Oklahoma (noncredit art course); Santa Fe Indian School, New Mexico.

ABOUT THE ARTIST: Though Hokeah painted during the time that the Kiowa Oklahoma style was being perfected, his portraits are not often characteristic of the full-figure Kiowa style. He was one of the Kiowa Five, a group of young Kiowa boys who all attended the University of Oklahoma and became famous because of their incredible artistic talent.

DELBRIDGE HONANIE

(a.k.a. Coochsiwukioma, "Falling Snow")

Hopi (1946–) Arizona
Artist—acrylics; carver-sculptor

AWARDS: Gallup Independent Marketplace Award (2001).

REPRESENTATION: Lovena Ohl Gallery, Scottsdale, Arizona; Shidoni Gallery, Tesuque, New Mexico.

ABOUT THE ARTIST: Honanie uses traditional Hopi symbols and pottery motifs in his work in order to link the present with the past. His sculptures are of Hopi daily life. His work has been held by the Museum of Northern Arizona.

RANCE HOOD
(a.k.a. Aut-Tup-Ta, "Yellow Hair")

Comanche (1941–) Lawton, Oklahoma
Artist—tempera

EDUCATION: Hood's style of painting is his own, though he learned some of his technique from Blackbear Bosin's work.

AWARDS: His numerous awards include First Award at the American Indian Artists Exhibition, Philbrook Art Center, Tulsa, Oklahoma (1970), and three Grand Awards at the Indian Art Exhibits in Anadarko, Oklahoma (1968, 1969, 1971).

ABOUT THE ARTIST: Hood paints Comanche scenes as they were in the past, a proud hunting and warring people. His painting style changes as he captures images of scenes that were gone long before he was born. He began exhibiting his work in 1962 and has, since then, shown it throughout the United States. Of his past and childhood images of peyote rituals, he says, "The wind comes blowing through you—it blows your sins away."

MICHAEL HORSE

Yaqui-Mescalero and Apache-Zuni (ca. 1951–) Arizona
Painter, carver, jeweler, ledger artist

AWARDS: Artist-in-residence, Southwest Museum, Los Angeles.

Michael Horse, painter, jeweler, carver, ledger artist, and actor with staff members at Gathering Tribes Gallery, Berkeley, CA. Courtesy of Gathering Tribes.

REPRESENTATION: Gathering Tribes Gallery, Berkeley, California; Smith-sonian Museum, Washington, D.C.

ABOUT THE ARTIST: Horse is best known for his acting roles in *Twin Peaks* and *North of 60*. He's also been in several movies, such as *Passenger 57* with Wesley Snipes, but his art is important enough to be noticed by the Smithsonian, where he has had his work exhibited, and to warrant an artist-in-residence stint at Southwest Museum. He has illustrated a children's book with his wife, Sandra. His jewelry work incorporates silver, gold, diamonds, coral, and turquoise. Horse has acted as judge for several art shows, and a 30-year retrospective of his work, "Dreams of Horses: The Collected Works of Michael Horse," was shown at the Southwest Museum in the spring of 1997.

OSCAR HOWE
(a.k.a. Mazuha Hokshina, "Trader Boy")

Yanktonai Sioux (1915–83) Crow Creek Reservation, South Dakota
Artist—various media

EDUCATION: The Studio, Santa Fe Indian School, New Mexico (1935); B.A., Dakota Wesleyan University, South Dakota; M.F.A., University of Oklahoma.

REPRESENTATION: Civic Fine Arts Center, Sioux Falls, South Dakota; University of South Dakota/University Art Galleries, Vermillion, South Dakota.

ABOUT THE ARTIST: Howe's style was cubist and surreal; however, he felt that his paintings were still in the mainstream of Native American art because his need to tell the Dakota Sioux's history was stronger than any other. He taught that cubism and surrealism are effective ways in which to relate the mystery and power of Native American beliefs. When he taught at the University of South Dakota, he mentored students who went on to become successful, like Arthur Amiotte, Colleen Cutschall, and Robert Penn.

JAMES HUMETEWA, JR.
(a.k.a. Saw-whu, "Morning Star")

Hopi (1926–) Arizona
Artist—watercolors

EDUCATION: Santa Fe Indian School (1945).

ABOUT THE ARTIST: Humetewa has painted Hopi traditions and ceremonial dances, often showing the spectators as well as the dancers. His work has been shown quite often, the first exhibit of which was in 1947 when the Museum of New Mexico chose his work for a one-man show.

JESSE HUMMINGBIRD

Cherokee (1952–) Talequah, Oklahoma
Artist—acrylic on canvas

AWARDS: Best of Division, painting, Heard Museum Indian Market; second place, painting, SW Arts Festival, Indio, California; Best of Division, two-dimensional art, Albuquerque Indian Art 2000 exposition; first place, painting and etching categories, SWAIA Indian Market, Santa Fe. Inter Tribal Ceremonial poster artist (1992); Bien Mur poster artist (1999).

ABOUT THE ARTIST: Hummingbird has published three children's coloring books with The Book Publishing Company, Summertown, Tennessee. In 1996 he was named artist of the year by the Indian Arts and Crafts Association and received a fellowship from SWAIA that same year. Jesse was featured in an article in the 1999 fall issue of *Native Artist* magazine. Interviews and his images have been featured in several published books. He paints in the flat native Oklahoman style, often using masks in his work.

JERRY INGRAM

Choctaw (1941–) Oklahoma
Artist—watercolors; beadworker; lithographer; graphic artist

EDUCATION: Chilocco Indian School, Oklahoma; Institute of American Indian Arts (1963); B.A., commercial art, Oklahoma State Tech (1966).

AWARDS: His first award was an honorable mention in the 1966 Annual American Indian Artists Exhibition at the Philbrook Art Center, the beginning of many awards and honors.

REPRESENTATION: Sunwest Silver, Albuquerque, New Mexico.

ABOUT THE ARTIST: Ingram has been exposed to many different Indian cultures and has relayed their mystic religious rites and customs through his art. He paints both historical and contemporary scenes in what may be described as a romantic style. A "peyote school" painter, he is one of the most experimental in Indian art. Ingram is also well known for his prizewinning beadwork. He has done shows all over the world and is included in many books on the subject of art.

ARNOLD JACOBS

(a.k.a. Nah-Gwa-Say)

Cayuga (1942–) Oshweken, Ontario, Canada
Painter—oils, acrylics

EDUCATION: Jacobs has taken special art classes at Central Technical School in Toronto.

AWARDS: Jacobs has shown his work from Canada to Cuba and won honors and recognition for it.

ABOUT THE ARTIST: Arnold developed his artistic skill in the commercial art field. Though he has worked with all types of media, he prefers oils and acrylics. His style varies from being very modern to realistic. His work usually includes the symbols of the earth and sky, spiritual forces that are vital to him. His painting "Creation" was used by the Iroquois Museum to raise funds to publish their directory of artists.

G. PETER JEMISON

Cattaraugus Seneca (1945–) Silver Creek, New York
Artist and illustrator—acrylics, various other media

EDUCATION: B.S., art education, State University of New York at Buffalo (1967); studied Italian art and culture at the University of Siena in Italy; self-imposed learning of Native culture from his own people; Ph.D., State University (2002).

ABOUT THE ARTIST: Jemison is considered one of the most active artists in the Northeast. He is dedicated to preserving Indian art and culture, illustrated *The Iroquois and the Founding of the American Nation*, has established community programs for Native Americans, directed the gallery of the American Indian Community House in New York City, and is a member of the New York State Iroquois Conference. His style emerged from the different types of training he had, showing his love for Matisse's cut-paper works, as well as his fascination in his own heritage. He continues to experiment with different artistic expressions.

WILLIE JOCK
(a.k.a. Shaklunia)

Mohawk (1946–) Hogansburg, New York
Painter—acrylics, watercolors, tempera, pen and ink, hide

EDUCATION: Jock took some art courses in high school, but is mostly self-taught.

ABOUT THE ARTIST: Jock has exhibited his work at the Native American Center for Living Arts, as well as at other shows and exhibitions. His work is held in private collections, and his cartoons have also been published. His work usually involves wildlife and nature scenes painted on deer hide or moose hide that has been stretched on barn board.

DAVID JOHNS

Navajo
Painter

EDUCATION: Concentration in printmaking, Northern Arizona University.
AWARDS: Lovena Ohl Foundation Award (1979), and others.
REPRESENTATION: Turquoise Tortoise, Sedona, Arizona; Lovena Ohl Gallery, Scottsdale, Arizona.
ABOUT THE ARTIST: Johns began painting full-time in 1980 and presented his fifth collection at the Lovena Ohl Gallery in the fall of 1984. A prolific, young painter, he is gaining a national reputation. His portraits of Navajo faces are drawn from his imagination.

JOSEPH KABANCE

Potawatomi (1945–) Horton, Kansas
Artist—mixed media

"The Elder" by David Johns. Acrylic. 60" × 48". $12,000.
Courtesy of the Turquoise Tortoise, Sedona, AZ.

"Composition—Plateau" by David Johns. Acrylic on canvas. 72" × 60". $9,400.
Courtesy of the Turquoise Tortoise, Sedona, AZ.

EDUCATION: Studied art ceramics at the Institute of American Indian Arts, Santa Fe, New Mexico (1963–64); majored in art, Fort Lewis College, Durango, Colorado (1964–65); B.A. in sociology, Wichita State University, Wichita, Kansas (1965–70).

AWARDS: Kabance's awards include first place in a ceramic competition at the South Dakota State Fair (1961–63).

ABOUT THE ARTIST: His work has been exhibited both at one-man and group shows. He has an almost abstract style that reminds one of trompe l'oeil and uses various types of media to create his art.

FRED KABOTIE
(a.k.a. Fred Nakavoma, "Day After Day")

Hopi (1900–86) Shungopovi, Second Mesa, Arizona
Artist and illustrator—various media; jeweler; silversmith

EDUCATION: Studied at the Santa Fe Indian School and was encouraged to explore art as a career by school superintendent John DeHuff. He went to

Santa Fe High School (1925), studied at the Museum of New Mexico, and took private lessons from Mrs. J. D. DeHuff of Santa Fe.

ABOUT THE ARTIST: Kabotie illustrated several picture books in the 1930s, worked for the Heye Foundation, and painted murals for some of the Fred Harvey Company's hotels. He painted the ceremonies and traditions of his people. He taught and/or inspired young artists to be innovative, as well as to continue the Hopi artistic traditions. Probably the best-known artist of the 1920s, Kabotie is thought to have been responsible for bringing traditional Indian painting into the forefront, gaining the support of wealthy collectors.

MICHAEL KABOTIE
(a.k.a. Lomawywesa, "Walking in Harmony")

Hopi (1942–) Shungopavi, Second Mesa, Arizona
Artist—mixed media

EDUCATION: Learned some of his technique from his father, painter and silversmith Fred Kabotie; studied with the Southwest Indian Art Project, University of Arizona, Tucson; and graduated in 1961 from the Haskell Institute in Lawrence, Kansas.

REPRESENTATION: Lovena Ohl Gallery, Scottsdale, Arizona; Kopavi International, Sedona, Arizona.

ABOUT THE ARTIST: Kabotie paints petroglyph images that reiterate basic Hopi beliefs and traditions. Symbols of his Hopi ancestors, such as clan symbols, rain clouds, snow, and other signs, are often incorporated into his paintings. He was one of the founders of the Artist Hopid in 1973. Kabotie's work has been exhibited throughout the United States, both in solo and group shows.

ERNIE KEAHBONE
(a.k.a. To-Gem-Hote, "Blue Jay")

Kiowa (1933–) Anadarko, Oklahoma
Artist—casein on illustration board

EDUCATION: Self-taught artist who began painting in 1966.

AWARDS: His many awards include the First Award in the Amateur Division, Indian Art Exhibit, at the American Indian Exposition in 1966.

ABOUT THE ARTIST: Keahbone is a member of the Ton-Kon-Ko Black Leggings Warrior Society. His simplistic, folk-art style is reminiscent of the ledger drawings of the Plains Indians. He has exhibited his work in group and one-man shows throughout the United States.

GEORGE CAMPBELL KEAHBONE
(a.k.a. Asaute)

Kiowa (1916–) Oklahoma
Artist—watercolors

EDUCATION: Santa Fe Indian School and Taos Valley School of Art.

ABOUT THE ARTIST: Keahbone has painted the Kiowa people as they were in the past. After his marriage, he lived with his wife's people at the Taos Pueblo. He has specialized in painting the stylized Indian figure and animals.

MICHAEL LACAPA

Apache/Hopi/Tewa; Phoenix, Arizona
Painter, storyteller

EDUCATION: Arizona State University; Northern Arizona State University.

REPRESENTATION: Sage Brush Limited Editions, Flagstaff, Arizona.

ABOUT THE ARTIST: Lacapa's traditions are as much incorporated into his paintings as they are into the stories he tells to classrooms full of children. He has illustrated and authored children's books. Many of the prints from those books have been made into limited editions. He has taught at the high school level, but left that position to work with the Apache tribe in a multicultural educational role that led him to work on children's books.

DOROTHY K. LAHACHE
(a.k.a. Kawannes)

Mohawk (1954–) Caughnawaga, Quebec, Canada
Painter, beadworker, leatherworker, silversmith, carver

EDUCATION: Elaine Lahache, Dorothy's mother, taught her some of her skills. Dorothy was also an arts major at Manitou Community College.

AWARDS: Lahache's career has been recognized with awards for her painting, beadwork, and dancing.

ABOUT THE ARTIST: Lahache's work has been exhibited, but her pieces are not for sale. She doesn't title any of her work.

ELGIN W. LAMARR

Wichita (1918–) Anadarko, Oklahoma
Artist—oils

EDUCATION: Studied art education and music at the University of Tulsa, Oklahoma (1945–49); graduate studies at the same school in 1950.

ABOUT THE ARTIST: Lamarr has passed on his skill to younger generations by teaching at the Indian City Pottery Works in Anadarko, Oklahoma. An abstract artist, he also has worked as a commercial illustrator.

JEAN LAMARR

Pitt River/Paiute (1945–) Susanville, California
Photographer and artist—mixed media

EDUCATION: Philco-Ford Technical Institute, Santa Clara, California; San Jose City College, California; University of California at Berkeley.

REPRESENTATION: Jerome Evans Gallery, Lake Tahoe, Nevada.

ABOUT THE ARTIST: Lamarr has created art in response to anniversaries (such as Christopher Columbus's arrival in America) and combines his photographs with other media.

FRANK LAPENA

Nomtipom Wintu (1937–) San Francisco, California.
Artist—acrylics, multimedia; poet; writer

EDUCATION: B.A., California State College, Chico (1965); Life Issue, Teaching Credential, San Francisco State University, California; M.A., anthropology, California State University, Sacramento.

AWARDS: LaPena has exhibited in solo and group shows since 1960, winning numerous honors. His work is held in permanent collections of the Heard Museum, Phoenix, Arizona; the Indian Arts and Crafts Board in Washington, D.C.; and others.

REPRESENTATION: Jerome Evans Gallery, Lake Tahoe, Nevada; Wheelwright Museum of the American Indian, Santa Fe, New Mexico.

ABOUT THE ARTIST: LaPena is a modernistic artist who paints the myths and traditions of Indian art. His work often shows how he is constantly searching for an understanding of the universe and its power, as did his people before him. In 1992 he created a work that was a response to the anniversary of Columbus's arrival in America. LaPena has acted as consultant to the Smithsonian, the California State Indian Museum, and the Ishi Project at Berkeley; has written and published poetry, as well as an arts column; is fluent in the Wintu language; and is now professor emeritus of art and ethnic studies and director of the Native American Studies Program at the California State University at Sacramento.

JAMES LAVADOUR

Walla Walla (1951–) Cayuse, Oregon
Artist—oil on linen, oil on wood

EDUCATION: Self-taught. Honorary doctorate from Eastern Oregon University.

REPRESENTATION: Works held by the Northwest Museum of Arts and Culture; Grover-Thurston Gallery, Seattle, Washington; James Baird Gallery, St. John's, Newfoundland, Canada; PDX Contemporary Art, Portland, Oregon.

ABOUT THE ARTIST: Lavadour uses many canvases to create his illusionistic landscapes. He applies paint thinly so that the spirit images he creates can become part of the real world. The artist has exhibited in many galleries and museums throughout the world.

JAMES LITTLE CHIEF
(a.k.a. Tsen-T'ainte, "White Horse")

Comanche/Kiowa (1941–) Lawton, Oklahoma
Artist—acrylics

EDUCATION: Studied painting at Cameron Junior College, Lawton, and at Oklahoma University, Norman.

AWARDS: Various awards include some won at the Indian Art Exhibit at the American Indian Exposition in Anadarko, Oklahoma (1966).

ABOUT THE ARTIST: Little Chief has had one-man shows in Oklahoma, where his distinct style (he often uses odd-shaped canvases) garner him a lot of attention.

CARM LITTLE TURTLE

Apache/Tarahumara/Mexican (1952–) Santa Monica, California
Photographer

EDUCATION: Graduated from Navajo Community College in 1978 as an R.N. Self-taught in photography.

AWARDS: Little Turtle has been exhibiting her work since 1981 and has won numerous honors. Her work is held in the Heard Museum, Phoenix, Arizona.

ABOUT THE ARTIST: The photographs Little Turtle creates are deft depictions of her personal history, and she is known for the way she uses light, manipulating it to her best advantage. She also paints on the image, making the photograph a mixture of the best of both the photographer's and artist's talents. Permanent collections of her work are held in many museums and universities, such as the Southwest Museum in Los Angeles and the Southern Plains Indian Museum in Anadarko, Oklahoma.

CHARLES LOLOMA

Hopi (1921–91) Hotevilla, Third Mesa, Arizona
Painter, potter, muralist, silversmith

EDUCATION: Studied under muralist Olaf Nordmark and received ceramics instruction at Alfred University, New York.

AWARDS: John A. Whiting Fellowship (1955); won awards in national and state competitions; Arizona Governor's Art Award "for his courage and innovation in changing the look of Indian jewelry" (1990).

REPRESENTATION: Wheelwright Museum of the American Indian, Santa Fe, New Mexico.

ABOUT THE ARTIST: Loloma instructed special classes at the University of Arizona and Arizona State. He exhibited at the Arizona State Fair, the Museum of Modern Art in New York City, and the New Mexico State Fair, as well as internationally. He started out as a muralist, painting for the Federal Building on Treasure Island in San Francisco Bay. Then he studied ceramics, focusing on the glazing properties of Hopi indigenous clays. He rented space at the Kiva Craft Center in Scottsdale, Arizona, where he and his wife, Otellie Pasivaya, sold their work. Then he began making jewelry in the 1950s.

A major force in Native American arts, he spoke about his work all over the world, taught at the Institute of American Indian Arts, was featured on television specials, and served as artist-in-residence in Japan and Korea for the National Endowment for the Arts. He also took on apprentices, such as his niece, Verma Nequatewa, and her sister, Sherian Honhongva, teaching them how to create, innovate, and combine colors. After an accident in 1989, Loloma was forced to retire.

LINDA LOMAHAFTEWA

Hopi/Choctaw (1947–) Phoenix, Arizona
Artist—various media

EDUCATION: Institute of American Indian Arts, Santa Fe; B.F.A. and M.F.A., San Francisco Art Institute, California.

AWARDS: Lomahaftewa has exhibited in national and international shows and several one-woman shows, and she has won many awards for her work.

REPRESENTATION: Heard Museum, Phoenix, Arizona.

ABOUT THE ARTIST: In addition to teaching jobs held at the San Francisco Art Institute, the University of California at Berkeley, and the Institute of American Indian Arts in Santa Fe, Lomahaftewa has been an active artist. She unites the ancient Indian world with the contemporary in her modernistic paintings and has done a series of abstract landscapes, which are considered the most powerful in her body of work. Her work is held in many private and public collections, such as the Millicent Rogers Museum in Taos; New Mexico, and the Southern Plains Indian Museum in Anadarko, Oklahoma, and her "Summer Harvest" is on the home page of the Institute of American Indian Arts Web site.

MILLARD DAWA LOMAKEMA
(a.k.a. Dawakema, "House of the Sun")

Hopi (1941–) Arizona
Artist—acrylics

EDUCATION: A member of the Hopi artist group, the Artists Hopid.

ABOUT THE ARTIST: In the 1960s Lomakema started to sell his work. Later he went to work for a detective agency, then returned to Hopi to become a police officer. Lomakema paints Kachinas and Kachina maidens and surrounds them with typical Hopi symbols. His work is an abstract interpretation of traditions within his tribe. He concerns himself with the spiritual and symbolic aspects of Hopi life.

GEORGE LONGFISH

Seneca/Tuscarora (1942–) Oshweken, Ontario, Canada
Painter, sculptor, filmmaker

EDUCATION: B.F.A. and M.F.A., Art Institute of Chicago (1972).

AWARDS: Longfish has participated in and/or directed many one-man and group shows since 1967 and has been given many honors.

REPRESENTATION: California State University at Hayward.

ABOUT THE ARTIST: Longfish has tried to incorporate European techniques with Indian traditions in his paintings. He uses mystical symbols on his large, unframed paintings, and they often resemble the sides of tepees painted by his ancestors. In 1983 he stated, "[I]t was this spirituality that made connections between making art and my cultural background." In addition to his artwork, Longfish has directed the graduate program in American Indian Arts at the University of Montana and is a professor of Native American studies at the University of California at Davis, as well as director of the C. N. Gorman Museum.

MARY LONGMAN

Saulteaux (1964–) Fort Qu'appelle, Saskatchewan, Canada
Artist—two- and three-dimensional artwork

EDUCATION: Concordia University (1990–91); Emily Carr College of Art and Design (1990–95); M.F.A., Nova Scotia College of Art and Design (1993). Doctoral student at the University of British Columbia.

AWARDS: Mungo Martin Award (1989), a Canada Council Award, and a Canadian Native Arts Foundation Award (1992).

REPRESENTATION: Kamloops Art Gallery, British Columbia, Canada.

ABOUT THE ARTIST: Longman specializes in the works of the First Nations, has exhibited extensively throughout Canada, and uses traditional aboriginal icons in her work to explore such powerful issues as suicide and AIDS.

CHARLES F. LOVATO

Santo Domingo (1937–87) Santo Domingo Pueblo, New Mexico
Painter, ceramist, sculptor, poet, jeweler

EDUCATION: Learned art by helping his grandmother, potter Monica Silva, decorate her pottery.

AWARDS: Honored posthumously with a show of his jewelry at the Wheelwright Museum, Santa Fe, New Mexico.

REPRESENTATION: Eagle Plume Gallery, Allenspark, Colorado.

ABOUT THE ARTIST: Lovato often used pottery designs in his work, a leftover influence of his early days of painting. He also incorporated traditional Pueblo images like the sun, mountains, and the plants of the Rio Grande Valley. He used incredibly small beads and was known for shading the colors in his necklaces so they shimmered. Lovato introduced other jewelers to the style of interchanging gold and turquoise with olive shell, white clamshell, sugilite, coral, and lapis lazuli.

F. BRUCE LUBO, SR.

Laguna (1911–) Old Laguna Pueblo, New Mexico
Artist—oils, watercolors, pastels

EDUCATION: Went to college for engineering and art; spent 30 years as an aircraft design engineer.

AWARDS: Many, including Best of Show in painting (twice) at the Eight Northern Pueblo Art Exhibit, New Mexico; 48 first, second, third, and honorable mention awards. Attended the Santa Fe Indian Market for 20 years and won Best of Class in pastels.

REPRESENTATION: In the past, Lubo's work has been represented by many Southwestern galleries, but since he lost his eyesight, he has not been working.

ABOUT THE ARTIST: A very active artist, Lubo has sold thousands of paintings during his career. In 1992 he was declared legally blind and now has to write using a magnifying glass. Before that time he attended many shows, sold works to collectors around the world, and was known for his roadrunner pictures (he is a member of the Roadrunner clan).

DONALD D. LYNCH

Cayuga (1948–) Oshweken, Ontario, Canada
Painter—oils, watercolors

EDUCATION: Lynch took art courses at Cornell University (1966) and at SUNY Geneseo (1967–69).

ABOUT THE ARTIST: Lynch likes to paint nostalgic views of the past. He often finds old photographs to use for ideas or plumbs his memory, imagining what the scene may have originally looked like. A talented man, Lynch was a biology major at Cornell and an English and journalism major at SUNY. He has spent most of his life at Six Nations.

OREN LYONS

(a.k.a. Jo-Ag-Quis-Ho)

Onondaga (1930–)
Painter—acrylics, oils, tempera, designer colors, pen and ink, pencil, charcoal, pastels; wood-carver

EDUCATION: B.A., Syracuse University, College of Fine Art (1954–58); M.A., Museum Technology and American History, Syracuse University.

AWARDS: Lyons has exhibited in many shows, has acted as director and codirector, has been commissioned to do silver medallion designs for the Franklin Mint, and won first prize for his illustrations in the children's book *Little Jimmy Yellow Hawk* from the Council of Interracial Books for Children.

ABOUT THE ARTIST: Lyons's work in the Iroquois Nation has been significant since he became involved with the Council of Chiefs at Onondaga in the 1970s. He has taught at SUNY Buffalo and been very involved with art exhibits. His work often depicts the Tree of Peace, the four winds, and clan animals. In 1993 he addressed the United Nations to open the Year of the Indigenous Peoples as Haudenosaunee Faithkeeper. As professor of

American studies, he directs the Native American Studies Program at the State University of New York at Buffalo.

MARIO MARTINEZ

Yaqui (1953–) near Scottsdale, Arizona
Painter

EDUCATION: B.F.A., Arizona State University (1979); M.F.A., San Francisco Art Institute (1985).

AWARDS: Won a San Francisco commission in 1995 to paint works based on Yaqui myths and legends.

REPRESENTATION: Jan Cicero Gallery, Chicago, Illinois.

ABOUT THE ARTIST: Martinez states that Monet, Kandinsky, and Picasso have influenced his vision of art, but he also delves into his own symbols from the Yaqui culture. His works are a combination of traditional and contemporary influences; they sometimes show his political leanings, and most often his feelings about the members of the Yaqui community. He calls himself an abstract painter and drawer and states that his "research has been based on imagery of cultural objects related to the cosmos and I have looked at work from my tribe and other tribes."

RICHARD MARTINEZ

(a.k.a. Opa Mu Nu)

San Ildefonso (1904–) San Ildefonso Pueblo, New Mexico
Artist, muralist

EDUCATION: One of the original students at the Santa Fe Indian School, Martinez helped paint a series of murals there in 1936.

ABOUT THE ARTIST: Most of his work was done between 1920 and 1950, and his subjects were often mythological or ceremonial. His work was exhibited with the Exposition of Indian Tribal Arts, Inc., in 1931, and collections are held by the Denver Art Museum, the Museum of New Mexico, the Chrysler Art Museum, and others.

GEORGIA MASAYESVA

Hopi; Arizona
Artist, photographer

EDUCATION: B.A. and master's degree in education, University of Arizona.

ABOUT THE ARTIST: Masayesva was the first female to be selected the poster artist for the Festival of Native American Art (1988). Her photography is sepia-toned black-and-white images that are hand-tinted as they were 100 years ago.

JEAN MCCARTY MAULDIN

Choctaw

Artist

EDUCATION: Mauldin's work has been influenced by Valjean Hessing, her sister and a well-known artist.

AWARDS: This artist's many awards come from exhibits such as the Gilcrease Museum (1968), the Philbrook Annual (1979), the Five Civilized Tribes Museum (1979), as well as many others.

ABOUT THE ARTIST: Mauldin has been included in *Who's Who in America* and *The Encyclopedia of American Indian Art*, and her work has been exhibited all over the United States. She also spent 25 years as a commercial artist and somehow found the time to raise four children.

SOLOMON MCCOMBS

(a.k.a. "Wolf Warrior")

Creek (1913-) Eufala, Oklahoma

Artist—watercolors

EDUCATION: Studied at Bacone with Acee Blue Eagle.

ABOUT THE ARTIST: McCombs worked for the Department of State for 17 years and traveled throughout Africa and Asia showing his paintings and telling the groups to whom he lectured about Indian culture. He focuses most of his interest on the Creek people and paints their customs and rituals. He is one of the artists who defined the traditional style of painting done by the Five Civilized Tribes.

J. D. MEDINA

Zia; Zia Pueblo, Arizona

Artist—tempera

REPRESENTATION: Sunshine Studio, Sante Fe, New Mexico.

ABOUT THE ARTIST: Brother of Raphael Medina. His work is hard to find.

RAFAEL MEDINA

(a.k.a. Teeyacheena)

Zia (1929-) Zia Pueblo, Arizona

Artist—watercolors

EDUCATION: Studied with Velino Herrera and José Ray Toledo.

ABOUT THE ARTIST: Medina has tried many styles of painting but is most successful when he works in the traditional Rio Grande style. He paints the Zia ceremonials and is an active spokesman for the Zia people. He is famous for his watercolor portraits of dancers.

ART MENCHEGO

Santa Ana Pueblo, New Mexico
Sculptor, Painter, Ceramicist; Charcoal drawer; Watercolorist

ABOUT THE ARTIST: Menchengo is known for painting/sculpting horses, particularly Paint Ponies of the American Southwest. His work often depicts warriors in full battle gear and is colorful and realistic.

"Buffalo Blessings" by Art Menchego. Courtesy of Tribal Expressions, American Indian Art Gallery, Arlington Heights, IL. www.tribalexpressions.com.

R. GARY MILLER
(a.k.a. Se-Honh-Yess)

Mohawk (1950–) Toronto, Ontario, Canada
Painter and printmaker—oils, watercolors, pen and ink

EDUCATION: Art classes at Glenhurst Gardens in Toronto, as well as at the Mohawk Institute Residential School and Burlington High School. In 1974 he was an honor graduate of Ontario College of Arts, and he took medical illustration and art history courses at the University of Toronto.

AWARDS: This artist has received much recognition for his work in the community and in exhibits. He even attended a dinner with the Queen of England and Prime Minister Trudeau for the Queen's Silver Jubilee (1977).

BRIAN MOHR
(a.k.a. Ga Hen Di')

Seneca (1959–) Salamanca, New York
Painter—oils, pencil, watercolors; beadworker

EDUCATION: Mohr learned beadwork skills from his grandmother, Deforest Abrams, Monroe Abrams, and others; studied painting and drawing in school; and studied silverworking at the Seneca Nation Organization for the Visual Arts.

AWARDS: Among Mohr's honors is a first prize for his work at the 1977 New York State Fair.

ABOUT THE ARTIST: In addition to painting traditional Iroquois life, Mohr also beads his own dance costumes and has learned to carve masks.

AL MOMADAY
(a.k.a. Haun Toa, "War Lance")

Kiowa (1913–) Mountainview, Oklahoma
Artist—various media

EDUCATION: Bacone College (1931–34); University of New Mexico, Albuquerque (1936–37); University of California at Los Angeles (1956); Famous Artists School correspondence course.

AWARDS: His numerous awards and honors include the Southwestern Indian Artists Award given by the Dallas Exchange Club (1956) and a Certificate of Appreciation awarded by the Indian Arts and Crafts Board, U.S. Department of the Interior (1967).

ABOUT THE ARTIST: The father of N. Scott Momaday, this artist was the grandson of a Kiowa medicine man, and thus knew the intricacies of tribal ceremonies, legends, and history. He brought some of this knowledge into his work and instructed others in art while at the Jemez Pueblo Day School in New Mexico. He illustrated some of his son's books. Momaday's work was commissioned by churches and other associations throughout the world and exhibited widely.

N. SCOTT MOMADAY

Kiowa (1934–) Lawton, Oklahoma
Illustrator, Drawer, Painter

EDUCATION: B.A., University of New Mexico (1958); M.A., Stanford (1960); Ph.D., Stanford (1963). Twelve honorary degrees.

AWARDS: Pulitzer Prize (literature), Guggenheim Fellowship, and numerous others.

REPRESENTATION: Horwitch LewAllen Gallery, Santa Fe, New Mexico.

ABOUT THE ARTIST: Momaday illustrates his own and other authors' books and lectures all over the world. He has held tenured positions at several U.S. universities and has won many writing awards, and his art has been exhibited widely, including a one-man, 20-year retrospective show at the Wheelwright Museum in Santa Fe during 1992–93.

DONALD MONTILEAUX

Oglala Sioux (1948–) South Dakota
Artist—acrylics

EDUCATION: Has studied under Oscar Howe, as well as at the Institute of American Indian Arts. Mentored by Herman Red Elk.

ABOUT THE ARTIST: Montileaux combines the traditional Plains painting on hide (using watercolors and quills) to abstract symbols that appear to be futuristic in tone. Though he frequently draws upon themes used by his Sioux forefathers, he often uses modern themes as well. His painting "Looking Beyond Oneself" was aboard the space shuttle *Endeavor*.

MARK D. MONTOUR

Mohawk (1952–) Caughnawaga, Quebec, Canada
Painter—acrylics, mixed media

EDUCATION: Architecture courses at City College of New York (1973); B.F.A. from Concordia University (1977).

ABOUT THE ARTIST: Montour has worked with many media, has taught art, has exhibited his work, and is a board member of the Native American Friendship Center in Montreal.

NANCY MONTOUR
(a.k.a. Skonwakwenni)

Mohawk (1934–)
Painter—oil pastels and oils

EDUCATION: Self-taught.
ABOUT THE ARTIST: Montour generally paints landscapes and sunsets.

ROSS MONTOUR
(a.k.a. Kakwiatkeron)

Mohawk (1954–) Caughnawaga, Quebec, Canada
Illustrator, beadworker, leatherworker, wood- and stone-carver

EDUCATION: Self-taught and has attended various classes.
AWARDS: Scholarship to attend School of Visual Arts.
ABOUT THE ARTIST: Montour's illustrations have been part of a number of books produced by Native people. He's also done beading on leather, as well as looms.

GERONIMA CRUZ MONTOYA
(a.k.a. Po-Tsunu)

San Juan; San Juan Pueblo
Artist—tempera

EDUCATION: Studied with Dorothy Dunn.
REPRESENTATION: Sunshine Studios, Sante Fe, New Mexico.
ABOUT THE ARTIST: Montoya assisted Dorothy Dunn at the Santa Fe Indian School from 1937 to 1947, then was director of the school after Dunn retired, keeping that position until 1962.

TOMMY EDWARD MONTOYA
(a.k.a. Than Ts'ay Ta)

San Juan
Painter

REPRESENTATION: Adobe Gallery, Albuquerque, New Mexico.
ABOUT THE ARTIST: Montoya has a subtle, ethereal style.

STEPHEN MOPOPE
(a.k.a. Qued Koi, Wood-Coy, "Painted Robe")

Kiowa (1900–74) near Anadarko (the Kiowa Reservation), Oklahoma
Artist—watercolors, other media

EDUCATION: His uncles taught him how to paint on hides, as well as the techniques of Kiowa painting. Mopope also studied with Susie Peters of the Kiowa Agency in Anadarko, Oklahoma, as well as at the University of Oklahoma, Norman (1926–29).

AWARDS: His many awards include a Certificate of Appreciation by the Indian Arts and Crafts Board, U.S. Department of the Interior (1966).

REPRESENTATION: Heard Museum, Phoenix, Arizona, and Fred Jones Jr. Museum of Art, University of Oklahoma, Norman.

ABOUT THE ARTIST: Mopope broke out of the Kiowa tradition of painting by including more figures in his narrative paintings. He was one of the Five Kiowas at the University of Oklahoma, his work is represented in *Kiowa Art*, and his paintings have been exhibited all over the world. His commissions include murals for the U.S. Department of the Interior, Washington, D.C. (1938), as well as works sponsored by the Works Progress Administration and the Public Works Administration.

MARY MOREZ
Navajo (1946–) Tuba City, Arizona
Artist—mixed media

EDUCATION: Southwest Indian Art Project, University of Arizona, Tucson. Morez is constantly going to school, taking new classes.

ABOUT THE ARTIST: Morez paints Navajo deities in a symbolic manner and often translates her dreams into her paintings. Her style is a bit abstract and combines traits from cubism, abstract expressionism, and the style of Joe Herrera. She takes some of her ideas from life (especially the Indian dancers) and portrays them colorfully. She states, "Everything I have learned over the years goes into my paintings: philosophy of the Navajo, the environment, religion, everything."

GEORGE MORRISON
Ojibway/Chippewa (1919–) Grand Marais, Minnesota
Painter, sculptor

EDUCATION: Studied art at the Minneapolis School of Art; got a honorary master's degree from that institution (now called the Minneapolis College of Art and Design); also studied at the Art Students League in New York City.

AWARDS: Fulbright Fellowship (1951) to study and work in France, Italy, and Spain.

REPRESENTATION: Bockley Gallery, Minneapolis, Minnesota; Minnesota Museum of American Art, St. Paul.

ABOUT THE ARTIST: Morrison's style is a conglomeration of those which he learned during his formal art training, as well as what he soaked up about his own quickly disappearing culture. His work has gone through many changes, and, as an artist, Morrison accepts those changes, works with them, and declares that he doesn't believe his art will make him immortal, that change is inevitable. He was the first Native artist on the faculty of the Rhode Island School of Design and the first Indian artist on the New York art scene.

NORVAL MORRISSEAU

Ojibway (1932–) Canada
Artist—acrylics

EDUCATION: One of the founders of the Ojibwa-Cree-Odawa School.

AWARDS: Order of Canada (1978). Elected to the Royal Canadian Academy of Arts.

ABOUT THE ARTIST: Morrisseau is considered one of Canada's premier painters and has influenced the next generation of artists. He founded the school of art called Woodland painting. Artists such as Tony Chee Chee and Leland Bell studied with Morrisseau. When he first began painting, he fought his tribe's tradition to prohibit painting certain subjects. His paintings and drawings are semiabstract visions of how he sees his culture's mystic ways.

JAMES MOSES

(a.k.a. Kivetoruk)

Eskimo (1900–82) near Cape Espenberg, Alaska
Artist—pen and ink, colored pencils, watercolors, mixed media

EDUCATION: Self-taught artist.

ABOUT THE ARTIST: Moses painted people he knew, experiences he'd had, and events he'd seen. His drawings and paintings of the land in which he lived reflect the cold and the animals with which the Eskimo shares his land. Moses did not begin painting until after he was injured in a plane accident in 1953.

RAYMOND NAHA

Hopi (d. 1974)
Artist—gouache, oils, pastels, inks

AWARDS: First Award at the Philbrook Show twice; Indian Arts Fund Award in Santa Fe, New Mexico; Bimson Grand Award at the Scottsdale National; and First Awards at the Gallup Ceremonials.

REPRESENTATION: Sunshine Studios, Sante Fe, New Mexico; Kiva Gallery, Gallup, New Mexico.

ABOUT THE ARTIST: Naha's work is much sought after in the art world. His paintings of Hopi dance scenes represent the whole scene, spotlighting key figures in the dance.

JOYCE LEE TATE NEVAQUAYA

(a.k.a. Doc Tate Nevaquaya, Nevaquaya, "One Who Is Tired of Looking Nice")

Comanche (1932–) Apache, Oklahoma
Artist

EDUCATION: Self-taught artist. Attended the Haskell Institute, Lawrence, Kansas (1951–52).

AWARDS: His awards include the Grand Award at the All Indian Art Show in Chicago in 1969, as well as many others.

REPRESENTATION: Eagles Roost Gallery, Colorado Springs, Colorado.

ABOUT THE ARTIST: Nevaquaya began painting professionally in the late 1950s and has exhibited his work in one-man, as well as group, shows all over the United States. He is also a self-taught flutist and composer who has played all over the world.

GUY NEZ, JR.

Navajo
Painter

REPRESENTATION: Quintana Galleries, Portland, Oregon; Native Arts Trading, Isle of Man, England.

ABOUT THE ARTIST: Nez paints Southwestern scenes, still lifes with pottery and baskets, and historical scenes. He has been painting for approximately 30 years, and many of his works hang in historic sites in Arizona and New Mexico.

REDWING T. NEZ

Navajo (1961–   )
Painter

AWARDS: First prize and Best of Show, Annual Navajo Artist's Exhibition, Museum of Northern Arizona (1987).

ABOUT THE ARTIST: Nez's painting "Her Precious Time" reflects his feelings about his grandmother (a weaver) and her work. He has also illustrated children's books, such as *Forbidden Talent*, published by Northland Publishing.

GEORGINA NICHOLAS
(a.k.a. Ga Han De Yosd)

Oneida (1928–   ) Southwold, Ontario, Canada
Artist—drawing, painting

EDUCATION: Took drawing and language classes at the Oneida Settlement Reserve.

AWARDS: Nicholas's many awards include first prize at the Oneida Fall Festival.

ABOUT THE ARTIST: Nicholas is multitalented. Not only does she draw and paint, but she has also knitted, crocheted, and done leather tooling, as well as helping her grandmother make cornhusk mats, dolls, and baskets. Furthermore, Nicholas is also a dedicated teacher, offering her knowledge of the Oneida language to her students.

PAT NICHOLAS

Oneida (1953–   ) Southwold, Ontario, Canada
Artist—pencil, oil pastels, chalk, acrylics, watercolors

EDUCATION: Self-taught.

ABOUT THE ARTIST: Nicholas does pencil portraits and watercolors of nature scenes. One of her designs graced the cover of *Three Generations*, a book about three generations of people on the reserve. She also does beadwork.

SHELLEY NIRO
(a.k.a. Shelley Doxtater)

Mohawk (1954–   ) Niagara Falls, New York
Painter, sculptor, photographer, filmmaker

EDUCATION: Trained in Durham College's Graphics Programme in Oshawa, Ontario (1978) and at the Ontario College of Art in Toronto.

REPRESENTATION: Sacred Circle Gallery of American Indian Art, Seattle, Washington, Daybreak Star Arts Center, Discovery Park, Seattle.

ABOUT THE ARTIST: Niro's collection of photographs entitled *Mohawks in Beehives* showed at Ottawa's Ufundi Gallery in 1991 and surprised viewers. Since that time, Niro's sense of humor in her photographs has been recognized nationally. A film that she wrote in 1992 (*It Starts with a Whisper*) starred her three sisters and won the Walking in Beauty Award at the Two Rivers Film and Video Festival in Minneapolis, Minnesota.

DENNIS NUMKENA

Hopi
Painter, architect

REPRESENTATION: Firehouse Gallery of Fine Arts, Bisbee, Arizona.

ABOUT THE ARTIST: Numkena designed sets and costumes for Mozart's opera *The Magic Flute*, an event held in Vienna. He also designed the Anasazi Plaza in Arizona.

J. NUMKENA-TALAYUMPTEWA

Navajo/Hopi; Tuba City, Arizona
Artist—watercolors and ink

ABOUT THE ARTIST: This artist's Native teachings came mostly from her father's side of the family, the Hopi side. She often illustrates Hopi ceremonies and traditions in her work, using soft colors that blend traditional style with contemporary.

LOREN PAHSETOPAH
(a.k.a. "Four Hills")

Cherokee/Osage (1935–) Pawhuska, Oklahoma
Artist—tempera and gouache

EDUCATION: Self-taught artist who began painting in 1941.

AWARDS: His awards include three Second Awards at the American Indian Artists Exhibition at the Philbrook Art Center in Tulsa, Oklahoma (1962, 1965, 1967).

ABOUT THE ARTIST: Pahsetopah's work has been exhibited nationally and internationally. His style is simple and natural, often focusing on the Native American family.

PAUL PAHSETOPAH
(a.k.a. Four Hills)

Cherokee/Osage (1932–) Pawhuska, Oklahoma
Artist

EDUCATION: Like his brother, Loren, Paul is a self-taught artist.

AWARDS: Pahsetopah's awards include a First Award from the American Indian Artists Exhibition at the Philbrook Art Center in Tulsa, Oklahoma (1967).

ABOUT THE ARTIST: He has exhibited his work throughout the United States in group shows. Pahsetopah also makes dance costumes and sings at various Native American events.

TONITA PENA
(a.k.a. Quah Ah)

San Ildefonso (1893–1949) San Ildefonso, New Mexico
Artist

REPRESENTATION: Adobe Gallery, Albuquerque, New Mexico.

ABOUT THE ARTIST: Part of the San Ildefonso Self-Taught Group, Pena started as an easel artist, painting ceremonial dances and everyday events. At first she signed her paintings with her Indian name. After 1915 she modified her signature. She was the mother of Joe Herrera.

RITA PHILLIPS
(a.k.a. Wita)

Mohawk (1929–) Caughnawaga, Quebec, Canada
Illustrator, painter, beadworker, dollmaker

EDUCATION: Self-taught.

ABOUT THE ARTIST: Phillips's illustrations have been published in books on Quebec Native Americans. She is also an educator who feels that Iroquois arts should be recognized as legitimate art forms. She has worked closely with others to produce Mohawk language books.

OQWA PI

San Ildefonso (ca. 1899–71) San Ildefonso Pueblo, New Mexico
Painter

EDUCATION: Untrained.

AWARDS: Received awards from both his constituents and exhibits.

ABOUT THE ARTIST: Pi began painting around 1919 and was encouraged to continue. Because he turned out a large number of paintings during this life, he made a good living at his art. His first exhibit was at the 1931 Exposition of Indian Tribal Arts in New York City, and, after that time, his work was shown throughout the U.S.

PITSEOLAK
Eskimo (1904–83) Hudson Bay area, Canada
Graphic artist—stone cuts, engravings and drawings with felt-tip pen
EDUCATION: Self-taught.
ABOUT THE ARTIST: Pitseolak created images of what she believed to be the past, about myths and monsters, and about Eskimo life as she knew it. The wife of a migrant hunter, she moved all over the Arctic region, teaching herself how to be an artist, making a living with her work, then passing on her skills to some of her 17 children (11 of them died).

OTIS POLELONEMA
(a.k.a. Lomadamocvia, "Springtime")
Hopi (1902–81) Shungopovi, Second Mesa, Arizona
Painter—watercolor on paper
EDUCATION: Santa Fe Indian School, New Mexico.
REPRESENTATION: Amerind Foundation Museum, Dragoon, Arizona.
ABOUT THE ARTIST: Polelonema and Fred Kabotie are said to have started the Hopi style of painting. Polelonema's delicate touch with the brush captured details of Hopi life. His and Kabotie's skills were an apex that generations of other artists attempted to reach. He started painting in 1917 and was active in the Works Progress Administration.

CHARLES PUSHETONEQUA
(a.k.a. Wawabano Data, "Dawn Walker")
Sauk-Fox (1915–) Tama City, Iowa
Painter
EDUCATION: Studied at Pipestone, Minnesota Indian School, Haskell Institute (Lawrence, Kansas) and Santa Fe Indian School.
REPRESENTATION: Museum of New Mexico.
ABOUT THE ARTIST: Pushetonequa actively participated in the Sauk and

Fox community's Indian Crafts organization at Tama. His paintings realistically depict the life and history of the Sauk-Fox people.

WILLIAM RABBIT

Cherokee; Oklahoma

Artist—oils

EDUCATION: He says he paints with the influence of Solomon McCombs, Fred Beaver, Blackbear Bosin, and Jerome Tiger.

AWARDS: Many, including first place at the Five Civilized Tribes Museum in Muskogee, Oklahoma (1981) and a number of prizes at the 61st Annual Gallup Ceremonial (1982). Poster artist for the 1985 "Trail of Tears" art show and for an exhibit at the Smithsonian.

REPRESENTATION: Gomes Gallery Inc., St. Louis, Missouri.

ABOUT THE ARTIST: Rabbit worked as a silversmith in the early years of his career, before producing the award-winning paintings for which he is well known. Collections of his work are held all over the world.

ROBERT REDBIRD

Kiowa (1939-) Lawton, Oklahoma

Artist—oils, watercolors

EDUCATION: Oklahoma State Tech, Okmulgee, Oklahoma (1960–62).

AWARDS: Best of Class in theme and first place in painting, Colorado Indian Market, Denver (1987). Named to the top five of "Best Investments in Indian Art under $1,000 for 1987." Has won numerous other international awards.

REPRESENTATION: Susan Peters Gallery, Anadarko, Oklahoma; Eagles Roost Gallery, Colorado Springs, Colorado; Antiques and Art, Seattle, Washington.

ABOUT THE ARTIST: Redbird is an associate pastor at the Tabernacle of Deliverance Church in Anadarko, Oklahoma. Collections of his work are held by Carnegie High School and by private collectors. He has exhibited in one-man and group shows throughout the United States.

ROBERT REDBIRD, JR.

Kiowa; Oklahoma

Artist—oils, watercolors

ABOUT THE ARTIST: Following in his father's footsteps, Redbird, Jr., has become a well-known artist. He plans to reside in Oklahoma and continue with his artwork.

LEONARD RIDDLES
(a.k.a. "Black Moon")

Comanche (1918–) Walters, Oklahoma
Artist

EDUCATION: Studied mural techniques at the Indian Art Center in Fort Sill, Oklahoma (1938–39).

AWARDS: His many awards include the First Award, Plains Division, from the Philbrook Art Center, Tulsa, Oklahoma (1969).

ABOUT THE ARTIST: Riddles has exhibited his traditional work in many group and one-man exhibits throughout the United States. He paints scenes of Indian life in a clear and precise manner, using watercolors, and signs them "Black Moon."

J. D. ROYBAL
(a.k.a. Oquwa, "Rain God")

San Ildefonso (1922–78) San Ildefonso Pueblo, New Mexico
Artist—tempera

EDUCATION: Santa Fe Indian School, New Mexico.

REPRESENTATION: Adobe Gallery, Albuquerque, New Mexico.

ABOUT THE ARTIST: Began painting in grade school, but did not devote time to the art until the 1950s. Roybal produced many paintings during the 1960s–70s. He was strongly influenced by San Ildefonso traditional painting styles, as well as Santa Fe Studio designs.

WILL SAMPSON

Creek (d. 1987) Oklahoma
Artist, actor

AWARDS: Won the Philbrook Art Center (Tulsa) art award in 1951, as well as many others.

ABOUT THE ARTIST: As a member of the Screen Actors Guild, he promoted the Indian in acting, directing, writing, and producing. He played the role of Chief Bromden in *One Flew Over the Cuckoo's Nest*. As an artist, Sampson sold his first painting at the age of three. He did landscapes and Western and Indian scenes in the style of Charles Russell and exhibited at the

Smithsonian, Library of Congress, Amon Carter Museum, and Creek Council House Museum.

ABEL SANCHEZ
(a.k.a. Oqwa Pi, "Red Cloud")—see page 73

PATRICK SANCHEZ
Zuni
Artist—acrylics

REPRESENTATION: Sunshine Studios, Sante Fe, New Mexico.
ABOUT THE ARTIST: Sanchez does some mandalas and is known for his intricate work.

PERCY TSISETE SANDY
(a.k.a. Kai Sa, "Red Moon")
Zuni (1918–74) Zuni Pueblo, New Mexico
Artist—watercolors

EDUCATION: Studied painting at the Albuquerque Indian School and the Dorothy Dunn Santa Fe Indian School.
REPRESENTATION: Sunshine Studios, Sante Fe, New Mexico.
ABOUT THE ARTIST: Sandy married a Taos woman and lived most of his life at Taos Pueblo, where he created authentic and realistic depictions of his people, often painting Kachinas in a detailed and meticulous manner. He is best known for his watercolors of dancers and wild animals.

ALLEN SAPP
Plains Cree (1929–) Saskatchewan, Canada
Artist—acrylics

EDUCATION: Elected to the Royal Canadian Academy of Arts. Sask Award of Merit (1985).
ABOUT THE ARTIST: Sapp's mother died, leaving him to be raised by his grandmother on the Red Pheasant Reserve in Saskatchewan. During his career Sapp has expanded his repertoire and gained success. Sapp paints in a realistic, narrative way. His works show how the Canadian Indians lived before World War II.

C. TERRY SAUL
(a.k.a. Tabaksi, "Ember of Fire")

Choctaw/Chickasaw (1921–76) Sardis, Oklahoma
Artist—acrylics, watercolors

EDUCATION: Studied at Bacone College with Woody Crumbo and Acee Blue Eagle; received a B.A. and an M.F.A. from the University of Oklahoma.

REPRESENTATION: Heard Museum, Phoenix, Arizona.

ABOUT THE ARTIST: As a painter, Saul turned to the legends and rituals of the Choctaw tribe for inspiration. His style made his figures light and floaty, creating a spiritlike, otherworldly feel to his paintings. He felt a strong responsibility as spokesperson for his tribe and tried to relate that through his painting. When he died he was chairperson of the art department at Bacone College.

EILEEN SAWATIS
(a.k.a. Looking for a Bluer Sky)

Mohawk (1943–) Hogansburg, New York
Painter, sandpainter, silk-screener, wood-carver, clothing designer, doll-maker, weaver

EDUCATION: Self-taught; learned some techniques from her mother and grandmother.

AWARDS: Sawatis has won many awards for her work at the Malone Fair in New York.

ABOUT THE ARTIST: Sawatis is a multitalented artist whose subjects include Iroquois legends, nature, scenery, wildlife, and portraits. She also sews Iroquois clothing ornamented with beads or ribbons, makes apple-faced dolls, and writes poetry and short stories.

GARY SCHILDT
(a.k.a. Lone Bull)

Blackfoot (1938–) Helena, Montana
Sculptor

EDUCATION: Studied commercial art and photography at City College, San Francisco.

REPRESENTATION: Meadowlark Gallery, Billings, Montana.

ABOUT THE ARTIST: Grew up on the reservation on his family's ranch in Montana. Influenced by Western art, such as that by Charles Russell. Schildt tries to give his sculptures the feeling of life that you might see below the surface. His bronzes are realistic and are often of the very young or very old. He lives and works in the Four Corners part of the Southwest.

FRITZ SCHOLDER

Mission/Luiseno (1937-) Breckenridge, Minnesota
Artist—oil on canvas; sculptor—bronze

EDUCATION: Studied under Francis Bacon. B.F.A., California State University, Sacramento; M.F.A., University of Arizona, Tucson; Southwest Indian Art Project, Tucson.

REPRESENTATION: Riva Yares Gallery, Scottsdale, Arizona; Louis Newman Gallery, Beverly Hills, California; Bishop Gallery, Allenspark, Colorado; Susan Duval Gallery, Aspen, Colorado; John A. Boler, Indian and Western Art, Minneapolis, Minnesota; Nevada Institute of Contemporary Art, Las Vegas; Albuquerque Museum of Art, History and Science, Albuquerque, New Mexico; Charlotte Jackson Fine Art, Santa Fe, New Mexico; Wheelwright Museum of the American Indian, Santa Fe; Ed Hill Gallery, El Paso, Texas.

ABOUT THE ARTIST: Scholder challenges every stereotype of Native Americans as a people and as artists. His feelings are that he is an artist, rather than an Indian artist. He purposely distorts his paintings of them so that he may relay the pain and confusion his people have felt. He believes that "[t]here is still real magic in the remnants of the American Indian" (*American Indian Painting & Sculpture* by Patricia Janis Broder). Scholder started instructing at the Institute of American Indian Arts in 1962 and was one of the original four to open the school.

HART MERRIAM SCHULTZ

(a.k.a. Nitoh Mahkwi, "Lone Wolf")

Blackfoot (1882–1970) Birch Creek, Minnesota
Painter, sculptor, illustrator

EDUCATION: Studied at the Art Students League, Los Angeles (1910) and the Art Institute of Chicago (1914). Influenced by Thomas Moran and Harry Carr (art critic of *Los Angeles Times*).

ABOUT THE ARTIST: Schultz's work was often compared to Frederic Remington's, as they both did active sculptures of men on horseback and of Wild West scenes. He painted in both oil and watercolor, painting scenes of Plains Indians. In addition to painting and sculpting, Schultz also illustrated some books by his father (white writer James Willard Schultz). Schultz was at the height of his career in the 1920s.

BERT D. SEABOURN

Cherokee (1931–) Iraan, Texas
Artist—oils

EDUCATION: Certificate of Art from Oklahoma C.U. in 1960 and studied with the Famous Artists Correspondence Art School.

AWARDS: Awards include three from ITIC.

ABOUT THE ARTIST: Seabourn has exhibited throughout the Southwest and has had one-man shows at Henson Gallery (Oklahoma) and Chandler Galleries (Oklahoma). The Oklahoma Art Center holds a collection of his work. His distinctive work often features the face of a Native American in an arrangement with some kind of wildlife.

DONALD HENRY SECONDINE, JR.

Cherokee/Delaware (1952–) Nowata, Oklahoma
Artist—gouache on illustration board

EDUCATION: Haskell Indian Junior College, Lawrence, Kansas (early 1970s); studied art with Loren Pahsetopah; attended a 1970 workshop given by Jim Burden in Washington, D.C.

AWARDS: His awards include an honorable mention from the Philbrook Art Center (Tulsa, Oklahoma) that was given to him when he was still in college.

ABOUT THE ARTIST: Secondine's work is his vision of what his ancestors may have looked like as they held court, as well as other scenes of Delaware or Cherokee life. He's a multitalented person: a flute player, as well as an artist.

DUKE WSAAJA SINE

Yavapi/San Carlos Apache (1955–) San Carlos, Arizona
Painter

EDUCATION: Learned the basics of art from his father, David V. Sine. Institute of American Indian Arts, Santa Fe, New Mexico (1973).

"Since the Beginning of Time" by
Duke Wsaaja Sine. White paint
and pencil on black paper. 14" ×
18". Private collection. Courtesy of
Tribe Azure Jewelry and Art,
Tucson, AZ.

AWARDS: Many awards, including commissions for posters for the White
Mountains Native American Arts Festival, the Indian Health Service, and
the Heard Museum, Phoenix, Arizona, as well as many others.

REPRESENTATION: Tribe Azure Jewelry and Art Gallery, Tucson, Arizona.

ABOUT THE ARTIST: A full-time artist for less than two decades, he uses watercolors and has tried to develop a distinct style by interpreting the ceremonial, social, and historical aspects of his culture. He uses fine details and
strong colors in his paintings. Sine's work has been exhibited all over the
Southwestern United States and is held in the permanent collections of

"The Sacred Prayers of White Shell Woman" by Duke Wsaaja
Sine. Watercolor, colored pencil, colored paint on paper.
18" × 12½". $4,500. Courtesy of Tribe Azure Jewelry and Art,
Tucson, AZ.

Portrait of Duke Wsaaja Sine.
Courtesy of Tribe Azure Jewelry and
Art, Tucson, AZ.

Arizona State Museum at the University of Arizona in Tucson and the
Heard Museum in Phoenix. His work has been published in many books
and articles.

ERNEST SMITH

Seneca (1907–75) Tonawanda Reservation, New York
Artist—oils, ink, watercolors

EDUCATION: Self-taught artist.

ABOUT THE ARTIST: Smith liked to paint stories of ancient legends, thus his
work became narrative. Though he had no formal training, his style was
delicate and finely executed.

JAUNE QUICK-TO-SEE SMITH

Flathead (1940–) St. Ignatius, Montana
Artist—various media

EDUCATION: B.A., Framingham State College, Massachusetts (1976);
M.F.A., University of New Mexico, Albuquerque (1980).

AWARDS: Among the many awards, Smith has won are honorary degrees
and commissions. She has also curated shows, organized cooperatives, and
been very active in her field.

REPRESENTATION: Horwitch LewAllen Gallery, Santa Fe, New Mexico; Jan
Cicero Gallery, Chicago, Illinois; Fort Wayne Museum of Art, Fort
Wayne, Indiana; Maine College of Art/The Baxter Gallery, Portland,
Maine; Yellowstone Art Center, Billings, Montana; Tamarind Institute,
Albuquerque, New Mexico; DEL Fine Art Galleries, Santa Fe, New Mex-
ico; Steinbaum Krauss Gallery, New York City; East Carolina Univer-
sity/Wellington B. Gray Gallery, Greenville, North Carolina.

ABOUT THE ARTIST: Smith's work shows her knowledge of the European
artists, as well as her ardor to show her Indian heritage. This effort often
comes out in her narratives, which are quite abstract. She is an outspoken
proponent of Native American issues, as well as environmental concerns,

and often brings those into her work. Her works are owned by the American Medical Association, AT&T, the Denver Art Museum, the National Museum of American Art, and many others.

LOIS SMOKY

(a.k.a. Lois Smokey, Bougetah, Bou Ge Tah)

Kiowa (1907–81) Anadarko, Oklahoma

Artist—mixed media

EDUCATION: Worked with Susan Peters at Anadarko Indian Agency; University of Oklahoma (1920s).

ABOUT THE ARTIST: Smoky was the only female of a group of five Kiowa Indians who became world renowned for their bold, broad style and knowledge of American Indian tribes and traditions during the 1920s when they studied at the University of Oklahoma. Their work represented the United States in the International Folk Art Exhibition in Prague, then the paintings and artists toured museums throughout the United States. Smoky stopped painting because of prejudice against her and is often left out of history books as one of the original Five Kiowas, but her work is in Jacobson's *Kiowa Indian Art* and *American Indian Painters*. Works are held by the Museum of the American Indian and McNay Art Institute in San Antonio, Texas.

CAROL SNOW

Allegany/Seneca; Allegany Reservation, New York

Artist—pen and ink

EDUCATION: Two degrees in zoology.

REPRESENTATION: Long Ago & Far Away Gallery, Manchester, Vermont.

ABOUT THE ARTIST: Snow draws wildlife because of her strong background in zoology. All of her art represents North American themes, and her series is called "Spirits of the Earth & Sky." Her paintings have been reproduced into prints as well as calendars.

CAROL A. SOATIKEE

Chiricahua Apache/Pima (1942–) Phoenix, Arizona

Artist—oil on canvas

EDUCATION: Studied art at Cameron College, Lawton, Oklahoma; art education at Central State College, Edmond, Oklahoma. She has three art degrees.

AWARDS: Her many awards include a first place at the Heard Museum (Phoenix, Arizona) in 1979 and a one-woman exhibit at the Southern Plains Indian Museum and Craft Center (Oklahoma) in 1973.

ABOUT THE ARTIST: Soatikee shared her knowledge of art by teaching the subject in the public school system of Anadarko, Oklahoma, and at the U.S. Indian School in Concho, Oklahoma. A fine poet and artist, she credits her mixed Native American background with giving her creativity, as well as her sensitivity to nature and devotion to God and family.

ALICE SOULIGNY

Cherokee/Delaware (1931–)
Artist

EDUCATION: Self-taught by watching the artists who lived nearby.

AWARDS: Souligny's list of awards is long and includes exhibits, TV and radio appearances, and publications.

ABOUT THE ARTIST: Alice started painting after raising her five children and now does portraits, as well as fantasies and abstracts. The colors she uses are vibrant and depict the heritage of her ancestors. She uses spiritualistic symbolism in her work, combining traditional values as well as contemporary.

KEVIN RED STAR

Crow (1943–) Montana
Artist—oil

EDUCATION: Graduated from the Institute of American Indian Arts in 1965.

AWARDS: Special award, Museum of New Mexico (1965).

REPRESENTATION: Custer County Art Center, Miles City, Missouri; 21st Century Fox Fine Art, Santa Fe, New Mexico. The Heard Museum (Phoenix, Arizona) and the Smithsonian Museum of the American Indian also own examples of Red Star's work.

ABOUT THE ARTIST: Red Star was exhibited at the Museum of New Mexico, as well as at the "First Annual Invitational Exhibition of American Indian Paintings" in 1965 and at the Riverside Museum (New York City) "Young American Indian Artists" (1966). The Indian Arts and Crafts Board holds a collection of his work. His paintings depict traditional scenes from Red Star's Crow background. He is considered one of the premier Northern Plains artists.

SUSAN STEWART

Crow/Blackfoot (1953–) Livermore, California
Painter, silk-screener

EDUCATION: Studied painting at the California College of Arts and Crafts, Oakland (1971–75); B.A. in fine arts from Montana State University (1981).

AWARDS: Stewart's work has been shown in many exhibitions, has been honored many times, and is held in permanent collections at the Museum of the Plains Indian in Browning, Montana, and the North Dakota Museum of Art in Grand Forks.

ABOUT THE ARTIST: Stewart has used watercolors and pastels, oils and monoprints, throughout her career. She likes to be spontaneous in her work and believes her paintings to be a "reflection of my inner visions." Her work has been influenced by Frank LaPena, George Longfish, Jean LaMarr, Kandinsky, and Klee.

DOROTHY STRAIT

Cherokee; Arizona
Painter

EDUCATION: Self-taught.

AWARDS: Strait has won many purchase awards, honorable mentions, prizes, and ribbons for her work.

ABOUT THE ARTIST: Strait works mostly in oils, but she does also use acrylics and watercolors and occasionally does portraits in pastels. She is a careful artist who researches her subjects completely so that she can incorporate their historic values in her work. Her paintings are held by many private collections and exhibited widely, including at the Annual Invitational at the Heard Museum in Phoenix, Arizona.

VIRGINIA STROUD

Cherokee (1949–) Tennessee
Artist—various media

REPRESENTATION: Eagles Roost Gallery, Colorado Springs, Colorado.

ABOUT THE ARTIST: Stroud's work draws upon her studies of all the different styles of Native American art, as well as the themes that originate within each tribe. Painting in the traditional manner, she does not add facial expressions or identities to her portraits. She paints the traditions and makes contemporary statements with her art. A writer as well, Stroud has written books for young adult readers.

THEODORE SUINA
(a.k.a. Kuperu, "Snow")

Cochiti (1918–) Cochiti Pueblo, New Mexico
Artist—tempera

EDUCATION: Santa Fe Indian School, studied with Geronima Montoya (Po-Tsuni).

ABOUT THE ARTIST: Permanently crippled by a fall from a horse, Suina began painting when a friend provided paints and paper, then went on to learn more about art. He has followed the basic designs of the Santa Fe Indian School, as well as abstract elements found on prehistoric pottery and petroglyphs. Suina is one of the muralists of the Southwest.

JOANNE SWANSON
(a.k.a. Kin'ughan)

Inupiaq Eskimo (July 23, 1952–) Unalakleet Village, Alaska
EDUCATION: Self-taught artist.

"Tusks and Tradebeads" by Joanne Swanson. Watercolor Giclee. Signed and numbered print $65. 13" × 17". Courtesy of Joanne Swanson.

"Danali, the Great One" by Joanne Swanson. Watercolor. 30" × 22". $1,000. Courtesy of Joanne Swanson.

"Two Girls Packing" by Joanne Swanson. Watercolor. Courtesy of Joanne Swanson.

REPRESENTATION: The Art Shop Gallery, Homer, Alaska; Dusty's Gold Gallery, Nome, Alaska; Alaska Native Heritage Center, Anchorage; Art-NatAm.com.

ABOUT THE ARTIST: Watercolor is Swanson's medium of choice. She says, "Challenge is a catalyst. I knew from the beginning if I didn't punch in the right numbers as you must in an algebraic equation I would not get it right. You need to know the basic principles of color and design to paint well. Never give up studying."

She continues, "My inspiration comes from having lived in rural Alaska. My ideas are endless. When someone views my paintings I want them to think 'I've been there . . . I remember.'" She has been helping Native organizations, such as Native radio stations, with donations from sales of her watercolors.

MARK SWAZO-HINDS
(*see* the "Sculpture" chapter for more photos of this artist's work, p. 431)

Tesuque; Tesuque Pueblo, New Mexico
Painter, sculptor

EDUCATION: Learned some of his techniques from his father, Patrick Swazo-Hinds.

Untitled pastel on paper by Mark Swazo-Hinds. Courtesy of Jill Giller, Native American Collections, Inc., www.nativepots.com. Photo by: Bill Bonebrake.

AWARDS: Many awards throughout the years.

REPRESENTATION: Native American Collections, Inc., Denver, Colorado.

ABOUT THE ARTIST: Swazo-Hinds is known for his bear fetishes, but he has done some more abstract sculptures and has also worked in watercolor on paper. He comes from an artistic family. His father, Patrick, was a well-known artist and mentor to many young artists.

TERRANCE TALASWAIMA
(a.k.a. Honvantewa, "Bear Making Tracks")
Hopi (1939–) Arizona
Artist—acrylics

ABOUT THE ARTIST: Talaswaima often paints about the spirit world, something that connects him strongly with his ancestors.

DANIEL J. TAULBEE
Comanche (1924–) Flathead Reservation, Montana
Artist

EDUCATION: Self-taught.

AWARDS: Taulbee has been the recipient of many awards and honors.

ABOUT THE ARTIST: This artist owned the Heritage American Gallery in Butte, Montana. His own work has been exhibited widely throughout the United States.

JOHN BIGTREE THOMAS
Mohawk (1958–) Hogansburg, New York
Painter—acrylics, pen and ink, pencil, tempera, charcoal; wood-carver

EDUCATION: Self-taught.

AWARDS: Thomas has been commissioned to do posters for the North American Indian Traveling College.

ABOUT THE ARTIST: Thomas started painting when his father, Frank, encouraged him. Now John paints the history of his people and their legends. Sometimes he does borders of his scenes, including geometric designs derived from peyote symbols used by the Native American Church. His family is active in working with the Akwesasne Library and Culture Center.

MARITA THOMPSON
(a.k.a. Kawenninon)

Mohawk (1956–   ) Cornwall Island, Ontario, Canada
Painter, basketmaker, beadworker, leatherworker, quilter

EDUCATION: Mostly self-taught, has taken some classes.

ABOUT THE ARTIST: Thompson can make baskets (she used to help her mother, Elizabeth, make them), does beadwork (floral designs on leather or felt), has made wooden rocking horses and other items, and also sews, crochets, and makes quilts. She demonstrates at fairs and craft shows, both in Canada and Florida. Her whole family is involved in arts and crafts, all working to help the Native Arts Cultural Organization spread information about their work and their people.

DANA TIGER

Cherokee-Creek/Seminole (1961–   )
Painter

AWARDS: Master Artist, Five Civilized Tribes Museum, Muskogee, Oklahoma (1997); Artist Choice Award and Peoples Choice Award, Colorado Indian Art Market, Denver (1998); Poster Artist, Attachments and Bonding Conference, Tulsa, Oklahoma (1998); Poster Artist, Honoring Her Gift, commemorating Wilma Mankiller's kidney transplant (1998); Spirit of Oklahoma Award, Masters Art Show, Five Tribes Museum, Muskogee (1999); Leadership Legacy Award, Oklahoma State University, Stillwater (1999); Poster Artist, Status of Women Study, State of Oklahoma (1999); Female Artist, Winter Camp Show, Cowboy Hall of Fame (January 2000); Poster Artist, Child Advocate Organization (June 2001); Spirit of Oklahoma Award, Masters Art Show, Five Tribes Museum, Muskogee (October 2001).

REPRESENTATION: NDN Art Gallery, Tahlequah, Oklahoma.

ABOUT THE ARTIST: Tiger is the daughter of famed Native American artist Jerome Tiger, and her work reflects the rich heritage with which she grew up. Her father died when she was five, so she turned to learning about his work when she got old enough to study art. Inspired by his legendary work, her paintings reflect what he taught her about her own heritage as well as her interest in Native American women's issues. She focuses on representing Native American women as strong and wise leaders. Her beliefs are evident in that she often donates her paintings to causes she finds worthy, such as the Nations Police Chiefs Conventions, AIDS Coalition for Indian Outreach, American Indian College Fund, American Cancer

Society, Indians in Medicine Project, National Organization for Women, and Conference of the American Family.

JEROME TIGER

Creek-Seminole (1941–67) Tahlequah, Oklahoma
Painter, sculptor

EDUCATION: Self-taught.
AWARDS: Top awards in the Printing Industries of America annual competition.
REPRESENTATION: Tiger Art Gallery, Muskogee, Oklahoma.
ABOUT THE ARTIST: Tiger was pretty much self-taught and, in the last five years of his life, produced hundreds of paintings. He had a colorful career, spending time as a fighter and a laborer. His career had just started to take off when he died in 1967 of a gunshot wound.

JOHNNY TIGER, JR.

Creek-Seminole; Tahlequah, Oklahoma
Painter, sculptor

AWARDS: Tiger has won many awards since he began working as an artist in 1967, including first place awards from many shows and fairs throughout the Southwest, the Governor's Award at the Five Civilized Tribes Museum (1977), Grand Prize, First Place, and the Heritage Award (as well as two others) at the 1978 Five Civilized Tribes Museum Annual Indian Exhibition, and many others (for both his paintings and sculptures).
REPRESENTATION: Tiger Art Gallery, Muskogee, Oklahoma.
ABOUT THE ARTIST: Johnny's brother, Jerome, was also a renowned artist. The two men learned about the Creek people and their native language from their grandfather. Tiger's work has been shown throughout the United States, as well as in England and Russia.

IRVING TODDY

Navajo; Chinle, Arizona
Artist—acrylics

AWARDS: Best-in-Class ribbon at the New Mexico State Fair in 1994.
REPRESENTATION: Sunshine Studios, Sante Fe, New Mexico, and many Southwest galleries.
ABOUT THE ARTIST: Toddy is the second son of Jimmy Toddy (Beatien Yazz). He is noted for detailed oil paintings of life on the Navajo reservation.

JIMMY TODDY
(a.k.a. Beatien Yazz, "Little No Shirt")

Navajo (1928–) Navajo Reservation, near Wide Ruins, Arizona
Artist—various media

EDUCATION: Studied with Yasuo Kuniyoshi at Mills College for two years; at the Santa Fe Indian School, New York; and at the Art Institute of Chicago.

REPRESENTATION: Tohono Chul Park, Tucson, Arizona; Sunshine Studios, Sante Fe, New Mexico.

ABOUT THE ARTIST: The most celebrated of the Navajo painters, Toddy has been written about in several books. Because of glaucoma, his last works were produced in the early 1990s. Toddy painted Navajo life on the reservations, featuring the traditions and ceremonies, using watercolors and natural colors. One of his paintings, done in 1946, pictured the Gallup Ceremonial Parade.

JOSÉ REY TOLEDO
(a.k.a. Sho-Bah-Woh-Hon, "Morning Star")

Jemez (1915–94) Jemez Pueblo, New Mexico
Artist—watercolors

EDUCATION: Started learning about art from his brother-in-law, John Sahmon, his uncle Juanito Moquino, and his cousin Velino. Received both B.A. and M.A. degrees in art at the University of New Mexico.

AWARDS: Has received awards at the Gallup Intertribal and the Philbrook Art Center, Oklahoma, as well as many others.

REPRESENTATION: Kiva Gallery, Gallup, New Mexico; Adobe Gallery, Albuquerque, New Mexico.

ABOUT THE ARTIST: Toledo regularly creates paintings of the Native American ceremonials and dance rituals. He tries to convey a deeper meaning to his paintings of those traditions. He shows the "far-away" look some Native American dancers have when they perform, and he tries to perfect his style. In 1992 the Museum of Indian Arts and Cultures mounted an exhibition of Toledo's work.

HERMAN TOPPAH
(a.k.a. All-Guat-Kou, "Yellow Hair")

Kiowa (1923–) Carnegie, Oklahoma
Artist

EDUCATION: Studied with muralist Olaf Nordmark at Indian Art Center, Fort Sill, Oklahoma; informal training from James Auchiah, Spencer Asah, Leonard Riddles, Archie Blackowl, and Cecil Murdock.

AWARDS: Among his awards are a Second Award in Special Category, American Indian Artists Exhibition, from the Philbrook Art Center in Tulsa, Oklahoma.

ABOUT THE ARTIST: Toppah has exhibited his work throughout the Southwest and is a member of the American Indian Artists Association.

LEE MONETT TSATOKE
(a.k.a. Tsa-Toke, "Hunting Horse")

Kiowa (1929–) Lawton, Oklahoma
Artist

EDUCATION: Self-taught.

AWARDS: Among Tsatoke's awards are a first prize, Indian Art Exhibit, American Indian Exposition, Anadarko, Oklahoma (1960).

ABOUT THE ARTIST: Tsatoke began painting in 1943 and has exhibited his works throughout the United States. He is also well known as a fancy war dancer in the Kiowa Dance troupe.

ANDY TSINAHJINNIE
(a.k.a. Yazzie Bahe, Andrew Tsinnajinne, "Little Gray")

Navajo (1918–) Rough Rock, Arizona
Artist—mixed media

EDUCATION: Studied with Dorothy Dunn at the Santa Fe Indian School in the 1930s.

AWARDS: Among this artist's many awards is a first prize in the 1962 Scottsdale National Indian Art Show for his painting "Slayer of Enemy Gods-Nayeinezani."

ABOUT THE ARTIST: One of the most influential Native American painters, Tsinahjinnie has a style that has been studied by artists of all generations (his and younger ones). His style and choice of medium have changed during his career, but his choice of subject matter has always been the same: the Navajo lifestyle.

HULLEAH TSINHNAHJINNIE

Seminole/Creek/Navajo (1954–) Phoenix, Arizona
Artist—multimedia

EDUCATION: Institute of American Indian Arts, Santa Fe; California College of Arts and Crafts, Oakland.

REPRESENTATION: San Francisco Art Institute Walter/McBean Gallery, San Francisco; Temple University, Tyler School of Art/Temple Gallery, Philadelphia, Pennsylvania; Sacred Circle Gallery of American Indian Art, Daybreak Star Arts Center, Discovery Park, Seattle, Washington.

ABOUT THE ARTIST: This artist is the daughter of Minnie McGirt of the Seminole and Muskogee nations and Andrew V. Tsinhnahjinnie of the Diné Nation. Hulleah uses her photography in conjunction with other media to produce pieces that often have significance, re: an anniversary (e.g., Columbus's arrival in America). She has taught at the University of California at Davis, San Francisco State University, the San Francisco Art Institute, and the Institute of American Indian Arts.

KEVIN SKYPAINTER TURNER

Choctaw (1958–) St. Louis, Missouri
Custom hand-painter—acrylics, oils, varnishes, etc.

EDUCATION: Self-trained sign painter and designer.

REPRESENTATION: Turner Artworks Trading Post and Art Gallery, DeSoto, Missouri; Red Cloud, St. Petersburg, Florida; Indian Sun, Sarasota, Florida; Dockside Gifts, Panama City Beach, Florida.

ABOUT THE ARTIST: Turner's unusual work includes creating a family coat of arms, Indian design fingernails (Turner is also a licensed manicurist), decorated crayfish pincher necklaces, earrings, pins, and shell amulet necklaces. He also makes arrowhead necklaces and chokers, as well as turtle shell wall hangings, paintings, and decorated skulls. Turner's work is sold through his catalog and the galleries that represent him.

JAMES TURPEN, JR.

Cherokee/Navajo (1930–) Winslow, Arizona
Painter, sculptor, jeweler

EDUCATION: University of Arizona.

ABOUT THE ARTIST: Turpen, who came from a family of traders, lived in the Southwest during his childhood, then moved after he married. While he traveled, he picked up a knowledge of art, continued to draw and to study Western and Indian history. His bronzes have been shown throughout the Southwest, and his jewelry is sometimes shown at Tobe Turpen's Indian Trading Company in Gallup, New Mexico (he manages the shop).

FRANK TUTTLE

Yuki/Wailaki/Koncow Maidu (1957–) Oroville, California
Painter—various media

EDUCATION: B.A. in fine arts, emphasis in Native American Studies, Humboldt State University (1981).

REPRESENTATION: Meridian Gallery Society for Art Publications of the Americas, San Francisco, California.

ABOUT THE ARTIST: Tuttle lectures in Native American art and studies at Medocino College and exhibits his work at Humboldt State University, as well as various other places. He experiments with different imagery and materials in his work, often combining the traditional with the contemporary. He has exhibited in solo and group exhibitions for many years at places including the Heard Museum, Phoenix, Arizona.

KYRATE TUVAHOEMA

Hopi (1914–42)
Artist—watercolors

REPRESENTATION: Sunshine Studios, Sante Fe, New Mexico.

ABOUT THE ARTIST: Tuvahoema created watercolors of Hopi ceremonial dances.

SHIRLEY VANATTA

Seneca (1922–75)
Painter—oils, watercolors, pastels, pen and ink

EDUCATION: Self-taught.

AWARDS: In 1972 Governor Nelson Rockefeller of New York presented Vanatta the award of Indian of the Year; she has also won many other honors.

ABOUT THE ARTIST: Vanatta's paintings and work in the Allegany community were appreciated by her community as well as the newspapers and magazines for which she illustrated during the 1950s–60s. She was also the publicist for the Seneca Nation and editor-in-chief of *O-He-Yah-Noh*. During her career she painted wildflowers, nature scenes, and portraits of famous Indians.

DONALD VANN

Cherokee (1952–) South Carolina
Artist—watercolors

EDUCATION: Self-taught.

AWARDS: Proclaimed "one of the best known Indian artists working in this century" by the Cherokee National Historical Society. The Smithsonian Institution's Museum of the American Indian top painting award for watercolor painting. First place ribbons in juried competitions at Oklahoma's Red Earth Exhibit, the Colorado Indian Market, and the National American Indian Arts Exposition.

REPRESENTATION: Eagles Roost Gallery, Colorado Springs, Colorado.

ABOUT THE ARTIST: Vann's paintings show the despair the Indians feel about how they've been deceived. He believes that his people have turned from their strong beliefs and are on the road leading to war, illness, violence, and despair. His paintings reflect a barren, stark landscape where it is always winter and always dreary.

PABLITA VELARDE
(a.k.a. Tse Tsan)

Santa Clara (1918–) Santa Clara Pueblo, New Mexico
Artist, muralist, portraitist—various media

EDUCATION: Velarde was the first full-time female student in Dorothy Dunn's art class at the Santa Fe Indian School (The Studio). Also studied with Tonita Pena.

REPRESENTATION: Amerind Foundation Museum, Dragoon, Arizona; Wheelwright Museum of the American Indian, Santa Fe, New Mexico.

ABOUT THE ARTIST: Velarde painted in the "traditional" style of Santa Fe and did accurate portraits of Indian life and culture. At first she worked in watercolor, but later learned how to prepare paints from natural pigments (a process called *fresco secco*). Velarde painted murals for the Bandelier National Monument in New Mexico (1939–48). She was also known to create art derived from the Navajo sandpainting tradition. Clara Tanner called her the "greatest woman artist in the Southwest." Velarde's daughter, Helen Hardin, was also quite well known.

PAUL VIGIL

Tesuque (ca. 1940–) Tesuque Pueblo, New Mexico
Artist—oils

EDUCATION: Learned some of his skills from father.

AWARDS: First place ribbon, Indian Market, Santa Fe, Mexico (1991).

ABOUT THE ARTIST: Vigil paints traditional Tewa dancers in the style of the early Pueblo artists, using delicate brushwork and geometric designs, as well as traditional motifs like corn, water, and Pueblo architecture. One of Paul's nine children (a son) is now learning to carry on the family's artistic tradition.

ROMANDO VIGIL
(a.k.a. Tse Ye Mu)

San Ildefonso (1902–72) San Ildefonso Pueblo, New Mexico
Artist—watercolor on paper

EDUCATION: Self-taught.

ABOUT THE ARTIST: A leader within the San Ildefonso Watercolor Movement, Vigil used a stylized design to represent ceremonial dances. He was a master at creating stylized images with a simple line. One of his many honors was being included in the first major exhibit of Native American art held in New York in 1931. He was employed at one point in the 1950s by Walt Disney Studios.

VIRGIL VIGIL

Tesuque; Tesuque Pueblo, New Mexico
Artist—oils

EDUCATION: Learned some of his skills from his father, Paul Vigil.

REPRESENTATION: Sunshine Studios, Sante Fe, New Mexico.

ABOUT THE ARTIST: Vigil's work is brighter than that of his father, but he is carrying on the tradition of painting Pueblo dancers.

KAY WALKINGSTICK

Cherokee (1935–) Syracuse, New York
Artist—mixed media

EDUCATION: B.F.A., Beaver College, Glenside, Pennsylvania; M.F.A., Pratt Institute, Brooklyn, New York.

AWARDS: WalkingStick has exhibited both solo and in museums. Her work is held in a number of public and private collections and has been honored by many awards.

REPRESENTATION: Wenger Gallery II at Hotel Nikko, Los Angeles; Wenger Gallery, Santa Monica, California; University at Albany/State University of New York/Rathbone Gallery, Albany, New York; Long Island University/Hillwood Art Museum, Brookville, New York; June Kelly Gallery,

New York City; State University College at Potsdam/Roland Gibson Gallery, Potsdam, New York; Cleveland State University Art Gallery, Cleveland, Ohio; Rainmaker Gallery, Bristol, United Kingdom.

ABOUT THE ARTIST: WalkingStick uses a diptych format, each painting needing the other to complete the picture. In 1987 she stated that she is "interested in the interrelationship between ideas and empirical reality." She is considered one of the leading contemporary Native American artists and is currently a professor of art at Cornell University, Ithaca, New York.

CARSON R. WATERMAN

Seneca (1944–) Salamanca, New York
Painter, graphics designer, printmaker, carver, sculptor

EDUCATION: Fine arts certified instructor degree, Cooper School of Art (1965–67); Smithsonian Institution internship program.

AWARDS: Honors include commissions from the Seneca Nation, the Department of Transportation, HUD, and others. One of his paintings (included in the exhibit "Famous Presidential Quotations") now hangs in the Lyndon B. Johnson Library.

ABOUT THE ARTIST: Waterman's mural paintings are well known in the Cattaraugus and Allegany nations' buildings. His work centers around Iroquois themes and at times has been political in content. He has extensive teaching experience, has acted as exhibit curator, has exhibited his own work, and was cofounder (with Pete Jemison) of the Seneca Nation Organization for the Visual Arts.

WA-WA-CHAW

(a.k.a. Wawa Calac Chaw, "Keep from the Water," Benita Nunez)
Luiseno (1888–1972) Valley Center, California
Artist, writer

EDUCATION: Self-taught.

ABOUT THE ARTIST: This artist was raised by Dr. Cornelius Duggan and his sister Mary because Wa-Wa-Chaw had been ill at birth. A child prodigy, she sketched Pierre and Marie Curie's experiments and started talking about her work and Indian matters to the public when still a teenager. Her oil paintings were done on large canvases and were usually portraits of people who were important at that time. A very active speaker on the equality of Indian women, she met many of the intellectuals and leaders of her day, including Sir Arthur Conan Doyle, General Richard H. Pratt, and Arthur C. Parker. After she married Manuel Carmonia-Nunez, she changed her name to Benita Nunez.

W. RICHARD (DICK) WEST
(a.k.a. Wapah Nahyah, Wah-Pah-Nah-Yah, "Lightfooted Runner" or "Lightfoot")

Cheyenne (1912–) near Darlington, Oklahoma
Artist—watercolors; sculptor—wood

EDUCATION: Studied with Acee Blue Eagle at Bacone College. West was the first full-blooded Indian to graduate from the University of Oklahoma (B.F.A., 1941; M.F.A., 1950). Also studied with the muralist Olaf Nordmark.

AWARDS: West has won many awards, including the Grand Award at the Philbrook Art Center (1955).

ABOUT THE ARTIST: For almost 25 years (1947–70), West taught and was director of Bacone College's art department. He has received honors for both his artistic and teaching abilities, as well as his painstaking research as tribal historian. His paintings show that knack for detail and historical accuracy. His career has often been said to reflect that of the entire Native American arts community—he has explored and experimented with a number of styles, techniques, and arts.

ANDREW WHITE
(a.k.a. Tekaronhaneka)

Mohawk (1947–) Hogansburg, New York
Painter—oils, charcoal, pencil

EDUCATION: Self-taught.

AWARDS: White has exhibited at the Iroquois Confederacy Arts and Crafts Exhibition.

ABOUT THE ARTIST: White has become well known for the paintings he does of Iroquois history, culture, and traditions. He sometimes also paints about other Indian cultures as well.

LARRY WHITE
(a.k.a. Kanatakeniate)

Mohawk (1945–) Hogansburg, New York
Painter—oils, acrylics, charcoal

EDUCATION: White is mostly self-taught; however, he has taken some community college classes in Texas and Nevada.

ABOUT THE ARTIST: White's brother, Andrew, encouraged him to start painting. He does mostly portraits or Native American scenes.

RANDY LEE WHITE

Sioux (1941–) North Dakota
Painter—mixed media

REPRESENTATION: MacLaren/Markowitz Gallery, Boulder, Colorado.

ABOUT THE ARTIST: Born Randy Whitehorse, White dropped the "horse" from his name. White roots his work in truth, though he often combines the past with the present in an abstract, mixed-media way. His paintings are frequently political in nature. White's style often reflects the stick figures Plains Indians used when drawing on ledger paper, but his figures might represent modern imagery rather than ancient. For example, in "Custer's Last Stand Revised," the narrative is of the battle, but the horses are replaced by cars and tanks.

EMMI WHITEHORSE

Navajo (1957–) Crownpoint, New Mexico
Artist—oil and chalk on paper, mounted in canvas

EDUCATION: B.A., University of New Mexico (1980); M.A., University of New Mexico (1982).

REPRESENTATION: Horwitch LewAllen, Santa Fe, New Mexico.

ABOUT THE ARTIST: Whitehorse brings abstract and Navajo metaphysical views into her paintings, her conceptualization sometimes denoted in recognizable symbols—snakes, spirals, leaves, and branches. Collections of her work are held by many institutions, including the Heard Museum (Phoenix, Arizona), the Wheelwright Museum of the American Indian (Santa Fe, New Mexico), and the U.S. Department of State.

ROLAND N. WHITEHORSE
(a.k.a. "Whitehorse")

Kiowa (1920–) Carnegie, Oklahoma
Artist, sculptor

EDUCATION: Bacone College, Muskogee, Oklahoma (1947–48); Dallas Art Institute, Texas (1951–52).

AWARDS: Among Whitehorse's awards are awards for his bronze sculptures and First and Second Awards given at the Oklahoma Indian Trade Fair (1970).

ABOUT THE ARTIST: Whitehorse has exhibited his work throughout the United States. He was an illustrator for the Fort Sill School Training Aids and also worked at the Fort Sill Museum, as well as acting as director of arts and crafts at the American Indian Exposition in Anadarko, Oklahoma.

ALFRED WHITEMAN, JR.
(a.k.a. "Sitting Bear")
Cheyenne/Arapaho (1928–) Colony, Oklahoma
Artist

EDUCATION: Certificate in commercial art, Oklahoma State Tech, Okmulgee, Oklahoma (1960–62).

AWARDS: Whiteman has been awarded prizes in exhibits throughout the Southwest and West.

ABOUT THE ARTIST: Whiteman worked as artist and designer for Oklahoma State University. He has exhibited his work throughout the United States.

BAJE WHITETHORNE
Navajo (1955–) near Shonto and Black Mesa, Arizona
Artist

EDUCATION: Learned his early painting skills from family.

REPRESENTATION: Sage Brush Limited Editions, Flagstaff, Arizona.

ABOUT THE ARTIST: Whitethorne's trademark is a small folding chair that he tries to include in all his paintings. The chair is part of what he remembers as a child living in a hogan. He says, "I recall my parents bringing home a new card table with four metallic blue chairs. In the summer I would put my face on the seats because they were cool. I started to include the chair in my paintings because that's what I remember as a boy. Now I don't mind that people want to see the chair. The chair draws people into the painting as they try to find it." He has had work exhibited in the Museum of Northern Arizona, the Heard Museum, and at the Santa Fe Indian Market. He likes to paint near his home and the Shonto and Tsegi Canyons.

ELIZABETH WHITETHORNE-BENALLY
Navajo; near Shonoto and Black Mesa, Arizona
Artist

EDUCATION: Learned from her family, especially Baje, her brother.

AWARDS: Merit Award, Lawrence Art Show (1995).

REPRESENTATION: Sage Brush Limited Editions, Flagstaff, Arizona; Sunshine Studio, Sante Fe, Arizona.

ABOUT THE ARTIST: Elizabeth's work often reflects the memories she has of watching her mother and grandmother weave rugs and take them to market. Other traditions are also incorporated into her work.

DAVID EMMETT WILLIAMS
(a.k.a. Tosque, Tos-Que, "Apache Man")

Kiowa/Tonkawa/Apache (1933–) Anadarko, Oklahoma
Artist—oil on canvas, tempera on illustration board

EDUCATION: Studied art at Bacone College, Muskogee, Oklahoma (1960–62).

AWARDS: Williams has won awards for his work throughout the United States.

ABOUT THE ARTIST: Williams, who is descended from the famous Kiowa chief Sitting Bear, has made his career with exhibits at such places as the Sporting Gallery in Williamsburg, Virginia, and Stouffer's Manor Gate House in Pittsburgh, Pennsylvania. He is a member of the Oklahoma Indian Arts and Crafts Cooperative.

ERROL WILSON

Oneida (1957–) Oneida, Wisconsin
Painter, beadworker, dollmaker, potter

EDUCATION: Painting major at the Institute of American Indian Arts (1975–78); art major at the University of Wisconsin, Milwaukee (1978). Also took beadwork classes and learned how to do cornhusk work from his grandmother Amelia Metoxin.

AWARDS: Among her awards is a Congressional Certificate of Merit in the painting category from the Institute of American Indian Arts.

ABOUT THE ARTIST: Wilson likes to work with oils for paintings and with pen and ink when doing illustrations. His scenes are frequently portraits of nature, which he sometimes borders with traditional Iroquois patterns.

CRYING WIND

Navajo; Arizona
Artist, freelance writer, lecturer

AWARDS: Received the "Distinguished Christian Service in the Highest Tradition of the American Indian" award from the CHIEF organization.

ABOUT THE ARTIST: Crying Wind achieved success with her first book, *Crying Wind*, and her second, *My Searching Heart*, a novelized biography about her and her family. Her paintings have been shown in museums and art shows.

CARL WOODRING
(a.k.a. Wasaba Shinga, "Little Bear")

Osage (1920–) Arkansas City, Kansas
Artist—watercolors

EDUCATION: Studied under Acee Blue Eagle.

AWARDS: Woodring won more awards in one year than any other competitor during the history of the Philbrook Museum's annual competitions.

ABOUT THE ARTIST: Woodring's narrative paintings, which often reflect the Osage ceremonies and rituals, have been exhibited both nationally and internationally.

BEATIEN YAZZ (SEE JIMMY TODDY ON PAGE 92)
(a.k.a. Jimmy Toddy, Bea Etin Yazz, Beatian Yazz, Beatian Yazzia, Beatin, Yazz, B. Yazz, "Little Shirt")

JOHNSON YAZZI
Navajo (1955–) Navajo Reservation
Artist—pastels, oils

EDUCATION: Inspired by his uncle, Clifford Beck. Certificate in Advertising Arts at Maricopa Technical Community College (Arizona). B.F.A., Northern Arizona University, Flagstaff.

AWARDS: Best-of-Class ribbons in prestigious shows including the Gallup Intertribal Ceremonial, the Heard Museum Show, and Santa Fe Indian Market.

REPRESENTATION: Sunshine Studios, Sante Fe, New Mexico.

ABOUT THE ARTIST: Yazzi's reputation as an artist is growing by leaps and bounds. He took his cue to become an artist from his uncle, Clifford Beck, a well-known Navajo painter, then went on to school and to win many awards. Sunshine Studios notes that Yazzi is "a versatile artist, [with] an exceptional understanding of composition and light, and his familiarity with his culture and the people allows an instant rapport with subjects who seem to come alive with the touch of his brush to canvas. His paintings speak with an eloquence of their own, and are often more than the simple portraits they may seem at first glance."

JIMMY YELLOWHAIR

Navajo
Artist

AWARDS:

REPRESENTATION: Trading posts throughout the Southwest; Sunshine Studios, New Mexico.

ABOUT THE ARTIST: Though Yellowhair is prolific, he has never become well known.

Paintings

Jimmy Abeita. 20" × 24" paintings are averaging $1,200.

———. "A Distant Warrior." 24" × 36". $3,500.

Gilbert Atencio. Watercolor of traditional dancers, dated 1956. 13½" × 19" image size, matted and framed. $5,500.

Sonja K. Ayres. "Moonlit Journey." Acrylic. $925.

Robert Becenti. "Gans Dancers." 12" × 24". $950.

Arthur C. Begay. "The Totem Pole." Tempera on board. 10" × 16". $450.

———. "Shepherdess at Monument Valley." 11" × 18". $375.

———. "I Can't Read but There's Lots of Fish." 10" × 14". $325.

———. "Monument Valley." 10" × 16". $375.

———. "On Our Way Home from Trading Post." 9½" × 23". $425.

———. "Monument Valley, Arizona." 8" × 20". $475.

Filbert Bowannie. "Kainakwe Ceremony." 12" × 14". $375.

Louis Brown. Tempera paintings of night dance ceremonies. Approximately 11" × 13". Average $300.

Clifford Brycelea. "The Northern Country Fall." Watercolor. 10" × 30". $3,500.

———. "Hopi Princess," 1979. Acrylic. 10" × 8". $500.

Jerome Gilbert Bushyhead. Original paintings start at $5,000.

Neil David. "Koshare Clown." Watercolor. 10" × 14". $550.

Duane Dishta. "Hopi Kachina, Wuyak-kuita, Broad-Faced Kachina." 12" × 24". $425.

Adelido Garcia. "Three Deer in Forest." 13¼" × 8⅜". $585.

Mike Kabotie. "Cloud/Lightning Chanting," 1998. Acrylic on canvas. 18" × 24". $2000.

———. "Eagle and River Chant," 1997. Acrylic on canvas. 22" × 28". $2500.

———. "Sikyati/Eagle Chant," 1997. Acrylic on canvas. 24" × 36". $3000.

James Lavadour. Paintings on wood, silk, various materials. Range from $2,000–$6,000.

J. D. Medina. "Night Dancer." Tempera. 7" × 10". $1,450.

Rafael Medina. "Buffalo Dancer." Watercolor. 7" × 10". $1,950.

Geronima Cruz Montoya. "In the Fall," 1996. Tempera. 11" × 8". $375.

———. Untitled. Tempera, brown speck on paper. 10¾" × 11¼". $360.

———. "Matachines Couple," ca. 1998. Shrink-wrapped. 11" × 8". $375.

Raymond Naha. "Peyote Dancer," ca. 1970. $1,350.

———. "Early Morning Scene with Ogre Kachina." 14½" × 19½". $1,200.

———. "Shalako Dance," ca. 1970. Tempera on paper. 30" × 20". $2,450.

Guy Nez, Jr. 18" × 24" paintings. Average $75.

Patrick Sanchez. Mandala style painting of a Rainbow Man, a Shalako, and two Mudheads under the sun in front of the sacred mountain of the Zunis, Dowa Yalanne. Acrylics on board. 9¾" diameter image. $375.

———. Painting on drum, acrylics on leather; it has the same fine detail as the preceding painting. 12" diameter × 7" tall. $375.

Peter Tsisete Sandy. Pair of watercolors of deer. 9" × 12". Set $850.

————. "Zuni Corn Dancer." Watercolor. About 8" × 14", slightly truncated in scanning. $450.

Irving Toddy. "Fall camping scene," 1992. Acrylic on board. 14" × 24". (Won a Best-in-Class ribbon at the New Mexico State Fair in 1994.) $1,700.

Jimmy Toddy. "Fawn," ca. 1980. Tempera on paper. 8½" × 10½". $600.

————. "Shiprock scene," ca. 1940. Tempera. 14" × 20". $850.

José Rey Toledo. "Ram Dancer," ca. 1992. 8 × 10". $295.

Andy Tsihnahjinnie. "Sandpainting ceremony inside a hogan," ca. 1963. Casein-tempera. 19½" × 14¼". $2,500.

Kyrate Tuvahoema. "Snake Dance." Watercolor. 5" × 8". $1,900.

————. "Home Dancer," condition, fair. 5½" × 8¼". $1,600.

Donald Vann. Watercolors. Average $650–$1,000.

Paul Vigil. "Katsina Dancers." Watercolor. 12" × 9". Pair $750.

Virgil Vigil. "Eagle dancer with drummer," ca. 1997. 16"x16". $275.

Jimmy Yellowhair. "Weathered Navajo man beside his paint horse near Shiprock, New Mexico," ca. 1970. Oil on canvas. 24" × 30". $425.

Prints

Clifford Beck. "Keeper of the Feather." Lithograph—Edition 150. 24" × 30". $450.

————. "The Legend." Lithograph—Edition 100. 24" × 30". $450.

Francis Blackbear Bosin. "Cairn of the Medicine Seeker." Poster. 27" × 32". $35.

————. "Prairie Fire." Poster. 22" × 29". $16.

Farrell Cockrum. "The Councilmen." 30" × 26." $55.

————. "Parasols—Spring of Summer." 24" × 34." $55.

————. "Evening News II." 30" × 26". $55.

Cecil Dick. "The Conjurer." 14" × 17". $40.

————. "Wild Deer Running Away." 14" × 17". $40.

W. B. Franklin. "Standing Horse Is Asked for a Dance in 1932." Limited Edition Giclée print no. 8/380. Image size 30" × 21", frame size 38" × 28". $450.

————. "Midnight Yeis." Limited Edition Giclée print no. 14/350. Image size 18" × 13", frame size 25" × 20". $250.

————. "Yei Mask." Limited Edition Giclée print no.1/360. Image size 11" × 9½", frame size 17" × 15½". $160.

Alyssa Hinton. Original works by this artist average $10,000 and up.

Bert D. Seabourn. "Eagle Mystic." Limited Edition: S/N: 950 prints. 23½" × 27½". $110.

CHAPTER 2

Baskets

When archeologists and anthropologists uncover a site once inhabited by Native Americans, they find pottery and, sometimes, remnants of baskets. Indian tribes have all made baskets at one point in time and for a variety of uses. For example, Apache water jars (ollas) were made to carry liquids; other types of basketry were meant for a more precious cargo, like babies. Baskets carried wheat, corn, fruit, or trinkets. They were bowls for eating, shelling beans, or mixing herbs. Basketry trays and plaques were created for ceremonial purposes—or even for gambling. Baskets acted as sifters to separate wheat from chaff, oat from grain, or they were used to catch fish or to act as saddlebags.

Baskets have long been part of Native American ceremonies, and the basket has its place and use in each tribal ritual. Navajo medicine men use baskets in their healing rites, as part of the wedding ceremony, and in religious practices. Apaches use baskets for gambling, and Hopis use baskets in wedding ceremonies.

All baskets fall into one of five major periods: Early, Classic, Transitional, Hiatus, or Contemporary. The Early Period refers to the first archaeological specimens of basketry to come from Native Americans' first contact with European influences. Classic baskets were made during the early years of contact with Europeans but before the European influence is seen in Native American arts. Transitional baskets were made between 1775 and 1875, while baskets of the Hiatus Period were created during the late 19th and early 20th centuries, when traditional basketmaking techniques began to degenerate. Contemporary baskets include those made from the early 20th century to today.

Many legends surround the art of basketry. Navajos have a myth about the Bat Woman and the strength of her baskets. Pueblo Indians tell a story of a young man being lowered over a cliff in a basket in an effort to obtain eagle feathers and of how he learned the eagle's secrets and lived with them. The Hopis tell the legend of Tiyo, the mythical snake hero.

Designs and their variances also abound. Geometric designs evolved as did others. Simple and square-edged at first, Greek key designs evolved into scrollwork that was eventually integrated into pottery designs. Other geometric designs mean different things to different tribes. For one tribe, an hourglass shape represents a bird, while another tribe may use two opposite triangles to signify the same animal. To the Thompson Indians, the cross depicts the intersection of trails, while to the Yokuts, it represents a battle, and to the Wallapis and Havasupai, it is a phallic symbol.

Materials also differ, according to tribe. Each group uses what's available to them. Each also uses a different style of weaving, as well as different colors and symbols. To make it easier to identify the tribe, and ultimately the artist that created the baskets you are collecting, utilize the following chart.

TRIBE	MATERIAL USED IN MAKING BASKETS
Cayuse, Umatilla, Nez Percé, and Wasco	Split cornhusks and wild hemp
Hopi	Yucca and fine grass
Klickitat	Roots of young spruce and cedar trees, squaw grass
Mono	Tender shoots, roots, and fibers
Nootka	Tough spruce roots, inner bark of red and yellow cedar, cattail or tule stems, wild cherry tree bark, mountain goat wool, duck down, dog wool, and various grasses, fern stems, and other native plants for decoration
Panamint	Young shoots of tough willow, sumac shoots, horns on pods of unicorn plants, and yucca roots
Paiute and Havasupai	Martynia (cat's claw), yucca, and amole
Pima and Maricopa	Sisal willow, squaw weed, skunk weed, tule root, and martynia
Pomo	Roots of slough glass
Salish	Same bark and plant fibers at Nootka, but especially prized mountain goat and dog wool
Southern California	Tule root and squaw weed
Tlingit	Spruce root, split and soaked in water

The colors used in basketry are also important and might indicate the tribe of the maker. Symbolic colors include the Cherokee's red, which is said to signify success or triumph, while blue signifies defeat. Red is considered sacred to almost all tribes. The chart that follows will help you identify not only the symbolism of the color but the tribe.

TRIBE	USE OF COLORS
Cahuilla	Exclusively uses yellow, white, black, and brown. The only one of these colors that is not natural is black. It is made by taking a pot of mud from nearby sulfur springs, boiling it, and stirring the mud and water together. Once the mud settles, the liquid is poured off and used to color the splints.
Havasupai	Uses the peeled pod of the martynia, which is black, but does not dye the willow they use in basketweaving.
Hopi	Uses plants, flowers, and roots as dyes, though much of their modern basketry uses aniline dyes.
Klickitat	The natural color of squaw grass, used in Klickitat basketry, is white. When soaked in water, it becomes yellow, and if soaked in hot water, it becomes brown.
Navajo	Uses a variety of colors. The order of color appearance has great significance in basketmaking, as in planting corn (i.e., the white goes first because it is the color of the east and has most importance; blue, the color of the south, goes next; yellow, the next color in the sun's movement, is planted after blue; and black is last).
Pomo	Dyes their basketry materials by a process that involves charcoal paste, willow ashes, and dirt. The process takes nearly 80 hours to produce what the Pomos consider a perfect dye.
Potawatomi	Produces baskets the color of gold sunset clouds.
Shasta	Dyes the white grass they use brown by adding an extract of alder bark. Maidenhair fern stem is used for black detailing.
Southeast	Uses plaited techniques with glossy cane splints. Reddish orange, black, neutral shades, and other colors, such as yellow and dark purple, occasionally used.
Yakima	Uses white, blue, and yellow as spiritual colors.
Zuni	Colors represent directions: Yellow is north, blue is west, red is south, and white is east.

Like most Native American artistic objects, baskets were originally created for everyday purposes and not appreciated as artistic until they became gifts for the tourist trade. Eventually, certain Indian tribes (such as the Pomo of California) began making baskets strictly for the tourist trade, showing off their weaving techniques.

Weaving techniques are different for each tribe, thus the various types of baskets and weaves are described in the next chart.

TRIBE	STYLE OF BASKETS
Aleut	Weaving is extremely delicate, yet strong. Lidded baskets often decorated with silk embroidery flosses or wool, grass embroidery, or bird feathers.
Anasazi	Prehistoric baskets. Twined, bag type.
Apache	Water jugs (*tuus*) and burden baskets are Apache basketry staples. Jugs are made of sumac or strawberry twigs twined and woven over each other. Juniper leaves and red ocher are used to fill in the cracks, and the jar is water-proofed with piñon pitch, applied with a brush made of cow's hair. Burden baskets are made of willow, cotton-wood, or wild mulberry and decorated with strips of buck-skin ended in tin cones that "tinkle" when the baskets move. Swastika or "whirling logs" design is common to Apache (and Pima) basketry.
Jicarilla	Use a five-rod coiling method in basketmaking and sew the coils together with gold sumac. No plaited work has been identified as Jicarilla.
Mescalero	Use a three-rod stacked coiling method to weave their baskets. Early attempts at basketry produced exclusively utilitarian objects. Weaving was coarse; colors and de-signs unimpressive. Once they began to make commercial baskets, their style improved, though their weaving in general is still not as fine as that of other tribes.
San Carlos and White Mountain	Expert weavers who incorporate intricate designs in their work. Most of their basketry work is coiled, and willow or twigs are used in weaving. Work includes water bottles (ollas), bowls, saucers, trinket baskets, and cradles.
Southern Apache	Use a simple coiling around the splint finishing.
California Mission	Three main types of vegetation used: juncus grass, sumac, and deer grass. Juncus grows beneath mountain oak trees and has a variegated stem that provides a variety of color combinations. Mission Indians often dye the grass a dark brown to accent patterns woven into their baskets. Sumac is a white color, thus providing the white needed for back-grounds and for outlining dark patterns. Deer grass, a material commonly found in southern California, was the grass-bundle foundation material. Other materials used include sedge root, willow, bulrush root, and redbud bark. Patterns used in California Mission baskets include geo-metrics, animal pictures (e.g., doves, burros, camels, fish, rats, mice, butterflies, lizards, and rattlesnakes). The most common design is the rattlesnake or the quail design (its plume represents an upside-down golf club); however, Mission Indian rattlesnake baskets were rare during the

late 1800s because they bore a stigma of evil. During the period when the baskets were made for the tourist trade, there were two styles: abstract (four in the Chumash, Monache, Panamint, Shoshone, Tejon, Kawaiisu, Yokut, and Tubatalabal) and a realistic version of the rattlesnake design sold in the late 19th century. By 1920 production of these baskets came to a halt because the Natives respected the rattlesnake's power and believed that blindness, untimely death, and other ill fortunes plagued the makers of this type of basket. Occasionally flowers and ferns are incorporated into their basketry. Most California Mission baskets are closely stitched and fine. Eighteen to thirty wrappings per inch are common, and there are many sizes, shapes, and designs. The baskets were never decorated with beads and only occasionally with feathers.

Chemeheuvi	Refined weaving, identified by designs (animals, butterflies, or animal tracks) considered the property of the weaver and not to be copied by other artisans. (Also see California Mission.)
Cherokee	Use the plaiting technique, bending warps over a hoop to make a rim. Rims usually bound with hickory bark. Use plain plaiting with oak splints, river cane twill plaiting, and some double twill plaiting. Oklahoma Cherokees use wicker plaiting. Many basket forms were developed by the Cherokee, such as melon baskets, gathering and processing baskets, storage baskets, fish baskets, sieves, trays, bottleneck, miniatures, and nesting baskets. North Carolina Cherokee use twill-plaited geometric patterns to decorate (most commonly used are the diamond patterns). Oklahoma Cherokee use brilliantly dyed wicker elements. North Carolina Cherokee use twill-plaited geometric patterns in decorating their baskets; diamond patterns are the most common. They use white oak splints, river cane, and sugar maple materials to make their baskets. The Oklahoma Cherokees use wicker elements brilliantly colored with aniline dyes. Both North Carolina and Oklahoma Cherokees use honeysuckle vine in wicker plaiting and hickory bark in binding hoops of rim finishes.
Chickasaw	Use a twill-plaiting style and often make winnowing and wall baskets. Produce twilled geometric patterns and often incorporate dyed splints in their work. They take advantage of natural and aniline dyes, especially red and black in decoration.
Chitimacha	Use twill plaiting (both single and double twill weave), and characteristic rim finish is compound binding, doubled twined, or braided selvage. During the Contemporary

Period, they used bundle coiling of pine needles with spaced thread stitching or cane splints. They use narrow river cane stem splints in plaiting their baskets and long leaf pine needles in coiling. Their baskets usually have square bases with rounded sides and rims. They also make flat trays with low sides, sieves, and winnowing baskets, lidded "cigarette case" basketry, and coiled trinket baskets with knobbed lids. Designs include zigzag and geometric patterns in black, red, yellow, dark purple, and orange. They also use colored thread in stitching the coiled examples of their baskets.

Choctaw	Basketmakers in Mississippi and Oklahoma make twill- and double twill-plaited baskets. Most common are double-mouth "elbow," triangular "cownose," winnowing, and wall baskets. Other types include egg, laundry, miniature, and storage baskets, as well as rimmed burden baskets used for harvesting. Choctaw patterns are similar to Chitimacha, but Choctaw decorations are simpler than Chitimacha. They use dyed red and black splints for decoration on a natural-dyed cane background. Narrow cane stem splints are used to make the baskets, as well as some oak splits (mainly by Mississippi Choctaw).
Creek	Plaiting technique is to twist the ends of the warp into a false braid. Though winnowing and wall baskets are the most common types, the Creek also make "elbow" baskets, "cownose" baskets, trays, and sieves. They use twill-plaited geometric designs in decoration, especially zigzag patterns, and dyed splints (black). Materials used include split cane stem splints and hickory splints. Oranges and browns are common colors.
Haida	Basketry is covered with totemic symbols and drawings, as are their other arts and crafts. Basketry forms include twined hats, plaited bags and mats, and wallets. All basketry is twined, sometimes with reinforcement and sometimes using open wrap twining. Sitka spruce is used for twining, and western red cedar bark for plaiting. Common colors include black, red, and some green. Bear grass used in false embroidery.
Havasupai	Most frequently made from 1900 to 1925, Havasupai baskets were finely made, but by the mid-1970s, there were only half a dozen basketmakers left in the Havasupai tribe. Basketmakers used three-rod coiling with a fine closed plan and diagonal twining. They utilized a starting knot of four warp elements. Some of their coiled rims were stitched with light overcasting, while others were black. Rims might consist of "herringbone" false braid borders

common to Apache, Paiute, and Navajo basketry. Types of baskets include trays, bowls, bottle jars, and burden baskets. Trays and bowls were made in coiling style, while bottle jars and burden baskets were made in twining style. Bottles have woven or horsehair handles and are waterproofed with piñon gum or pitch. Designs are less complex than Apache designs, but Havasupai basketmakers used black boldly and favored concentric circles or simple geometric patterns. During the 1930s basketmakers used life-forms as decoration. Some of the materials used include willow, black devil's claw, acacia, shrub strawberry, and sumac. Devil's claw was used in patterns, and dyes of red, gold, yellow, and black were used during the Contemporary Period.

Hidatsa	Wove their baskets from box elder and willow bark, using willow splints for coiling, and twill painting with black willow and box elder for weaving. Four ash saplings formed the U-shaped framework for their twill burden baskets. Pieces were dyed before being woven together to form geometrically patterned baskets. Types of baskets include gambling trays and burden baskets.
Hopi	Considered the greatest basket producers of the Pueblo Indians, they practice all three types of weaving and characteristically produce a great variety of baskets in all types of designs. Because baskets are used in trade, occasionally a Navajo pattern will show up on a Hopi basket and vice versa. Hopi basketry has gone through periods of change in both design and types of dyes used. They began using aniline dyes in the late 1800s and early 1900s. By 1906 the Hopis had shifted from Old Oraibi to Hotevilla and went back to using natural dyes and large coils. During the late 1920s and 1930s they reduced the size of their coils and improved their designs. Patterns grew more elaborate and structured. By the early 1960s the wedding tray became an established form, the basketmakers' work had improved overall and it continues to improve today, partially because today's weavers are practicing more elaborate designs. Materials used include galleta grass and yucca. Sumac is used for warp and several types of rabbit brush for wefts. Design patterns are basically geometric or in a sunburst style with rays extending to the edge of the basket, though themes (including clouds, with or without rain, and Kachinas) have been used. The most common designs are the lightning symbol and the rain clouds, but mountain and valley symbols are often used, and butterflies, eagles, and Kachinas may be woven into basketry

pieces. The types of baskets produced include the afore-mentioned wedding tray, wicker bowls, trays (e.g., piki, peach, and gambling), burden baskets, and ceremonial baskets.

Hupa	Use open and closed plain twining to manufacture their baskets. The materials used include hazel, alder, willow, cottonwood, wild grape, and sometimes digger and yellow pine, or lowland spruce roots imported from the coastal Yuroks. In the late 1800s they used willow to make smaller, finer baskets. Their decoration consisted of half-twist overlays in yellow, red, white, and black, and geometric designs relied on a horizontal dividing line through the center of the main pattern. They also used horizontal bands of triangles at the base or rim of the caps. The types of baskets produced include openwork cradles and utility baskets, wood baskets, dippers, cooking and storage and serving baskets, fish baskets, burden baskets, sifts, mats, and caps.
Iroquois	Use the plaiting technique, usually incorporating two black ash splints to make a double hoop that holds the upper ends of the warps. One material distinctive to this tribe's baskets is cornhusks. They use husks to make ceremonial masks and small bottles to hold salt and tobacco. Occasionally they use bark to make ladles and bowls. Their styles often resemble other tribes' baskets, such as the Cherokee melon and storage baskets.
Jemez	One of the only Rio Grande pueblos still active in basket-making, both men and women of the tribe make baskets. They use yucca as their main material source, but sumac is used in the rim of the basket. Yucca is the only material used for decoration. Most Jemez baskets are round because almost all of the mats are woven in squares. The types of baskets made include shallow ring baskets for winnowing, as well as twill-plaited mats and rings for carrying water jars on one's head, winnowing baskets, and other useful basketry items.
Navajo	The types of baskets made include water bottles (*tus jeh*), the Navajo wedding basket, and gambling baskets. Materials used are similar to the basketry produced in the Pueblos and by Apaches.
Northwest Coast	Often weave their twined baskets upside down and depict fish in their basketmaking. The Coast Salish groups especially prize mountain goat or dog wool in their weaving. They pick out the long, coarse guard hairs from the wool and discard them; then the wool is collected in loose hanks, and a core of yellow cedar bark string added for

strength. The wool was spun into two-ply yarn. Sometimes they use bird down or the soft cotton pappus of certain plants in their baskets. Their most common weaving technique is twining. Plain twining is used to make spruce root basketry containers, hats, and capes, as well as robes and capes of red and yellow cedar bark yarn. The baskets are so fine that they are watertight and used as containers for liquids and sometimes for cooking. Hats made with this twining technique are waterproof and decoration applied with bleached or dyed grasses and splints of black fern stems to produce geometric designs. Some Coast Salish tribes (e.g., Pentlatch, Sanetch, Cowichan) make baskets with twined openwork that incorporates crossed or zigzag warp elements. Coiled basketry (sewn rather than woven) was made by a few Northwest Coast groups, but is thought to have been introduced to these tribes by the Plateau tribes.

Paiute	Painte basketry bowls (also called Navajo wedding baskets or Apache medicine baskets) have a border woven in a diagonal whip stitch, often called herringbone. This stitch is the distinguishing mark of Paiute, Navajo, and Havasupai weaving. They use aromatic sumac, yucca, and martynia materials. Incorporated into their basket design is the belief that the Paiute came from an underworld (a "lower" world) that corresponds to the hills and valleys of the upper world. The communication link between the two (Shipapu) is represented by the basket's opening. If the opening is closed, the basketmaker would make it impossible for any more of her people to be born into the upper world.
Papago	Early Papago baskets, sturdy black trays of martynia (devil's claw) were used for parching corn with live coals. Modern baskets are made of yucca leaves, coiled over bear grass or yule stem foundations. Baskets are made by the bundle-coiling technique with closed, spaced, or split stitching. Spaced stitching was used until 1900, and split stitching was used after 1934. Types of baskets include shallow coiled bowls, twill-plaited mats, head rings, baskets with and without lids, jars, trays, storage baskets, trinket baskets, and miniature baskets (made of horsehair or yucca). Black devil's claw designs or geometric horizontal figures decorate their baskets. Natural green and red colors were used to decorate coiled wares, while aniline dyes were used between 1920 and 1943. Today's Papago basketweaver makes items like wastebaskets, hampers, and covered baskets.

Pima/Maricopa	Baskets are similar to Paiute, Havasupai, and Apache baskets, though the work is coarser. The border stitch is a distinctive forward and backward kind of stitch, and the designs incorporate the Greek fret and circular swastika forms. The types of baskets include shallow, medium-size bowls, closely woven of cattail, over which the basketmaker will sew strips of willow shoots and devil's claw. Designs used include the fret, star, butterfly, squash blossom, swastika, and whirlwind. Miniatures of their creations are also made, and many are held by museums. A good Pima miniature might take up to three months to make.
Pomo	Nine distinct weaves were used in their basketry between 1880 and 1920, and five other weaves were found in earlier baskets. The first weave to produce patterns was the "bam-tush." The weave process, a one-rod coiling method, was an increasing spiral, and the basket eventually showed spaces that required extra ribs that would be filled in with stitches made by a bone awl. A change of thread was required to make the pattern, and often rings of *ti* stitches were worked in. (*Ti* in the Pomo language means ponderous, stable, and unyielding, and describes the Pomo double weave, which is actually twined weaving.) Seed baskets were a fine weave, water baskets were finer still, and gathering acorns or larger items. Plain baskets held food; decorated or fanciful ones held gifts.
Skokomish	Use an open and closed plain and wrap twining. In the late Classic Period, some of the baskets were coiled. Types of baskets include cylindrical bags or berry baskets with looped rims. An all-over half-twist overlay in vertical geometric patterns was used to decorate the baskets. On four-legged figures, if the tails turn up, the animal is a dog; if the tail is down, the animal is a wolf.
Tlingit	Use twining and plain plaiting. Decorations are usually stylized animals (e.g., raven, wolf) in native pigments, such as the black of sulfur spring mud, hemlock bark, and iron scrapings; the red of alder bark or sea urchin juice; the yellow of lichen or wolf moss; the green-blue of hemlock bark with copper oxide; the purple color of huckleberries; the blackish purple of maidenhair fern; the brown of undyed Sitka spruce root; and the white of undyed grasses.
Yavapai	Baskets are strong and fine enough that food can be boiled in them. Because they did not have horses, the Yavapai made an abundance of burden baskets. Materials used include willow twigs (for coiling), split willow, and devil's claw for sewing. The three-rod coiling method was

used to create bowls, plaques, trays, and deep jars. Designs are geometric and of animal and human figures that are usually not used on the item more than once. Colors are black and, sometimes, red.

Zuni	Plaited baskets were made at the turn of the century and were still being made during the 1930s; however, wicker baskets are more readily available. The Zuni are not known for making coiled baskets, but they made coiled water bottles, twill-plaited shallow ring baskets, and fancy openwork wicker bowls. They use a willow or sumac rod with a yucca bundle as the foundation for their baskets, incorporating wick and twill plaiting in their decoration. Little decoration is done on Zuni baskets.

Before Native Americans started participating in the tourist trade, most basketmakers remained anonymous, but as the trade became established, certain weavers came to the forefront. Because most baskets aren't signed, there is often insufficient information on basketweavers, but we have attempted to bring all of the major weavers to the forefront in the biographies that follow.

The Artists

ELIZA ABRAHAM

Haida; Masset, British Columbia, Canada
Basketmaker

ABOUT THE ARTIST: Gathers roots and bark for her baskets in the summer (usually the month of August).

MARY ADAMS

Mohawk (1942–) St. Regis, Quebec, Canada
Basketmaker, splint worker, quilter

EDUCATION: Learned how to weave baskets by watching her mother, Gertrude Gray.

AWARDS: New York State Iroquois Conference award (1975); first prizes at New York State Fair; and many others.

ABOUT THE ARTIST: Adams creates many types of baskets, using black ash splints, sweet grass, natural or plastic twine, and cloth. She has taught others, demonstrated, and exhibited her basketry throughout the Northwest, as well as at Brigham Young University.

SALLY ANNE ADAMS

Mohawk (1943–)
Basketmaker, quilter

EDUCATION: Learned her trade from her mother, Agnes Sunday.

ABOUT THE ARTIST: Adams uses black ash splints and sweet grass for her baskets and cloth for her quilts. She prefers the smaller-sized baskets, gathering the sweet grass herself and using natural dyes. She has taught basketry to grade school children.

AGNES ALFRED

Kwakiutl, Mamalelekala Tribe; Village Island, British Columbia, Canada
Basketmaker

ABOUT THE ARTIST: Alfred is one of only a few people who make cedar root and cedar bark handled baskets. She states, "[W]e used to make big ones for clams, fish and berries" (*Artists at Work* by Ulli Steltzer).

ELSIE COMANCHE ALLEN

Pomo (1899–1990) Santa Rosa, California
Basketmaker

EDUCATION: Allen learned from her mother, Annie Burke, and her grandmother.

ABOUT THE ARTIST: Allen worked in the fields as a laborer during much of her childhood, and after her marriage and the birth of her four children, she returned to that work. In 1924 her grandmother died, and she realized that she needed to carry on the family basketmaking tradition. When her mother died, Allen had to battle Pomo tradition to keep her mother's wish that her baskets *not* be buried with her, but instead should be studied by future generations of basketweavers. Allen not only respected her mother's wishes but carried on the tradition in an admirable way, teaching at California's Mendocino Art Center and working to promote education and cultural tradition. She became known as the "Pomo sage" and in 1972 authored a book entitled *Pomo Basket Making: A Supreme Art for the Weaver*. Later, she became associated with the Native American Advisory Council and was so important to Pomo culture that a school in Santa Rosa was named after her. She died at the age of 91, a truly valued member of her community.

JOSEPHINE ANGUS
(a.k.a. Ka En Ten Ha Wi)

Mohawk (1920–) St. Regis, Quebec, Canada
Basketmaker, splint worker, quilter

EDUCATION: Angus's grandmother taught her.

REPRESENTATION: Mohawk Craft Fund, New York.

ABOUT THE ARTIST: Angus makes a number of different types of baskets, including cone-shaped doll baskets, comb holders, and strawberry baskets. She usually uses natural splints. A founding member and president of Akwesasne Homemakers and Cultural Committee, she often shares her skills with others in the community.

ANNIE ANTONE

Navajo (ca. 1965–) Gila Bend, Arizona
Basketry

EDUCATION: Learned from her maternal relatives and made her first basket in her teens.

AWARDS: Many awards at the Santa Fe Indian Market and the Heard Museum Indian Fair, including Best of Show.

REPRESENTATION: Cristof's, Santa Fe, New Mexico.

ABOUT THE ARTIST: Antone creates traditional vegetal baskets and miniature horsehair pieces, using the hair from the tail of Arabian horses. Antone believes that it takes maturity to have the patience to create baskets.

NORMA ANTONE

Tohono O'odham
Basketmaker

REPRESENTATION: Penfield Gallery of Indian Arts, Albuquerque, New Mexico; eSouthwest, Albuquerque.

ABOUT THE ARTIST: Antone makes miniature horsehair baskets in the Papago style. Her work is detailed and fine.

MARIA ANTONIA

Diegueno
Rattlesnake baskets.

EDUCATION: Self-taught.

ABOUT THE ARTIST: Antonia is credited with designing the first rattlesnake basket (in 1898), although others before her may have made cruder versions of the same design.

CHRISTIE ARQUETTE
(a.k.a. Kia Wenh Toe)

Mohawk (1924–) Hogansburg, New York
Basketmaker, splint worker

EDUCATION: Arquette learned from her mother.

REPRESENTATION: Mohawk Crafts Fund, New York, and Margaret David (Arquette's mother).

ABOUT THE ARTIST: Arquette uses black ash splints and sweet grass in her baskets, making strawberry baskets that are pink, red, or natural in color.

JAKE ARQUETTE
(a.k.a. Zock)

Mohawk (1905–)
Basketmaker

EDUCATION: Learned his skills from his father.

REPRESENTATION: Mohawk Crafts Fund, New York, and Arquette himself.

ABOUT THE ARTIST: Arquette makes lunch baskets, as well as market, laundry, pack, and fancy baskets. He uses black ash splints, sweet grass, and hickory. Though he taught his children how to make baskets, they have not continued the tradition.

MARGARET ARQUETTE

Mohawk (1915–) Hogansburg, New York
Basketmaker, quilter

EDUCATION: Arquette learned from her sister, Christie; her mother, Anne Thompson, and three other sisters are also basketmakers.

AWARDS: Has won first prizes for both her baskets and her quilts at the New York State Fair.

REPRESENTATION: Mohawk Crafts Fund, New York.

ABOUT THE ARTIST: Arquette uses black ash splints and sweet grass to make sewing, fancy, strawberry, wastepaper, and button baskets, as well as flowerpots, filing trays, purses, and matchbook holders. She often dyes the splints different colors and is very skillful combining the splints to make attractive baskets. Arquette demonstrates or exhibits her work whenever she can.

MARY BENSON

Pomo (1890–)
Basketmaker

EDUCATION: Self-taught.

REPRESENTATION: National Museum of the American Indian, New York.

ABOUT THE ARTIST: Benson is considered one of the foremost Pomo basketmakers in the early twentieth century. Quite a few of her pieces have
ended up in such museums as the Grace Hudson Museum and the Museum of the American Indian. She and her husband, William, were well
known for their coiled baskets because of the fine and tight stitching.
They created both miniatures and regular sizes and often decorated them
with feathers. One coiled basket held by the National Museum of the
American Indian has a light and dark design and more than 100 stitches
to the inch.

SUSAN BILLY

Pomo (1951–) Santa Rosa, California
Basketweaver, beader, educator

EDUCATION: Learned Pomo basketry from her mother.

AWARDS: Selected one of 200 American women designers of the 20th century; acts as consultant for the Smithsonian.

REPRESENTATION: Bead Fever, Ukiah, California.

ABOUT THE ARTIST: Billy's great-aunt (Elsie Allen) taught her about the art
of basketmaking, a craft she had learned from her mother, Annie Burke.
Billy showed up on her great-aunt's doorstep one day and announced
she'd like to learn about baskets. Allen, 74 at the time, was surprised because young members of the Pomo tribe had shown no interest for quite a
while. Billy worked with Allen until her death, learning all she could
about the native craft. Now Billy is guest curator, consultant, and demon-
strator for the Smithsonian National Museum of the American Indian Exhibit "Pomo Indian Basket Weavers: Their Baskets and the Art Market."
A contemporary artist with her roots deep in tradition, Billy exhibited one
of her Pomo feathered baskets in "Women Designers in the USA,
1900–2000: Diversity and Difference" at the Bard Graduate Center for
Studies in the Decorative Arts, Design, and Culture, New York City.

AGNES BLACK

Navajo
Basketmaker

ABOUT THE ARTIST: Daughter of Mary Holiday Black, Agnes uses deer, butterflies, and human forms to decorate her traditionally coiled trays.

LORRAINE BLACK

Navajo; Monument Valley, Arizona
Basketmaker

EDUCATION: Learned how to create baskets from her famous mother, Mary Holiday Black.

REPRESENTATION: Twin Rocks Trading Post, Bluff, Utah.

ABOUT THE ARTIST: Black began creating ceremonial baskets at the age of 13. Like her sister Agnes, Lorraine Black decorates her traditionally coiled trays with deer, butterflies, and human forms. She is the third daughter of Mary Holiday Black and well known in her own right for her Horned Toad story basket, a piece that won first place in the Navajo Show at the Museum of Northern Arizona in Flagstaff, as well as an award at the Gallup Ceremonials.

MARY BLACK

(a.k.a. Mary Holiday Black)

Navajo/Ute
Basketmaker

EDUCATION: Learned how to weave from a relative of her grandmother when she was 11 years old.

AWARDS: Utah Governor's Folk Art Award (1995); National Heritage Fellowship Award from National Endowment for the Arts (1996), presented to her by First Lady Hillary Clinton.

REPRESENTATION: Twin Rocks Trading Post, Bluff, Utah.

ABOUT THE ARTIST: Black is credited with the revival of Navajo basketry and has taught her large family how to weave. She began weaving in 1960, when most of the Navajo women were weavers. Only a handful of basketmakers existed on the reservation. Since that time, she has woven her stories into her baskets, some of which sell for almost $10,000. She has also taught many others how to create baskets.

SALLY BLACK

Navajo; Monument Valley, Arizona
Basketry.

EDUCATION: Learned from her mother, Mary Holiday Black.
REPRESENTATION: Native American Collections, Inc., Denver, Colorado.
ABOUT THE ARTIST: Black is the eldest daughter of Mary Holiday Black, an important Navajo basketweaver. The Black family is recognized as being responsible for the revival in Navajo basketry, and Sally is one of the premier Navajo weavers.

CHRISTINE BOBB

Northwest Coast (1890–) Boothroyd Reserve, British Columbia, Canada
Basketmaker

ABOUT THE ARTIST: Bobb gathers her own materials to make her decorated baskets.

ANNIE BURKE

Pomo (1876–1962) California
Basketmaker

ABOUT THE ARTIST: Burke spent much of her life trying to teach others about the Pomo way of life and about her craft. She passed her skills on to her daughter, Elsie Allen, and also asked her not to destroy her baskets after her death.

Basket by Sally Black. 12" wide, $550. Courtesy of Jill Giller, Native American Collections, Inc., www.nativepots.com. Photo by: Bill Bonebrake.

ELSIE CHARLIE

First Nations; Yale, British Columbia, Canada
Basketmaker

EDUCATION: Charlie's mother taught her how to weave baskets, telling her to speak to the tree to make sure it realizes she would not waste any of it. Charlie still uses her mother's tools.

ABOUT THE ARTIST: Charlie makes all kinds of baskets, including decorated baby baskets. She uses deer-bone awls as tools (just as her ancestors did) and makes baskets out of cedar roots, white straw, and wild cherry bark.

FLORENCE COOK

(a.k.a. Ana)

Mohawk (1930–) Hogansburg, New York
Basketmaker, quilter

EDUCATION: Her mother taught her basketmaking; however, she learned how to quilt in grammar school.

AWARDS: She has won first prizes for her quilts at the New York State Fair.

REPRESENTATION: Mohawk Craft Fund, New York; Akwesasne Notes; Christina Jock.

ABOUT THE ARTIST: One of the unusual shapes Florence creates is a square handkerchief basket; however, she makes a wide variety of shapes and sizes and uses black ash splints, sweet grass, and dyes. She often uses green, brown, orange, and red, but will make a grass out of very white splints if she has enough. Her quilts have been recognized nationally and have even been exhibited at the New York Metropolitan Museum of Art Gift Shop. They are brightly colored, sometimes in appliqué form, or in star, fan and crazy quilt designs.

JULIUS COOK

(a.k.a. Jo Jo)

Mohawk (1955–) Hogansburg, New York
Basketmaker

EDUCATION: Cook learned by watching his mother, Florence Cook, and his grandmother Josephine Lazore. Norwich University, Vermont (business administration).

REPRESENTATION: Mohawk Craft Fund, New York.

ABOUT THE ARTIST: Julius prepares the splints, pounds the logs, and carves the handles for the baskets he creates. He doesn't use a mold and makes all types of baskets in various sizes.

CECILIA CREE

Mohawk (1920–)
Basketmaker, quilter

EDUCATION: Anna and Richard Sunday, Cree's parents, taught her.
REPRESENTATION: Mohawk Craft Fund, New York.
ABOUT THE ARTIST: Cree makes lighter baskets, instead of the large ones
  with wood handles. She prefers to work with naturally colored and
  brown-dyed splints. Occasionally she demonstrates her craft and teaches
  children at a local grammar school.

CLARA DARDIN

Chitimacha (ca. late 1800s–early 1900s) Bayou Teche, Louisiana
Basketry

EDUCATION: Self-taught.
ABOUT THE ARTIST: Dardin wove in the style of the Southeast culture,
  using the double twill-plaited technique with splints of river cane. She
  was particularly talented in manipulating weaving elements and incorporated different colors into her designs, such as "bottom of basket" (*kaxt-
  ma'xta*), "cross marks" (*nakc-apcta'nk'in'ic*), "eyes of cattle" (*wa'ct'ik-ka'ni*),
  and "something around" (*hakc-koksko'ksn*). Dardin worked from the late
  1800s to the early 1900s, and at least one of her designs is held by the
  Peabody Museum at Harvard University.

FLORENCE DAVID

Mohawk (1934–) Hogansburg, New York
Basketmaker, splint worker, quilter, leatherworker, beadworker

EDUCATION: Eva Point, David's mother, taught her.
REPRESENTATION: Mohawk Craft Fund, New York.
ABOUT THE ARTIST: David produces a wide variety of basketry items, usu-
  ally featuring plain splints, but sometimes using some colors in her work.
  She also is a skilled sewer, knitter, crocheter, beadworker, and leather-
  worker, and has passed her skills down to her children.

FLORENCE DAVIDSON

Haida (1896–) Masset, British Columbia, Canada
Basketmaker

ABOUT THE ARTIST: Davidson personally collects the cedar bark and spruce
  roots, then hangs them to dry on clothesline strung in her backyard. She

works her baskets and hats the way the Raven taught her people in the beginning. In 1992 Davidson contributed to an autobiographical work entitled *During My Time: Florence Edenshaw Davidson: A Haida Woman*. Margaret Blackman, a cultural anthropologist at State University of New York at Brockport, took down Davidson's history and translated it into book form.

CHARLOTTE DELORMIER
(a.k.a. Warisarot Kenetahawi)

Mohawk (1910–) Cornwall Island, Ontario, Canada
Basketmaker, splint worker, quilter

EDUCATION: Self-taught.

ABOUT THE ARTIST: Delormier makes sewing, strawberry, button, bingo chip, and thimble baskets, using black ash splints, sweet grass, and rope. She collects her sweet grass in the summer, then works on making baskets throughout the winter. Her mother, Josephine Thompson, and her sisters, Minnie Delormier and Mary Leaf, are also basketmakers. Delormier has taught others and has held demonstrations of basketmaking.

MINNIE DELORMIER

Mohawk (1921–) Cornwall Island, Ontario, Canada
Basketmaker, splint worker

EDUCATION: Josephine Thompson, Delormier's mother, taught her.

ABOUT THE ARTIST: Delormier has been making baskets since her adolescent years and still uses her mother's distinctively styled molds. She uses many colors in her work and creates many different types of baskets. She now passes her skills on to her own daughters.

CHARLOTTE DIABO
(a.k.a. Warisaro Wasontanoron)

Mohawk (1921–) Caughnawaga, Quebec, Canada
Basketmaker

EDUCATION: Learned from her mother.

REPRESENTATION: Akwesasne Notes.

ABOUT THE ARTIST: All members of Diabo's family were basketmakers from the St. Regis reservation. She learned a lot from them and has returned the favor by passing on her skill to her granddaughter. Charlotte makes colorful baskets, using all the colors of the rainbow, often attaching flowers and leaves made from sweet grass and splints.

MAVIS DOERING

Cherokee; Oklahoma
Basketmaker

AWARDS: Red Earth "Honored One." Many awards for her work, including a commission from the Oklahoma Governor's Arts Awards.

REPRESENTATION: Mittie Cooper Gallery, Oklahoma City, Oklahoma.

ABOUT THE ARTIST: Doering uses wicker in unusual colors, such as pink and purple (natural dyes), and adds feathers for decoration. She gathers materials for both her baskets and dyes on her mother's property in eastern Oklahoma and weaves her works of art into either double wall pieces (a method that is unique to her tribal people) or splint creations. She incorporates feathers, beads, pieces of wood, or strips of leather to implement certain ideas and thoughts. The materials she uses for baskets include buckbrush, reed, honeysuckle, white oak, ash, cane, and cattails. Substances used for dyes are blueberry, black walnut hulls, hickory hulls, mulberry, peach leaves, sumac bark and root, sassafras bark and root, pokeberry, bloodroot, wild plum leaves, pecan hulls, wild cherry leaves, almond hulls, elderberry, and huckleberry. She also utilizes aniline dyes. Her work has been included in exhibits in the Southern Plains Indian Museum, Coulter Bay Indian Art Museum, Wheelwright Museum of the American Indian, Museum of Fine Art at the University of Oklahoma, Oklahoma Historical Society, Kennedy Center in Washington, D.C., and Smithsonian Folklife Festival.

FRANCES EDGAR

Northwest Coast; Nitinat, British Columbia, Canada
Basketweaver

EDUCATION: Self-taught.

REPRESENTATION: Black Tusk Gallery, Vancouver, British Columbia, Canada.

ABOUT THE ARTIST: Edgar collects her own swamp grass, cedar bark, and three-corner grass for the baskets she creates. She began making baskets at the age of eight and then used cedar baskets for gathering berries, kindling, and seafood.

DELFINA FRANCISCO

Basketmaker

AWARDS: Francisco was designated one of Arizona's Indian Living Treasures in 1994. The Heard Museum holds photographs of her and her works.

MARY MITCHELL GABRIEL

Passamaquoddy (1909–) Passamaquoddy Indian Reservation, Maine
Basketmaker

EDUCATION: Her grandmother taught her the art of basketweaving.

AWARDS: Gabriel is the first Maine Indian basketmaker to win the National Heritage Fellowship of the National Endowment of the Arts. In 1994 she was given the Maryann Hartman Award.

ABOUT THE ARTIST: Gabriel creates sweet-grass and ash round baskets, some covered with sweet-grass patterns and the lids topped with a "frog" handle. She is keeping the basketmaking tradition alive by teaching some of her seven children the art of weaving.

SYLVIA GABRIEL

Passamaquoddy (1930–) Maine
Basketmaker

EDUCATION: Sylvia's mother, Mary Mitchell Gabriel, taught her how to weave a basket.

ABOUT THE ARTIST: Gabriel creates sweet-grass baskets, which are usually round and topped with a lid. Her styles often imitate those her mother taught her.

DORINA GARCIA

Tohono O'odham (Dorina: 1959–)
Basketmaker

ABOUT THE ARTIST: Dorina weaves miniature baskets. She began weaving in 1990. She uses Arabian horsehair to make her baskets because it's fine and easy to work with. Dorina's work has been included in such volumes as Tryk and Nohl's *Santa Fe Indian Market* and Jerry and Lois Jacka's *Beyond Tradition*. Her sister is basketry artist Ruby Thomas.

AGNES GARROW

Mohawk (1900–99) St. Regis, Quebec, Canada
Basketmaker, splint worker

EDUCATION: Learned from her mother.
REPRESENTATION: Mohawk Craft Fund, New York.
ABOUT THE ARTIST: Garrow makes a variety of baskets, using black ash splints, sweet grass, ribbon, and rope. She has a reputation for fine craftsmanship, creating sewing baskets usually made with undyed splints (sometimes she uses a brown dye).

AGNES GEORGE

Carrier; Nautley Reserve, British Columbia, Canada
Basketmaker

ABOUT THE ARTIST: George creates birch-bark baskets, some shaped like bowls.

PAT COURTNEY GOLD

Tlingit/Wasco (1939–) Warm Springs, Oregon
Basketmaker

EDUCATION: Learned basketry from local basketweavers in Oregon and Washington in 1991 and 1992; B.A. in mathematics-physics, Whitman College.
AWARDS: Invited to participate in Governor Barbara Roberts and Oregon Arts Commission show, June–August 1991; special invitation to the "Ancient Images of the Columbia River Gorge" show at the Maryhill Museum, March–July 1992; received the Timberline Purchase Award at the Tribal Member Art Show at the Museum of Warm Springs, Oregon, September 1993–January 1994.
REPRESENTATION: Snow Goose Assoc., Inc., Seattle, Washington; Ancestral Spirits Gallery, Port Townsend, Washington; Perry House Galleries, Alexandria, Virginia; Indian Way Gallery, Olympia, Washington; Lelooska Gallery, Ariel, Washington.
ABOUT THE ARTIST: When this artist had had enough of the business world, she and her sister Bernyce started a business—reviving the art of Wasco basketweaving. The business, called the Sally Sisters, means to preserve the art for future generations. Gold has exhibited and sold her work, as well as taught the art of basketry, throughout the western United States.

GERTRUDE GRAY

Mohawk (1917–) Hogansburg, New York
Basketmaker, quilter, clothing designer

EDUCATION: Gray learned by helping her mother, Mary Adams.

AWARDS: She has won prizes at the New York State Fair for her work and has a small bassinet on exhibit at the United Nations building in New York.

ABOUT THE ARTIST: Gray's first basket was an Easter basket, but she made a wide variety of sewing baskets (often made with a velvet lining and a pincushion on top), as well as flower baskets decorated with ribbons and large hampers decorated with sweet grass.

TOM GRAY

(a.k.a. Kaion Ha Te Ni Or)

Mohawk (1895–) Hogansburg, New York
Basketmaker

EDUCATION: Gray is self-taught.

AWARDS: The New York State Fair has awarded Gray's baskets many times.

ABOUT THE ARTIST: Gray uses black ash splints to make large pack baskets. His nephew helps him pound the logs, but Gray still carves his own handles.

LINDA GUZMAN

Apache
Basketweaver

ABOUT THE ARTIST: Guzman weaves fine baskets in the Apache style. Most of her work sells for thousands of dollars. She creates ollas and other types of baskets with figural and traditional designs.

LIZ HAPPYNOOK

Northwest Coast; Bamfield, British Columbia, Canada
Basketmaker

EDUCATION: Taught how to weave baskets by her aunt.

ABOUT THE ARTIST: Her baskets are often in the shape of bottles, created with designs she learned from family members.

LINDA HENDRICKS

Tohono O'odham (ca. 1955–) Chuischu, Arizona
Basketry

EDUCATION: Self-educated.

REPRESENTATION: Cristof's, Santa Fe, New Mexico.

ABOUT THE ARTIST: Hendricks creates miniature horsehair baskets as well as full-size yucca baskets. She is an innovative weaver who uses a lot of sorrel horsehair and depth in her designs. Her work has been featured in quite a few publications.

MARY HERNE

Mohawk (1928–)
Basketmaker, quilter

EDUCATION: Learned from her mother, Josephine Lazore, and shared experiences with her sisters, Florence Cook and Sarah Lazore.

REPRESENTATION: Mohawk Crafts Fund, New York.

ABOUT THE ARTIST: Mary's baskets are usually made of black ash splints and sweet grass. She makes sewing and wastepaper baskets that are done in natural colors. Her quilts are made in a variety of patterns.

ELIZABETH HICKOX

Karuk (1875–1947)
Basketry

ABOUT THE ARTIST: Hickox met premier basket dealer and collector Grace Nicholson in 1908. Because of Nicholson's excellent documentation, photos exist of almost all of Hickox's baskets produced before 1922. Hickox specialized in baskets for the higher-end collector, producing a signature lidded gift basket with an undulating profile and high knob. *The Grove Dictionary of Art* states that "she delineated main designs with supreme attention to the relationship of positive and negative elements and embellished them with a complex scheme of bordering designs and shifts in weaving technique." After 1922 Hickox produced mostly miniatures, and in 1934 Nicholson stopped buying from Hickox, who subsequently stopped weaving. The information Nicholson collected has been divided between the Phoebe Apperson Hearst Museum of Anthropology at the University of California at Berkeley and the Huntington Library in San Marino, California.

DOROTHY JEFFREY

Nuu-cha-nulth (October 5, 1946–) Victoria, British Columbia, Canada
Basketry

EDUCATION: Learned from her mother, Effie Tate.

REPRESENTATION: Coastal Peoples Fine Arts Gallery, Vancouver, British Columbia, Canada.

ABOUT THE ARTIST: Jeffrey's family crest symbol is the killer whale. She's one of a few women from her generation to keep the art of basketweaving alive and follows the tradition passed down to her from her mother, Effie Tate. Jeffrey was only 10 when she began weaving. Using three-corner grass, white grass, and cedar bark from Vancouver Island, she creates baskets with the traditional designs of the Nuu-cha-nulth Nation, such as birds, whales, and canoe hunting.

THERESA JEMISON
(a.k.a. Teres Kanawiosta)

Mohawk (1918–) Basom, New York
Basketmaker, beadworker

EDUCATION: Learned some of her basketmaking skills from her mother and grandmother and learned loom beadwork at the National Youth Association Training Camp.

ABOUT THE ARTIST: Jemison has lectured on the art of basketry, has taught the art, and has owned her own craft shop. She's been recognized in local publications. Her baskets are made from black ash splints. Jemison also does loom beadwork, occasionally making a piece for one of her friends. She has taught the Mohawk language and continually researches her heritage.

MATILDA JIM

Mount Currie (ca. 1890–) Mount Currie, British Columbia, Canada
Basketmaker

EDUCATION: Jim learned her skills from fellow family members.

ABOUT THE ARTIST: Jim continued making baskets until she was well over 100 years old. Her daughter, Julianna Williams, learned the art from Jim.

CHRISTINA JOCK
(a.k.a. Ka Wennite)

Mohawk (1920–) Hogansburg, New York
Basketmaker, leatherworker, beadworker, porcupine quillworker

EDUCATION: Learned her basketry skills from her mother. Malone School of Practical Nursing (1968); A.A., education, Mater Dei College (1975).

ABOUT THE ARTIST: Jock began selling Iroquois baskets in the 1960s, creating hampers as well as other types. She sometimes dyes her own splints and usually uses sweet grass. In addition, this multitalented artist makes pipestone and heishi shell necklaces (sometimes glass beads, too). She is also dedicated to teaching the Mohawk language to others and passing on her skills to whoever wants to learn.

TERROL DEW JOHNSON

Tohono O'odham
Basketry

EDUCATION: Learned how to weave in school on the reservation. Three teachers (including Clara Javier) taught him some of the finer details of their weaving.

ABOUT THE ARTIST: Most of Johnson's work is done on commission. When he started the TOCA (Tohono O'odham Community Action), he cut down the number of shows he does. He states that his tribe is known for its weaving and that the work being produced currently is mostly for tourists. Collector pieces are commissioned and rare. Johnson creates both miniature and larger baskets, incorporating the techniques he's learned through the years.

CHARLENE JUAN

Tohono O'odham (ca. 1965–) Chuischu, Arizona
Basketry

EDUCATION: Self-taught.

REPRESENTATION: Cristof's, Santa Fe, New Mexico.

ABOUT THE ARTIST: Juan comes from a family of basketweavers. She weaves miniatures and has created some woven horsehair masterpieces. She is versatile, using a variety of designs she creates using the coil method. Her work has been recognized in such publications as *Beyond Tradition* by Jerry and Lois Jacka.

LENA JUMBO

Northwest Coast; Ahousat, British Columbia, Canada
Basketmaker

EDUCATION: Her grandmother started to teach her how to weave when Jumbo was five.

ABOUT THE ARTIST: Jumbo often creates pocketbook-style baskets, complete with zippers, and decorated with eagles, whales, and other typical Northwest Coast designs. She is a tribal elder whose craft is important to her town of Ahousat and her people, and she attempts to pass it along as her grandmother did to her.

BEATRICE KENTON

Apache
Basketmaker

ABOUT THE ARTIST: Kenton incorporates traditional animal, figural, and geometric designs into her burden baskets.

MADELINE LAMSON

Hopi
Basketmaker

AWARDS: Won Best of Show at the Annual Museum of Northern Arizona Hopi Artist's Exhibition (1986).

ABOUT THE ARTIST: Lamson creates traditionally coiled Hopi baskets and trays.

AGNES LAZORE

(a.k.a. Ka He Ro Ton Kwas)

Mohawk (1924–) St. Regis, Quebec, Canada
Basketmaker, splint worker

EDUCATION: Learned how to make baskets at Akwesasne Homemakers and Cultural Committee.

REPRESENTATION: Mohawk Craft Fund, Quebec, Canada.

ABOUT THE ARTIST: Lazore often makes large stars from splints. She likes to use white or orange colored splints. Her basketry specialty is small sewing baskets, but she also knows how to make other types.

MARGARET R. LAZORE

(a.k.a. Kon Wa Ke Ri Saionatonti)

Mohawk (1923–) St. Regis, Quebec, Canada
Basketmaker, splint worker

EDUCATION: Learned by watching her mother, Dorothy Curry.

ABOUT THE ARTIST: Lazore uses black ash splints, sweet grass, and twine to make various types of baskets, both large and small. She likes using colored splints, but usually bends to the customer's preference. She often teaches basketry classes.

SARAH LAZORE

Mohawk (1918–) St. Regis, Quebec, Canada
Basketmaker, splint worker, clothing designer, quilter

EDUCATION: She learned from her grandmother and mother.

REPRESENTATION: Mohawk Craft Fund, Quebec, Canada.

ABOUT THE ARTIST: Lazore makes a wide variety of baskets, including baskets in the shape of turtles, as well as lampshades and woven chair seats. Lazore also creates dance costumes, quilts, and other types of clothing. The costumes are made for the Katerie Dance Group, to which she belongs.

MARY LEAF

Mohawk (1925–)
Basketmaker, splint worker, lacrosse stick weaver

EDUCATION: Learned her skills from her mother, Josephine Thompson.

AWARDS: Some of Leaf's work is held by the North American Indian Traveling College in Ontario.

ABOUT THE ARTIST: Leaf began making baskets at the age of eight, helping her mother. She creates sewing accessory baskets, as well as a variety of other types. Her work is well known and has been photographed for television and for the North American Indian Traveling College.

DAT SO LA LEE

(a.k.a. Mrs. Louisa Kayser)

Washo (ca. 1850–1924) Lake Tahoe, Nevada
Basketmaker

EDUCATION: Self-taught.

ABOUT THE ARTIST: Dat So La Lee learned to make baskets with her people and worked odd jobs as a domestic maid and laundress. When she was 60 she was recognized by Abe Cohn, an emporium owner from Carson City, Nevada. He became her business agent, providing her and her husband with a home, food, clothing, and medical payments in exchange for her baskets. Her weaving was tight and even, and her baskets are considered classics by the experts. Her triangular and flame-shaped motifs are perfectly spaced to the field on which they are placed. Some of her baskets incorporate symbols that represent sunrise or the midday ascending heat waves. Because she could not sign her name, she used a handprint as her signature. Cohn listed, numbered, and titled Dat So La Lee's baskets based on his conversations with her, and his efforts made it easier to study her development as an artist. In 1919 Dat So La Lee brought her work to the St. Louis Exposition and became one of its stars.

MIRIAM LEE

Seneca (d. 1993)
Basketmaker, beadworker, quilter

EDUCATION: Lee's mother-in-law taught her how to make baskets. She taught herself beadwork.

AWARDS: New York State Iroquois Conference Award, seventh annual Award to Iroquoian Individual (1976).

ABOUT THE ARTIST: Lee was one of the last Allegany basketmakers, and her specialties were corn washing, hominy, flower, and sewing baskets made in a twill or wicker weave from black ash splints. She demonstrated her craft and taught others how to create baskets.

GRACE LEHI

San Juan/Paiute
Basketmaker

REPRESENTATION: Blair's Dinnebito Trading Post, Page, Arizona.

ABOUT THE ARTIST: Lehi sometimes patterns her baskets after the traditional Navajo wedding basket.

ADELINE MANUEL

Tohono O'odham (ca. 1963–)
Basketry

EDUCATION: Learned how to weave from Norma Antone.

REPRESENTATION: Cristof's, Santa Fe, New Mexico.

ABOUT THE ARTIST: Manuel weaves miniature horsehair baskets and prefers to use the long, fine hair from Arabians. She comes from a family of weavers and is related to the Antone family. She weaves the tray shape as well as olla and vase in many of the traditional designs.

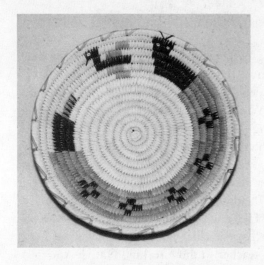

Tohoho O'odham (Papago) coiled
basket by V. Lopez (ca. 1960s)
Unusual design. A collector's item.
Courtesy of Jay Sadow, The Eastern
Cowboys, Scottsdale, AZ.

RITA MCDONALD

Mohawk (1938–) Hogansburg, New York
Basketmaker

EDUCATION: Her mother, Josephine Sunday, taught her.

REPRESENTATION: Mohawk Craft Fund, New York.

ABOUT THE ARTIST: In the past, McDonald made some baskets with her sister, Agnes Phillips, but now works alone. She uses black ash, sweet grass, and rope to create sewing baskets, as well as other types. She usually uses undyed splits.

MARY MITCHELL

Mohawk (1906–) St. Regis, Quebec, Canada
Basketmaker, quilter

EDUCATION: Learned by watching her mother.

REPRESENTATION: Mary Peachin's Art Company, Tucson, Arizona.

ABOUT THE ARTIST: Mitchell once created larger baskets, but as she grew older, she started making smaller baskets. She used sweet grass, black ash splints, and dyes.

TU MOONWALKER

Apache (1948–)
Basketmaker, beadworker, leatherworker, weaver—willow, grasses, beads, feathers, leather, wool, etc.

EDUCATION: B.A. in anthropology, B.S. in biochemistry, M.A. in museum science, and M.S. in geology.

AWARDS: First place, miniature baskets, Gallup Ceremonial (1986, 1987, 1988); first place, baskets, Denver Indian Market (1986).

REPRESENTATION: Andrews Pueblo Pottery, Albuquerque, New Mexico; Evelyn Siegel Gallery, Fort Worth, Texas; Maison des Maison, Denver, Colorado; Serendipity Trading Company, Estes Park, Colorado.

ABOUT THE ARTIST: Moonwalker is considered the premier Apache basketweaver in the Southwest, using her skills to produce miniature baskets, which have won almost all the awards given to basketweavers at shows throughout that area. In addition to her weaving, she teaches, lectures, and writes on the art. Her grandmother Dorothy Naiche Moonwalker is a descendant of the Apache chief Cochise. Moonwalker is also considered a major spiritual teacher to those seeking Native American religious guidance.

CHARLOTTE MOREY

Mohawk (1912–) Potsdam, New York
Basketmaker

EDUCATION: Learned by helping her mother, Margaret Brown Oaks.

REPRESENTATION: Mohawk Craft Fund, New York.

ABOUT THE ARTIST: Morey uses black ash splints, sweet grass, and rope to make a variety of baskets, as well as covered lamps and shades. She has taught basketry in New York and Massachusetts, has exhibited throughout the United States, and has been recognized as a talented artist by some local newspapers.

THERESA OAKES

(a.k.a. Ta Ka Ne Ten Ha Wi)

Mohawk (1916–) St. Regis, Quebec, Canada
Basketmaker, quilter

EDUCATION: Learned by helping Mary Adams.

ABOUT THE ARTIST: Oakes uses black ash splints and sweet grass to make small, fancy sewing baskets. An active basketmaker, she also teaches and creates quilts in her spare time.

ALICE PAUL

Northwest Coast; Victoria, British Columbia, Canada
Basketmaker

ABOUT THE ARTIST: Paul returns to her original home in Hesquiat every year to pick cedar and grass to make her baskets. She uses the whale in her designs because her people always considered it a vital part of their lives since they used every bit of it in trading and making things for personal or household use.

VICTORIA PHILLIPS

Mohawk (1946–) Hogansburg, New York
Basketmaker, splint worker

EDUCATION: Took basketmaking classes at the Akwesasne Library in 1969.
REPRESENTATION: Mohawk Crafts Fund, New York.
ABOUT THE ARTIST: Phillips uses black ash and sweet grass to make her sewing, fancy, strawberry, and button baskets. She also creates wastepaper baskets and doll bassinets, as well as splint work bells and pincushions. She has attended many craft shows, powwows, and fairs.

MAMIE RYAN

Oneida (1903–) Oneida, Wisconsin
Basketmaker, beadworker, jeweler, leatherworker

EDUCATION: Ryan's mother, Elizabeth Summers, taught her basketry. Ryan learned beadwork on her own.
REPRESENTATION: Oneida Nation Museum, Oneida, Wisconsin.
ABOUT THE ARTIST: Ryan is one of the last experienced basketmakers in Oneida. Her baskets are made solely of black ash splints (some natural, some dyed). She has passed on her skills to others in the hopes that the art will not die. She also created cornhusk dolls, beadworked clothing and jewelry, and enthusiastically promotes all Native American arts. She often created her work on commission, thus didn't have enough baskets to take to a fair.

JOYCE SAUFKIE

Hopi/Water Clan; Shongopavi Village
Basketmaker

AWARDS: Best of Basketry, Albuquerque Indian Market (2000).
ABOUT THE ARTIST: Saufkie makes Hopi wedding trays with interesting designs, such as the piece for which she won first prize from the Albuquerque Indian Market, a coiled basket with a water maiden design. She began making plaques at the young age of 15. After she was initiated into the Lalkan

society, she began making plaques, baskets, and yucca baskets. Since attending a show in Santa Fe, New Mexico, in 1982, she has focused on making coil plaques. She has won numerous awards and makes collector baskets.

JOYCE SHARROW
(a.k.a. Te Kon Wa Ren Ken Nionh)

Mohawk (1949–) St. Regis, Quebec, Canada
Basketmaker

EDUCATION: Learned from her mother, Margaret R. Lazore.

ABOUT THE ARTIST: Sharrow makes mail and wastepaper baskets, sometimes working alongside her mother. She has passed on her basketry skills to her own children as well.

MARY SNYDER

Chemeheuvi
Basketry

EDUCATION: Self-taught.

ABOUT THE ARTIST: Snyder was well known throughout Arizona for making the rattlesnake basket using a unique combination of Chemeheuvi and Cahuilla materials. Though her baskets look like those made by Southern California Indians, different materials were most likely used. Chemeheuvi basketmakers almost always used willow for white stitches and devil's claw for black details. True Mission weavers never used these materials.

AGNES SUNDAY
(a.k.a. Ka Ra Kwine)

Mohawk (1909–) St. Regis, Quebec, Canada
Basketmaker, quilter

EDUCATION: She learned from her mother, as well as from her mother-in-law, Annie Sunday.

AWARDS: One of Sunday's baskets was on display at a United Nations exhibit held in 1977.

REPRESENTATION: Mohawk Craft Fund, Quebec, Canada.

ABOUT THE ARTIST: Sunday was a founding member of the Akwesasne Homemakers and Cultural Committee. She uses black ash splints, sweet grass, dyes, and hickory when making her sewing, shopping, and pack baskets (as well as others).

CECILIA SUNDAY

Mohawk (1919–) St. Regis, Quebec, Canada
Basketmaker

EDUCATION: Learned by watching her father and mother-in-law.
REPRESENTATION: Mohawk Craft Fund, Quebec, Canada.
ABOUT THE ARTIST: Sunday has been making baskets since she was 13. She
uses black ash splints, sweet grass, and white ash handles for shopping,
picnic, pie, clothes, pack, bushel, and corn-washing baskets as well as
hampers. She has taught basketry to others and often works with her husband, Joe. They have taught their eldest daughter and granddaughter
how to create baskets.

MARY TEBO

(a.k.a. Wen Ni Si Ri Io Sta)

Mohawk (1906–) Rooseveltown, New York
Basketmaker, splint worker

EDUCATION: Learned from Minnie Thompson, her mother.
ABOUT THE ARTIST: Tebo has been creating baskets all her life and has
passed her skills on to her five children. She often works with her daughter Annabell, traveling to exhibits and demonstrations. She has also taught
classes on basketry in her home. Tebo uses black ash splints and sweet
grass to make a variety of baskets, including sewing baskets, jardinieres,
and hampers. She also makes splint bookmarkers.

CECILIA THOMAS

Mohawk (1899–) St. Regis, Quebec, Canada
Basketmaker

EDUCATION: Learned from John and Marion Adams, her parents.
AWARDS: Thomas has presented one of her baskets to the Queen of England
(1973) and has one first prize at the New York State Fair.
ABOUT THE ARTIST: Thomas learned how to weave baskets at a young age
and started selling her own baskets when she was in her early 20s. Her husband often helped her with the bindings on her laundry baskets. She creates quite colorful, memorable baskets, often naming her original designs.

FRANCES THOMAS

Tohono O'odham
Basketweaver

REPRESENTATION: Penfield Gallery of Indian Arts, Albuquerque, New Mexico.

ABOUT THE ARTIST: Thomas does some woven horsehair plaques with figural designs on them, including rattlesnakes.

MARY THOMAS
(a.k.a. Wa Rie Wa Thon Tha)
Mohawk (1901–) St. Regis, Quebec, Canada
Basketmaker

EDUCATION: Learned her skills from her parents.

ABOUT THE ARTIST: Thomas has taught others the Mohawk names for her baskets. She began making them at a very young age and can weave a wide variety of baskets, often creating new styles. She works with black ash and sweet grass to create such items as sewing, Easter, shopping, and clothes baskets.

RUBY THOMAS (RUBY GARCIA)
Tohono O'odham (ca. 1965–) Casa Grande, Arizona
Basketry

EDUCATION: Learned to weave from her mother.

REPRESENTATION: Cristof's, Santa Fe, New Mexico

ABOUT THE ARTIST: Though she learned how to make yucca and bear grass baskets, she prefers to make miniature horsehair baskets. Her designs include the traditional Man-in-the-Maze, as well as unique landscape scenes and plates and bowls. Her baskets are fine and detailed. Her sister is basketmaker Dorina Garcia.

ELIZABETH THOMPSON
(a.k.a. Katsitsainnie)
Mohawk (1916–) Cornwall Island, Ontario, Canada
Basketmaker, splint worker, lacrosse stick lacer, textile worker

EDUCATION: Thompson learned her basketry skills from her mother, Christie Phillips, and her stick-lacing skills from her husband and mother-in-law.

ABOUT THE ARTIST: Thompson has passed on her skills to her daughter, as well as others. She makes a variety of baskets, including an egg-shaped knitting basket that has a hole in one end through which the yarn is pulled. She is always trying new styles.

ELLA THOMPSON

Northwest Coast ( ) Ucluelet, British Columbia, Canada
Basketmaker

ABOUT THE ARTIST: Thompson states that all the women she knew created baskets long ago, but that the number who weave today has dwindled. Thompson makes smaller baskets with designs woven in.

MIKE TOM AND JOSEPHINE TOM

Northwest Coast; Canada
Basketweavers and carvers

ABOUT THE ARTISTS: This couple makes totem pole–style baskets, masks, canoes, and other smaller wooden carved items. Josephine's basketmaking also extends to mats, which she might design with whales and halibut, both part of Northwest Coast legends.

NETTIE WATT

(a.k.a. Ah Wen Non Gon)

Seneca (1901–99) Steamburg, New York
Basketmaker, dollmaker, beadworker

EDUCATION: Learned her skills by watching her in-laws and through experimentation.

ABOUT THE ARTIST: One of the last basketmakers at Allegany, Nettie passed her skills on to her daughter Ruth. Nettie made baskets since the Depression days, making most of them during the winter months. The majority of her baskets are made of black ash splints; however, she does make some sweet grass and sea grass rope. She also created cornhusk dolls and tried to pass those skills on to others so that the craft would not die. One of the elders of the Cornplanter reservation, Watt endeavored to keep her culture alive by doing such things as passing on seeds for Seneca Hominy corn to the Eastern Native Seed Conservancy.

RUTH WATT

Seneca (1921–) Steamburg, New York
Basketmaker

EDUCATION: Ruth's mother, Nettie Watt, taught her how to make basket bottoms. Later, Ruth learned how to make the rest of the basket on her own.

ABOUT THE ARTIST: Watt makes market, cake, shopper, and mail baskets out of black ash splints. They have rope or hickory handles. She often uses colored splints to give accents to the basket, but most are made from natural fibers. Ruth also makes colored corn necklaces.

JESSIE WEBSTER

Northwest Coast; Ahousat, British Columbia, Canada
Basketweaver

EDUCATION: Webster watched her grandmothers weave hats. One of them would start a project for her, then she worked on it later.

ABOUT THE ARTIST: Webster creates woven basketry hats: fancy ones for the chief, and plain varieties for the people.

GLADYS WHITE

Mohawk (1942–)
Basketmaker, quilter

EDUCATION: White learned her basketmaking skills at the Akwesasne Homemakers and Cultural Committee.

ABOUT THE ARTIST: White makes planters and 4-inch baskets in natural splints and a simple pattern. She also sews quilts.

Hopi coiled basket. Multi-chrome Heheya design by Ione Yoycestewa. Typical example of basketwork from the Hopi Mesas of Arizona. Courtesy of Jay Sadow, The Eastern Cowboys, Scottsdale, AZ.

Seneca/Mohawk woven sweetgrass covered basket, from the Whitehawk family, ca 1950s. Courtesy of Jay Sadow, The Eastern Cowboys, Scottsdale, AZ.

JULIANNA WILLIAMS

Mount Currie; Mount Currie, British Columbia, Canada
Basketmaker

EDUCATION: Learned the skills of basketmaking from her mother, Matilda Jim.

ABOUT THE ARTIST: Williams makes lidded and unlidded baskets, as did her mother before her.

Prices

Joyce Addington. Unusual Hopi Mudhead Kachina design coil plaque. Approximately 10". $500.

Norma Antone. Woven horsehair plaque shows the Friendship Circle and the Yokats Friendship basket. 6½" in diameter. $2,400.

Lorraine Black. Positive Stars basket. 15". $400.

———. Snake Yeis basket. 15" wide. $875.

———. Underground Dogs basket. 21". $2,250.

Mary Holiday Black. Night Sky People basket. 14½". $620.

Sally Black. Hozho Crosses. 15". $1100.

———. Eagle. 16½". $1150.

———. Kokopelli Vessel. 12⅜" tall × 15" wide. $3,600.

Linda Guzman. White Mountain Apache Tus twined weave basket, made of Devil's Claw and Yucca, ca. 1990s. 17" × 26". $2,500.

Alice Honanie. Hopi wicker plaque with an interesting geometric design in green, red, yellow, blue, and brown. Approximately 12". $540.

Grace Lehi. Paiute basket with exceedingly fine decoration of a spiral of black and red. Approximately 16". $1,000.

Ruby Saufkie. Hopi coil plaque. Approximately 11". $1,150.

CHAPTER 3

Beadwork

When considering beadwork, the best way to tell the difference between the items created by different tribes is to observe the types of material used, the construction or pattern, the medium used to decorate the item, the technique, the colors, and the design. Because this type of decoration was used to identify everything from dresses and moccasins to bridles and gun holders, the collector can discover a plethora of materials in this category. Following is a breakdown of the recognizable characteristics of each tribe's beadwork.

TRIBE	CHARACTERISTICS
Assinboin, Sarcee, and Blackfoot	Beadwork designs were exclusively geometric.
Blackfoot and Crow	Used geometric spot-stitching beadwork designs until floral motifs became popular (about 1870). Examples of Crow work were often triangular and sewn on red cloth. Crow beadworkers rarely made tobacco bags; however, they did make beautiful gun cases.
Chippewa	Used a variety of techniques to produce beadwork. A wood heddle separated the warps so that the beaded weft could be inserted. Other beadwork was made with a needle, producing either single- or double-weft weaving. This sewing style was also used by the Winnebago tribe.
Iroquois	Crowded their beads together and padded their designs to create a raised, textural effect. This type of beadwork was done mostly on velvet pieces.
Micmac	Delicate, double-curving forms. Imitated European embroidery in their beadwork.
Nez Percé	Made a distinctive four-tabbed beaded leather bag that was widely traded. A similar bag was made by the Athabascan tribes.
Northeast, Lakes, and	Created intricate designs by laying strung beads

Northern Plains	in a pattern and sewing them into place. Produced shaded floral designs to decorate all kinds of clothing, bags, moccasins, and turbans. Northeastern beadwork has a lacy and stylized appearance. Floral work is common among tribes such as the Penobscot, Iroquois, and Micmac.
Northwest Coast	Influenced by the styles of the Northern Plains and distinguished by designs one sees repeated in their painting, sculpture, and rugs: geometric patterns drawn from oceanic life and featuring seals, whales, eagles, bears, and ravens.
Plains	Used "lazy stitch" sewing: beads strung together, then attached to the garment at the ends of short lengths of beads. In other words, each bead was not individually fastened to the material. Pony beads were larger and used from about 1800 on. Seed beads became popular around 1840.
Sauk and Chippewa	Used bilateral symmetry in their boldly styled beadwork.

The Artists

JEANNINE AARON
Iroquois (1956–)
Beadworker

EDUCATION: Self-taught.

ABOUT THE ARTIST: Aaron shows her work at powwows, schools, and other places. Her whole family practices beadwork, and Aaron has been experimenting with new techniques.

D. MONROE ABRAMS
(a.k.a. Ten Nooshagh, "Sugar Bear")
Seneca (1948–) Steamburg, New York
Beadworker, leatherworker, featherworker, porcupine quill designer, carver, dollmaker

EDUCATION: Learned many of his skills from his parents; attended Ithaca College, New York.

ABOUT THE ARTIST: This multitalented artist does beadwork medallions, necklaces and earrings, wristbands, watchbands, belts, headbands, chokers, and necklaces. He also decorates his leather vests, purses, and costumes with beadwork; makes porcupine quill chokers and earrings; carves wooden statuettes, pipes, hatchets, and basket handles; makes rattles from turtle, horn, and hickory; and makes cornhusk dolls. In addition, he is a dancer and takes his work with him when he travels to dancing ceremonies.

EULA ANTONE

Oneida (1917–) Southwold, Ontario, Canada
Beadworker, leatherworker, quilter, rug maker

EDUCATION: Mostly self-taught; took beadwork classes in 1965.

AWARDS: Various prizes for her beadwork and pipes from the Oneida Fall Fair and the Homemakers' Convention.

ABOUT THE ARTIST: Antone has taught beadwork and exhibited her work extensively. She especially likes to use turtles, eagles, and wolves on her medallions and bolo ties. During the winter Antone's husband, Russell, helps her with loomwork, and both their children also bead. Antone is deeply involved with Oneida affairs.

CHARLA BACH

Seneca (1946–) Salamanca, New York
Beadworker, dollmaker

EDUCATION: She has taught herself and also has taken classes in working with cornhusks at the Allegany Indian Arts & Crafts Co-op.

REPRESENTATION: Allegany Indian Arts & Crafts Co-op.

ABOUT THE ARTIST: After being hospitalized in the late 1970s, Bach became interested in beadwork and now sells her craftwork. She also makes cornhusk dolls and takes her work to fairs and festivals. Bach, like many other Indian artists, encourages young people to carry on Iroquois crafts.

RUTH BAIRD

Oneida (d. 1900)
Beadworker, quilter

EDUCATION: Self-taught.

ABOUT THE ARTIST: Baird watched members of her family make baskets, but did not get interested in creating her own items until the 1970s, when she learned how to do beadwork. She received orders for both her freehand and loomed jewelry and medallions. She often used green and yellow (Green Bay Packers colors). An active member of the Oneida community, Baird has headed the Oneida Indian Singers and often teaches the Oneida language.

VIRGINIA (HILL) BEAVER

Mohawk (1930–)

Beadworker, weaver, leatherworker, cornhusk worker, basketmaker, porcupine quill decorator

EDUCATION: Beaver learned beadwork from her grandmother; finger weaving from Audrey Spencer, and basketry from Mary Adams and Margaret Torrence; she has taught herself other crafts.

AWARDS: She has won several grants for different types of research and work.

ABOUT THE ARTIST: A prolific craftsperson, Beaver has done beadwork since a child and has passed on what she knows by teaching classes on the subject. She has done quite a bit of research about the traditional crafts, discovering that the beadwork used on antique Native American clothing was subtle in color. She has also educated herself and others about the Indians who lived in the Grand River area before the Six Nations settled there.

MARY ANN BEGAY

Navajo; Red Mesa, Arizona

Beadworker

EDUCATION: Learned beading from her aunt. Received her bachelor's degree and teaching certificate and is working on her master's.

REPRESENTATION: Twin Rocks Trading Post, Bluff, Utah.

ABOUT THE ARTIST: Begay has practiced making beaded baskets since she was a child and weaves her baskets in yucca, then covers them with leather, upon which she patterns her beads. As a child, she learned how to weave rugs from her grandmother and learned Navajo philosophy from her grandfather, who was a medicine man. She does not use sacred cultural or religious themes in her work, concentrating on working with earth tone color schemes.

DOROTHY M. BISCUP

(a.k.a. Gain Ee)

Seneca (1911–) Steamburg, New York

Beadworker

EDUCATION: Biscup's aunt, Kathryn Jamerson, taught her. The artist also taught herself some skills.

ABOUT THE ARTIST: Biscup was a president of the Iroquois Senior Citizens and also taught Seneca at the Haley Community Building. She was a member of the Allegany Indian Arts & Crafts Co-op from its inception. She finds making beadwork chokers, daisy chains, and ladder-stitch necklaces to be quite relaxing, and she prefers to use brightly colored glass beads in her work.

WINONA ESTHER BLUEYE
(a.k.a. Ko Woo Wiitha')

Seneca (1903–) Basom, New York
Beadworker, leatherworker

EDUCATION: Self-taught, with some classes.

AWARDS: Among Blueye's honors is the recognition she received from the New York Iroquois Conference in 1975, when they named her one of the Ten Prominent Women of the Year in New York state.

ABOUT THE ARTIST: Blueye has exhibited her work at powwows and art exhibits. She prefers to do beadwork medallions, but has also worked with leather. She teaches the Seneca language at several area schools.

GRACE BONSPILLE
(a.k.a. Takahawakwen)

Mohawk (1930–) Oka, Quebec, Canada
Beadworker, leatherworker

EDUCATION: Bonspille took classes in beadwork and leatherwork, as well as leather tooling.

ABOUT THE ARTIST: Bonspille has made beaded belts, necklaces, watchbands and headbands, leather moccasins, jackets, vests, and purses and has decorated leather change purses, key holders, and wallets. Her whole family is involved in the arts, especially her mother, Margaret Etienne, a basketmaker.

PERRY BONSPILLE

Mohawk (1960–)
Beadworker, leatherworker

EDUCATION: Took classes in beadwork and leatherwork.

ABOUT THE ARTIST: Like his mother, Grace, Perry has been doing craftwork since a young age. He likes to use stars and geometric patterns in his beadwork designs and continues to experiment with different media.

ARLENE BOVA
(a.k.a. Gah Na Sah Gnaha)

Seneca (1961–) Salamanca, New York
Beadworker

EDUCATION: Learned from her mother, Ella Bowen.

ABOUT THE ARTIST: Bova has been doing beadwork since she was nine years old. She prefers loom beadwork because it allows her to work with many different colors and designs. She tries to never use the same design twice with the same colors. Bova took a number of art courses at Salamanca Central School, and she also dances with the Seneca Dancers. She is active in the Seneca Nation and has been an Allegany councillor.

DARLENE BOVA
(a.k.a. Gay Yeh Na)

Seneca (1960–) Salamanca, New York
Beadworker, porcupine quill designer

EDUCATION: Learned her skills from her mother, Ella Bowen, and her aunt, Delores Oldshield.

ABOUT THE ARTIST: Bova has been working with beads since she was nine years old. She especially likes to make porcupine quill and bead earrings in the peyote stitches.

MAMIE BROWN
(a.k.a. Gan Nah Jah Leet)

Oneida (1921–) Afton, New York
Beadworker, quillworker, dollmaker, featherworker

EDUCATION: Learned from her mother.

ABOUT THE ARTIST: Brown's mother was quite an active craftsperson at Onondaga. Her father carved wood basket handles and axe handles. Brown has made baskets, but she now does mostly quillwork and beadwork, as well as cornhusk dolls. She dresses her dolls in traditional clothing and often makes male and female pairs. One such doll went into Rose Kennedy's collection. Brown exhibits at the New York State Fair and travels to shows all over the country.

HELEN BURNING

Onondaga (1918–) Oshweken, Ontario, Canada
Beadworker, clothing designer, leatherworker

EDUCATION: Learned from Huron Miller.

AWARDS: Best in Show, beadwork, Six Nations Fall Fair (1977).

ABOUT THE ARTIST: Burning makes beaded jewelry, barrettes, and hair and
bolo ties. She also does beadwork decoration on Native clothing and moccasins. Burning travels extensively to fairs, festivals, and powwows to sell
the work that she and her daughters, Shirley and Ruth, have created.
Burning shades and blends her beads, striving for an original design and
style. She experiments with beadwork and also holds classes in the art.

DORIAL CLARK

Tuscarora/Cayuga (1940–)
Beadworker, wireworker, headdress designer

EDUCATION: Murial Hewitt, Clark's cousin, taught her.

ABOUT THE ARTIST: Clark uses a variety of beading techniques to fill her orders and uses as many as 200 colors, in addition to making her own patterns. She has been especially influenced by the beadwork made on
Manitoulin Island.

KAREN CLARK

Seneca (1948–) Steamburg, New York
Beadworker

EDUCATION: Though mostly self-taught, Clark learned the daisy chain
stitch from her mother, Martha Bucktooth, and learned different skills by
watching other artists.

ABOUT THE ARTIST: An experienced beadworker, Clark uses porcupine
quills with her beadwork medallions, necklaces, and earrings. She almost
never uses the same pattern more than once and enjoys working with
whatever pattern her customer suggests or designs. She has decorated costumes with beadwork and has also beaded leather purses. In addition, she
makes turtle rattles and passes on what she has learned to others.

DARELYN CLAUSE

Mohawk/Algonquin (1957–) Sanborn, New York
Beadworker

EDUCATION: Took beading classes from Doris Hudson.

ABOUT THE ARTIST: Clause has exhibited her work at the New York State Fair, the Erie County Fair and Exhibition, and other fairs, since the early 1970s. Her beadwork includes barrettes, medallions, hair ties, jewelry, lighter covers, and key chains. She also decorates pipe stems with beadwork.

RUTH CONKLIN

Seneca (1936–) Irving, New York
Beadworker, dollmaker

EDUCATION: Learned some beadwork skills from Virginia Snow; taught herself additional beadwork designs and how to make cornhusk dolls.

ABOUT THE ARTIST: Conklin has been creating beadwork since the early 1970s, preferring the older beaded designs done on velvet. She uses raised beading in her medallions. She also makes cornhusk dolls and is passing on her skills to her son.

CARL COOK

Mohawk (1942–) Hogansburg, New York
Beadworker

EDUCATION: Self-taught and also learned some basic techniques in school.

ABOUT THE ARTIST: Cook designs his own patterns to create beadwork on belts, wristbands, and watchbands. His designs often portray the Mohawk longhouse or clan animals. Cook also takes special orders.

TONI COOKE

(a.k.a. Gus Ah Doong Gwas)

Oneida (1961–) Onondaga Nation, Nedrow, New York
Beadworker, porcupine quill decorator, clothing designer, painter, potter, weaver

EDUCATION: Took pottery classes at Lafayette Central School (1975–79); art major at Cazenovia College, New York.

AWARDS: Many, including the Gold Key Award and Mony Scholastics Award.

ABOUT THE ARTIST: A multitalented artist, Cooke has been selling her beadwork since the age of 14. She experiments with different forms and traditions, as well as arts. She incorporates what she learns into the clothing, beadwork, quillwork, weaving, pottery, and painting she creates.

KATHLEEN D'ARCY

Seneca (1935–)
Beadworker, porcupine quill designer

EDUCATION: Learned her skills while attending Thomas Indian School, Cattaraugus.

AWARDS: Several, including first prize for a barrette at the Indian Fall Festival.

ABOUT THE ARTIST: D'Arcy experiments with new designs and forms in her beadwork, using both traditional and modern styles. She creates jewelry and barrettes with her beadwork and has made porcupine quill chokers and earrings. Turquoise, black, and white are her favorite color combinations. She sells from her home and does not attend fairs.

AGNES DECAIRE

Mohawk (1951–) Caughnawaga, Quebec, Canada
Quillworker, beadworker

EDUCATION: Learned beadwork from Nora Deering.

ABOUT THE ARTIST: A founding member of the Kanawake Handicrafts Workshop, Decaire makes a wide variety of items, including quill chokers and earrings, beaded chokers, earrings, medallions, barrettes, and bone chokers. She works closely with her mother, Isabell Myiow, when selling her work.

KRISTEN DEER

Mohawk (1963–) Caughnawaga, Quebec, Canada
Beadworker

EDUCATION: Learned her beadworking skills at the Caughnawaga Boys & Girls Club.

ABOUT THE ARTIST: Deer does most of her work on a loom, though she can also do freehand items. She likes blue and white beads, and though some of her designs are geometric, she has been known to make moose or eagle patterns. She also likes to make ribbon shirts.

NORA DEERING

Mohawk (1911–76)
Beadworker, dollmaker, basketmaker, knitter, seamstress

EDUCATION: Self-taught.

ABOUT THE ARTIST: This well-respected craftswoman attended quite a few fairs, taught her craft to anyone who wanted to learn, worked to keep the Mohawk language alive, and accepted any creative challenge given her. She experimented with new techniques and often gave some materials to others to make their works. Her most important contribution to Iroquois culture was a dictionary of the Mohawk language and a grammar book that she coauthored.

DIANE DEMARCO

Tuscarora (1937–)
Beadworker, dollmaker, painter, carver

EDUCATION: Learned from her grandmother Harriet Pembleton.
ABOUT THE ARTIST: Since the early 1970s Diana has made beaded items in the raised and flat style and has exhibited her work at the Tuscarora Indian Culture Night and Earl Bridges Art Park. Her work includes beaded light covers, barrettes, medallions and jewelry, and velvet cushions, along with cornhusk dolls and other items. She also paints and does stone-carving.

LUELLA DERRICK

Onondaga (1925–) Nedrow, New York
Beadworker, textile worker

EDUCATION: Learned some of her skills from her grandmother Minni Shanadore.
AWARDS: Derrick has won many awards at the New York State Fair for her sewing.
ABOUT THE ARTIST: An active creator, Derrick attends fairs and exhibits with her items. She makes beaded jewelry, headbands, key chains, belts, and wristbands, as well as ribbon shirts and other types of clothing.

ALICE DIABO

Mohawk (1906–) Caughnawaga, Quebec, Canada
Beadworker, leatherworker, dollmaker, headdress creator

EDUCATION: Learned from her mother.
ABOUT THE ARTIST: Diabo created many of her items with the traditional raised beadwork-on-velvet style. Though she often substituted leather for the traditional turn-of-the-century velvet, she preserved the old designs. As others, Diabo has taught the young, so that the Iroquois traditions will

not be lost. In 1990 she starred in a movie entitled *Strangers in Good Company*, with a group of women who had never acted before.

MARJORIE DIABO

Mohawk (1937–) Caughnawaga, Quebec, Canada
Beadworker, dollmaker, porcupine quill decorator

EDUCATION: Diabo's mother, Alice, taught her some skills and she also took beadwork classes from Nora Deering.

ABOUT THE ARTIST: Diabo makes beaded chokers, key chains, barrettes, and watchbands, working both freehand and on the loom. She also works with leather, quilts, crochets, knits, and hooks rugs. A founding member of the Kanawake Handicrafts Workshop, Diabo wants children to learn the art of beadwork.

VICTOR K. DIABO

Mohawk (1956–) Caughnawaga, Quebec, Canada
Leatherworker—beads; painter; carver; sculptor; silversmith

EDUCATION: Mostly self-taught, Diabo also learned some of his skills from his grandmother Alice Diabo and learned about soapstone sculpture from Olga Korper.

ABOUT THE ARTIST: Diabo has traveled to many places to demonstrate his crafts and to teach others. Some of his work is held in private collections in Switzerland, Australia, Scotland, and Canada. He is noted for his original designs and never uses the same design twice. He gets ideas for his paintings from the people, animals, and land around him, and his soapstone carvings are delicately carved.

BETTY DOXTATOR

Mohawk (1960–) Oshweken, Ontario, Canada
Beadworker, clothing designer

EDUCATION: Self-taught.

ABOUT THE ARTIST: Doxtator started becoming more prolific with beadwork when she began beading her own dress costumes. She makes Native clothing for men, women, and children in both the Iroquois and Western styles. Additionally, she creates breastplates, gauntlets, headbands, and belts.

LAURA DOXTATOR

Oneida (1935–) Southwold, Ontario, Canada
Beadworker, leatherworker, knitter, crocheter, quilter

EDUCATION: Doxtator has taken various classes, including beadwork. Her mother taught her how to sew, and Doxtator taught herself how to work with leather.

AWARDS: Doxtator has won various prizes for her work at the Oneida Fall Fair.

ABOUT THE ARTIST: Some of the items Doxtator makes include medallions, necklaces, neckties, guitar straps, belts, wallets, key chains, belts, and purses. She creates new patterns and is always experimenting with the decorating she does on leather. In addition to creating her own new work, Doxtator teaches craft classes, as well as the Oneida language.

DEBORAH DROUIN

Mohawk (1953–)
Beadworker, leatherworker, dollmaker

EDUCATION: Learned how to create beadwork from Nora Deering and Elaine Lahache.

ABOUT THE ARTIST: A founding member of the Kanawake Handicrafts Workshop, Drouin started working with leather at the age of 15, when a neighbor gave her a pattern for a vest. She does both raised and flat beadwork and is teaching her children the art.

NANCY DIABO DROUIN

Mohawk (1926–) Caughnawaga, Quebec, Canada
Beadworker, leatherworker, dollmaker

EDUCATION: Self-taught.

ABOUT THE ARTIST: Drouin is a founding member of the Kanawake Handicrafts Workshop and did not begin making Indian crafts until that shop opened in 1976. She works with silver and bone, quality beads, and other material to make necklaces and chokers. She also makes fringed and decorated leather vests.

SHANNON ELIJAH

(a.k.a. Guna Da How)

Oneida (1952–) Southwold, Ontario, Canada
Beadworker

EDUCATION: Mostly self-taught, Elijah has also taken some beadwork classes.

AWARDS: Received a grant from the Young Canada Works program in 1975; has won many prizes at fairs and festivals; and work illustrated in *Redbook* magazine.

ABOUT THE ARTIST: An innovative artist, Elijah creates her own patterns for the freehand and loom beadwork she makes. Her beaded wallets, change purses, and cuffs are unusual. Though she uses flower or feather designs, she also incorporates traditional Iroquois designs into her clothing. She exhibits widely and does shows in the Northeast.

GAIL ELLIS

Oneida (1953–) Oneida, Wisconsin
Beadworker, porcupine quill designer, weaver

EDUCATION: Institute of American Indian Arts (1969–72); University of New Mexico (1975–76); University of Wisconsin, Green Bay (1979).

AWARDS: Received the Vincent Price Award for her poetry.

ABOUT THE ARTIST: When she returned home from college, Ellis studied under Josephine Wapp, learning traditional weaving techniques and the history of other Native American crafts. Her preference is beadwork, and she constantly studies the old designs. Her work recalls the wampum belt work done in the early days. She specializes in making leather pouches and teaches not only the crafts of the Oneida but the language as well to children in grammar schools.

ADELINE ETIENNE
(a.k.a. Nikawonna A)

Mohawk (1950–) West Oka, Quebec, Canada
Beadworker, leatherworker, weaver

EDUCATION: Etienne took beading classes.

REPRESENTATION: Kanesatake Indian Arts & Crafts, Quebec, Canada.

ABOUT THE ARTIST: A multitalented woman, Etienne prefers beadwork, though she has made many other items. She uses floral and geometric designs when decorating her leather tooled pieces and floral designs in her loomwork. She also weaves rugs and ponchos.

KAREN ETIENNE
(a.k.a. Whentenhawi)

Mohawk
Beadworker, leatherworker

EDUCATION: Largely self-taught; however, took some classes in leatherwork and tooling.

ABOUT THE ARTIST: Etienne's whole family is working in the arts. Her talents lie in creating beaded and quill earrings, feathered hair ties, and duffle garments that are embroidered, as well as decorating leatherwork with tooled designs.

IDA GABRIEL
(a.k.a. Kwatsitsaienni)

Mohawk (1938–) Oka, Quebec, Canada
Beadworker, leatherworker

EDUCATION: Gabriel's sister, Violet, taught her.

ABOUT THE ARTIST: Gabriel beads men's ties, necklaces, headbands, daisy chains, and rosettes, as well as leather hair ties and vests. She does most of her work during the winter and passes on that piece of Iroquois culture to others.

MILDRED GARLOW
Seneca (1889–1965)
Beadworker, dollmaker, basketmaker

EDUCATION: Learned how to bead from her mother-in-law and how to make cornhusk dolls from her mother.

ABOUT THE ARTIST: Garlow made unique items, such as beaded pincushions, velvet dolls, cornhusk dolls, and other items that she sold at Prospect Point, Niagara Falls, for more than 60 years. She had a distinct beadwork style, elaborating on the raised beadwork styles. Her red velvet dolls were made from cloth Queen Victoria gave to Garlow's mother, Deerfoot. In the 1950s Garlow wrote letters about the Demarcation of the Five Nation Confederacy to various members of the U.S. government.

RUTH GARLOW
(a.k.a. Yah Wenh Gwas)

Seneca (1914–) Lewiston, New York
Beadworker, dollmaker, leatherworker

EDUCATION: Learned how to bead from her grandmother and mother, how to make beaded velvet birds from her cousin, and how to create cornhusk dolls from her grandmother.

AWARDS: Garlow has received numerous prizes for her beaded birds at the New York State Fair.

ABOUT THE ARTIST: Garlow's specialty is her velvet and satin beaded birds, which she tries to make as realistic-looking as possible. Because of the great demand for her work, Garlow has been able to devote her time solely to creating items to sell to her customers.

SARAH GARROW

Mohawk (1954–) Bombay, New York
Beadworker, porcupine quill designer

EDUCATION: Learned beadwork from her sister, Martha Cook, and learned loom beadwork at Salmon River Central School in the late 1970s.

ABOUT THE ARTIST: Garrow uses beads, sequins, pearls, and porcupine quills to create both loom and freehand beadwork. Some of the items she makes include beaded key chains, earrings, medallions, hair ties, watchbands, and barrettes. She also does porcupine quill–designed earrings and chokers. Garrow believes it is important for Iroquois children to know the old ways and crafts, thus she teaches the culture at the Salmon River Central School, as well as at the Twin Rivers School in Massena.

FIDELIA GEORGE

Seneca (1955–)
Beadworker

EDUCATION: Learned by watching her mother.

ABOUT THE ARTIST: George creates beaded jewelry, as well as bolo ties, wristbands, barrettes, hair ties, belt buckles, and cigarette cases. She has exhibited her work and is always trying something new. She also dances and sings, spreading the Iroquois traditions whenever she gets the chance.

MILDRED GEORGE

Seneca (1916–)
Beadworker

EDUCATION: George learned how to bead by watching others.

ABOUT THE ARTIST: She creates beaded jewelry, preferring to make clan medallions in patterns she has created.

LEONA GRAY

Mohawk (1959–) Hogansburg, New York
Beadworker, porcupine quill designer, carver

EDUCATION: Learned some of her skills from a friend and developed her other skills personally.

ABOUT THE ARTIST: Gray taught herself how to bead as a young child of seven, then learned other stitches at the longhouse. She does freehand and loomwork and uses geometric, as well as floral, designs. In addition, Gray carves cradleboards from red pen. She also teaches crafts in the Native American Program in Rochester and has worked with that city's language program.

IRENE GREENE

Oneida (1925–) Nedrow, New York
Beadworker, clothing designer, leatherworker

EDUCATION: Self-taught.

AWARDS: Greene has won prizes for her work at the New York State Fair.

ABOUT THE ARTIST: Greene creates beaded jewelry and other items, children's Native clothing, and beaded leather wristbands. She has been working at her craft since a youngster and has also taught her own children how to bead. She rarely exhibits her work.

MARY HALFTOWN

(a.k.a. Jo Yan Non)

Seneca (1903–)
Beadworker

EDUCATION: Learned beadwork from a friend.

ABOUT THE ARTIST: Mary has sold her beadwork at a number of fairs, creating medallions, bolo ties, and necklaces, in addition to decorating leather purses and vests with beadwork. She has made baskets and cornhusk dolls. Her daughters also make baskets and beadwork.

HAZEL HARRISON

Seneca (1933–) Jamestown, New York
Beadworker

EDUCATION: Harrison has learned some techniques from a friend and others through a class at the Allegany Indian Arts & Crafts Co-op.

ABOUT THE ARTIST: A full-time emergency medical technician for the Seneca Nation, Harrison fills her free time with beadwork. She has passed on her skills to her sons and daughters. She usually makes clan medallions, medallions, and daisy chain and other types of necklaces.

LOUISE HENRY

Tuscarora
Beadworker, clothing designer

EDUCATION: Her sister, Doris Hudson, gave Henry classes on how to bead.

ABOUT THE ARTIST: Henry has decorated velvet, cloth, and leather with her beadwork and has also passed on what she knows by teaching beading classes at conferences, colleges, and churches. She has exhibited at the New York State Fair with her beaded medallions, bolo ties, barrettes, velvet picture frames and cushions, Iroquois clothing, and leather purses and moccasins.

MARGIE HENRY
(a.k.a. Kawinetá)

Cayuga; Ohsweken, Ontario, Canada
Beadworker, weaver, cornhusk dollmaker, silverworker

EDUCATION: Mostly self-taught; however, Henry has taken classes in silversmithing and finger weaving, and was taught how to work with cornhusk by her mother.

ABOUT THE ARTIST: Henry's work is held in collections at the Woodland Indian Cultural Educational Centre and the North American Traveling Indian College. She is very active within her community, teaching all kinds of classes, as well as the Cayuga language. Her work is traditional, and she makes beadwork jewelry, finger-woven sashes, felt and cornhusk dolls, and silver jewelry.

ETHEL HILL
(a.k.a. Gah Wonh Ho Donh)

Seneca (1910–)
Beadworker, clothing designer

EDUCATION: Self-taught.

AWARDS: First prize for a woman's Native dress shown at the New York State Fair in 1977.

ABOUT THE ARTIST: Hill began beading in the mid-1950s and exhibited regularly after that time. She used her own designs for clan medallions and often took orders for Native costumes that she designed and sewed herself. She taught her daughter and grandchildren the skills she'd learned.

ROSEMARY HILL

Iroquois-Tuscarora/Beaver Clan; Tuscarora Reservation, New York
Beadworker

EDUCATION: Learned how to do beadwork at the age of seven with her mother, Margaret Elaine Williams, her aunt, Gertrude Rickard Hill Crew, and her grandmother Hattie Bissell Williams. Attended beading classes taught by Marylou Printup and Penny Hudson at the Tuscarora Indian School.

ABOUT THE ARTIST: Hill works in raised beadwork and uses all glass or natural beads in her art pieces. In 1993, following a family tragedy, Hill began beading full-time and created her own style. She designs pieces for ceremonies, gifts, and clothing. She follows the philosophy her mother taught her: "You will never starve as long as you can sew."

Glengarry Bonnet by Rosemary Hill. Beaded in Iroquois raised beadwork style. Black velvet with floral beaded pattern. 4" h × 8" w × 13". $500. Courtesy of Rosemary Hill and copyright by D. Wood.

Portrait of beadwork artist
Rosemary Hill with beaded
pincushion held by the British
Museum in London, England.
Courtesy of Rosemary Hill and
copyright by D. Wood.

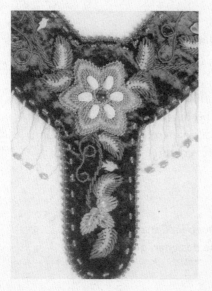

Beaded horse bridle by Rosemary
Hill. Done on commission.
Courtesy of Rosemary Hill and
copyright by D. Wood.

PENNY HUDSON
Tuscarora (1956–) Sanborn, New York
Beadworker, weaver

EDUCATION: Learned from her mother, Doris Hudson.

AWARDS: Hudson has won numerous awards for her beaded work at the New York State Fair and the New York State Iroquois Conference.

ABOUT THE ARTIST: From a very young age, Hudson began to help her mother with beadwork and attended the New York State Fair. She uses geometric designs or clan animals to decorate. She prefers to use blacks, reds, yellows, and browns in her designs, utilizing both regular or cut glass beads; however, she does special orders.

GŌWA 'DJŌWA ALSEA ISAACS
(a.k.a. Gonwaka 'son)
Cayuga (1959–) Ohsweken, Ontario, Canada
Beadworker

EDUCATION: Learned how to bead from her father.

ABOUT THE ARTIST: Alsea's family ran a crafts shop called Iroqcrafts. She learned at a young age to do beadwork and tend the store. She chooses to work with pony beads and large beads that she strings on sinew, making chokers, earrings, yoke necklaces, and danglers. She often uses bone, brass, and glass beads, as well as leather, shell, or beaded rosettes.

CONNIE JACOBS
Mohawk (1936–) Caughnawaga, Quebec, Canada
Beadworker

EDUCATION: Self-taught.

REPRESENTATION: Kanawake Handicrafts Workshop, Quebec, Canada.

ABOUT THE ARTIST: Jacobs began beading on velvet in 1976 and uses only floral designs. She uses her mother's patterns and lets her daughter watch her work so that she'll learn how to continue the tradition.

MARY SCOTT JACOBS
(a.k.a. Kanekenhawi)
Mohawk (1907–) Caughnawaga, Quebec, Canada
Beadworker, leatherworker, costume designer, quilter

EDUCATION: Self-taught.

ABOUT THE ARTIST: Jacobs has exhibited all over Canada and the United States and has sold her work in her own shop, as well as from door-to-door. She beads velvet and satin cushions and change purses, makes leather moccasins and beadwork medallions, designs Native costumes, and sews quilts that have Indian designs. She is active in the community, was elected as one of the first women counselors in 1964, and has been president of the Retarded Children Association.

JACQUELINE "MIDGE" JAMISON

Mohawk (1934–) Irving, New York
Beadworker, dollmaker

EDUCATION: Self-taught.

ABOUT THE ARTIST: Jamison learned how to do beadwork in the 1960s, preferring variety in all she does. She does most of her beadwork in the winter, creating medallions, necklaces, Indian head rings, watchbands, wristbands, and pincushions. She also makes stand-up cornhusk dolls.

FIDELIA JIMERSON

Seneca (1915–)
Beadworker, clothing designer, dollmaker, basketmaker

EDUCATION: Jimerson is mostly self-taught; however, she learned basketry from her grandmother and how to work with cornhusks from her grandmother and Dorothy Jimerson.

ABOUT THE ARTIST: Jimerson, a well-known speaker on Indian traditions, music, and dance, is also a talented craftsperson. She has made and sold baskets, began doing beadwork in the late 1940s, and makes Native clothing, moccasins, and beaded cloth picture frames. She and her husband were very involved with longhouse affairs and have taught the Seneca language and Iroquois culture at high schools and colleges in New York, Pennsylvania, and Massachusetts.

DARLA JOHNSON

Seneca (1945–) Salamanca, New York
Beadworker, featherworker, costume designer, dollmaker, painter

EDUCATION: Self-taught.

ABOUT THE ARTIST: Johnson began doing loom beadwork when she was seven and wanted to learn how to work with leather when she saw her father working. As a child, she did beadwork for the Indian Village in Onoville, then stopped for a while. When she became a member of the Allegany Indian Arts & Crafts Co-op, she began beading again. She has made beaded medallions, chokers, necklaces, earrings, belts, hatbands, headbands, watchbands, and leatherwork clothing. She also creates feathered war bonnets, fancy dance costumes, bone and bead chokers, and cornhusk dolls. In addition, she paints.

EVELYN JONATHAN

Seneca (1934–)
Beadworker, porcupine quill designer

EDUCATION: Jonathan took classes at the Tonawanda Indian Community House.

ABOUT THE ARTIST: Jonathan has exhibited her work quite regularly and has passed on the skills she learned to others. She makes beaded jewelry, often decorated with geometric and floral designs. In addition, she does appliqué beadwork on clothing and is investigating other crafts.

CELESTE (ROONEY) KETTLE

Seneca (1956–)
Beadworker, clothes designer, porcupine quill designer

EDUCATION: Learned from parents and self-taught.

ABOUT THE ARTIST: Rooney began making beadwork pieces in the 10th grade and continued to expand her repertoire after that time. She has mastered the challenge of weaving porcupine quill designs into leather and cloth and also draws and does some finger weaving.

IVY KIBBE

(a.k.a. Wasontiio)

Mohawk (1949–)
Beadworker, leatherworker

EDUCATION: Most of what Kibbe knows was learned from her mother; however, she has also attended classes for beadwork and leather tooling.

ABOUT THE ARTIST: Both of Kibbe's parents, as well as her siblings, have been involved in Iroquois arts. Kibbe uses Indian designs and flowers on her loomwork and leather pieces.

SHIRLEY KILLS-IN-SIGHT

Navajo; Monument Valley, Arizona
Beader

EDUCATION: Self-taught.
AWARDS: Many awards, including first and second place awards at the
Gallup Intertribal Ceremonial.
REPRESENTATION: Twin Rocks Trading Post, Bluff, Utah.
ABOUT THE ARTIST: Kills-in-Sight creates museum-quality beaded pieces,
using small beads that other beaders rarely use. She often weaves 200
beads to a square inch, an incredible feat and very time-consuming. In her
repertoire are beaded baskets, belts, and moccasins and the traditional
clothing that her children wear at Native American dances.

BRENDA LAUGHING

Mohawk (1957–) Hogansburg, New York
Beadworker, leatherworker

EDUCATION: Learned from her parents, Ida and Angus Laughing.
ABOUT THE ARTIST: Laughing's whole family are active in crafts and often
travel together to exhibits, including the New York State Fair. She makes
men's and women's leather outfits, beaded pieces (especially on clothing)
in both raised and flat style, and bone beads, which she works on with her
brother. She is very active in the American Indian Nationalist Movement
and travels all over to promote Indian causes and arts.

JUANITA LAY

Seneca (1905–?) Irving, New York
Beadworker, dollmaker

EDUCATION: Learned from her mother.
ABOUT THE ARTIST: Lay beads clan and other medallions, necklaces, lighter
covers, and rings. Her medallions often feature animals such as the turtle,
hawk, beaver, heron, snipe, bear, deer, and wolf. She also uses some flower
designs. She and her daughters often work together to create items that
they sell at Indian functions.

DOROTHEA LEROY

Seneca (1904–?)
Beadworker, leatherworker, quillworker

ABOUT THE ARTIST: Leroy's specialty is clan medallions, and she creates designs that include bear, heron, turtle, wolf, snipe, deer, beaver, and eel. She started doing beadwork through the Seneca Historical Society and has since designed some of the costumes and beadwork and has learned to make cornhusk dolls. In addition, Leroy can crochet and knit and makes quilts.

MARILYN LEROY

Mohawk (1943–) Irving, New York
Beadworker, leatherworker

EDUCATION: Dot LeRoy, Marilyn's mother-in-law, taught her some of her skills.

AWARDS: Marilyn's awards include second place for a necklace at the 1976 Indian Fall Festival and a third place the following year.

ABOUT THE ARTIST: LeRoy became involved with the Seneca Historical Society in the late 1960s and took some beadwork and leather classes there. Her first attempt at selling her work was from a stand set up outside her house. She creates beaded jewelry, papoose dolls, and leatherwork items such as vests, jackets, and belts. She also teaches, passing on what she's learned to new students.

DAVID R. MARACLE
(a.k.a. Kanatawakhon)

Mohawk (1952–)
Beadworker, leatherworker, artist, basketmaker, potter, quillworker

EDUCATION: Mostly self-taught, though he has learned basketry from women on the reservation.

ABOUT THE ARTIST: A multitalented man, Maracle makes beadwork-decorated items such as belts, medallions, necklaces, cloth bandolier bags, tobacco bags, and moccasins. He also paints and sketches, has worked in clay, creating pipes or pots with old Iroquois-incised designs, has written articles about the Iroquoian people, and has encouraged others to use the traditional Iroquois designs in their crafts. Maracle has also prepared various reference and curriculum materials on Mohawk (Iroquoian, New York and Canada) traditions for the Centre for Research & Teaching of Canadian Native Languages, University of Western Ontario.

ROBIN MARR

Mohawk (1959–) Hagersville, Ontario, Canada
Beadworker, leatherworker, wireworker

EDUCATION: Largely self-taught, though she has taken classes in beadwork, painting, leatherwork, cornhusk crafts, and copper enameling at the Six Nations Arts Council.

ABOUT THE ARTIST: Marr uses her talents to try to reach mentally retarded children by teaching them crafts. She makes a number of beadworked crafts, including jewelry, headbands, and strips. She makes beaded strips. She also makes moccasins, pouches, necklaces, and plant hangers out of leather, and she makes bone chokers and wirework chairs, tables, and rings.

LOUISE MCCOMBER

Mohawk (1919–) Caughnawaga, Quebec, Canada
Beadworker, quilter

EDUCATION: Learned basic beading techniques from her mother and loomwork beading from a kit she had bought for her children.

ABOUT THE ARTIST: McComber began selling her jewelry when one of her children's teachers admired a necklace McComber had given her. McComber's rope necklaces are usually united by a beaded rosette that has a design on it. She sells directly to her customers. During the 1930s McComber met the famous French entertainer Maurice Chevalier, who came through her village on a tour and sang the song "Louise" to her.

SANDRA MCCOMBER

Mohawk (1939–) Caughnawaga, Quebec, Canada
Beadworker, leatherworker, dollmaker, ceramist

EDUCATION: Largely self-taught, but has attended classes for sewing, papier-mâché, macaroni art, beading, drawing, and ceramics.

REPRESENTATION: Thunder's Child, Kahnawake, Quebec, Canada.

ABOUT THE ARTIST: McComber opened a crafts store in 1976 and has continued to work with her own style. She makes beaded leatherwork, beaded jewelry, and Indian dolls; decorates tomahawks and toys that her husband makes; and makes ceramic figures.

BETTY MCLESTER

Oneida (1940–) Oneida, Wisconsin
Beadworker, porcupine quillworker, clothing designer, knitter, crocheter

EDUCATION: Learned from her friends, as well as by attending crafts classes.

ABOUT THE ARTIST: McLester makes beaded jewelry, belts, wristbands, and headbands and designs Native clothing and porcupine quill earrings. She is active in an Iroquois social dance group, often making costumes for the dancers.

THERESA MITTEN

(a.k.a. Guh Gwi Suh)

Seneca (1916–) Caledonia, Ontario, Canada
Beadworker, cornhusk dollmaker, clothing designer

EDUCATION: Though she taught herself how to bead, she learned to work with cornhusks from Isabell Skye.

ABOUT THE ARTIST: Mitten began beading during the late 1960s, remembering how her grandmother did beadwork on velvet. She beads both freehand and on a loom, creating jewelry, belts, key chains, wristbands, watchbands, headbands, armbands, and other items. She also makes Native ribbon clothing, action cornhusk dolls, and bone and bead chokers.

BERNICE NORTON

Navajo; Navajo Reservation, Utah
Beadworker

EDUCATION: Learned how to bead from her parents, Alice and Tom Toney.

REPRESENTATION: Twin Rocks Trading Post, Bluff, Utah.

ABOUT THE ARTIST: Norton learned how to bead before reaching adolescence and has also picked up silversmithing, as well as rug weaving. At 13, she created her first beaded piece—a feather—for a peyota ceremony. She sold her work with her family at the Four Corners National Monument and eventually became recognized in her own right and was commissioned to do beaded baskets. After that time, she continued to achieve success in her art, garnering awards for her beaded baskets and other work. She is a stay-at-home mom and is teaching her children the Native arts she has mastered through the years.

DELORES OLDSHIELD

Seneca (1931–) Steamburg, New York
Beadworker, dollmaker, basketmaker

EDUCATION: Some of Oldshield's skills were learned from her mother and
sister Ella; she also took cornhusk classes, then learned how to make cloth
costumes in classes taught by Dorothy Jimerson and Fie Jimerson, and took
basketry classes from Nettie Watt, Kathryn Jamerson, and Miriam Lee.

ABOUT THE ARTIST: Oldshield, a prolific craftsperson, creates beaded
medallions, necklaces, chokers, rings, earrings, and bracelets, as well as
cornhusk dolls and black ash splint baskets. She spends a lot of her time
promoting Seneca arts and crafts, teaching beadwork classes, and helping
the Allegany Arts & Crafts Co-op.

ALICE PAPINEAU
(a.k.a. De Wa Senta)

Onondaga (1912–) Onondaga Nation, Nedrow, New York
Beadworker, jeweler, basketmaker, leatherworker, dollmaker

EDUCATION: Papineau learned most of the Iroquois traditions by working
with Mrs. Menros, a missionary whom Alice knew in her teenage years.
Papineau joined the American Indian Village group in 1964, traveling
widely with the group, giving talks about herbs, and caring for their traveling museum of Indian relics. After she returned to her home, she ran the
Onondage Trading Post. She played a Huron woman in the movie *The
Last of the Mohicans*. She is Clan Mother of the Onondaga Nation.

JUNE PETERS
(a.k.a. Ga Yah Don Nes)

Seneca (1963–)
Beadworker

EDUCATION: Learned her beadworking skills from her grandmother Ethel
Hill.

ABOUT THE ARTIST: Peters makes beaded jewelry and has exhibited her
work at the New York State Fair.

MYRTLE PETERSON
(a.k.a. Tidiwe: Nosah)

Seneca (1912–) Allegany Reservation, New York
Beadworker, dollmaker, leatherworker

EDUCATION: Though Peterson learned most of her skills from her mother and grandmother, she also took some classes at the Allegany Indian Arts & Crafts Co-op.

ABOUT THE ARTIST: Peterson is well respected for her large variety of beadwork pieces, as well as her cornhusk dolls, baskets, and corn and acorn necklaces. She travels to fairs to sell her work. Concerned with preserving Seneca history, as well as its language, she has instructed and was working to compile a Seneca dictionary in the late 1970s. She is also well known for her storytelling, a skill she learned from her grandmother.

DONNA PHILLIPS

Oneida (1941–) London, Ontario, Canada
Beadworker, Native clothing designer, leatherworker, knitter, crocheter

EDUCATION: Phillips took some beadwork classes.

ABOUT THE ARTIST: Phillips learned about her culture from an Oneida woman in the States and began using old Iroquois design elements and symbols in her own beadwork. She uses beaded eels, wolves, thunderbirds, deer, turtles, and bears in her designs. She has created dance costumes that are beaded and has decorated leather goods with traditional Iroquois designs. Phillips teaches crafts as well as cultural topics.

ESTHER KANE PHILLIPS
(a.k.a. White Dove)

Mohawk (1920–)
Beadworker, weaver, dollmaker

EDUCATION: Learned how to bead from her grandmother and mother.

ABOUT THE ARTIST: Phillips makes beaded necklaces, headpieces, medallions, and rings. She weaves pillows, dresser scarves, and wall hangings and also makes small leather dolls. She had a career in show business before returning to her craftwork and is an active member of a Mohawk dance and song group. Phillips also teaches the Mohawk language and encourages others to carry on Iroquois traditions.

MORGAN PHILLIPS
(a.k.a. Kahentonni)

Mohawk (1962–) Caughnawaga, Quebec, Canada
Beadworker

EDUCATION: Learned how to bead from a friend.

ABOUT THE ARTIST: Phillips began loom beadwork at the age of 10 and uses her own patterns or standard designs she sees in books. She prefers to let her customers choose their own colors.

CONNIE PIERCE

Seneca (1932–)
Beadworker

EDUCATION: Learned how to do beadwork, leather tooling, fabric stenciling, and cross-stitch work at the Thomas Indian School.

ABOUT THE ARTIST: Pierce prefers to make bead jewelry, often using porcupine quills as accents in her designs. She does much of her work on a loom. Her medallion patterns include the wolf, turtle, bear, beaver, and snipe. The buyer decides what colors she should use. Pierce has taught her daughter and her sister how to do beadwork.

DAVID PIERCE

Seneca (1961–) Gowanda, New York
Beadworker, porcupine quill designer, featherworker

EDUCATION: Self-taught.

ABOUT THE ARTIST: Pierce has exhibited his beadwork and god's eye pieces at the Indian Fall Festival. He creates his own Native clothing and uses feathers, porcupine quills, claws, furs, and shells in his beadwork. Though he specializes in loomwork, he takes orders for anything a customer may want. He has experimented with many craft forms, always expanding on his art background. He also dances and sings in the longhouse and is now teaching his brothers and sisters both traditions so that they may keep them alive.

RODNEY PIERCE

Seneca (1961–)
Beadworker

EDUCATION: Self-taught.

ABOUT THE ARTIST: Pierce has made bone beadwork breastplates and chokers and loom beadwork belts and wristbands, and he also works with feathers. A dancer who travels regularly to festivals and fairs, Pierce takes his items with him to show new customers. He has learned about his culture by being a guide at the Seneca Iroquois National Museum and passes on what he has learned to whoever wants the knowledge. His grandmother Nettie Watt was a well-known basketmaker; she taught him to make baskets.

AMIE POODRY

Seneca (1954–) Basom, New York
Beadworker

EDUCATION: Learned how to bead from her mother, Doris Sundown.

ABOUT THE ARTIST: Poodry does both loom and freehand beadwork, creating men's ties, headbands, wrist- and armbands, jewelry, and barrettes. Usually she uses patterns from craft books or her mother's designs, but she sometimes relies on her own inspiration. She also makes Native outfits for children and intends to become more involved with Iroquois crafts as time passes.

NANCY POODRY

Cayuga (1951–)
Beadworker, dollmaker

EDUCATION: Though largely self-taught, Poodry learned how to make cornhusk dolls from Edna Parker and Betsy Carpenter.

AWARDS: Include a first prize award in 1976 at the New York State Fair for a cradleboard and coverings.

ABOUT THE ARTIST: Poodry and her husband began making traditional items in the early 1970s. Ken made cradleboards that Nancy decorated with beaded pieces. They both made cornhusk dolls, which Nancy dressed and beaded, using traditional materials, colors, and designs.

KAREN POWLESS

Seneca; Cattaraugus Indian Reservation, New York
Beadworker, moccasin designer, porcupine quillworker

EDUCATION: Taught herself a lot of techniques, but also learned from her brother and friends. Majored in the arts and received an Associate in Arts degree from Jamestown Community College.

ABOUT THE ARTIST: Powless is known for the variety in the types of beadwork she creates. The items she decorates include hair ties, necklaces, rings, medallions, key chains, lighter covers, belts, headbands, chokers, wrist- and watchbands, and barrettes. Her porcupine quillwork is an added talent, as are the bead chokers and earrings, bone chokers, and hair ties she makes.

KIM PRICE

Pawnee/Otoe/Kaw/Kiowa (1957–) Pawnee, Oklahoma
Beadworker—leather and fabrics

EDUCATION: Two years in college.

REPRESENTATION: The Turquoise Lady, Wichita Falls, Texas; Frye Back-roads, Republic, Kansas.

ABOUT THE ARTIST: Price's beaded work is a combination of contemporary and traditional styles. Though she often works with leather, as her ancestors did, she also creates beadwork-decorated denim jackets, pillows, earrings, vests, and bags. Her work has been sold to customers in the United States and Europe.

ANNETTE PRINTUP

Cayuga/Tuscarora (1958–) Lewiston, New York
Beadworker, wireworker, porcupine quill designer, graphic artist

EDUCATION: Learned by watching her mother, Marlene, and her grandmothers.

AWARDS: Printup has won awards for her beadwork and graphics at the New York State Fair and New York State Iroquois Conference.

ABOUT THE ARTIST: Printup often uses her own designs, though she'll make whatever her customers desire. She creatively blends the colors and designs in her beadwork so that her work is easily recognizable. Her beadwork adorns barrettes, bolo ties, necklaces, collars, picture frames, leather purses, and many other items. Her etchings, engravings, and woodcuts have also been award-winners.

DORIS PRINTUP

Cayuga (1930–) Lewiston, New York
Beadworker, leatherworker, porcupine quill designer, wireworker, clothes designer

EDUCATION: Learned most of her skills from her mother-in-law, Minnie Printup, and Inez Green. Doris also picked up other techniques on her own.

AWARDS: Among her prizes is a first prize from the 1977 New York State Fair for a pair of beaded moccasins.

ABOUT THE ARTIST: Printup began making small decorated moccasin pins when in her 20s and later began making rings. From there, she stepped into other crafts, usually incorporating a floral design into her work. She is a master craftswoman who also teaches her arts to others.

MARLENE PRINTUP

Cayuga (1938–)
Beadworker

EDUCATION: Learned from Harriet Pembleton, her husband's grandmother.

ABOUT THE ARTIST: Printup has made beaded medallions, belt buckles, jewelry, watchbands, picture frames, and cushions, working to decorate both cloth and leather items with her designs. She has exhibited at the New York State Fair, as well as other fairs, festivals, and crafts shows.

MARY LOU PRINTUP

Tuscarora (1939–) Lewiston, New York
Beadworker, clothing designer

EDUCATION: Learned from her mother.

AWARDS: Among her awards are first and second prizes won at the New York State Fair for her beaded cushions.

ABOUT THE ARTIST: Printup is surrounded by family members who are proficient at beadwork, and she follows in their tradition. She does shows and conventions and takes orders for her belt buckles, medallions, jewelry, and beaded cushions. In addition, she makes ribbon shirts and beadwork designs on clothing. She encourages her children to follow in her footsteps.

TOM PRINTUP

Seneca (1940–)
Beadworker, leatherworker, dollmaker, basketmaker

EDUCATION: Tessie Snow taught Printup the art of beadwork, while his grandmother taught him how to make cornhusk dolls.

ABOUT THE ARTIST: Printup experiments in both technique and creative detail with his designs. He does both flat and raised beadwork and creates decorative accents on costumes and leather purses, besides making beadwork jewelry. He likes using the traditional Iroquois or woodland floral designs. Prolific in his work, Printup also makes baskets, has carved masks, and teaches his skills to others.

AUDREY RAY

Seneca (1949–) Jimmersontown, New York
Beadworker, porcupine quill designer, dollmaker

EDUCATION: Self-taught.

ABOUT THE ARTIST: Ray works mostly with beading, though she has learned other crafts. She features clan animals and floral or geometric patterns in the wrist- and watchbands she makes. Her dolls are created from cornhusk, made with braided arms, and sometimes dressed in traditional clothing. She also has made baskets.

ELNORA REUBEN
(a.k.a. Joh Wehl Ah)

Seneca (1937–) Basom, New York
Beadworker, dollmaker

EDUCATION: Learned by watching her stepfather.

ABOUT THE ARTIST: Reuben began actively working with beads in the mid-1960s. She designs her own medallion patterns; one of her specialties is a cameo medallion. She often surrounds storebought cameos with fancy beadwork. She also makes Native clothing and costumes by order. Reuben has taught her children and others her crafts.

MARGARET RICKARD

Tuscarora (1926–)
Beadworker, featherworker, wireworker, dollmaker, clothing designer

EDUCATION: Learned from her mother, Hattie Williams.

ABOUT THE ARTIST: Rickard sells her beaded leather, felt, and velvet items and her feather earrings, wirework items, dolls in Iroquois dress, ribbon shirts, and cloth drawstring purses at Prospect Point, Niagara Falls, the New York State Fair, and many crafts shows in her area. She has taught her children her skills and also takes orders for special items, such as quilts.

WILMA LEE ROBERTS
(a.k.a. Ga Sen Neé Daeh)

Seneca (1919–) Steamburg, New York
Beadworker, dollmaker, basketmaker

EDUCATION: Roberts's mother, Miriam Lee, taught her how to make baskets and beaded pieces; Roberts's sister, Doris Kenyon, taught her additional beadwork skills; and Roberts took cornhusk craft classes at the Allegany Indian Arts & Crafts Co-op.

ABOUT THE ARTIST: Roberts's whole family has been involved in creating Iroquois products. Her efforts in creating beaded jewelry, loom beadwork, cornhusk dolls, and baskets continue that tradition.

CHERYL SCHAPP

Seneca (1954–)
Beadworker, leatherworker, artist

EDUCATION: Learned how to bead and make cornhusk dolls from Clara Redeye and Dorothy Jimerson. Leland John taught Schapp loom beadwork. She received a certificate in art from Salamanca Central High School in 1972.

ABOUT THE ARTIST: Schapp has always experimented with different styles and techniques, no matter what medium she is working with. She beads jewelry, does loom beaded work, creates beaded designs on leather, makes deer tail roaches, and draws and paints. She has been very involved in the Allegany Indian Arts & Crafts Co-op and teaches her skills to her children so that they may carry on the Iroquois tradition.

MAISIE SCHENANDOAH AND FAMILY

(a.k.a. Wah-Lee)

Oneida (Maisie: 1932–) Oneida, New York
Beadworker, clothing designer, featherworker, cornhusk worker, potter, carver, painter, silverworker, stonecarver

EDUCATION: Maisie learned from her mother and, in turn, she has taught her five daughters and one son.

AWARDS: The Indian Arts and Crafts Board in Washington, D.C., holds some of this family's work.

ABOUT THE ARTISTS: The Schenandoah family, led by matriarch Maisie, combine their talents in both the visual and performing arts to present programs in schools, museums, and cultural centers throughout the United States. They also make a number of objects that have been exhibited at powwows and craft shows throughout the United States.

KATHERINE SKYE

Cayuga (1957–) Ohsweken, Ontario, Canada
Beadworker, featherworker, leatherworker

EDUCATION: Self-taught.

ABOUT THE ARTIST: Skye began doing beadwork in the late 1970s, but her specialty is dance costume items. She works with beads, feathers, and leather to decorate the costumes.

RUTH SKYE

Onondaga (1932–) Hagersville, Ontario, Canada
Beadworker, wireworker

EDUCATION: Learned from her mother.

AWARDS: Include a second prize for an Indian head medallion she entered at the Caledonia Fair.

ABOUT THE ARTIST: Skye opened her own shop (Indian Crafts) in her home in 1974. She sold her own, as well as her husband Wilbur's, work. Skye has taught others how to bead and is a member of the Independent Indian Handicrafters, and has also exhibited at fairs and powwows in the Northeast.

VIRGIE SMITH

Oneida (1911–)
Beadworker, quilter, crocheter

EDUCATION: Smith learned beadwork from her father, and her mother-in-law taught her how to quilt.

ABOUT THE ARTIST: Smith learned how to make baskets from her uncle and how to do embroidery as a young girl. Beadwork took over her interests as she grew older. She has made medallions, bolo ties, hair ties, jewelry, belts, and other items, as well as quilts.

VIRGINIA G. SNOW

Seneca (1909–)
Beadworker, moccasin maker, dress designer, silverworker, dollmaker

EDUCATION: Snow learned beadwork from Lenora George, dressmaking from Maud Hurd, and silverwork from Mrs. Barcus.

ABOUT THE ARTIST: Snow has lectured on Iroquois culture and crafts and has taught classes in beadwork, silverwork, cornhusk doll construction, and dress- and moccasin making. She has also judged costumes at the Indian Fall Festival. An active woman, Snow has been particularly generous with her time and teaches anyone interested in Iroquois art and crafts.

NANDELL SPITTAL
(a.k.a. Giyā Nu 'Ndyā, "Invisible Footprints")

Cayuga (1960–) Ohsweken, Ontario, Canada
Beadworker

EDUCATION: Learned from her father, Buck Spittal.

ABOUT THE ARTIST: Spittal's whole family works in crafts. Her own beadwork includes jewelry made out of large beads, hairpipe bone beads, and
   leather. She also makes wolf headdresses and porcupine quill earrings. In
   addition, she sketches animals and horses.

SHAWNEE SPITTAL
(a.k.a. Nyu Din 'Don, "Hanging Lake")

Cayuga (1958–) Ohsweken, Ontario, Canada
Beadworker, soapstone carver, painter

EDUCATION: Learned the basics of his crafts from his father, Buck Spittal.

ABOUT THE ARTIST: Spittal makes bone and beadwork necklaces, soapstone
   pendants, and carvings, but his specialty is breastplates that are made from
   hairpipe bone beads, grass and glass beads, and leather. He has been active
   in Native American affairs and in movies including Native actors.

ELSIE M. STEFFANS
Mohawk (1917–) Sanborn, New York
Beadworker

EDUCATION: Self-taught.

AWARDS: Include a first prize for a turtle medallion at the Optimist Club in
   Lockport, New York.

ABOUT THE ARTIST: Steffans has exhibited at powwows throughout the
   United States, taking her beaded jewelry, clan medallions, bolo ties, headbands, chokers, jackets, and wristbands. She also makes ribbon shirts and
   rattles. Excited about what she makes, Steffans shares information about
   her art with whoever is interested.

DORIS SUNDOWN
(a.k.a. Gie Onh Won Noeh)

Seneca (1925–) Basom, New York
Beadworker, clothing designer

EDUCATION: Learned from Malinda Parker.

AWARDS: Her talent was recognized when the New York State Iroquois

Conference commissioned her to make the bolo ties given to honor famous Iroquois in 1976.

ABOUT THE ARTIST: Sundown makes beaded medallions, bolo ties, hair ties, barrettes, jewelry, belt buckles, and lighter covers. Her designs are original, and though she may start with a pattern in mind, it often changes as the work progresses. She has taught others how to bead.

MOLLIE SUNDOWN

Seneca (1950–) Basom, New York
Beadworker

EDUCATION: Taught by her mother, Doris Sundown.

ABOUT THE ARTIST: Sundown has exhibited her work and taught others how to bead. She does both loom and freehand beading, creating jewelry, key chains, cigarette cases, and other items. She uses both beads and porcupine quills in her designs. Sundown usually gets together with her family to bead and show her work.

MAISA PARKER TAHAMONT
(a.k.a. Ko Noh So Tyooh)

Seneca (1895–)
Beadworker, rug maker, basketmaker

EDUCATION: Learned from some of her friends.

ABOUT THE ARTIST: Tahamont, a versatile craftsperson, created beadwork jewelry, hooked rugs, pillows and wall hangings, baskets, and cornhusk wreaths. She also ran a crafts shop from 1920 to 1940, helped her husband when he headed the WPA Indian Arts and Crafts Project, and continued to support the Iroquois Nation's activities by actively participating in organizations, such as the National Conference on Aging, where, in 1971, she represented the New York State Native Americans.

HAZEL THOMPSON
(a.k.a. Deh Gah Nego Wes)

Seneca (1933–)
Beadworker

EDUCATION: Taught by Rose John and her husband, Philip.

ABOUT THE ARTIST: Thompson started making necklaces and loomwork in the late 1960s and didn't begin going to shows with her work until almost 20 years later. Her medallion designs include clan animals, as well as geometric and floral patterns. She is active in longhouse activities, teaches the Seneca language, and works with her husband, who creates traditional Iroquois items. She also has passed on some of her beading techniques to her son.

NOWETAH TIMMERMAN

Cherokee/Susquehanna (1947–) Strong, Maine
Beadworker

REPRESENTATION: Nowetah's Indian Store, New Portland, Maine.

ABOUT THE ARTIST: Timmerman, who creates beaded earrings, moccasins, jackets, and other clothing in a traditional Cherokee style, started her store in 1969 in Connecticut. When she moved to Maine 13 years later, she began a store/museum, combining her own work with the work of other New England Indians. She's an Indian dancer and craftswoman, who has supported her seven children with her store and crafts. She works to educate others in the history of her craft and people.

LORRAINE TOME

Seneca (1933–) Salamanca, New York
Beadworker

EDUCATION: Self-taught, in addition to some classes taken at the Allegany Indian Arts & Crafts Co-op.

AWARDS: One of Tome's belts and necklaces was presented to Mrs. Krupsack, lieutenant governor of the state of New York in 1977, as well as to Miss Cattaraugus County 1977.

ABOUT THE ARTIST: Tome creates her own patterns, usually geometric and in red, white, blue, or turquoise, for her medallions. She also uses floral designs for loom beadwork. Her mother taught her to make dolls when she was a child (which she sold at a stand in front of her house). Tome has passed her own skills on to two of her children.

EVON TRUJILLO

(a.k.a. Snowflake; Evonne Trujillo; Evon Snowflake Trujillo; Evon Martinez; Evone Rae Trujillo; Evon Sno-Flake Martinez; Evon Sno-Flake Trujillo)

Cochiti/San Ildefonso (January 2, 1959–) New Mexico
Clothing designer; potter—storytellers

EDUCATION: Learned pottery making from her mother, Kathy Trujillo. New Mexico State University (1 year); Bacone Jr. College (1 year).

AWARDS: Second place, SWAIA Fashion Contest (1986).

ABOUT THE ARTIST: Trujillo comes from a long line of potters, including her grandmothers, Rosalie Aguilar and Helen Cordero, her grandfather Jose A. Aquilar, her aunts, Florence A. Naranjo and Annie A. Martinez, her uncles, Alfred Aguilar and Jose V. Aguilar, Sr., and her cousin, Becky Martinez. Evon began making storytellers in the late 1970s, but her major interest is sewing and clothing design. She makes traditional and contemporary fashions decorated with beads, which she enters in the Indian Market.

MADELINE WHITE

Mohawk (1917–) Caughnawaga, Quebec, Canada
Beadworker, carver

EDUCATION: Self-taught. Continues to expand on her knowledge by studying books and traditional Iroquois designs.

ABOUT THE ARTIST: White likes to use dark colored beads when making her medallions, Indian head ties, and clan animal patches. She has also carved cradleboards. White teaches her art at home and promotes Iroquois crafts.

HATTIE WILLIAMS

Tuscarora (1908–)
Beadworker, dollmaker

EDUCATION: Learned from her mother.

AWARDS: Among the awards Williams has received are some from the New York State Fair for her beadwork.

ABOUT THE ARTIST: Williams helped her mother sell her crafts in Niagara Falls before she started beading herself. She mostly creates raised beadwork style items on velvet.

TOM WILLIAMS AND FAMILY

Cayuga
Beadworkers, carvers

EDUCATION: Tom is largely self-taught, though his children have attended craft classes.

ABOUT THE ARTISTS: The Williams family is talented and diverse. Janice, mother of the six children, makes beaded items, both freehand and on a loom. She often creates her own designs or helps friends fill orders. Her daughters, Arlene, Darlene, and Sharon, crate woodwork and the boys,

Duane and Richard, carve soapstone pendants. Tom, the eldest son, is a leathercrafter.

Values

Rosemary Hill. Glengarry bonnet. Velvet with white and beige beadwork in raised beadwork style; floral pattern. 4" × 8" × 13". $500.

Shirley Kills-in-Sight. Beaded basket. Round with "button" top; pastel colors. 5¼" tall × 5¼" wide. $1,250.

————. Beaded basket. Shallow bowl done in pastel colors with starburst design in center. 8". $1,050.

————. Beaded basket. Lidded; pastel colors, mostly blue. 1⅜" tall. $245.

Bernice T. Norton. Creation of Bees and Wasps basket. 8½". $1,350.

————. Beaded basket. Mostly blue; water design. 6½" tall × 7½" wide. $1,250.

————. Beaded basket. Pastels, mostly yellow. 1¾" × 2". $175.

CHAPTER 4

Carving

In different areas of North America, various materials are used by Native Americans use to create the artistic objects covered in this book. Because of the natural materials available to them, pottery is created by tribes in desert-like regions, where clay is plentiful. For the tribes from the Northeast and Northwest regions of North America, the natural materials they work with are usually from the forest. Thus, most of the carvings created by Native tribes come from areas in the Northeast or Northwest. The most recognized of these artists are largely from the Northwest Coast, where the indigenous tribes utilize large trees to produce such items as carvings, totem poles, and canoes.

Native Americans use everything Mother Earth gives them, never taking more than they give back, thus animals provide food, clothing, and shelter; grasses weave clothing, blankets, and baskets; shells are transformed into utensils, tools, and ornamentation; and trees give shade, wood for shelter, ornamental items, tools, and transportation. Naturally, Native Americans not only create utilitarian items out of wood but also add their own artistic elements to those items.

Following are some examples of the types of items the artists in this chapter create.

| Bowls | Bent-corner bowls made by Northwest tribes were used for serving food. Early examples were made from birch bark, but later (19th century) pieces were usually made of yellow or red cedar. Characteristic of these bowls was an undulating rim—high at the ends with dipping sides. Created in all sizes, from individual containers to great feast dishes up to 20 feet long, they are decorated, painted, carved, or embellished with shells. Their sides can be joined in many ways: pegs, lacing, lashing, or fitted with tenons and scarfs. The sides are bent by steaming the wood until it becomes flexible. Once carved with an adze and shaped with a knife to form the high-ended form, the sides are joined to a red |

cedar base. Brass tacks and shells are a popular form of decoration used around the rims of these bowls.

Boxes	Northwest Coast tribes make boxes for storage, for cooking, and as coffins. Some are painted and carved, some are trimmed with shellwork, and others are simply painted. The sides are connected to the box in a rather unique way: sewn with spruce root. Ends of thicker wood boxes are joined with small wooden pegs. Northwest Coast tribes use straight-grained red and yellow cedar, spruce, and yew, as well as other woods. The wood for the boxes is split with a wooden or antler edge, adzed to the specified thickness or thinness, and shaved with a knife to achieve a flat surface. Other tribes, such as the Cherokee, make boxes out of cedar wood, but they are usually small and designed to hold fetishes or other trinkets of significance. Often the boxes are painted with decoration.
Canoes and Paddles	Canoes and paddles made by the Northwest Coast Indians are as decorative as they are useful. The early models are characterized by a low bow, while later ones have an upswept bow. Detail in the geometric painting of these canoes is extremely important and mimics the work done on Northwest Coast Indian masks. The animal's head is painted toward the front (bow) of the canoe, and its hindquarters are depicted at the back (stern). The paddles are decorated, usually in black and red. Eastern Forest Indians made birch-bark canoes by stripping the bark off birch trees that grew in the Great Lakes region.
Headdresses and Masks	Northwest Coast Indians are masters in carving and decorating wooden objects, such as headdresses and masks. Dance headdresses are made of a cylindrical frame. Down the back hangs a long panel of ermine skins, while the front is an incredible plaque of hardwood, painted and decorated (usually with abalone). The frontlet (or plaque) represents a mythical creature, and on Haida and Tlingit headdresses, it is often framed by rows of orange and black feathers with a band of iridescent green and black mallard head skin across the forehead. Other masks made by the Northwest Coast tribes vary in form, shape, and purpose and may be used to celebrate times of change (e.g., birth, death, or marriage). The Skhwaikhwey mask is owned by one person and is passed on to that person's descendants. It is used in the cleaning ritual of the Salish. The Kwakiutl tribe uses a Goomokwey mask (chief of the undersea world), made of wood and cedar bark. The thunderbird, a favored subject of that tribe, is used in a dance that celebrates the power of ancestors who had contact with supernatural beings.
Spoons	Northwest Coast spoons are usually made of alder, maple, or yew, and they resemble ladles. Most are plain, but some are decorated or embellished with carving, painting, or inlay. Northeast-

ern tribes used wooden spoons and bowls made from the burls of trees, burnt and scraped until they were just a thin shell.

Totem Poles	Northwest Coast tribes carve totems in two distinct types: memorial poles to honor past leaders and house poles that are installed within the house itself. House poles display the lineage crests of the homeowners and record family history. Their carvings are more detailed and complex, and the poles are physically broader than memorial posts. Heraldic (or true totem) poles are freestanding storytelling poles that tell of mythical and historical pasts by carving one figure on top of another and painting them brilliantly. The characters most commonly depicted on totem poles are the raven, the eagle, the thunderbird, the grizzly, the frog, the wolf, the beaver, and the whale.

The Artists

BRUCE ALFRED

Kwakwaka'wakw (August 24, 1950–) Alert Bay, British Columbia, Canada
Carver

EDUCATION: Learned some of his art from his cousins, the Hunt brothers, and other artists such as Wayne Alfred, Beau Dick, Richard Hunt, and Doug Cranmer.

REPRESENTATION: Coastal Peoples Fine Arts Gallery, British Columbia, Canada.

ABOUT THE ARTIST: Alfred's specialty is steam-bent wood boxes and chests, though he has been part of several huge projects like the building of a replica of a Haida village (planned by Bill Reid and Doug Cranmer, two renowned carvers of the region) and the erection of a 30-foot totem pole for Fort McNeil, his village. Alfred's boxes and chests are highly sought after by collectors.

PATRICK AMOS

Mowachaht Band/Nuu-chah-nulth Nation (1957–) Nootka Island, British Columbia, Canada
Carver, painter, printmaker

EDUCATION: Apprenticed with Tony Hunt, Sr., at the Art of the Raven Gallery in Victoria, British Columbia, as well as with Tim Paul at the Royal British Columbia Museum carving shed in Victoria.

AWARDS: Solo exhibits include Gallery Indigena, Stratford, Ontario (1991);

Native Heritage Center, Duncan, British Columbia (1992); and many others throughout Canada.

REPRESENTATION: Coghlan Studio & Gallery, Aldergrove, British Columbia, Canada.

ABOUT THE ARTIST: Amos began selling his work through galleries and museum shops as early as 1976. He has assisted in creating totem poles throughout Canada and even as far away as New Zealand (1990 with Tim Paul). He has been commissioned for larger works, such as a mural for the Mount Klitsa Junior Secondary School, in Port Alberni, British Columbia (1995); a 14-foot totem pole for the Alberni District Secondary Scholl, in Port Alberni (1997); an 8-by-20-foot painted mural for the HA-HO Payuk Elementary School on the Tsahahe reserve in Port Alberni; and a 7-foot totem pole for the Gallery Indigena in Stratford, Ontario. In addition to creating his art, Patrick teaches carving and art in British Columbia.

JOHNSON ANTONIO

Navajo (1932–) New Mexico
Carver

REPRESENTATION: Pennfield Gallery of Indian Arts, Albuquerque, New Mexico.

ABOUT THE ARTIST: Antonio carves wooden dolls that are folk art in design and which are now becoming collectors' items. The dolls capture the Navajo spirit through authentic clothing and costumes. His work has been shown at the Wheelwright Museum of the American Indian in a one-man show and at other museums and galleries.

JOMIE APEELIE

(September 11, 1963–) Iqaluit, Baffin Island, Canada
Carver

EDUCATION: Completed eighth grade, then went to work.

ABOUT THE ARTIST: Apeelie comes from a long line of carvers. His father, Sepee Ipeelie, was a carver, as was his great grandfather and his father. Jomie started carving when he was a teenager and now carves Antarctic animals and hunters out of medium-sized stone.

DEMPSEY BOB

Tahltan-Tlingit (1948–) Telegraph Creek, British Columbia, Canada
Carver

EDUCATION: A self-taught artist, Bob uses the ancient art of carving, the old designs, and drawings.

REPRESENTATION: Blue Wolf Arts, Ltd., British Columbia, Canada.

ABOUT THE ARTIST: Dempsey Bob works with wood because he likes the feel of it. He uses alder for masks, bowls, and spoons (because it has no taste); red cedar for canoes, houses, and large totem poles; and birch for rattles. He carves human figure bowls and all other types of wooden objects, using the old designs that were once incorporated into blankets, rattles, drums, and masks. Because his work is so well respected, it is held by major government buildings throughout Canada, such as the Indian and Northern Affairs Collection in Ottawa, the Museum of British Columbia, the Vancouver International Airport, and the Centennial Museum in Ketchikan. He states on his Web site (www.dempseybob.com) that he is currently studying bronze after working with wood for more than 30 years. Bob is considered the artistic spokesman for his people.

GENE BRABANT

Cree (October 16, 1946–) Victoria, British Columbia, Canada
Carver

EDUCATION: Worked with Tony Hunt, Sr., and John Livingston at Arts of the Raven in the 1970s.

REPRESENTATION: Coghlan Studio & Gallery, Aldergrove, British Columbia, Canada.

ABOUT THE ARTIST: Brabant lived close to the Hunt family in Victoria and grew up with Henry Hunt's children. When Tony Hunt, Sr., offered him the opportunity to learn to carve, Brabant took it and went to work with Hunt. Brabant states he's "always been interested in the old style of carving." His work has been included in many gallery shows, including some at the Seattle Art Museum and the Museum of Osaka, Japan. Though he carves in all styles from the Northwest Coast, he prefers Kwaguilth and Bella Coola. He is considered one of the best carvers by his peers, and his work is collected worldwide.

JAY BRABANT

Cree (January 5, 1970–) Victoria, British Columbia, Canada
Carver

EDUCATION: Studied as a preteen under his father, Gene, and the Hunt family.

REPRESENTATION: Coghlan Studio & Gallery, Aldergrove, British Columbia, Canada.

ABOUT THE ARTIST: Though Brabant is most influenced by the simple style of Kwaguilth carvers, he is accomplished in all forms and known for his clean execution of the style. He works at home in Surrey, British Columbia, and at Coghlan Studio & Gallery.

STEPHEN BRUCE

Namgis/Kwakwaka'wakw (1968–) Alert Bay, British Columbia, Canada
Carver

EDUCATION: Learned how to carve in his teens with artists such as Ned Matilpi, Beau Dick, and Wayne Alfred.

AWARDS: Commissions include works designed for the Campbell River Museum, the Namgis First Nation Cemetery, the Canadian National Railroad, and many others.

REPRESENTATION: Coastal Peoples Fine Arts Gallery, British Columbia, Canada.

ABOUT THE ARTIST: Bruce has worked on many commissions for totem poles and has completed solo and group exhibitions all over Canada and in other countries as well (e.g., Holland and Japan). His traditional totem poles are quite large, often standing more than 20 feet tall.

DALE CAMPBELL

Tahltan (1954–) Telegraph Creek, British Columbia, Canada
Carver

EDUCATION: Apprenticed under Dempsey Bob; took courses from Henry Green, Victor Reece, and Rick Adkins in the 1970s. Influenced by Fred Diesing and Glen Wood.

AWARDS: Her eagle design was chosen as the logo for the Museum of Northern British Columbia.

REPRESENTATION: Coastal Peoples Fine Arts Gallery, British Columbia, Canada.

ABOUT THE ARTIST: Campbell's clan affiliation is Wolf on her mother, Peggy's, side and Raven on her father, Harry's, side. She currently lives in Prince Rupert, but she travels to participate in major exhibitions throughout the country, such as the "Indian Woman Art Show" held at the Museum of Northern British Columbia. Dale and her brother Terrence have carved and raised several totem poles, one adjacent to the Museum of Northern British Columbia and another in Kowloon Park, Hong Kong. Campbell also engraves, creates jewelry, and has even designed and constructed a button blanket, but her major talent lies in creating poles, masks, and jewelry.

LYLE R. CAMPBELL

Haida; Haida Gwaii (Queen Charlotte Islands), Canada
Carver, painter

EDUCATION: Two years of Native designing, several years as an understudy with the north coast's premier artists, carvers, and sculptors. Graduate of the Kitanmax School of Northwest Coast Indian Art, Hazelton, British Columbia, Canada.

REPRESENTATION: Coastal Peoples Fine Arts Gallery, British Columbia, Canada.

ABOUT THE ARTIST: Campbell is a member of the Haida Nation of the Sta-Sta-aas Eagle clan of the Songalth tribe of the Kaighani Haida from Kiusta, Langara Island, Haida Gwaii (Queen Charlotte Islands). His family name is It-in-su, which is pronounced "Edenshaw." He works in argillite and wood, is considered a first-class carver, but is also a jewelry designer and sculptor. Currently, he lives in Victoria, British Columbia.

WAYNE CARLICK

(a.k.a. Yon-Deck Kin Taith, "Flying Raven")

Tlingit (October 13, 1958–) Atlin, British Columbia
Carver, pen and ink artist

EDUCATION: Attended college for carpentry. Studied with Dempsey Bob and Ted Harris (pen and ink artist).

REPRESENTATION: Coastal Peoples Fine Arts Gallery, British Columbia, Canada.

ABOUT THE ARTIST: Carlick has worked as a counselor in alcoholism and drug addiction centers as he continues to hone his skills as an artist. He's known for his carving and makes bowls, totem poles, regalia, and wood prints. He has appeared on ABC Television's *Good Morning America* and the BBC and is currently a member of a dance group.

JIM CHARLIE

Coast Salish/Squamish Band (September 10, 1967–) North Vancouver, British Columbia, Canada

EDUCATION: Comes from a long line of artists (Dominique Charlie was his grandfather). Studied under Phil Janze, a well-known Northwest Coast artist.

REPRESENTATION: Coastal Peoples Fine Arts Gallery, British Columbia, Canada.

ABOUT THE ARTIST: A versatile artist, Charlie enjoys creating works that depict legends and myths of the Northwest Coast peoples. His gallery says that "his style is refined, uncomplicated, dimensional with a northern influence."

SIMON CHARLIE

Coast Salish/Malahat Tribe (November 15, 1919–) Cowichan Bay, Canada
Carver

EDUCATION: Self-taught.

AWARDS: Awarded the Order of British Columbia (2001).

REPRESENTATION: Simon Charlie Consulting, British Columbia, Canada.

ABOUT THE ARTIST: Charlie listened to his family tell him of hiring men to carve potlatch figures. The figure would have two open hands, welcoming the friends who were coming to the potlatch. By listening to his uncle's description, Charlie has been able to reproduce the figures. In 1950 Charlie created his first commissioned totem pole for the Department of Highways. In 1974 Charlie made a replica of a decaying house board that was used at the University of British Columbia. In the 30 years that he's been carving, the government of British Columbia estimates he's carved "the equivalent of 22 logging truckloads of cedar logs." His totem poles stand in Canada, the United States, New Zealand, Australia, and Holland, and his masks and other artworks are held in collections throughout the world. He teaches his heritage and culture to his people and others.

DOUG CRANMER

Haida/Namgis; Canada
Carver, painter

EDUCATION: Worked with Bill Reid.

ABOUT THE ARTIST: One of the poles Cranmer worked on was one that Bill Reid resurrected on Anthony Island. Cranmer assisted Reid in recarving and painting the pole, which was finished in 1959. He also worked with Reid on several others that were also part of the collection held by the University of Columbia's Museum of Anthropology. Cranmer was also responsible for carving a memorial pole for his father, Dan Cranmer. Cranmer is considered a world-class artist, and his history has been included in a book about him and his work written by a doctoral student, Eden Robinson.

JOE DAVID

Haida/Nuu-chah-nulth (May 30, 1946–) Opitsaht, Meares Island, British Columbia, Canada
Carver, painter

EDUCATION: Formally trained in commercial and fine arts, and also worked with Bill Holm and Duane Pasco.

REPRESENTATION: Douglas Reynolds Gallery, Vancouver, British Columbia, Canada.

ABOUT THE ARTIST: David recalls certain Northwest Coast legends in his paintings. He has done some totem pole carving, notably a pole carved by Art Thompson (David assisted) for the University of British Columbia's Museum of Anthropology. Considered one of the finest singers of his tribe, David also produces fine masks and headdresses in a style distinctly his own.

REG DAVIDSON

Haida (1954–) Masset, British Columbia, Canada
Carver

EDUCATION: Learned the finer carving skills from his father, Claude Davidson, and his brother, Robert Davidson, his role model.

ABOUT THE ARTIST: Davidson works mostly with wood. One of his totem poles was erected at Tamagawa University in Japan. He is also known for painting drums, creating silk screens, and being a founding member of the Rainbow Creek Dancers.

ROBERT DAVIDSON

(a.k.a. Guud San Glans, Jaa-daa Guulx)
Haida (November 4, 1946–) Hydaburg, Alaska
Carver, artist, printmaker

EDUCATION: The artist's father urged him to begin carving at a young age in order to continue a family tradition. Bringing his work one step further, Davidson visited museums to learn about the carved items his ancestors had made and was guided by Bill Reid and Bill Holm.

AWARDS: In 1993 Davidson became the second Northwest Coast artist to have a one-person exhibit at a major gallery. In 1997 the governor-general of Canada bestowed the Order of Canada upon Davidson.

REPRESENTATION: Douglas Reynolds Gallery, Vancouver, British Columbia, Canada.

ABOUT THE ARTIST: Called a great innovator by his contemporaries, Davidson carves large totem poles, masks, bowls, and other items. He paints the items and often uses alder wood with an abalone inlay. He also carves on silver, making jewelry, spoons, boxes, and other items. Davidson continues to learn about his culture, often lectures on the subject, and passes on his education to the new generation of Haida carvers.

FRED DAVIS

Haida; Masset, British Columbia, Canada
Carver

ABOUT THE ARTIST: Davis creates wooden and argillite carvings that are often mythical in subject matter. He sells his services out of a building on Loop Road in Masset.

BEAU DICK

Kwakwaka'wakw (November 23, 1955–) Kingcome Inlet, British Columbia, Canada
Carver, painter

EDUCATION: Attended school in Vancouver and studied with Doug Cranmer and Henry Hunt. Learned some of the basics from working with his father, Ben Dick, and his grandfather Jimmy Dick.

REPRESENTATION: Douglas Reynolds Gallery, Vancouver, British Columbia, Canada.

ABOUT THE ARTIST: Dick started as an artist working on very large canvases, but he also carves masks in various tribal styles, primarily in the Kwakwaka'wakw style. He comes from a long line of carvers. His father is Ben Dick and his grandfather is Jimmy Dick. Together they created the largest totem pole in the world in Alert Bay. The work Beau Dick creates today is collected by people all over the world. He currently resides in Kingcome village.

JIMMY DICK

Kwakiutl; Kingcome Inlet, Canada
Carver

EDUCATION: Self-educated.

ABOUT THE ARTIST: Dick carves masks, poles, and other pieces of art from wood. He often colors and paints them. His totems are in the Campbell River and Victoria area. The largest totem pole in the world, located in

Alert Bay, British Columbia, and standing at 173 feet tall, was carved under his direction and completed by 1972.

SIMON DICK-TAHNIS

Kwakwaka'wakw (1951–) Alert Bay, British Columbia, Canada
Carver, painter

EDUCATION: Apprenticed for four years with Tony Hunt, Sr., at Art of the Raven workshop in Victoria. Worked with Bill Reid to carve 24-foot cedar canoe.

REPRESENTATION: Coghlan Studio & Gallery, Aldergrove, British Columbia, Canada.

ABOUT THE ARTIST: Simon Dick is immersed in the culture and language of his people and spent quite a bit of his early carving years learning the tricks of the trade under several masters. By 1986 he'd honed his own skills enough to create the 40-foot high by 30-foot wide thunderbird carving that held the amphitheater for the Canadian pavilion at the Worlds Fair Exposition in Vancouver, British Columbia. He pays his ancestors back by passing on his own skills to young apprentices, as well as instructing them in the old traditions.

FREDA DIESING

Haida (1925–) Prince Rupert, Canada
Artist—carver, jeweler, printmaker, button designer

EDUCATION: Studied at the Kitanmax School of Northwest Coast Indian Art in 'Ksan (Hazelton, British Columbia, Canada).

ABOUT THE ARTIST: Diesing often decorates totem poles carved by others (e.g., Freda Diesing and Josiah Tait) in the Northwest Coast tradition. In 1967, when she was already 42 years old, she created her first Northwest Coast style carving. Since then she has also carved decorated masks, bowls, and other items, but she is best known for her portrait masks, which she calls "imaginary persons." Diesing is one of the few women carvers in the Northwest Coast to carve totem poles. She instructs students in the arts at 'Ksan Indian Art School, Hazelton, British Columbia, and in Prince Rupert and Terrace, British Columbia.

PAT DIXON

Haida (1938–) Skidegate, British Columbia, Canada
Carver—stone, wood, other materials; jeweler

REPRESENTATION: Black Tusk Gallery, Whistler, British Columbia, Canada.

ABOUT THE ARTIST: Her carvings imitate the totems common to the Northwest and are done in minute detail.

TOM ENEAS
Salish (October 4, 1970–) Penticton, British Columbia, Canada
Carver, painter

EDUCATION: Studied Northwest Coast form and design in 1991 and began painting in 1993. Worked with Kevin Cranmer later that year.

REPRESENTATION: Douglas Reynolds Gallery, Vancouver, British Columbia, Canada.

ABOUT THE ARTIST: Eneas began working in the mid-1990s and has redesigned and painted the Esquimalt band's longhouse, as well as being part of carving a totem pole in front of the Vancouver Technical School in Vancouver, British Columbia.

STAN GREENE
Coast Salish (1953–) Canada
Carver, watercolorist, silk-screener

EDUCATION: Spent six months in 1975 living in Hazelton and learning carving. His teachers were Walter Harris, Ken Moatt, Earl Muldoe, and Vernon Stevens.

REPRESENTATION: Coghlan Studio & Gallery, Aldergrove, British Columbia, Canada.

ABOUT THE ARTIST: Because the Coast Salish did not have totem poles that displayed crests, Greene's carvings are often simple posts that may have acted as support beams for dance houses in the Northwest. He replicated one such pole in 1986 for the Expo in Vancouver. He is one of the first Salish artists to carve.

RON HAMILTON
(a.k.a. Ki-Ke-In)
Northwest Coast (1948–) Port Alberni, British Columbia, Canada
Carver—slate, wood

EDUCATION: Apprenticed with Henry Hunt.

ABOUT THE ARTIST: He carves some pieces on slate from the Campbell River, stating that it is harder than the pieces the Haida people use in their carvings. He also states that his style of carving and design is more realistic than the tribes further north. He uses the sea serpent in his work on a regular basis. Hamilton lives in the Ahaswinis reserve.

RICHARD HARRIS

Gitxsan; Canada
Carver

EDUCATION: Harris learned some of his carving skills from his father, Walter Harris. This is unusual since most Gitxsan carvers traditionally train their nephews.

ABOUT THE ARTIST: Harris worked with his father on a pole that was commissioned by Sunrise Films of Toronto. The film showed the traditional skills of making a totem pole and the raising of the pole on August 24, 1980.

WALTER HARRIS

Gitxsan; Kispiox, British Columbia, Canada
Carver

EDUCATION: Studied under Duane Pasco.

ABOUT THE ARTIST: Walter is married to blanket maker Sadie Harris. He often provides the designs for the blankets she creates in addition to the carvings he produces. He has carved doors for the Royal Centre in Vancouver and has also done masks, some with abalone inlay and movable parts, and totem poles. He and his son, Richard, were part of a film made by Sunrise Films of Toronto in 1980. The documentary followed the making of a pole for a University of British Columbia outdoor exhibit. Harris also guided the 'Ksan carvers who made the carved folding doors at the Museum of Anthropology's entrance. Harris is the hereditary chief of the Kispiox.

JAMES HART

Haida; Canada
Artist, carver, silk-screener

ABOUT THE ARTIST: Hart has carved totem poles for the Museum of Anthropology of the University of British Columbia. One, which was originally a house pole carved before the turn of the century, was resurrected by Hart and it took him almost a year to complete the carving. It was officially raised in 1982.

BILL HENDERSON

Kwakiutl (March 21, 1950–) Canada
Carver

EDUCATION: Henderson learned some of his skills from his father, Sam Henderson.

ABOUT THE ARTIST: Henderson is known for helping his father to carve some house posts, such as the one at one end of the traditional plank house erected in Campbell River's Foreshore Park (British Columbia). He has carved totem poles and masks by the thousands, and his work is in public and private collections all over the world. He and his brother, Ernie, worked with their father on totems, then went on to carve their own.

ERNIE HENDERSON

Kwakiutl; Canada
Carver

EDUCATION: Ernie learned some of his carving skills from his father, Sam Henderson.

ABOUT THE ARTIST: Henderson and his brother, Bill, assisted their father in carving two house posts and crosspieces for a traditional plank house erected in Campbell River's Foreshore Park (British Columbia).

JOHNATHAN MAXWELL HENDERSON

Campbell River Band (1969–) Alert Bay, British Columbia, Canada
Carver, painter

EDUCATION: Watched his grandfather Sam Henderson carve, then studied Kwaguilth art styles with his father, Dan Henderson, and also his uncles, Mark and Bill Henderson.

REPRESENTATION: Coghlan Studio & Gallery, Aldergrove, British Columbia, Canada.

ABOUT THE ARTIST: Henderson makes masks and model poles in red and yellow cedar, and he also paints and does serigraph prints. In addition to his artwork, he's a Native singer and a chef. He lives with his family in Victoria and carves at the Royal Museum of British Columbia.

MARK HENDERSON

Kwakiutl (1953–) Canada
Carver, artist

EDUCATION: Henderson learned some of his carving skills from his father, Sam Henderson.

REPRESENTATION: Black Tusk Gallery, Whistler, British Columbia, Canada.

ABOUT THE ARTIST: Henderson and his brothers have carried on the carving tradition their father began. In fact, Mark was responsible for repainting one of his father's poles. Mark began painting at the young age of 11 and does his artwork during the winter, since he spends his summers fishing.

SAM HENDERSON

Kwakiutl (1905–82) Canada
Carver, dancer, composer, singer, speaker

EDUCATION: Henderson learned his carving skills from members of his family.

ABOUT THE ARTIST: Considered one of the most renowned of the Northwest Coast carvers, Henderson passed on the traditions he'd learned to other members of his family (sons Ernie and Bill), as well as to many others. He carved totem poles that now stand along the Campbell River.

JERETT HUMPHERVILLE

Cree; Queen Charlotte City, Haida Gwaii, Canada
Carver, painter

EDUCATION: Apprenticed with established carvers since his early teens. Learned some of his skill from his uncle, Ken, and his brother, Jeremy, and inherited some of his talent from his father, grandparents, great-uncle, and great-aunt.

REPRESENTATION: Coastal Peoples Fine Arts Gallery, British Columbia, Canada.

ABOUT THE ARTIST: For the past decade, Humpherville has been creating bentwood items such as canoes, boxes, and sculpture, from red and yellow cedar, alder, and yew wood. He utilizes his years in log home construction to give him the knowledge he needs to select the right wood for each project.

KEN HUMPHERVILLE

Metis, Cree (1948–) Saskatoon, Saskatchewan, Canada
Carver, painter

EDUCATION: Influenced by Dempsey Bob, Heber Reece, and Henry Green.

AWARDS: First prize for artwork in a show judged by First Nation.

REPRESENTATION: Coastal Peoples Fine Arts Gallery, British Columbia, Canada.

ABOUT THE ARTIST: Humpherville's artistic talents are supported by his wife, a Tsimshian woman who has had a Native art shop in Prince Rupert since 1990. Because of her, he studies the Tsimshian culture and art. He uses his carpentry and contracting skills in his work and was finally "discovered" at an art show in Alaska in 1994. Once he gained representation in Portland, Oregon, collectors started seeking out his work. He makes steam-bent chests that are elaborately detailed, as well as bentwood bowls, masks, paddles, and large-scale wall panels.

CALVIN HUNT

Kwakiutl, Nootka (1956–) Alert Bay, British Columbia, Canada
Carver, jeweler, printmaker, painter

EDUCATION: Apprenticed with his uncle, Henry Hunt, his cousin, Tony Hunt, and Douglas Cranmer.

REPRESENTATION: Black Tusk Gallery, Whistler, British Columbia, Canada.

ABOUT THE ARTIST: Hunt is the grandson of renowned carver Mungo Martin. Hunt's work is found all over the world. He was responsible for carving the pole that was erected in Comox reserve in 1989 and dedicated to Andy Frank, the past chief of the Comox reserve.

HENRY HUNT

Kwakiutl (d. 1985) Fort Rupert, British Columbia, Canada
Carver

EDUCATION: Learned some of his skills from his step-grandfather-in-law, Mungo Martin. Hunt passed on his own knowledge to four of his six sons.

AWARDS: His pole in Swartz Bay was awarded first prize in the "Route of the Totems."

ABOUT THE ARTIST: Hunt was the chief carver at the Royal British Columbia Museum in Victoria for 14 years. His poles—all sizes—are parts of collections all over the world. He is considered one of the finest carvers in the world. With Mungo Martin and Dave Martin, Hunt created the tallest totem pole in the world, erected in Victoria, British Columbia, in 1956. Recently, the pole was designated at risk and the city parks department issued a statement that got some activists interested in saving it.

JASON HUNT

Kwaguilth (1973–) Fort Rupert, British Columbia, Canada
Carver, painter

EDUCATION: Business administration at Camosun College; influenced by his father Stan Hunt.

REPRESENTATION: Coghlan Studio & Gallery, Aldergrove, British Columbia, Canada.

ABOUT THE ARTIST: Hunt didn't start carving until he went home for break in 1994 and started watching his dad design and carve traditional Kwaguilth pieces. Once Hunt became interested in learning more about his culture, he began to offer explanations of his work. He utilizes the traditional methods of carving as much as possible, leaving the power tools for pure necessity.

RICHARD HUNT

Kwakiutl (1951–) Fort Rupert, British Columbia, Canada
Carver, jeweler

EDUCATION: Taught by his father, Henry Hunt.

ABOUT THE ARTIST: Hunt comes from a long line of carvers, including his grandfather Mungo Martin and father, Henry Hunt. He carves colorful tall and small totem poles. Hunt acts as head carver at the Provincial Museum, makes ceremonial potlatch masks, and is a dancer of the highest regard.

STAN HUNT

Kwaguilth (September 25, 1954–) Fort Rupert, Vancouver Island, Canada
Carver, painter

EDUCATION: Worked with his father, Henry Hunt.

REPRESENTATION: Coghlan Studio & Gallery, Aldergrove, British Columbia, Canada.

ABOUT THE ARTIST: Born into the talented Hunt family, this artist learned how to carve boats and canoes, then talked to his father about being a carver. When his father told him to learn how to make his own tools, Hunt spent the next couple of years learning the techniques and assisting his father on six totem poles, then went out on his own. He doesn't use any power tools and carves in the Kwaguilth style. He's been part of Coghlan Studio since 1988.

Portrait of carver Stan Hunt with two of his
masks: Raven mask and Rattle. Courtesy of
Tribal Expressions, American Indian Art Gallery,
Arlington Heights, IL.
www.tribalexpressions.com.

STANLEY E. HUNT III

Kwakwaka'wakw (March 24, 1958–) Alert Bay, British Columbia, Canada
Carver, painter

EDUCATION: Learned from his grandfather Charlie Willie.

REPRESENTATION: Coastal Peoples Fine Arts Gallery, Vancouver, British
   Columbia, Canada.

ABOUT THE ARTIST: Hunt carves masks and potlatch objects, having
   learned how to do so from his grandfather. He is now passing those skills
   on to his son, Willis Charles Henry Hunt. Stan's most recent work is to
   produce carvings of the old Hamatsa Raven masks, some of which echo
   the style of Willie Seaweed. Both Hunt's miniature and full-size Hamatsa
   masks are found in collections all over the world.

TONY HUNT

Kwakiutl (1942–) Alert Bay, British Columbia, Canada
Carver

EDUCATION: Learned from parents and apprenticed with his uncle, Mungo Martin, master carver, for 10 years. His father, Henry Hunt, was also a master carver.

REPRESENTATION: Orca Aart Gallery, Chicago; Coghlan Studio & Gallery, Aldergrove, British Columbia, Canada. Hunt also has his own gallery in the Northwest.

ABOUT THE ARTIST: Hunt works in the Northwest Coast style. He carves certain animals, fish, and birds, as well as other symbols. Hunt has passed on the skills he has to others, who have gone on to become accomplished carvers. His work has been featured in exhibits held around the world; he has also carved totem poles for Mexico and for European and South American cities and universities. Hunt has done work for the Royal British Columbia Museum. One of his poles, located in Sidney on Vancouver Island, is on the "Route of the Totems."

TONY HUNT, JR.

Kwaguilth (December 4, 1961–) Victoria, British Columbia, Canada
Carver, painter

EDUCATION: Apprenticed at Arts of the Raven workshop under his father, Tony Hunt.

REPRESENTATION: Coghlan Studio & Gallery, Aldergrove, British Columbia, Canada.

ABOUT THE ARTIST: Hunt is a Kwaguilth dancer, as well as carver, and can trace his family heritage back to his grandfather Henry Hunt and his great-grandfather Mungo Martin. Though his carvings are traditional, he infuses them with his own creativity. His work is collected throughout the world, and he's been part of several major exhibitions.

TREVOR HUNT

Kwaguilth (March 9, 1975–) Fort Rupert, British Columbia, Canada
Carver, painter

EDUCATION: His father, Stan Hunt, and brother, Jason, taught Trevor how to paint and carve.

REPRESENTATION: Coghlan Studio & Gallery, Aldergrove, British Columbia, Canada.

ABOUT THE ARTIST: Hunt began painting and carving at the young age of 10. Recently, his work has been chosen for major businesses, and he's been published after a search for young artists. He and his family live in Fort Rupert, where he continues to study his art.

SIMON JAMES
(a.k.a. Winadzi, "Raider")

Kwakwaka'wakw (February 18, 1969–) Alert Bay, British Columbia, Canada
Carver, painter, sculptor

EDUCATION: Learned how to carve from his father, Simon Dick, as well as other artists such as Wayne Alfred, Beau Dick, Max Chickite, and Patrick Logan.

REPRESENTATION: Coghlan Studio & Gallery, Aldergrove, British Columbia, Canada; Douglas Reynolds Gallery, Vancouver, British Columbia; Howling Wolf Productions.

ABOUT THE ARTIST: James was given his Native name of Winadzi (Raider) by his grandfather Chief James Aul Sewid. The son of Simon Dick, James has been carving, painting, and sculpting since 1995. He is also an accomplished dancer, drummer, singer, and computer animator.

CHAD JOE

Coast Salish (July 23, 1967–) Sechelt, British Columbia, Canada
Carver, engraver

EDUCATION: Studied under Victor Herson, who taught him how to engrave.

REPRESENTATION: Coastal Peoples Fine Arts Gallery, Vancouver, British Columbia, Canada.

ABOUT THE ARTIST: Joe's family crest symbol is sisutl, the double-headed sea serpent. Though he's only been carving for a short time, he strives for perfection and collectors value his work.

JIMMY JOHN

Nootka (ca. 1873–1987) Friendly Cove, British Columbia, Canada
Carver

EDUCATION: Learned how to carve from family members and passed his skills on to his son, Norman John.

ABOUT THE ARTIST: John, a direct descendant of Chief Maquinna, carved for close to 100 years. He was estimated to be around 114 years old when he died. His body of work includes masks, headdresses, totem poles, and feast bowls.

NORMAN JOHN

Nuu-Chah-Nulth; Friendly Cove, British Columbia, Canada
Carver

EDUCATION: Learned most of his carving skills from his father, Jimmy John.

ABOUT THE ARTIST: John assisted his father in carving some of the larger totem poles, such as the one in Nanaimo, on the north end of the Pearson Bridge, one of the poles located on the "Route of the Totems."

JAMES JOHNNY, JR.

Kwakwaka'wakw/Coast Salish Nation (July 5, 1973–) Victoria, British Columbia, Canada
Carver, painter

EDUCATION: Began drawing at age 13 and learned how to carve from father, Jim Johnny.

REPRESENTATION: Coastal Peoples Fine Arts Gallery, Vancouver, British Columbia, Canada.

ABOUT THE ARTIST: Johnny's family crest symbol is the killer whale. He is a young artist who works in red and yellow cedar wood and relies on his carving to make a living. Quite a few private collectors own pieces of Johnny's work, and he's begun to make a name for himself because of his attention to detail.

TRACY JOHNSON

(a.k.a. Ahosta)

Tuscarora (1940–) Lewiston, New York
Carver, beadworker, leatherworker, collage maker—acrylics, deerskin, leather, bone, stone, quills, feathers, horsehair, fur, ermine tails, beads, ironwood, elk, moose horn, caribou

EDUCATION: Johnson learned most of his skills by watching his parents, Norma and Tracy Johnson.

ABOUT THE ARTIST: Johnson draws on his heritage to make various items, such as cradleboards, collages, clan staffs, pipe bowls, knife cases, and bracelets. His family is also active in the arts. He has exhibited his work throughout the Northeast.

Crooked beak mask. Yellow Cedar, Cedar Bark, Cord, and Paint. 10" l × 7½" h × 4" d (including base). Miniature with a movable beak. Courtesy of Black Tusk Gallery, Vancouver, B.C.

AUBREY JOHNSTONE

Kwakwaka'wakw; Alert Bay, British Columbia, Canada
Carver, painter

REPRESENTATION: Black Tusk Gallery, Whistler, British Columbia, Canada.

KLATLE-BHI (PRONOUNCED "CLOTH BAY")
(name translates to "head killer whale of a pod of killer whales")

Kwakwaka'wakw/Coast Salish (March 21, 1966–) Vancouver, British Columbia, Canada
Carver, painter

EDUCATION: Mostly self-taught, with some guidance from Richard Baker, Wade Baker, Rick Harry, and Simon Dick.

REPRESENTATION: Douglas Reynolds Gallery, Vancouver, British Columbia, Canada.

ABOUT THE ARTIST: Klatle-Bhi has been carving for approximately 15 years and incorporates his spiritual beliefs into his work. He is also currently president of the Squamish Nation Sea-going Society and paddles in a 45-foot canoe.

DOUG LAFORTUNE

Coast Salish (August 25, 1953–) Bellingham, Washington
Carver

EDUCATION: Completed college course in fine arts after school in Victoria, British Columbia, then went on to learn from Simon Charlie.

REPRESENTATION: Coastal Peoples Fine Arts Gallery, British Columbia, Canada.

ABOUT THE ARTIST: Though LaFortune learned some of his technique from Simon Charlie, he developed his own style and has been creating totems, masks, feast dishes, small figures, and other carved items for the past three decades. One of his most impressive accomplishments has been to carve a Salish Welcome Figure that was presented to Queen Elizabeth at the Opening Ceremonies of the XV Commonwealth Games held in Victoria, British Columbia. LaFortune's family crest symbol is the owl, and he and his family are members of the Tsawout band and live on tribal territory in Saanichton, British Columbia. His work resides in collections in Japan, Europe, and Canada and throughout the United States.

GREG WHITE LIGHTBOWN

Haida; Masset, British Columbia, Canada
Carver

EDUCATION: Learned from watching other carvers and studying the ancient carvers' works.

REPRESENTATION: Coastal Peoples Fine Arts Gallery, British Columbia, Canada.

ABOUT THE ARTIST: Lightbown often uses argillite in his work and has been known to carve pieces that tell one of the Haida myths or legends.

GERRY MARKS

Haida; Masset, British Columbia, Canada
Carver—wood; jeweler—silver and gold

ABOUT THE ARTIST: Marks finds creating repoussé is one of the "more challenging techniques" (*Indian Artists at Work* by Ulli Steltzer). He makes his own tools and shapes them to his hands or to a particular job. In 1977–78 Marks assisted Reg and Robert Davidson in carving the Charles Edenshaw Memorial Housefront & Houseposts in Masset, British Columbia.

MUNGO MARTIN
(a.k.a. Chief NaKePenkim)

Kwakwaka'wakw (ca. 1881–1962) Fort Rupert, British Columbia, Canada
Carver

EDUCATION: Learned his carving skills from his father, Charles James.

AWARDS: Canada Council Medal, posthumously.

ABOUT THE ARTIST: Martin, one of the premier carvers in the Northwest, taught many other Northwest Coast carvers the art of creating totem poles. He worked with his tools so well that he never cut himself. Considered a master among Northwest Coast carvers, Martin was responsible for passing on what he'd learned to many others, including his stepgrandson-in-law, Henry Hunt. He was personally responsible for helping museums and anthropologists salvage and restore various facets of his culture. As chief, he created new feast dishes and recorded songs and oral histories. He carved totem poles, masks, and a half-scale replica of the house in which he was born. Some of his poles are located in Beacon Hill Park, Victoria, British Columbia; Vancouver, British Columbia; Windsor Great Park, London; and Courtenay, British Columbia.

JAMES H. MICHELS

Metis (1964–) Merritt, British Columbia, Canada
Carver, painter, miniaturist

EDUCATION: Self-educated.

REPRESENTATION: Coastal Peoples Fine Arts Gallery, British Columbia, Canada; Douglas Reynolds Gallery, Vancouver, British Columbia.

ABOUT THE ARTIST: At the age of 16, Michels started studying Native art and was able to learn from other artists while he was on the road as a musician. In 1994 Michels became adept with woodworking tools while employed at a log home company, and soon after, he utilized those techniques in his own carving and painting. He started creating steam-bent cedar boxes, then began producing miniatures and medium boxes, perfecting his craft.

GARY MINAKER RUSS

Eagle Clan (1958–) Masset, Queen Charlotte Islands, Canada
Carver, painter, sculptor

EDUCATION: Learned to carve from his brother Ed and sister-in-law Fay.

REPRESENTATION: Coastal Peoples Fine Arts Gallery, British Columbia, Canada.

ABOUT THE ARTIST: In 1980 Minaker Russ started working on his art and began carving unpolished pieces on a gray-black matte surface. His work shows his cultural heritage and keeps in line with the Haida three-dimensional form. He works in argillite, soapstone, wood, and silver, and his art has been included in international exhibits and collections.

FLORITA MITCHELL

Navajo; Gallup, New Mexico
Carver, sculptor, jeweler

EDUCATION: Learned how to carve fetishes from her aunt.

REPRESENTATION: Native Artists United, Thoreau, New Mexico.

ABOUT THE ARTIST: Mitchell began carving in about 1990. After first creating pottery bowls decorated with fetishes, she turned to making fetish treasure necklaces. Her current artwork is assorted fetishes (e.g., turtle, buffalo, bear, frog, and horse). She uses turquoise, fish rock, serpentine, orange and white alabaster, and black jet.

NORVAL MORRISSEAU

Ojibway (March 14, 1932–) Sand Point Ojibwe Reserve, British Columbia, Canada
Carver, painter

EDUCATION: Self-taught.

AWARDS: Received Order of Canada (1978). Elected to the Royal Canadian Academy of Arts.

REPRESENTATION: Coghlan Studio & Gallery, Aldergrove, British Columbia, Canada.

ABOUT THE ARTIST: Morrisseau is responsible for introducing the Woodland style (also called Legend or Medicine Painting) and is considered one of the most important artists Canada has produced. He paints the myths of the eastern woodlands that were originally passed down orally. Though he was told it was taboo to draw the myths, he did so anyway, developing his own style and incorporating bright color in his art. When he brought them to Toronto, they were accepted with high praise and now hang in galleries, museums, and private collections all over the world.

BRIAN MULDOE

Gitxsan; British Columbia, Canada
Carver

EDUCATION: Often assisted Earl Muldoe and learned some of his carving skills.

ABOUT THE ARTIST: Brian worked with Earl Muldoe to carve a pole that now stands at the entrance to VanDusen Gardens in Vancouver.

EARL MULDOE

Gitxsan; British Columbia, Canada
Carver, painter, printmaker

EDUCATION: Kitanmax School of Northwest Coast Indian Art (1969).

ABOUT THE ARTIST: Muldoe carves such items as the Raven Transformation mask, a mask that, when closed, is shaped and designed like the Northwest Coast raven—when strings are pulled, the mask opens to show a man's face. In Northwest Coast Indian folklore, the raven came to Earth and became reborn as a man. Muldoe has also created totem poles such as the one carved for the entrance to the VanDusen Gardens in Vancouver in 1986. A well-known artist, he works in wood, bone, horn, ivory, and gold and silver metal.

BOB NEEL

Kwakiutl; Canada
Carver

EDUCATION: The son of Ellen Neel, Bob learned some of his trade from his mother, as well as from other members of his family.

ABOUT THE ARTIST: Using the knowledge his mother gave him, Neel carved a pair of house posts for Foreshore Park's traditional plank house, as well as other works of art.

DAVID NEEL

Kwakiutl (1960–) Fort Rupert, British Columbia, Canada
Carver, jeweler, photographer

EDUCATION: Learned some of his skills from his grandmother Ellen Neel and father, David Neel, Sr.

ABOUT THE ARTIST: Neel comes from a long line of artists, including his mother's grandfather, carver Charlie James. He utilizes woods like cedar and alder in his carvings, but is versatile enough to use gold, silver, platinum, abalone, and precious gems in his jewelry. His masks are highly collectible and found in major collections throughout North America.

ELLEN NEEL

Kwakiutl (d. 1966) Fort Rupert, British Columbia, Canada
Carver

EDUCATION: Learned some of her skills from her grandfather Charlie James. Also worked with her uncle, Mungo Martin.

REPRESENTATION: Douglas Reynolds Gallery, Vancouver, British Columbia, Canada.

ABOUT THE ARTIST: Neel was one of the first woman carvers and left her mark on the art world through her own work and that of the men in her family who came after her.

AMOS OWEN

Sioux/Dakotah (August 1916–June 1990) Sisseton, South Dakota
Pipe carver

EDUCATION: Learned from the old Sioux men who carved.

ABOUT THE ARTIST: Owen carved pipes for the sacred pipe ceremony, as well as for collectors. Though he had studied the old ways, he used modern tools such as an electric drill, and sandpaper and beeswax for polishing. He got his stone from the Pipestone Quarries in Pipestone, Minnesota. The site is a place where many tribes have mined their sacred stone, just as their ancestors before them. Each pipe Owen made was blessed before being given to a person for ceremonial use. He was well respected in the Dakotah community for his wisdom and his leadership. A garden dedicated to him is located at Mankato State University in Mankato, Minnesota.

CHESTER PATRICK
(a.k.a. Chaz)

Gitxsan (March 11, 1958–) Hazelton, British Columbia, Canada
Carver, painter

EDUCATION: Certificate in art from 'Ksan art school, Hazelton, and independent study with Vernon Stephens, Earl Muldoe, Art Sterritt, Ken Mowatt, and Walter Harris.

REPRESENTATION: Coastal Peoples Fine Arts Gallery, British Columbia, Canada.

ABOUT THE ARTIST: Since the mid-1970s, Chester has worked on his art, concentrating on his designing and painting skills first, then working on his carving skills. He uses red and yellow cedar wood with little or no paint and pays a great deal of attention to detail and design. His work is highly sought after among Northwest Coast collectors.

TOM PATTERSON

Nuu-chah-nulth (June 13, 1962–) Victoria, British Columbia, Canada
Carver, painter

EDUCATION: Learned how to carve at Arts of the Raven workshop under Tony Hunt, Sr. Has been influenced by Tim Paul, Don Yeomans, and Art Thompson.

REPRESENTATION: Coghlan Studio & Gallery, Aldergrove, British Columbia, Canada.

ABOUT THE ARTIST: Patterson is strong in the Kwaguilth style of carving, even though he's Nuu-chah-nulth, and he studies the styles created by the Bella Coola, Tlingit, and Tsimshian, as well. He has taught carving in his home village of Kyuquot and also at the Idyllwild School of Music and the Arts in California.

TIM PAUL

Nuu-chah-nulth (1950–) Experanza Inlet, Vancouver, Canada
Carver

EDUCATION: Learned carving from Ben Andrews and John Livingston at the Arts of the Raven studio in Victoria, British Columbia, Canada.

REPRESENTATION: Coastal Peoples Fine Arts Gallery, Vancouver, British Columbia, Canada; Black Tusk Gallery, Whistler, British Columbia, Canada.

ABOUT THE ARTIST: In 1977 Paul became the assistant carver to Richard Hunt at the Thunderbird Park at the Royal British Columbia Museum. In 1984 he became senior carver, the only person other than Hunt family members to do so. When he went to work for Vancouver Island, running a Native education program in 1992, he began accepting totem pole commissions. Some of the poles he carved include one installed at the Great

"Eclipse" by Tim Paul. Red Cedar and Paint. 24" h × 15" w × 6" d. Courtesy of Black Tusk Gallery, Vancouver, B.C.

Hall of the Canadian Museum of Civilization in Hull, Quebec, and in Auckland, New Zealand, as a presentation to commemorate the 1990 Commonwealth Games. He has also worked on other projects and commissions throughout the world.

GEORGE PENNIER

Coast Salish (1957–)
Carver, painter, printer

EDUCATION: Trained under Tony Hunt and worked with Beau Dick.

REPRESENTATION: Coastal Peoples Fine Arts Gallery, Vancouver, British Columbia, Canada; Coghlan Studio & Gallery, Aldergrove, British Columbia.

ABOUT THE ARTIST: Pennier is a Sto:Lo artist known for his stylistic and detailed masks, totem poles, frontelets, ceremonial dishes, rattles, drums, original paintings, and limited edition prints.

SUSAN A. POINT

Coast Salish (1952–) Vancouver, British Columbia, Canada
Carver, painter

REPRESENTATION: Rainmaker Gallery, Bristol, United Kingdom; Coastal Peoples Fine Arts Gallery, Vancouver, British Columbia, Canada; Stonington Gallery, Anchorage, Alaska and Seattle, Washington; Canada House Gallery, Banff, Alberta, Canada.

ABOUT THE ARTIST: Point has created a vivid, contemporary design of her own that echoes traditional Coast Salish art. She works in many media, including precious metals, glass, wood, stainless steel, and concrete, and her work can be found in collections all over the world.

GLEN RABENA

Yakima; Yakima Reservation, Washington
Carver, illustrator, engraver, painter

EDUCATION: Studied at the Kitanmax School of Northwest Coast Indian Art at 'Ksan (1975–76).

REPRESENTATION: Black Tusk Gallery, Whistler, British Columbia, Canada; the Legacy Ltd., Seattle, Washington.

ABOUT THE ARTIST: After Rabena completed his studies at the Kitanmax School, he illustrated a book called *The Birds of Ksan* by Susan Marsden, which proved to be the basis for a series of serigraphs of birds he has done. During the late 1980s he worked with Robert and Reg Davidson to complete several commissions and totem poles for PepsiCo's world headquarters in New York. He and Reg were artists-in-residence at Headlands Center for the Arts in San Francisco in 1990, and his project was a 30-foot cedar canoe. Though Rabena is Yakima, he carves in the Gitxsan style. Often he uses birch for his masks. A multitalented artist, Rabena works in silver and gold, carves wood and ivory, and paints on wood and hide.

HEBER REECE

Tsimishian (1955–) Klemtu, British Columbia, Canada
Carver

EDUCATION: Self-taught and some studies at 'Ksan school, Hazelton, British Columbia.

REPRESENTATION: Coghlan Studio & Gallery, Aldergrove, British Columbia, Canada; Pacific Editions Ltd., Victoria, British Columbia.

ABOUT THE ARTIST: Reece's family crest symbol is the killer whale. He comes from a long line of carvers and continues to preserve his heritage through this artwork. In his carving, he uses alder and cedar wood to create rattles, masks, grease bowls, and paddles. He has also aided in the carving of totem poles in British Columbia and Washington.

VICTOR REECE

(a.k.a. Whe'X Hue, "Big Sky")

Tsimshian; Prince Rupert, British Columbia, Canada
Carver

EDUCATION: Self-educated.

REPRESENTATION: Coastal Peoples Fine Arts Gallery, Vancouver, British Columbia, Canada.

ABOUT THE ARTIST: Reece is a member of the Wolf clan and an educator who has been employed by the Vancouver School Board as storyteller and Native liaison educator. He carves masks, bowls, rattles, and sculpture and is sought after by many collectors.

BILL REID

Haida (January 13, 1920–March 12, 1998) Vancouver, British Columbia, Canada
Carver, jeweler

EDUCATION: Formal education was at Victoria College and lasted one year (1937). Largely a self-taught artist, he built on traditional forms with his own innovative style.

REPRESENTATION: Douglas Reynolds Gallery, Vancouver, British Columbia, Canada.

ABOUT THE ARTIST: Even though Reid started out in radio broadcasting, he used that time to study jewelry making at Ryerson Institute of Technology, intending to be a jeweler until he saw the Northwest Coast Native Art collection at the Royal Ontario Museum. That visit sparked an interest to study the art of his mother's people. Reid is one of the best-known carvers in the Northwest, creating everything from abstract jewelry to housefront poles, and 4½-ton wooden sculpture. He has done jewelry, as well as small and large carvings, utilizing the crests known to the Haida people (e.g., the raven, eagle, beaver, bear, and killer whale). His larger carvings often end up at public buildings, such as the Vancouver Public Aquarium and the University of British Columbia. He is often given credit for the revival in Haida culture and has received many honors for his contributions to Northwest Coast art. When he passed away in 1998, he was laid to rest in his mother's village (Tanu) in the Queen Charlotte Islands.

LIONEL SAMUELS

Haida (1963–) Masset, Queen Charlotte Islands, British Columbia, Canada
Carver

EDUCATION: Taught carving by family members.

REPRESENTATION: Coastal Peoples Fine Arts Gallery, Vancouver, British Columbia, Canada.

ABOUT THE ARTIST: Samuel takes the raven as his family crest symbol. He started carving when he was 20 and works in argillite, cedar, silver, and gold. Usually his argillite pieces are carved on both sides and his sculptures have a four-dimensional quality that collectors admire.

RONALD SEBASTIAN

(a.k.a. Gwin Butsxw, from the house of Spookw of the Lax Gibuu clan)

Gitxsan and Wet'suwet'en; Hagwilget, British Columbia, Canada
Carver, painter, jeweler

EDUCATION: Kitanmax School of Northwest Coast Indian Art at 'Ksan Village, Hazelton, British Columbia.

REPRESENTATION: RAS Fine Arts, Hazelton, British Columbia, Canada.

ABOUT THE ARTIST: Sebastian started carving in the 1970s and produces wood carvings that include masks, bowls, bentboxes, rattles, talking sticks, rhythm canes, murals, and totem poles of all sizes. Some of his prints have appeared in art books. In 1977 three murals carved by Sebastian and Earl

Muldoe were installed in the main lobby of Les Terrasses de la Chaudiere, home of the Department of Indian Affairs in Hull, Quebec. Sebastian and his brother Robert have carved cedar panels for public buildings. Some of his carved masks are decorated. For example, a birch porcupine mask he made for the 'Ksan Dancers was decorated with actual quills. He opened his own gallery in 1993 and fills it with his work.

CECIL SEPPILU

ABOUT THE ARTIST: This sculptor gained recognition with his miniature sculpture of Binky, the polar bear at the Alaska Zoo who became famous when a tourist/visitor got too close. The tourist lost his shoe, the bear made national headlines, and Alaskans still laugh over the event. The sculpture of the bear shows him with the bloodied tennis shoe in his mouth.

TERRY STARR

Tsimshian (March 2, 1951–) Prince Rupert, British Columbia, Canada
Carver, painter

EDUCATION: College business course; learned to carve and paint from Tim Paul and Richard Hunt.

REPRESENTATION: Coghlan Studio & Gallery, Aldergrove, British Columbia, Canada.

Carving of Binky (right side) by Cecil Seppilu. Courtesy of Tribal Expressions, American Indian Art Gallery, Arlington Heights, IL. www.tribalexpressions.com.

ABOUT THE ARTIST: Starr's family crest is the eagle (mother's side) and killer whale (father's side). When carving wood, he prefers to use alder. His prints are based on Tsimshian imagery. He uses traditional pigments and lines in his masks but deliberately only paints part of the mask so that the grain of the wood can show through. His art is collected internationally.

ART STERRIT

Gitxsan; British Columbia, Canada
Carver

ABOUT THE ARTIST: Sterrit carves decorated masks for the 'Ksan Dancers (such as a sun mask made of alder) and other wooden items. He made a pole for the VanDusen Gardens in Vancouver, which was raised on June 11, 1976. The pole told the story of the Black Bear crest of the Killer Whale clan. He's responsible for teaching quite a few younger artists.

DONALD SVANVIK

Kwakwaka'wakw (1958–) Alert Bay, Vancouver Island, British Columbia, Canada
Carver, painter

EDUCATION: Learned how to carve from Beau Dick, Sam Johnson, Wayne Alfred, Sandy Johnson, Bruce Alfred, Harold Alfred, Doug Cranmer, and Calvin Hunt.

REPRESENTATION: Coastal Peoples Fine Arts Gallery, Vancouver; British Columbia, Canada.

ABOUT THE ARTIST: Svanvik's father is Finnish-Swedish, but his mother, Alice Whonnock, came from Alert Bay. Svanvik was strongly influenced by his participation in potlatches and carves ceremonial pieces and masks for them. He's also worked on totem poles.

NORMAN TAIT

Nisga'a; Kincolith, Nass River, Canada
Carver, sculptor, jeweler

EDUCATION: Learned some of his carving skills from his father, Josiah Tait. Educated himself about Nisga'a art by traveling to museums and universities across the country.

AWARDS: Exhibited by the Museum of Anthropology in British Columbia in 1977.

REPRESENTATION: Stonington Gallery, Spirit Wrestler Gallery, Vancouver, British Columbia, Canada.

ABOUT THE ARTIST: Tait began seriously carving in the 1970s. He has made totem poles utilizing tools that are the same type his ancestors used. One of his poles, made for the Port Edward community, included all of the community's family crests. His commissions include sculptures, masks, prints, bracelets, and even doors. His work resides in collections all over the world.

JAMES TAYLOR

Kwakwaka'wakw (March 21, 1966–) Vancouver, British Columbia, Canada
Carver, jeweler

EDUCATION: Learned from and apprenticed with many different artists, such as Tony Hunt, Jr., Patrick Amos, Beau Dick, Don Lancaster, and Tony Hunt.

REPRESENTATION: Coastal Peoples Fine Arts Gallery, Vancouver, British Columbia, Canada.

ABOUT THE ARTIST: Taylor is a member of the Nimpkish band, and his family crest symbols are the butterfly and the wolf. He's been carving cedar and silver since the early 1990s and makes miniature as well as full-size pieces. His style is traditional and he carves with an eye on detail and high quality. His jewelry is gold and silver, and he's been designing for more than 15 years.

ROY VICKERS

Tsimshian (June 1946–) Canada
Carver, painter, printmaker, designer

EDUCATION: Studied traditional First Nations art and design at the Kitanmax School of Northwest Coast Indian Art in Hazelton, British Columbia, Canada.

AWARDS: Named first artist included in *Maclean's* magazine's Annual Honour Roll of Extraordinary Canadian Achievers (1994); appointed to the prestigious Order of British Columbia by the Province of British Columbia (1998).

REPRESENTATION: Orca Aart Gallery, Chicago, Illinois; Eagle Aerie Gallery, Vancouver, British Columbia, Canada; Roy Henry Vickers Gallery, Vancouver; Coastal Peoples Fine Arts Gallery, Vancouver.

ABOUT THE ARTIST: Vickers creates crests for family use, often incorporating Northwest Coast animals, such as the killer whale, in his designs. He has acted as artistic adviser in the building of Saanich Commonwealth Place and the refurbishment of Vancouver International Airport. This artist's style is a blend of the traditional and contemporary, and he likes to incorporate his Eagle Moon and various suns on some of the pieces he creates. Vickers has created a number of monumental works in wood and has participated in many events relating to his Tsimshian background. He also founded Vision Quest Recovery Facility, established to help people overcome addictions, and is known as a prestigious speaker.

CONNIE WATTS

Tseshaht and Mamalilikla and Gitxsan Nations; Campbell River,
British Columbia
Carver, painter, printer

EDUCATION: Bachelor of Interior Design, University of Manitoba (1991); B.F.A. in Intermedia, Emily Carr Institute of Art and Design (1996).

AWARDS: Awards and grants for the computer animation "Witness," from the Vancouver Foundation and the Canada Arts Council. Commissions to complete and install the large thunderbird sculpture "Hetux," for the Vancouver International Airport.

REPRESENTATION: Stonington Gallery, Anchorage, Alaska and Seattle, Washington; Quintana Galleries, Portland, Oregon.

ABOUT THE ARTIST: Watts has exhibited in many shows throughout Canada and the United States.

SEAN WHONNOCK

Kwakwaka'wakw (March 16, 1966–) Alert Bay, British Columbia, Canada
Carver, painter

EDUCATION: Took a carving course from George Hunt, Jr., in 1978, apprenticed with Simon Dick, and has been influenced by Beau Dick and Wayne Alfred.

REPRESENTATION: Black Tusk Gallery, Whistler, British Columbia, Canada.

ABOUT THE ARTIST: Whonnock has been carving since 1984, crediting his cousin, Joe Peters, with being his strongest influence. He is always working on developing his style and has carved totem poles, as well as a number of other projects, including ceremonial items that are in collections throughout the world. He is best known for his traditionally carved shaman's rattles. A recent project is a reproduction of a 42-foot canoe his relative Jonathan Whonnock made during the early 1900s (on display at the Thomas Burke Museum in Seattle, Washington).

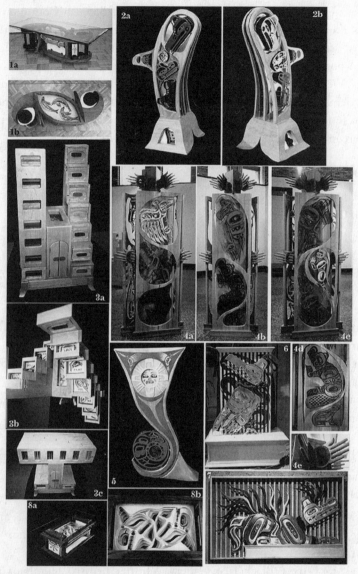

Collection of works by Connie Watts, Courtesy of Connie Watts.   1) "Curiosity"
Edition Size: 1st of 5 (edition of 6), including one artist proof: the artist proof and the
second of the edition have sold to private collectors, one in Vancouver and one in
Seattle. Approx Dim: 30" × 54" × 16" Materials: Mahogany, Aluminium, Alder, &
Baltic Birch. Images: Three seals, a sun, a moon, and two hummingbirds.   2) "Play"
One of a Kind Dimensions: 1'¼" × 1'4" × 3'0" Materials: Powder coated Aluminium &
Mahogany. Images: Outline of the killer whale, a yellow eagle, three seals (one blue
and two red), two green bears, a purple wolf, a blue raven, a silver salmon, and a
moon.   3) "Ha!" One of a Kind Dimensions: 1'6" × 3'0" × 2'8" (5'0" when open)
Materials: Cherry, Baltic birch & Glass. Images: abstractions of the animals used in the

LYLE WILSON

Haisla/Kwakiutl (1955–) Canada
Carver, artist

EDUCATION: Wilson learned about carving from his uncle, Sam Robinson, as well as by his own research in the study of graphic design.

ABOUT THE ARTIST: In his work, Wilson often uses a multishade pencil, which is a new medium for Northwest Coast artists. His work represents the Beaver, Fish, Blackfish, Raven, and Eagle (his own crest) clans.

GEORGE YELTATZIE

Haida; Masset, British Columbia, Canada
Carver—wood, stone; jeweler

ABOUT THE ARTIST: Using the traditional Northwest Coast animal symbols, Yeltatzie often creates pieces that are narrative in nature. He believes that his art reaches people and helps them to understand who he is.

DON YEOMANS

Haida (1957–) Prince Rupert, British Columbia, Canada
Carver, artist, jeweler

EDUCATION: Studied fine arts at Langara College, Vancouver, Canada. Apprenticed under his aunt Freda Diesing. Worked with Robert Davidson on the Charles Edenshaw Memorial Longhouse and completed a jewelry apprentice with Phil Janze.

---

other sculptures in the series.   4) "Remember." One of a Kind. Dimensions: 2'2¾" × 2'7¼" × 6'3". Materials: Red cedar, Tiger wood, Stainless steel, Baltic birch, Mahogany & Powder coated Aluminium. Images: Six blue moons, six red hummingbirds, a yellow thunderbird, a red wolf, a blue killer whale, a red eagle, a blue beaver, a green frog, a green raven, a yellow woman, and a red bear.   5) "Fly." *Fly* is dedicated to the young talented director/writer, Zoe. One of a Kind. Dimensions: 7½" × 2'0" × 3'1½". Materials: Mahogany, Powder coated aluminium & Marble. Images: Two red eagles, a blue moon, two yellow suns, and four blue hummingbirds (two on each side).   6) "Radiant Raven." One of a Kind. Approx. Dim: 30" × 22" × 36". Materials: Aluminium, Maple, and Fabric. Images: A silver Raven.   7) "Whimsical Wolf." One of a Kind. Approx. Dim: 36" × 64" × 8". Materials: Brass, Maple wood. Images: One brass wolf.   8) "Incorporation." *Incorporation* stands for the structure of business. Edition Size: 1st of 10 (edition of 11), including one artist proof: the artist proof sold to private collectors in San Francisco. Approx. Dim: 30" × 56" × 16". Materials: Black walnut, Baltic birch, Glass and Metal tacks. Images: Two killer whales and two suns.

REPRESENTATION: Douglas Reynolds Gallery, Vancouver, British Columbia, Canada.

ABOUT THE ARTIST: Yeomans carves masks, small totems, and other wooden items from his home in Prince Rupert. The head of the Fine Arts Department where Yeomans studied asked him to carve a totem pole for the college's entrance. It was only his second pole, but he had already established himself as an artist. Yeomans crafts exquisite jewelry pieces in gold and silver, paints Haida designs on paper, produces prints, and is one of the finest carvers.

Prices

Bruce Alfred. Bentwood chest, Legend of T'Iisalagi'lakw—Mink, Son of the Sunshine. Chest is carved and painted red, black, and white with this well-known legend. $8,500–$9,000.

Johnson Antonio. Male Navajo figure with dog. 16½" tall, 5⅓" wide, and 4⅓" deep. $775–$850.

Stephen Bruce. Shaman Transformation. Mask of shaman in black, red, and white. $12,000–$12,500.

————. Thunderbird Human Transformation. Thunderbird face mask, protruding beaklike nose, human eyes, decorated with raffia and feathers. Colors of mask: red, yellow, orange, green, black, beige, and white. $5,000–$5,500.

Douglas David. Ling Cod Swallows the Moon. Wood mask of sun face, stylized decoration around the outer edges. Colors are terra-cotta, yellow, blue, and white. $8,000–$8,700.

Johnathan Maxwell Henderson. Killerwhale Transforming into Raven Cradle Rattle. Wooden rattle in a cylindrical design. Simple stylized decoration in red and black. Rattle resembles a spindle, with no extensive carvings. $2,000–$2,600.

Charles McKay. Raven, Frog, Watchman Transformation. Appears to be a whale bone carving depicting the raven, frog, watchman transformation. $600–$750.

Henry McKay. Raven, Frog Transformation. Carving of a spoon on a wooden rest. Decorated with raven and frog transformations. $500–$650.

James H. Michels. Bent Wood Boxes. Hand-carved and painted red cedar. Bear, frog, and eagle designs. 4½" × 4½" × 6½" Each $100–$150.

Gary Minaker Russ. Eagle Spirit Box. Black carved box with white abalone inlay designs. $10,000–$10,500.

Victor Reece. Red Ochre Woman. Ochre-colored mask with simple red decoration across the woman's forehead (no hair) and a protruding lower lip. $3,000–$3,600.

Isabel Rorick and Reg Davidson. Raven Transforming into Human Ceremonial Hat. Carving of a ceremonial hat decorated with stylized ravens encircling it in black and red. $13,000–$13,400.

Ed Russ. Raven Releases the Light. Carved statue of a stylized raven. No painted decorations. $1,000–$1,800.

Peter Smith. Raven Transformation. Mask of raven face surrounded by raffia. The colors are powder blue, black, red, and beige. $7,000–$7,500.

Don Svanvik. Frog Man. Green and red stylized frog face mask, protruding snout. Backboard with some stylized decoration. $14,000–$14,500.

Christian White. Grizzly Bear Song Pipe. Intricately carved pipe with four grizzly bears facing each other and abalone shell inlaid eyes. $16,000–$16,500.

————. Raven and Killer Whale Box. Intricately carved box with carving of raven, boat, and killer whale atop it. $20,000–$22,500.

Sean Whonnock. Chief's Raven Rattle. Wood carving of rattle on top of wooden block. Colors are red, black, and beige. Carving extends right up the arm of the rattle, and head of the rattle is a raven. Handle is turned rope carving. $5,000–$5,500.

CHAPTER 5

Dolls and Kachinas

In the field of Native American collectibles/art, dolls and Kachinas are in the same category. The wooden Kachinas are called "dolls" because they're often given as gifts during the planting season. Though Kachinas are by and large made by Hopis, there are other types of dolls made by other tribes, and those dollmakers are also included in this chapter. Dollmakers from tribes other than the Hopi tribe utilize various materials, and the style is not necessarily particular to the tribe. However, the Kachinas are usually Hopi (though some are made by the Navajo tribe), so that said, we will concentrate on providing information about Hopi Kachinas here.

Kachinas are benevolent Hopi spirits said to exist in the San Francisco Peaks. The Hopi people believe the spirits rehearse in those peaks and prepare themselves for their main function: the making of snow or rain. Kachinas represent the spirit essence of the natural world: plants, animals, food, insects, birds, power, and weather. They are extremely important to Hopi society, thus the San Francisco Peaks are considered sacred.

Kachinas traditionally appear in villages after the winter solstice when the kivas (underground ceremonial chambers that the Hopis believe are entrances to the underworld) are opened. They join with the men there to dance in the kiva and pray for the new year. Until late July, when the path to the kiva is closed, the Kachinas dance in one of the 12 Hopi villages. As August approaches, the villages host Niman (home dance) ceremonies for the Kachinas to return to their homes in the mountains. This dance is the time when Hopi brides, dressed in white cotton robes traditionally woven by their husbands' uncles, are presented to the Kachinas.

The Hopis hold three main ceremonies: the Soyal ceremony in December (opening of Kachina season); the Powamu ceremony in February (to celebrate the false advent of spring and prepare for the new growing season); and the final ceremony, held when the corn is ready for harvest and the Kachinas are sent home to their mountain peaks.

Because of their sacred place in Hopi society, Kachinas are never photographed, thus the Kachina dolls are largely the product of Hopi carvers' memories of the gods.

Gifts of Kachinas are given to young children by their male relatives during the planting season. Because the times when a Hopi child receives presents are few and far between, children learn to give to those who give to them, mainly by returning good thoughts and behavior. Children start getting initiated into the Kachina cult around the age of eight in the Powamu ceremony, which introduces the child to his ancestors, the Kachinas, as his birth introduced him to his father, the sun. Every Hopi over 10 years old is initiated into the cult in order to teach the child the difference between the supernatural and the real and the child's role in the scheme of things. After the ritual, boys join one or more of the secret societies, and girls join those of their ceremonial aunts.

During the season when the Kachinas take part in the dances and festivals held in the Hopi villages, the Hopis are reacquainted with the approximately 500 Kachinas who exist in the religion. More than 300 are currently active, and about 200 make infrequent appearances. The men of the tribe act as the Kachinas, using masks and costumes to resemble the Kachina spirit they represent. When the men are representing their Kachinas, they are said to be invested with the particular Kachina's spirit.

Though Hopi men are traditionally the Kachina carvers, Oraibi women have been known to make Kachinas. Old Kachinas were carved from cottonwood (ba'ko) and painted with natural colors. They were usually decorated with real feathers, and pieces of leather were used as skirts or tops. Fabric was used to make other accessories. Today's Kachinas are extremely beautiful carvings, usually created from one piece of cottonwood. Instead of being completely painted, as the old ones were, they are only partially decorated, and sometimes no other materials adorn the dolls.

Following is a list of some of the more common Kachinas.

Aholi appears in the company of Eototo, but only on the Third Mesa during the Powamu ceremony.

Bear Kachinas have red *nakwakwosi* (prayer feathers) placed on their heads. The bear is a warrior, and all warriors have red feathers.

The **Buffalo Kachina** is always masked and dances for the life and population of the buffalo. He usually holds a lightning stick and rattle.

Chief Kachinas are the most important and have jurisdiction over other Kachinas, as well as over village life. They appear at every ceremony, but dolls are not usually made in their likeness.

Deer Kachinas are very popular in the Plaza Kachina dances. They pray for an increase in the deer population and have power over the rain.

The **Eagle Kachina** or **Kwahu** dances during one of the March night ceremonies or during the Powamu. The dancer imitates the eagle as closely as possible.

Eototo appears every year on each of the three mesas. He is the equivalent of the village chief and the "father" of the Kachinas.

One of the best-known Kachinas is the **Hemis Kachina**. He is said to come from the Jemez Pueblo and dances a stately dance in the final dance of the ceremonies.

Kokopelli is the humpbacked Kachina who plays a flute. His silhouette has graced quite a few decorative elements for houses decorated in the Southwestern style in recent years.

Kokosori is one of the oldest-recorded Kachinas and is always portrayed by a boy.

Mudhead Kachinas are cult clowns whose function is to lighten the atmosphere and tease some of the more serious Kachinas.

The only masked Kachina who is truly a woman is **Pahavuin Mana**. She brings bean sprouts into the village during the Pachavu ceremony.

Talavai Kachinas wake up the people in the village by singing in pairs on the rooftops.

Tawa Kachina or **Sun Kachina** appears with a spruce tree in his left hand and a bell in his right. He is not often impersonated.

Warriors or **Police Kachinas** make sure the public does not interfere with the dancers or venture into the wrong areas.

The angry-looking **Wuyak-kuita** is one of the police or guards who protects the ceremonies. He is often at the rear of the Bean Dance Procession, and his appearance terrifies the clowns.

The Artists

LAWRENCE LEALLEN ACADIZ

Hopi (January 11, 1964–) Tucson, Arizona
Kachina carver, painter

EDUCATION: Institute of American Indian Art, Santa Fe, New Mexico.

AWARDS: First place national honors for painting during stint with Job Corps; awards at annual yearly Indian Market in Santa Fe, Gallup, New Mexico Ceremonial, Heard Museum in Phoenix, Arizona State Museum in Tucson, Northern Arizona Museum in Flagstaff, and many other art show competitions.

REPRESENTATION: Cristof's Art Gallery, Santa Fe, New Mexico.

ABOUT THE ARTIST: Acadiz comes from a long line of artists, including his great-grandmother Ella Sommah, a potter; his great-grandfather Fritz Soomah, a Kachina carver; his grandmother Amelia Martin, a potter; his great-uncles Guy and Alfred Fritz and uncles Lorenzo and Johnny Martin, all well-known Kachina doll carvers.

ROBERT ALBERT
(a.k.a. Sakhomenewa, "tobacco laid out straight to dry")

Hopi (ca. 1964–) Phoenix, Arizona
Kachina carver, painter

EDUCATION: Institute of American Indian Arts in Santa Fe from 1984 to 1986 and graduated with a fine arts degree in two-dimensional art. He then went to a commercial art school, graduating in 1989.

AWARDS: First place, Kachina doll, American Indian Art Festival and Market, Dallas, Texas (1991); second place, Kachina doll, American Indian Art Festival and Market, Dallas (1993); first place, miniature Kachina doll, Museum of Northern Arizona Hopi Show, Flagstaff, Arizona (1993); third place, Kachina doll, Gallup Ceremonial (1994); second place, Kachina doll, Santa Fe Indian Market (1997).

REPRESENTATION: Cristof's Art Gallery, Santa Fe, New Mexico.

ABOUT THE ARTIST: Albert specializes in carving Kachinas and comes from a family of artists. His father, Stephen Albert, Jr., was a carver and artist. Albert started carving full-time in 1990 and now sells to collectors all over the country. He uses both traditional and modern techniques to carve his dolls, such as acrylic paints and a wood sealer so that the wood will be protected. He faithfully re-creates the clothing and other attributes of his Kachinas. Cecil Calnimptewa's approach to carving more realistic Kachinas has inspired Albert to do the same.

CLARA BEGAY
Navajo (1961–) Gallup, New Mexico
Kachina carver, dollmaker, painter

Portrait of Kachina artist Robert Albert with one of his works. Courtesy of Cristof's, Santa Fe, NM

EDUCATION: Self-taught and influenced and inspired by the works of cloth doll artists such as Lisa Lichtenfels, Antonette Cely, and Akiko Anzai.

REPRESENTATION: Native Artists United, Thoreau, New Mexico.

ABOUT THE ARTIST: Begay likes the medium of cloth because she says "it's forgiving." She sculpts Native American dolls out of cloth, paying special attention to their faces. She uses a sewing machine only minimally. Some of her dolls resemble Cabbage Patch children, while others are in the tradition of storytellers.

CECIL CALNIMPTEWA

Hopi (1950–) Moenkopi, Arizona
Carver—Kachinas

EDUCATION: Learned carving from father.

AWARDS: Calnimptewa's awards are numerous, including many won at the Santa Fe Indian Market for his lifelike Kachinas.

REPRESENTATION: Adobe Gallery, Albuquerque, New Mexico; Canyon Country Originals, Tucson, Arizona; Arizona Tribal Collectors, Phoenix; Grey Dog Trading Company, Tucson; Southwest Art Collection, Wheatland, Oklahoma.

ABOUT THE ARTIST: Calnimptewa is well known for his true one-piece carved Kachinas, as well as for his understanding of draping materials and attention to musculature. He has passed on his knowledge to his own students, such as Dennis Tewa, winner in the Kachina carving category of the 1983 Gallup Intertribal Ceremonial. The artist's innovations have given new nuances of artistic rendering to his Kachina carvings. In a recent interview, Calnimptewa says, "I listen to the spirit of the doll as I carve it, and that gives me new ideas. They don't become alive until I carve the eyes, and when I open them, I feel they become a real spirit." He teaches young carvers, including his children, and feels he is serving to introduce artists who will create even more realistic-looking Kachinas.

MANUEL CLEVELAND

Hopi/Navajo (September 4, 1964–) Second Mesa, Arizona
Kachina carver

EDUCATION: Learned from his father.

REPRESENTATION: Cristof's Art Gallery, Santa Fe, New Mexico.

ABOUT THE ARTIST: Cleveland is known as one of the better Hopi Hano clown/koshare carvers. His work was featured on the cover of *Clowns of the Hopi* by Barton Wright. He is married, has four children, and lives in Tsayatoh, New Mexico.

EUGENE DALLAS

Hopi (1958–) Hotevilla, Third Mesa, Arizona
Kachina carver, painter

EDUCATION: Self-taught.

REPRESENTATION: Cristof's Art Gallery, Santa Fe, New Mexico.

ABOUT THE ARTIST: Dallas began carving as an adult and has a style that is unique because he uses deep, rich colors and shading on his Kachinas. He signs his work on the bottom with crossed feathered arrows.

Portrait of Kachina artist Manuel Cleveland with one of his Koshare Kachinas. Courtesy of Cristof's, Santa Fe, NM.

NEIL DAVID, SR.

Hopi (1944–   ) First Mesa, Arizona

Painter, carver—various media

EDUCATION: David is a third-generation artist.

REPRESENTATION: Arizona Tribal Collectors, Phoenix; Tribal Expressions, Arizona; Cristof's Art Gallery, Santa Fe, New Mexico; Native American Traders, Decatur, Georgia; McGee's Indian Art Gallery, Keams Canyon, Arizona.

ABOUT THE ARTIST: David belongs to the Artist Hopid, a group of Hopi artists, and may have been the first to convert the painted Kachina into a three-dimensional being. He is prolific and versatile and brings to his Kachina figures a feeling of reality that makes them truly appear alive.

Clown by Neil David. Courtesy of Cristof's, Santa Fe, NM.

White Buffalo Kachina by Dion Fox, Hopi Carver. One of the few Kachinas with a more human face. Courtesy of Jay Sadow, The Eastern Cowboys, Scottsdale, AZ.

His paintings are geometric and often use both traditional and modern designs. Well known for his koshare carvings, David lives in Polacca, on the First Mesa. He's just as comfortable painting as he is carving Kachinas.

DION FOX

Hopi
Kachina carver, painter

EDUCATION: Self-taught.

REPRESENTATION: Eastern Cowboys, Scottsdale, Arizona.

ABOUT THE ARTIST: Fox tends to carve the more popular Kachinas in the traditional way with good use of colorful paint.

JAMES (JIM) FRED

Hopi (1945–) Bacavi, Third Mesa, Arizona
Carver—Kachinas

REPRESENTATION: Adobe Gallery, Albuquerque, New Mexico.

ABOUT THE ARTIST: Fred creates realistic all-wood Kachinas, even carving the feathers that adorn his creations. He began carving full-time after spending some time working for the Hopi Center for Human Services, teaching the mentally handicapped. He tries to carve the dolls the way they move during the traditional dances, capturing certain motions. He does not attempt to carve unless he's "in the mood to carve a particular type of doll."

MALCOLM FRED

Hopi (1960–) Bacavi, Third Mesa, Arizona
Kachina carver, painter

EDUCATION: Learned quite a bit about carving Kachinas by watching his brothers, Verlan, Henry, and Jim Fred, while he was in high school.

AWARDS: Won an award for Zuni Fire God entered into the 1996 Arizona State Fair.

REPRESENTATION: Arizona Tribal Collectors, Phoenix; Cristof's Art Gallery, Santa Fe, New Mexico.

ABOUT THE ARTIST: Well known for his one-piece carvings and fine detail, Fred attempts to create accurate costumes on his ceremonial Kachinas. His traditions and beliefs infuse all his work and have created a demand among collectors for his work. He is featured in Theda Bassman's *Kachina Dolls and Their Carvers*. He signs his Kachinas with a hallmark that is distinctively his.

JOHN FREDERICKS

Hopi
Carver

ABOUT THE ARTIST: Fredericks carves stylistic, rather than realistic, Kachinas.

THOMAS J. FREDERICKS

Hopi; Kykotsmovi, Third Mesa, Arizona

EDUCATION: Learned some of his craft from his father, master carver John Fredericks.

REPRESENTATION: Arizona Tribal Collectors, Phoenix, Arizona.

ABOUT THE ARTIST: Fredericks finishes his Kachinas with a stain, giving them a different "look." Though he usually carves full-figured dolls, sometimes he follows the flow of the wood and will carve a more stylistic Kachina. He signs his work "Thomas J. Fredericks, Kykotsmovi, AZ."

ARMAND FRITZ

Hopi/Fire Clan (ca. 1949–) Walpi, First Mesa, Arizona
Kachina carver, painter

EDUCATION: Learned from family members, such as father Alfred, another carver.

AWARDS: Several Santa Fe Indian Market awards, including a first in 1999.

REPRESENTATION: Cristof's Art Gallery, Santa Fe, New Mexico.

ABOUT THE ARTIST: Fritz comes from a long line of artists, like his father, carver Alfred Fritz, and his mother, Masayse, a potter. Fritz began carving for an income in 1993, but he only carves two or three pieces a year. He's a Hopi activist, spending much of his time on tribal activities. Because he spends so much time on his activism, he often carves smaller and less detailed Kachinas to generate an income.

ROS GEORGE

Hopi
Carver

REPRESENTATION: Grey Dog Trading Company, Tucson, Arizona; Adobe East Gallery, Delray Beach, Florida.

Portrait of Armand Fritz with Eagle Dancer Kachina.
Courtesy of Cristof's, Santa Fe, NM.

ABOUT THE ARTIST: George carves one-piece Kachinas. His work appeared on the cover of *Arizona Highways* magazine in October 1998. Some of his work is in museum collections, such as the Arizona State Museum.

RICHARD GORMAN

Hopi/Navajo (April 4, 1962–) Keams Canyon, Arizona
Carver—Kachinas; painter

EDUCATION: Became interested in wood-carving when he saw the work of Bavarian wood-carvers. Influenced by Neil David, Sr., Helen Hardin, and Charles Loloma.

AWARDS: Several awards for painting and Kachina carving from Kansas Indian Market, White Mountain Native American Art Festival, and the Gallup Ceremonial.

REPRESENTATION: Cristof's Art Gallery, Santa Fe, New Mexico.

Portrait of Richard Gorman with two of his
Kachinas. Courtesy of Cristof's, Santa Fe,
NM.

ABOUT THE ARTIST: Gorman is considered Hopi, though his mother is
Hopi and his father is Navajo, because both tribes believe the children are
born into the mother's tribe/clan/family. He is not related to R. C. Gorman. He's known for his abstract-style paintings, but he also carves Kachinas and was responsible for Cristof's reintroduction of Kachinas into their
collection.

PHILBERT HONANIE

Hopi/Coyote Clan; Hotevilla, Third Mesa, Arizona
Kachina carver, painter

REPRESENTATION: Cristof's Art Gallery, Santa Fe, New Mexico.

ABOUT THE ARTIST: Honanie has been carving since the mid-1980s, after a
turbulent childhood spent in foster care. At first he sold sculptures at the

Portrait of Kachina artist Philbert Honanie. Courtesy of
Cristof's, Santa Fe, NM.

Hopi Cultural Center, then he started selling in retail stores. In the late
1980s he started learning how to make dolls/Kachinas, and his work soon
appeared in galleries and shows. He treats each Kachina as individually as
the spirit it embodies.

HONOWA

Hopi (January 6, 1963–) Hotevilla, Third Mesa, Arizona
Kachina carver, painter

EDUCATION: Learned from his father, Jerry Honawa.

REPRESENTATION: Cristof's Art Gallery, Santa Fe, New Mexico.

ABOUT THE ARTIST: Honowa has been carving Kachinas full-time since
1992, but he never carves the Chief Kachina, such as Ahole. He and his
family live near Tuba City, Arizona.

BRIAN HONYOUTI

Hopi (1947–) Bacavi, Third Mesa, Arizona
Carver—Kachinas

EDUCATION: Honyouti learned how to carve from his father and often carves Kachinas with his brothers Ronald and Loren.

REPRESENTATION: Arizona Tribal Collectors, Phoenix; Adobe East; Adobe Gallery, Albuquerque, New Mexico.

ABOUT THE ARTIST: Honyouti began carving in 1978 and was the first Kachina artist to use wood preservatives and varnish as a sealer. He carved a Crow Mother emerging from the kiva which is said to be one of the first wood Kachinas that was only partially painted (Howato did the other). He prefers to let the wood grain represent flesh tones and signs his pieces "BH." He lives in Hotevilla, Arizona.

RONALD HONYOUTI

Hopi; Bacavi, Third Mesa, Arizona
Carver—Kachinas

AWARDS: Best of Class, Gallup Intertribal Ceremonial (1983).

REPRESENTATION: Adobe East; Arizona Tribal Collectors, Phoenix; Hozhoni, Naperville, Illinois; Adobe Gallery, Albuquerque, New Mexico.

ABOUT THE ARTIST: Brother of Brian Honyouti, Ronald began carving after Brian. He does realistic Kachinas.

WALTER HOWATO

Hopi; Arizona
Carver—Kachinas

EDUCATION: Self-taught.

REPRESENTATION: Bahti Indian Arts, Salt Lake City, Utah.

ABOUT THE ARTIST: One of the first Kachina carvers to partially paint his figures, Howato entered his Kachina in the Santa Fe Indian Market in the early 1970s. He's been creating Kachinas in the old style since the 1950s and is still selling them.

DUANE DEAN HYEOMA

Hopi (ca. 1969–) Polacca, First Mesa, Arizona
Kachina carver, painter

EDUCATION: Self-taught.

AWARDS: Several awards in judged competitions.

REPRESENTATION: Cristof's Art Gallery, Santa Fe, New Mexico.

ABOUT THE ARTIST: Hyeoma has been carving Kachinas since his teenage years and is known for carving active and detailed figures. He sometimes signs his dolls with his middle name.

ALVIN JAMES, SR.
(a.k.a. Makya)

Hopi (ca. 1930–) Old Oraibi, Third Mesa, Arizona
Carver

EDUCATION: High school, Carson City, Nevada; studied under Peter Shelton.

REPRESENTATION: Sherwood's Spirit of America, Santa Fe, New Mexico.

ABOUT THE ARTIST: James creates lifelike features on his Kachinas and doesn't cover the wood's natural qualities. He is one of the first to produce bronze castings of his work. Makya considered his Kachinas something that "makes my living worthwhile." During the early 1970s, Makya Kachinas were not on the market, but those that had been sold earlier brought four-figure prices.

LAWRENCE JACQUEZ

Navajo (1965–) Nageezi area of Navajo Reservation, New Mexico

EDUCATION: Self-taught.

AWARDS: First place and Best of Division, Santa Fe Indian Market.

REPRESENTATION: Cristof's, Santa Fe, New Mexico.

ABOUT THE ARTIST: Jacquez is a carver, sculptor, and painter who has been rendering sculptures of Navajo sandpainting. He often carves *yeibachai* and *yendalooshi* (skin walker) figures. After his entire family was killed in an automobile accident in the early 1990s, Jacquez began painting. He went from large murals to three-dimensional sandpaintings to wood sculpting. In addition to wood sculpting, he also sculpts in stone and plays the guitar. He often carves pieces in honor of his children, saying that they are with him in spirit and he hopes that they "see and understand my visions."

DARRIN KEWANYAMA

Hopi
Kachina carver

EDUCATION: Self-taught.

Portrait of Lawrence Jacquez working on unfinished carving. Courtesy of Cristof's, Santa Fe, NM.

Portrait of Lawrence Jacquez with Kachina holding Eagle. Courtesy of Cristof's, Santa Fe, NM.

REPRESENTATION: Eastern Cowboys, Scottsdale, Arizona.

ABOUT THE ARTIST: Carves Kachinas in the traditional way for the tourist trade.

VERN MAHKEE
(a.k.a. Kuwanwisiwima)

Hopi/Corn Clan (November 13, 1963–) Oraibi, Third Mesa, Arizona
Kachina carver

EDUCATION: Learned from watching his relatives, for example, his uncle Alvin James (Makya).

AWARDS: Has won awards at Santa Fe Indian Market and Gallup Ceremonial.

REPRESENTATION: Cristof's Art Gallery, Santa Fe, New Mexico; Adobe Gallery, Albuquerque, New Mexico; Hoel's Indian Shop, Sedona, Arizona.

ABOUT THE ARTIST: Mahkee began carving Kachinas for sale in 1979. He's

Owl Kachina by Hopi Carver
Darrin Kewanyama. Courtesy of Jay
Sadow of the Eastern Cowboys,
Scottsdale, AZ.

Kweo (Wolf) Kachina by Vern
Mahkee. Courtesy of Tribal
Expressions, American Indian Art
Gallery, Arlington Heights, IL.
www.tribalexpressions.com.

known for his ultra-fine detail and balance. He signs his name (Vern Mahkee) on the base of his Kachinas.

REGINA NAHA TSOSIE

Hopi (ca. 1948–) Teesto, Arizona
Kachina carver

REPRESENTATION: Cristof's Art Gallery, Santa Fe, New Mexico.

ABOUT THE ARTIST: Tsosie's parentage is Hopi, but she married a Navajo. She is related to Sylvia Naha and Helen Naha, both potters, and to Henry Naha, a Kachina carver. This artist has been carving Hano clowns since 1975. Tsosie's son Gerald is also a carver.

CHRISTINE NAHSONHOYA

Hopi (December 24, 1958–) First Mesa, Arizona
Kachina carver

EDUCATION: Learned her craft from Armand Fritz.

REPRESENTATION: Cristof's Art Gallery, Santa Fe, New Mexico.

ABOUT THE ARTIST: A relatively new carver, Nahsonhoya has been creating Kachinas since 1998. She is also a potter.

WATSON NAMOKI

Hopi (ca. 1970–) Kykotsmovi, Third Mesa, Arizona
Kachina carver, painter

EDUCATION: Learned by watching other carvers, such as his father, Bob Namoki.

REPRESENTATION: Cristof's Art Gallery, Santa Fe, New Mexico.

ABOUT THE ARTIST: Namoki has been carving seriously since 1994. He carves smaller figures and makes sure he is quite accurate in color and design. He creates the full range of Kachinas for a living and lives with his family on the Second Mesa.

ORIEL NAVASIE

Hopi/Spider Clan (ca. 1960–)
Kachina carver, miniaturist, painter

EDUCATION: Learned from family members, including her grandmother Joy Navasie and her sister, Muriel Navasie.

REPRESENTATION: Cristof's Gallery, Santa Fe, New Mexico.

Portrait of Christine Nahsonhoya with one of her
Kachinas. Courtesy of Cristof's, Santa Fe, NM.

ABOUT THE ARTIST: Navasie prefers to carve miniatures and doesn't favor
any particular Kachina.

VAL PAHONA

Hopi
Kachina carver, painter

EDUCATION: Self-taught.
REPRESENTATION: Eastern Cowboys, Scottsdale, Arizona.
ABOUT THE ARTIST: Pahona attempts to put as much detail into his painted
Kachinas as possible. Creates Kachinas in the traditional way.

TED PAVATEA

Hopi (July 5, 1952–) Hano, First Mesa, Arizona
Kachina carver, painter

Eagle Dancer by Hopi Carver Val Pahona. One of the most popular of all the Kachinas made on the Hopi reservation. Courtesy of Jay Sadow of the Eastern Cowboys, Scottsdale, AZ.

EDUCATION: Self-taught and Institute of American Indian Arts in Santa Fe. Influenced by other artists, such as Neil David.

REPRESENTATION: Cristof's Art Gallery, Santa Fe, New Mexico.

ABOUT THE ARTIST: Pavatea started painting and exhibiting at the young age of six. Since that time, he has worked in many different arenas, including illustrating children's books, and became a full-time artist in 1994. He carves both miniatures and larger dolls, and enjoys creating Navajo clowns, as well as koshares.

LOREN PHILLIPS

Hopi (1942–) Moencopi, Arizona
Kachina carver, painter

EDUCATION: Self-taught.

AWARDS: Consistently wins Best of Show Awards at annual Hopi Artists exhibition at the Museum of Northern Arizona.

REPRESENTATION: Adobe Gallery, Albuquerque, New Mexico; Arizona Tribal Collectors, Phoenix; Cristof's Art Gallery, Santa Fe, New Mexico.

ABOUT THE ARTIST: Phillips gets anatomy books from the library and studies the muscles and ligaments so that his carved Kachinas are more lifelike. He is meticulous about his carving, using pocket and hunting knives to create fine details in his work. He is also quite particular about the sanding and finishing of his Kachinas.

ERWIN PINO

Hopi (ca. 1964–) Polacca, First Mesa, Arizona
Kachina carver, painter

EDUCATION: Learned how to carve from an uncle, Meldon Hayah.

REPRESENTATION: Cristof's Art Gallery, Santa Fe, New Mexico.

ABOUT THE ARTIST: Pino lives in New Mexico with his wife, a Laguna Pueblo native. He comes from a long line of Kachina carvers, including his grandparents Billy Hayah and Blanch Dewakakuku. Pino started early, selling his first Kachina at the young age of 11. He attempts to improve his artistry with every piece he carves.

MARLIN PINTO

Zuni-Tewa (1957–) Zuni, New Mexico
Carver—Kachinas

EDUCATION: Self-taught.

REPRESENTATION: Blue Rain Gallery, Taos, New Mexico; Cristof's Art Gallery, Santa Fe, New Mexico.

ABOUT THE ARTIST: Pinto specializes in miniature Zuni, Hopi, and Tewa dolls, since those tribes interchange Kachinas. Every time he carves a Kachina, he purposely makes a mistake to let the spirit out. He uses a pocket knife as his main tool and uses acrylic paint to make his dolls more realistic. His family includes well-known potters like his grandmother Nampeyo.

LESTER QUANIMPTEWA

Hopi (1962–) Third Mesa, Arizona
Kachina carver, painter

EDUCATION: Self-taught.

AWARDS: Best of Show Award at the prestigious Eight Northern Pueblo Show in New Mexico.

REPRESENTATION: Cristof's Art Gallery, Santa Fe, New Mexico.

ABOUT THE ARTIST: Quanimptewa has been carving Kachinas since 1991, but he will not carve the sacred Kachinas. He pays meticulous attention to the Kachina costume and color.

ANDREW L. SAHMIE

Tewa/Hopi (ca. 1960–) Polacca, First Mesa, Arizona
Kachina carver, painter

EDUCATION: Learned from his brothers Finkle and Randall Sahmie.

REPRESENTATION: Cristof's Art Gallery, Santa Fe, New Mexico; Arizona
Tribal Collectors, Phoenix.

ABOUT THE ARTIST: Sahmie has been carving since 1990 and has accomplished a high sense of refinement in his work. He comes from a long line of artists, include his first cousin Dan Namingha, an award-winning artist, and his great-great grandmother Nampeyo, a famous potter. He lives in Keams Canyon, Arizona.

HENRY SHELTON

Hopi; Arizona
Carver—Kachinas

AWARDS: Seniors Division Best of Kachina Dolls, Museum of Northern Arizona Hopi Show (2001).

REPRESENTATION: Old Town Gallery, Flagstaff, Arizona.

ABOUT THE ARTIST: Shelton was first persuaded to carve a raw wood *Ho-ote* about 40 years ago and proceeded to term it "very difficult," but during the mid-1960s he went on to carve two Snake Dancers and an Eagle Dancer, both of which were eventually cast in bronze. His Kachina figures caused other artists to change the way they carved the dolls.

LOWELL TALASHOMA

Hopi (January 23, 1950–) Moenkopi, Arizona
Kachina carver, painter

EDUCATION: Self-taught.

REPRESENTATION: Tribal Expressions, Arlington Heights, Illinois

ABOUT THE ARTIST: Talashoma started carving Kachinas at the age of 10. He tends to work with one piece of cottonwood, creates stocky, large figures, and is adept at carving in muscle tone and specific details.

ELI TAYLOR

Hopi/Corn Clan (ca. 1955–) Third Mesa, Arizona
Kachina carver, painter

EDUCATION: Self-taught.

Kaisale Kachina by Talashoma. Courtesy of Tribal Expressions, American Indian Art Gallery, Arlington Heights, IL. www.tribalexpressions.com.

Koyemsi by Talashoma. Courtesy of Tribal Expressions, American Indian Art Gallery, Arlington Heights, IL. www.tribalexpressions.com.

REPRESENTATION: Cristof's Art Gallery, Santa Fe, New Mexico; Arizona Tribal Expressions.

ABOUT THE ARTIST: Taylor's been carving Kachinas since 1970 but carves fewer than a dozen a year. He likes to create Maiden Kachinas and finishes his dolls with acrylic washes for a muted color finish. Prices of his dolls make them very collectible.

DENNIS TEWA

Hopi; Arizona
Carver

REPRESENTATION: Gallery 10, Inc., Santa Fe, New Mexico; Blue Rain Gallery, Taos, New Mexico; Bashas Art Gallery, Taos, New Mexico, Tucson, Arizona; Adobe East, Summit, New Jersey.

ABOUT THE ARTIST: Tewa believes that the Kachinas he carves may someday no longer exist (according to Hopi prophecy). By carving them, perhaps people will remember them and what they stood for.

STEVE TSANNAJINIE

Hopi
Kachina carver, painter

EDUCATION: Self-taught.

REPRESENTATION: Eastern Cowboys, Scottsdale, Arizona.

ABOUT THE ARTIST: The Tsannajinie/Tsannajinnie family have been
known Kachina carvers for generations.

OLIVER TSINNIE

Hopi/Fire Clan (ca. 1966–) Polacca, First Mesa, Arizona
Kachina carver, painter

EDUCATION: Self-taught. Watched his grandfather and uncles.

AWARDS: Won awards at the annual Santa Fe Indian Market, the Museum
of Northern Arizona Indian Show, and the Gallup Ceremonial.

REPRESENTATION: Cristof's Art Gallery, Santa Fe, New Mexico.

ABOUT THE ARTIST: Tsinnie has been carving since about 1990 and carves
all of his Kachinas both in miniature and very large sizes. He especially

Navajo Cottonwood carving
representing two Hopi Kachinas:
the Pahlik Mana and the Sunface
by Steve Tsannajinie, 2001.
Courtesy of Jay Sadow and the
Eastern Cowboys, Scottsdale, AZ.

likes the deer and ogres, and like the majority of the Hopi Kachina, he hopes to sculpt in stone and bronze.

BESS YANEZ

Hopi (ca. 1965–) Hotevilla, Third Mesa, Arizona
Kachina carver, painter

EDUCATION: Learned carving from her mother. College in California, Arizona, and New Mexico.

REPRESENTATION: Cristof's Art Gallery, Santa Fe, New Mexico.

ABOUT THE ARTIST: Yanez has been creating miniature Kachinas decorated with thread, feathers, and paint since 1983. She spends little time on the Hopi reservation.

RON YAVA

Kachina carver, painter

REPRESENTATION: Eastern Cowboys, Scottsdale, Arizona.

Hopi "Cradle" Dolls by Ron Yava. Kachina images given to children to remember the ceremonies. Courtesy of Jay Sadow and the Eastern Cowboys, Scottsdale, AZ.

Portrait of Elmer Yungotsuna and Kachinas. Courtesy of Cristof's, Santa Fe, NM.

ELMER YUNGOTSUNA

Hopi/Tewa (April 18, 1953–) Hano, First Mesa, Arizona
Kachina carver, painter

EDUCATION: Self-taught.

REPRESENTATION: Cristof's, Santa Fe, New Mexico.

ABOUT THE ARTIST: Yungotsuna has been carving since 1990 and uses mostly hand tools. Has been on the art show circuit only a short time but has won some awards, is going to college to get a teaching degree, and intends to pass his artistic knowledge on to his children.

Sample Prices

Cecil Calnimptewa. "Buffalo Maiden." Carved from cottonwood root. Signed on base. 13½" tall. $4,875–$5,200.

————. "Matsau'u Katsina." Carved from single piece of cottonwood. Signed on base. 18" tall. $7,000–$7,250.

Neal David, Sr. "Getting Ready." Butterfly maiden carved in 1988. An unusual carving for the artist, as he is usually associated with his clown (koshare) carvings. 15" tall. $2,250–$2,400.

————. Koshare trying to stay cool with a fan and water bottle. Koshare or koyala is the name of a Rio Grande clown that is often seen on Hopi mesas. 7" tall. $875–$925.

Armand Fritz. Longhair Katsina, and Longhair Maiden Cottonwood Root. 16.625" tall. $1,000–$1,250.

Brian Honyouti. Navajo Maiden Kachina (Tasap Kachin' Mana) dancing with Tasap Kachina. Carved from one piece of cottonwood with no additions. 10" tall. $2,850–$3,000.

Ronald Honyouti. Maiden. 13" tall. $1,875–$2,000.

Walter Howato. Traditional cottonwood root carving of the Hopi Hilili katsina. $11\frac{3}{4}$" tall. $950–$1,000.

Alvin James, Sr. (Makya). Hopi "Imitator" Kachina (Kwikwilyaka), 1985. 19" tall. $4,500–$4,800.

Vern Mahkee. "Motsin" (disheveled Kachina). 12" tall. $2,500–$2,800.

Loren Phillips. "Ogre Lady." 14" tall from the base to the top of the knife. $6,450–$6,800.

Marlin Pinto. "Hard Luck Soft Ball." $13\frac{1}{2}$" tall. $3,200–$3,500.

Andrew L. Sahmie. "Colorful Clown"/Kaisale. 13" tall. $975–$1,000.

Henry Shelton. Kahaila Kachina and Clown. 14" high. Each $500.

Eli Taylor. Kocha Hanau or White Bear Kachina. $10\frac{1}{4}$" tall. $2,250–$2,500.

Bess Yanez. Miniature White Ogre. $38–$45.

CHAPTER 6

Jewelry

Since Native American jewelers have distinctive characteristics, the best information to offer here is an overview of the general attributes of each tribe's jewelry. Naturally, the individual makers usually find a way to sign their work with a hallmark or an actual signature. If that signature is known, it will be noted in the jeweler's biography; if not, it is best to rely on the dealer or seller from whom you buy your item for some information about the piece's maker.

Hopi

The Hopi people learned how to work with silver after the Navajo and Zuni tribes. Lanyade, the Zuni silversmith who learned his trade from Atsidi Chon in 1872, taught a Hopi named Sikyatala (Yellow Light) the trade in 1890. Early pieces mimicked those made by Navajo and Zuni smiths, but as time went on, the Hopi's distinctive style began to emerge.

The majority of Hopi jewelry as we know it today was produced after the 1930s, when a conscious effort was made to get the tribe to produce more silverwork and to develop an overlay style. Dr. Harold Colton and Mary Russell Colton, his wife, began a project in 1938 at the Museum of Northern Arizona that encouraged Hopi jewelers to create their own style. These artisans used designs that had originated in Hopi basketry, pottery, and textiles.

After World War II, Hopi people who wanted to learn silversmithing were able to take classes on the GI Bill. In 1949 the Hopi Silvercraft Guild was founded. It acted as both a workshop and commercial outlet for the jewelers.

The overlay process simply means that two sheets of silver are soldered together after designs are cut out of the top layer. The bottom layer is oxidized (blackened) and textured with chisel marks or stamp-work. Afterward the pieces are usually buffed to give the silver a soft matte finish.

Hopi work is of high quality, and designs are traditionally abstract. Though Hopi silversmiths generally do not use stones in their work, there are exceptions to the rule, and one should not attempt to identify a piece of jewelry as the work of another tribe on that basis. First, look at the style. Occasionally a Hopi jeweler will choose to include turquoise, red coral, or shells in his or her work.

Iroquois

Though the Navajo and Zuni are the best-known Native American silversmiths, the Iroquois were also known to work with silver. They began working with silver around 1800 and first produced hammered coins and ingots, decorating them with stamped designs.

Brooches made in the shape of hearts were often called the Iroquois National Badge. A design that incorporated the much-used heart with a crown was called "Owl" or "Guardian of the Night." Brooches and dangling earrings were popular and worn by both males and females.

Navajo

It is said that Mexican silversmiths taught Navajos how to make jewelry, yet the Indians did not use the Mexican-style filigree. The stamped designs found on Navajo jewelry are similar to Mexican leatherwork designs, and even the swastika and arrow motifs are attributed to Mexican sources.

Atsidi Sani was the first Navajo silversmith. His teacher was a Mexican blacksmith named Nakai Tsosi who worked near Mount Taylor during the mid-1800s. Tsosi taught Sani ironworking and silversmithing techniques; however, neither made jewelry. The Navajo came up with the idea of making and wearing jewelry after their release from Bosque Redondo in 1868.

Sani taught at least nine other people his trade, including his son, Red Smith. His work training others provided a new way for the Navajo to boost their economy, and the sale of their jewelry soon provided a surplus income, as well as adornments for themselves.

Before 1850 the Navajo people acquired silver ornaments through trade or battles with neighboring Spanish or Mexican settlers. After 1850 the jewelers began using American coins as a source of silver, but after 1890, law stated they could no longer deface U.S. coins. Though they stopped melting U.S. coins, they continued to melt Mexican pesos up until 1930, when the coins were no longer exported to the United States. By 1935 jewelers were buying their silver in sheets and wire forms. Today most jewelers use the same type of silver for their work.

The application of decoration has changed throughout the years. Prior to 1880 decorations were applied by rocker engraving or cutting the design into the metal with a file. Previously, a cold chisel was used, and after 1885 stamping was common. To stamp a design onto metal, a piece of worn-out file made of carbon was heated until it glowed, then was pulled from the fire and shaped with hammering. After the desired shape was formed, the piece was reheated and slowly cooled. The smith could then file final design details. The tool was cleaned and gently heated, and once more quenched. This process gave the piece the hardness needed to keep it from bending, yet kept it soft enough to stop splitting or chipping when struck.

Navajos made silver pieces by pouring molten silver or by hammering down silver ingots directly into carved stone molds. It took time to carve a design into a mold, so the technique was not used often.

To make a good cast, a two-piece mold was necessary, with a spruce hole and air vents. It had to be coated with fine charcoal (or smoked) so that the hot metal would flow evenly into the design and not stick in the deeply carved spaces. The cooled piece was then filed and sanded until smooth.

This technique was used to produce buckles, bracelets, buttons, rings, *najas* (crescent-shaped pendants), and *ketohs* (pronounced "gatos"; bow guards worn around the wrist).

Soldering is one of the hardest jewelry-making tasks to master, even for those jewelers of today who have modern torches and the help of chemical engineers who formulate fluxes. Indians had to make their own solder by combining silver filings with brass filings from old pans or cartridge cases. The mixture was placed at the soldering point, along with borax (used as a sedimentary flux). The pieces were put into the red-hot coals of a forge just below the material's melting point. If the silversmith was lucky, the solder would melt and the pieces would hold together when cooled. Sometimes pieces weren't heated sufficiently and had to go back to the forge. If the pieces became oxidized, the process was begun over again.

Jewelry became so important to the Navajo that no Navajo felt properly dressed without it. It became a sign of wealth. Navajo often exchanged jewelry for livestock, food, fabric, or medical services.

By the early 20th century, the Navajo made lighter pieces for sale to tourists traveling to the Southwest. The era of tourist trade had begun.

Northwest Coast

Northwest Coast tribes wore metal jewelry made of copper or silver long before the arrival of the white man, and although they used stone hammers and anvils, the results they achieved were far from crude. Tlingit shamans wore silver bracelets incised with straight lines, geometric shapes, and stylized animals that are instantly recognizable as Northwest Coast decoration. In the early 19th century, silver and gold replaced copper as the metal of choice because they were easier to work with and obtain.

Tlingit history states that their first blacksmith was a Chilkat woman named Shukasaka. Her skill working metal had won her that name, which means "half man."

Tlingit used silver coins, brought to them by traders, to make nose and finger rings. Silver coins, the traders' money, had no value in their society, nor did any object without a practical use. They chose to present such things to each other as gifts, and in the language of the Tlingit, Haida, and Kwakiutl, the word "silver" is a variation on the English word "dollar."

The Haida tribe was most proficient with silver, producing silver articles such as rings, earrings, bracelets, spoons, and napkin rings. Of all the jewelry, Haida bracelets continue to be most popular. They are heavy and deeply carved, whereas Tlingit bracelets are bands of even width and are lighter in weight.

Northwestern tribes commonly wear nose rings and other jewelry as symbols of status.

Before the 20th century, white influences or motifs were used as frequently as Native designs. For example, the American eagle was an oft-used motif. Haida eagles are generally more geometric than the realistic forms of Tlingit eagles.

Tlingit whale designs are distinctive and best recognized by the segmented, fingerlike flipper that reveals the skeletal structure beneath its skin.

Plains

The common adornments of the Plains Indians (e.g., concha belt, *naja*, and metal bridle) were eventually adopted by Southwestern tribes. The

Plains tribes wore their own metal decorative pieces by the end of the 19th century, using silver and brass until German silver was introduced in the 1860s. They worked with metal until the 1880s, when such ornaments were readily available and the need to produce them diminished.

Conchas were originally hair ornaments that were attached closely to the scalp, but the decoration grew until the hairplate reached as long as 6 feet. When a man sat down, the hairplate was often pulled around his shoulders and across his lap, resembling a belt. Plains women often wore these ornaments as belts and let the extra length trail down one side.

The Navajo adopted the use of concha belts from the Plains but changed the material from German silver to silver and applied Mexican-style decoration to the discs.

Naja decoration was constantly used by the Plains Indian on ear pendants, headstalls, and other items. When the Navajo made bridles, the construction was almost identical to that used by the Plains Indians.

Seminole and Choctaw

Seminole and Choctaw silver jewelry is simple and consists mainly of brooches and pendants. The Seminole were also known to use watch chains as jewelry (though they seldom used watches), but these chains were of European and not Indian manufacture.

Seminoles have produced coin necklaces since before the Second Seminole War. Necklaces had anywhere from one to nine coins on them, and most of the coins (usually Liberty quarters and Mercury dimes) were placed in the front of the necklace, but in the early 1900s, the coins encircled the whole necklace from front to back. Sometimes women wore more than one of these necklaces at a time.

The Seminoles wore pierced silverwork earrings and pendants during the 1920s and 1930s.

Zuni

This tribe learned to work with copper and brass in about 1830, though excavations by archaeologist F. W. Hodge proved that the Zuni peoples had been using pieces of turquoise in their jewelry long before this time.

The Navajo silversmith Atsidi Sani traded with the Zuni in the 1870s and eventually taught his trade to a Zuni man called Lanyade. As a result, Zuni forms and settings are very similar to those made by Navajo jewelers.

Frank Hamilton Cushing, an explorer and historian who lived with the Zunis from 1879 to 1881, reported that the Zuni drew plates made from deep scapulae to form silver and copper wire from silver and copper rods. The thinning, bending, stamping, and drawing of wire was done when the metal was cold, as heating made the metal weak and crumbly.

The Zuni smith Keneshde was the first to use turquoise from the Cerrillos mines during the 1890s. It is believed that Zunis made their jewelry strictly for personal use up until the 1930s, when they began creating pieces for sale to tourists.

The Zuni have been carving stone and shells for hundreds of years and making jewelry from shell, jet, turquoise inlay, mosaic on shell, wood, stone, bone, and ceramics almost as long. Silver is merely a vehicle to hold turquoise, with very little ornamentation. They make light pieces, often by using twisted wire, raindrops, wire scallops, or stamping. Zuni earrings are often long and dangly with pieces of stone or silver hanging from the wire.

Zunis excel in mosaic work and incorporate jet, turquoise, coral, and shell in their designs. They are known to carve small figures in their jewelry. Needlepoint, a practice that began in the 1940s, made with tiny, oval, pointed-end stones, is a specialty of the Zuni jewelry makers.

The Zuni jewelry decorations are lighter and finer than those of the Navajo, whose jewelry has a massive look and feel to it. The Zuni tribe also is well known for fetishes, often carving necklaces that consist of fetish animals and birds.

The Artists

VICTORIA ADAMS
(a.k.a. He On E Va, "Woman Who Lights the Pipe")

Southern Cheyenne/Arapaho (1950–) Oakland, California
Jeweler

EDUCATION: Apprenticeship with William Burke, Golden Balance Fine Jewelry, Mill Valley, California; Revere Academy of Goldsmithing, San Francisco, California; independent study in London, England; University of Nevada at Reno; San Francisco Art Institute, California.

AWARDS: Best of Division, jewelry, lapidary, and Best of Classification, large necklaces, Heard Museum Indian Market, Phoenix (1999); Best of Division, nontraditional jewelry, and first place, large necklaces, Santa Fe Indian Market (2000); Best of Division, nontraditional jewelry, and first place, large necklaces, Santa Fe Indian Market (2001).

Pendant by Victoria Adams.
Courtesy of Tribal Expressions,
Arlington Heights, IL.

REPRESENTATION: Tribal Expressions, Arlington Heights, Illinois; Eagle
  Plume Gallery, Allenspark, Colorado; Morning Star Gallery, Santa Fe,
  New Mexico; Bjorges Gallery, Big Fork, Montana; Adobe East Gallery,
  Delray Beach, Florida and Millburn, New Jersey; Blue Rain Gallery, Taos,
  New Mexico.

ABOUT THE ARTIST: Adams thinks seriously about incorporating natural el-

Butterfly Man Pendant by Victoria
Adams. Courtesy of Tribal
Expressions, Arlington Heights, IL.

ements into her work. She says, "Sightings of deer, antelope, birds, bugs, berries and my own horses can set one day very much apart from another. Cheyenne religious ceremonies are not complete without the inclusion of plants and animals. We honor them. They governed our survival in ancient times, and today they are still an integral part of our traditional and contemporary cultures."

ALVIN ADKINS

Haida (January 19, 1959–) Prince Rupert, British Columbia, Canada
Jeweler

EDUCATION: Self-taught, but has been mentored by Dempsey Bob, Freda Diesing, Bill Reid, Robert Davidson, and Don Yeomans. Worked most closely with Freda Diesing.

REPRESENTATION: Douglas Reynolds Gallery, Vancouver, British Columbia, Canada; Coastal Peoples, Vancouver; Deschutes Gallery, Bend, Oregon.

ABOUT THE ARTIST: Adkins, who began his career in 1971, works in gold, silver, wood, and argillite. Since that time, he has established himself and become one of the best known of the Northwest Coast jewelers. His pieces are highly sought after and respected for preserving the heritage of the Haida people.

MARIE AGUILAR

Santo Domingo (1924–)
Jeweler

EDUCATION: Learned some of her craft from family members.

AWARDS: During the 20 years she has entered the Indian Market, she has won many prizes for her necklaces.

REPRESENTATION: Wright's Collection of Indian Art, Albuquerque, New Mexico.

ABOUT THE ARTIST: Aguilar works almost exclusively with coral, sometimes adding Navajo tooled beads to her necklaces.

TONY AGUILAR

Santo Domingo (1919–)
Jeweler

EDUCATION: Worked at Skip Maisel's Indian Jewelry and Craft, Inc., Albuquerque, New Mexico, as a silver polisher, then took a course from Wilfred Jones, a Navajo silversmith, at the Santa Fe Indian School, New Mexico.

REPRESENTATION: Elaine Horwitch Gallery, Santa Fe, New Mexico; Wadle Galleries Ltd., Santa Fe; Tanner Chaney, Santa Fe.

ABOUT THE ARTIST: Aguilar creates classic heishi pieces with unique touches, such as metal, turquoise, coral, and jet.

JERI ALDACO

Navajo (May 20, 1968–) Navajo Reservation near Bloomfield, New Mexico
Jeweler, silversmither, beadworker.

EDUCATION: Younger sister, Cheryl Arviso, taught her silversmithing. Mother taught her beadworking.

REPRESENTATION: Native Artists United, Thoreau, New Mexico.

ABOUT THE ARTIST: The jewelry business is part of Aldaco's family history, and though she learned silversmithing from her sister, she turned to beadwork in 1999, trying to remember what her mother had taught her during her childhood. Aldaco's jewelry has been exhibited at the Jeanette Iles-North in Rochester, Kent, England, the Beth Friedman Shop in Tucson, Arizona, the Cibola Arts Council/Double 6 Gallery, and many other places. She states that her trademark is including four green beads on every piece she makes.

VICTOR BECK

Navajo (1941–) New Mexico
Jeweler

EDUCATION: Beck was one of the first young artists to participate in an art internship at the Museum of Northern Arizona Art Institute (in 1975).

AWARDS: Awarded the Heard Museum's Ted Charveze Memorial Award in 1991. Commissioned by Pope Paul VI in 1978 to create a rosary. Best of Division at the Museum of Northern Arizona, and the Jewelry Division at the Santa Fe Market, along with Best of Show at the Navajo Tribal Fair. Similar awards have been received from the Heard Museum in Phoenix, Arizona.

REPRESENTATION: Gallery 10, Inc., Scottsdale and Carefree, Arizona, and Santa Fe, New Mexico; Squash Blossom Gallery, Aspen, Vail, and Denver, Colorado; Merrill B. Domas American Indian Art, New Orleans, Louisiana; Four Winds Gallery, Pittsburgh, Pennsylvania.

ABOUT THE ARTIST: Beck creates contemporarily styled jewelry, using the same stone (turquoise) as his ancestors, as well as some other semiprecious stones. He was strongly influenced by Charles Loloma's and Kenneth

Begay's work and is especially known for his side inlay rings in silver and gold, as well as for his unusual bolo-tie designs.

MARY (THOMPSON) BECKMAN
(a.k.a. Jostwi)

Onondaga; Nedrow, New York
Jeweler, painter, beadworker, Native clothing designer

EDUCATION: Took painting classes at Roosevelt School in Syracuse, New York, as well as at the Cayuga Museum.

ABOUT THE ARTIST: Beckman's work has been exhibited throughout New York. She also teaches and writes. Her paintings are landscapes, still lifes, wildlife, and, sometimes, portraits.

ALVIN AND LULA BEGAY

Navajo (Alvin: 1956–) (Lula:) Navajo Reservation, Arizona
Jeweler

EDUCATION: Alvin apprenticed under Navajo silversmiths Tommy Singer and Abraham Begay and found that he had a real talent for making jewelry after learning painting under Billy Betoney and rug-weaving from his mother, Ada Kai Begay.

AWARDS: First, second, and third place awards, Santa Fe Indian Market; Best of Division, Heard Museum; second place award, Gallup Intertribal Indian Ceremonial; first place award, Navajo Nation Fair; Red Earth Art.

REPRESENTATION: Native Hands, Santa Fe, New Mexico.

ABOUT THE ARTISTS: One of the most accomplished husband-and-wife jewelry teams, the Begays create mostly needlepoint designs and silver jewelry. Alvin creates the design and does the basic carving, while Lula sets the stones and does the cutting and polishing. He incorporates his mother's rug-weaving patterns, borne of the Southwestern landscapes, into his designs. In addition to being a well-known jeweler, Alvin was also a champion bull rider in his youth.

HARVEY BEGAY

Navajo (1938–) New Mexico
Jeweler

EDUCATION: Harvey learned most of his jeweler's skills from his father, Kenneth Begay, as well as apprenticing with Pierre Touraine. B.S., Arizona State University.

REPRESENTATION: Lovena Ohl Gallery, Scottsdale, Arizona; Gallery of the American West, Sacramento, California; Galeria Capistrano, San Juan Capistrano, California; Indian Craft Shop, Washington, D.C.; Beckwith Gallery, Wellesley, Massachusetts; Adobe East Gallery, Millburn, New Jersey; La Fonda Indian Shop & Gallery, Santa Fe, New Mexico; Red Rock Trading Company, Alexandria, Virginia; Elk Ridge Art Company, Golden, Colorado.

ABOUT THE ARTIST: Begay incorporates traditional styles with modern techniques, often utilizing the textile patterns he learned from his mother, Eleanor Begay, a weaver. In the 1970s he opened a shop called the Navajo Craftsman in Steamboat Springs, Colorado, where he sold work created by Native American artists. Eventually, Begay's jewelry began to take over, and he soon earned his living from what he created. He is adept at all types of casting, works in silver and gold, and uses precut, as well as polished, stones in his pieces. Also a metalcraft artist, he creates flatware, plates, and goblets.

KENNETH BEGAY

Navajo (1914–77) New Mexico
Jeweler

EDUCATION: Taught by Fred Peshlakai at the Fort Wingate Boarding School for Native Americans during the 1930s.

AWARDS: Begay won many awards for the work he did with John C. Bonnell and built a national reputation for his work. SWAIA 2000 Lifetime Achievement Honoree.

ABOUT THE ARTIST: Begay was responsible for creating a style of Navajo jewelry that was simple and designed with bold lines around a single stone. He worked with John C. Bonnell at the White Hogan in Arizona from 1946 to 1950. They collaborated to created metalwork of all kinds, each piece with its own distinct design. After leaving the White Hogan, Begay taught silversmithing at the Navajo Community College, where he influenced the new generation of jewelers. He is called the Father of Modern Navajo Jewelry.

NORMAN BENTLEY

Haida (1968–) Skidegate, British Columbia, Canada
Jeweler

EDUCATION: Apprenticed with Tony Cavelit, world-renowned jeweler.
REPRESENTATION: Coastal Peoples, Vancouver, British Columbia.

ABOUT THE ARTIST: Bentley's family crest is the eagle. He began making jewelry in 1983 and today creates detailed, exquisite pieces that reveal his talent in carving.

CHARLIE BIRD

Laguna/Santo Domingo (1943–) New Mexico
Jeweler

EDUCATION: Comes from a family of artists, but did not develop his own style of jewelry until the 1970s. Taught himself mosaic work.

REPRESENTATION: Dewey Galleries, Ltd., Santa Fe, New Mexico; Packard's Indian Trading Co., Inc., Santa Fe; Museum of New Mexico Shops, Santa Fe.

ABOUT THE ARTIST: Bird is inspired by nature. Some of his jewelry reflects the designs he sees in places like the Chaco Canyon and the cliffs at Jemez Pueblo.

GAIL BIRD AND YAZZIE JOHNSON

Bird: *Santo Domingo/Laguna* (1949–) California
Johnson: *Navajo* (1946–) Arizona
Jewelers

EDUCATION: Self-taught.

AWARDS: Fellowship from the Southwestern Association on Indian Affairs (1980); Best of Show, Santa Fe Indian Market (1981). Work is held by the Museum of Man, San Diego, California; the Wheelwright Museum; the Millicent Rogers Museum; Albuquerque International Airport.

REPRESENTATION: Joanne Lyon Treasures, Aspen, Colorado; Dewey Galleries, Ltd., Santa Fe, New Mexico; Susan Duval Gallery, Aspen.

ABOUT THE ARTISTS: Bird designs the jewelry and Johnson fabricates the pieces. They have worked in brass, silver, copper, and gold and have used precious and semiprecious beads and stones from all over the world. Bird keeps a notebook of her designs, as well as clippings of ideas for future pieces.

MIKE BIRD

San Juan Pueblo (1946–) New Mexico
Jeweler

EDUCATION: Basically self-taught, Bird was inspired to create jewelry after watching Julian Lovato.

AWARDS: Awards at the Santa Fe Indian Market for his petroglyph figural pins.

REPRESENTATION: Gallery 10, Inc., Scottsdale and Carefree, Arizona, and Santa Fe, New Mexico; Federico on Montana, Santa Monica, California; Galeria Primitivo, Santa Monica; Merrill B. Domas American Indian Art, New Orleans, Louisiana; Dewey Galleries, Ltd., Santa Fe; Four Winds Gallery, Pittsburgh, Pennsylvania.

ABOUT THE ARTIST: Bird did not take up jewelry as a career until in his mid-30s. He and his wife, Allison, research Navajo and Pueblo traditional styles, then Bird uses their designs to create his own jewelry. He has even copied some petroglyph designs and re-created them, giving them new life as pieces of jewelry. His work is held in the Millicent Rogers Museum.

BLACK EAGLE

(*see* biography in the "Leather" chapter, p. 315)

CAROLYN BOBELU

Zuni; Arizona
Jeweler

EDUCATION: Self-taught.

Warrior's Loop Necklace by Black Eagle. Necklace is made in the classic Shoshone design, using brain-tanned smoked deerskin in its creation. The strands are made with antique clam shell and decorated with antique glass trade beads. Highly polished gold-lipped mussel shell at the top of the necklace creates a background for more antique bead decorations. Braided deerskin neck ties and a waist tie are strong. Courtesy of Black Eagle.

AWARDS: 1983 Indian Arts and Crafts Association Artist of the Year.

ABOUT THE ARTIST: Bobelu often uses intricate inlay designs in her work.

"CA W'IN" JIMMY CALABAZA

Santo Domingo (1949–) New Mexico
Jeweler

EDUCATION: Self-taught silversmith.

AWARDS: Judges' Choice Award, Southwest Indian Art Fair Juried Competition (2002).

ABOUT THE ARTIST: Calabaza makes jewelry in the Santo Domingo Pueblo craft tradition. He is well known for his polished turquoise necklaces. At the end of the 1990s, he also started using silver in his necklaces, and his signature piece became a silver side box.

JOE AND ROSEY CATES

Santo Domingo (Joe: 1944–) (Rosey: 1948–) New Mexico
Jewelers

EDUCATION: This husband-and-wife team learned some of their techniques from family members. Rosey also studied at the Institute of American Indian Arts in Santa Fe, New Mexico.

REPRESENTATION: Dewey Galleries, Ltd., Santa Fe, New Mexico; Packard's Indian Trading Co., Inc., Santa Fe, New Mexico; Wheelwright Museum of the American Indian/Case Trading Post, Santa Fe.

ABOUT THE ARTISTS: The Cates's trademark is the addition of a *jacla* (means "ear string" in Navajo) to their heishi necklaces. The *jacla* can be worn as earrings or can be left attached to each side of the necklace.

RIC CHARLIE

Navajo (1959–) New Mexico
Jeweler

EDUCATION: Self-taught.

AWARDS: Best of Show and Best of Division, "Navajo Show," Museum of Northern Arizona (1999, 2000). Awards at the Santa Fe Indian Market include Best of Show, Best of Division, Best of Classification, and Most Creative Design, to name a few.

REPRESENTATION: Sherwoods, Beverly Hills, California; Hoel's Indian Art Shop, Sedona, Arizona.

ABOUT THE ARTIST: Charlie creates one-of-a-kind gold pieces, using tufa casting and setting them with semiprecious stones. He carves his design on the tufa with dental tools and often applies patinas to his metals. Charlie often creates *yeibichai* designs on his jewelry.

ELIZABETH CHARVEZE-CAPLINGER

Isleta; Isleta Pueblo, New Mexico
Jeweler—gold, diamonds, precious/semiprecious stones

EDUCATION: Ted Charveze, Elizabeth's father, taught her.

REPRESENTATION: Killgore Gallery, Scottsdale, Arizona; Koshari Gallery, Scottsdale; Whitehills Indian Arts, Camp Verde, Arizona; Turquoise Tortoise, Sedona, Arizona; Indian Jewelry Center, Sacramento, California; Galleria Capistrano, San Juan Capistrano, California; Squash Blossom Gallery, Aspen and Vail, Colorado; White Horse Gallery, Boulder, Colorado; Village Goldsmith, Estes Park, Colorado; Tanners Indian Art, Wheat-Ridge, Colorado; Kansas Fine Arts, Topeka, Kansas; Stone Flower, Detroit, Michigan; American Legacy Gallery, Kansas City, Kansas; Santa Fe East, Santa Fe, New Mexico.

ABOUT THE ARTIST: At the age of 14, Elizabeth started making jewelry. She has continued to improve and is already considered important enough to be included in major art books. Charveze-Caplinger shows in major galleries.

TED CHARVEZE

Isleta (1936–90) Isleta Pueblo, New Mexico
Jeweler

EDUCATION: Studied with Pierre Touraine, a French jeweler.

AWARDS: Featured artist, Heard Museum, Phoenix, Arizona.

REPRESENTATION: Killgore Gallery, Scottsdale, Arizona; Koshari Gallery, Scottsdale; Whitehills Indian Arts, Camp Verde, Arizona; Turquoise Tortoise, Sedona, Arizona; Indian Jewelry Center, Sacramento, California; Galleria Capistrano, San Juan Capistrano, California; Squash Blossom Gallery, Aspen and Vail, Colorado; White Horse Gallery, Boulder, Colorado; Village Goldsmith, Estes Park, Colorado; Tanners Indian Art, Wheat-Ridge, Colorado; Kansas Fine Arts, Topeka, Kansas; Stone Flower, Detroit, Michigan; American Legacy Gallery, Kansas City, Kansas; Santa Fe East, Santa Fe, New Mexico.

ABOUT THE ARTIST: Charveze's jewelry is owned by royalty, including the queen of Denmark and the princess of Luxembourg. He has designed for Cartier in Paris and Imperial Enterprises in Japan. He taught his daughter, Elizabeth, who has become a major jewelry designer in her own life-time.

RICHARD CHAVEZ

San Felipe (1949–) New Mexico
Jeweler

EDUCATION: Studied architecture at the University of New Mexico. Learned how to make jewelry from his grandfather.

AWARDS: Grand Prize at the Eight Northern Indian Pueblo Artist and Craftsman Show (1975); Fellowship from Southwestern Association on Indian Affairs (1981); many awards and honors until 1990, when he decided not to enter any more competitions.

REPRESENTATION: Squash Blossom Gallery, Aspen, Vail, and Denver, Colorado; Merrill B. Domas American Indian Art, New Orleans, Louisiana; Beckwith Gallery, Wellesley, Massachusetts; La Fonda Indian Shop & Gallery, Santa Fe, New Mexico; October Art Ltd., New York; Four Winds Gallery, Pittsburgh, Pennsylvania; Texas Art Gallery, Dallas.

ABOUT THE ARTIST: Chavez began making heishi and turquoise necklaces more than 20 years ago, but switched to silver because the price of silver was low. He taught himself how to smith and has been influenced by the simplistic manner of Scandinavian jewelry. He only uses three colors at a time and often perfects the sculpture of his jewelry by working outward before filling the pieces in with color.

JOHN CHRISTIANSEN
(a.k.a. Keokuk)

Sac and Fox; Michigan
Jeweler

EDUCATION: Self-taught.

ABOUT THE ARTIST: Christiansen creates fine necklaces of turquoise and other semiprecious stones. He also creates miniature (stone) beads that are hand-rolled and hand-polished.

CARL AND IRENE CLARK

Navajo (Carl: 1952–) (Irene: 1950–) Arizona
Jewelers

EDUCATION: Carl learned how to make jewelry by observing silversmiths when he managed a jewelry production shop in Winslow, Arizona.

AWARDS: The Clarks have exhibited all over the world and have won awards at the Gallup Intertribal Ceremonial, the Museum of Northern Arizona, and the Heard Museum competitions.

REPRESENTATION: Gallery 10, Inc., Scottsdale and Carefree, Arizona, and Santa Fe, New Mexico; Many Hands, Sedona, Arizona; Southwest Trading Company, St. Charles, Illinois.

ABOUT THE ARTISTS: This couple has researched historical jewelry styles, then incorporated Navajo themes into their designs. They often use Yei figures in their jewelry, creating those figures with thousands of microscopic stones so that they look like sandpaintings. Their work has appeared in at least seven books. Irene does the design work, while Carl does the lapidary work.

VICTOR COOCHWYTEWA

Hopi
Jeweler, silversmith

AWARDS: Designated one of Arizona's Indian Living Treasures in 1994. Some of his work is held in museums, including the British Museum in London.

ABOUT THE ARTIST: Coochwytewa uses gold, diamonds, and Hopi symbolism, an unusual combination.

RITA JOE CORDALIS

Navajo (1954–) New Mexico
Jeweler

EDUCATION: Grew up in a family of silversmiths.

REPRESENTATION: Dewey Galleries, Ltd., Santa Fe, New Mexico; October Art Ltd., New York; Gallery 10, Inc., Scottsdale, Arizona.

ABOUT THE ARTIST: Cordalis has chosen to create jewelry that she hopes will be "multicultural," more contemporary than traditional, and that is made out of wood, ivory, malachite, and other nontraditional materials.

CIPPY CRAZY HORSE

(a.k.a. Cipriano Quintana)

Cochiti (1946–) New Mexico
Jeweler, silversmith

EDUCATION: Observed his father, Joe H. Quintana, a silversmith who worked in Santa Fe's production shops in the 1930s. Also taught himself silversmithing techniques and how to make all his own tools.

AWARDS: He has won top honors for all his work—jewelry as well as canteens and buckles—at the Santa Fe Indian Market and has acted as curator for an exhibit shown at the Museum of Indian Art and Culture in Santa Fe, New Mexico.

REPRESENTATION: Interior Craft Shop, Washington, D.C.; Dewey Galleries, Ltd., Santa Fe, New Mexico; Packard's Indian Trading Co., Inc., Santa Fe, New Mexico; Indian Post, Allentown, Pennsylvania; Texas Art Gallery, Dallas.

ABOUT THE ARTIST: Cippy did not start making jewelry until 1974 when he was left partially disabled after an accident at work. He uses early Navajo and Pueblo patterns for his work and likes the First-Phase jewelry style. His designs are drawn from items he sees every day.

GORDON CROSS

Haida; Skidegate, British Columbia, Canada
Jeweler, carver

ABOUT THE ARTIST: After an accident in 1965, Cross gave up his fishing business and began carving silver. He carves the Haida animal symbols into his pennants, bracelets, pins, and rings.

NELSON CROSS

Haida; Skidegate, British Columbia, Canada
Jeweler, carver

ABOUT THE ARTIST: Cross creates silver jewelry and believes the piece must speak to him, that he must feel the urge to create, and that what he does is not just a job.

RAMON DALANGYAMA

Hopi (January 26, 1954–) Grand Canyon Village, Arizona
EDUCATION: Self-taught. Institute of American Indian Arts, Santa Fe, New Mexico.

REPRESENTATION: Tribal Expressions, Arlington Heights, Illinois.

ABOUT THE ARTIST: Dalangyama began working with silver in 1978 when he returned to Hotevilla after spending some time in the Marine Corps. At first, he signed his name with the stylized initials "RA," but he had problems selling his work because his last name wasn't recognizable as Hopi. He uses typical Hopi designs in his work, like thunderclouds, thunderbolts, and rain.

Selection of jewelry by Ramon Dalangyama. Courtesy of Tribal Expressions, Arlington Heights, IL.

Selection of jewelry with Hopi symbols by Ramon Dalangyama. Courtesy of Tribal Expressions, Arlington Heights, IL.

CHALMERS DAY
(a.k.a. Dap-Hong-Va)

Hopi (1956–) Polacca, First Mesa, Arizona

EDUCATION: Participated in a program for silversmithing conducted by Preston Monongye in 1976–77. Later continued to work with Monongye.

AWARDS: First, second, and third ribbons at Santa Fe Indian Market (1982), and many others since then.

REPRESENTATION: Cristof's Art Gallery, Santa Fe, New Mexico.

ABOUT THE ARTIST: Day's grandfather was Robert S. Satala, Sr. His jewelry tells the story of his people, their migrations, their ceremonies, and their lore. He creates award-winning silver and gold jewelry heavily influenced by Preston Monongye. The jewelry is filled with images of the Corn Water clan to which Day belongs, incorporating rain, clouds, Hopi Kachinas, ollas, and Native dancers.

DENNIS AND NANCY EDAAKIE

Zuni; Arizona
Jeweler, silversmith—silver, turquoise, jet, coral, mother-of-pearl, other inlays

AWARDS: First place, Gallup Intertribal Ceremonial (1972), as well as many others.

REPRESENTATION: McGee's Indian Art Gallery, Keams Canyon, Arizona; Gallery of the American West, Sacramento, California; Interior Craft Shop, Washington, D.C.; Tanner Chaney Gallery, Albuquerque, New Mexico; Joe Milo's Trading Company, Vanderwagen, New Mexico.

ABOUT THE ARTISTS: The Edaakies create silverwork and inlaid belt buckles and jewelry in their studio in Zuni, New Mexico. Dennis does all the figurative work, while Nancy inlays the borders. He has experimented with new designs, such as cardinals and blue jays, and in 1985 made his first koshare figure. Dennis, who led the way in refining the Zuni inlay technique, is Jake Livingston's uncle. They stamp both of their names (one above the other) into their work as their signature.

CHRISTINA EUSTACE

Zuni/Cochiti (1954–) Albuquerque, New Mexico
Jeweler

EDUCATION: Learned her trade by helping her parents, both of whom were jewelers. She also studied fine arts at the University of New Mexico and took some stained-glass classes in New York in 1976.

REPRESENTATION: Gallery 10, Inc., Scottsdale and Carefree, Arizona, and Santa Fe, New Mexico; American Indian Contemporary Arts, San Francisco; Galeria Primitivo, Santa Monica, California; Dewey Galleries, Ltd., Santa Fe; Wadle Galleries, Ltd., Santa Fe; October Art Ltd., New York.

ABOUT THE ARTIST: Eustace uses petroglyphs to design some of her jewelry. She uses a variety of stones and does all her own lapidary work. Her

stained-glass background has influenced her jewelry designs. She has
made masks as pins and concha belts.

RAYMOND AND BARBARA GARCIA

Santo Domingo; New Mexico
Jewelers

EDUCATION: Self-educated.

AWARDS: Three blue ribbons, Indian Market (1990).

ABOUT THE ARTISTS: Raymond cuts and grinds the shells for their 20- to 40-
strand necklaces. Barbara then drills the shells and strings the beads on wire.
Their necklaces are finished with a "squaw wrap" (they intertwine the ends
of their strands, then wrap them tightly in cotton) rather than with commercially made clasps. They sell most of their work directly to collectors.

CARMEN GOERTZEN

(a.k.a. Tlaajang Nung Kingaass)

Haida (June 1963–) Vancouver, British Columbia, Canada

EDUCATION: Learned how to make tools with Robert Davidson, a Northwest Coast carver.

REPRESENTATION: Coastal Peoples, Vancouver, British Columbia, Canada.

ABOUT THE ARTIST: Started carving at the age of 11 and gradually moved
into jewelry making, though he's also a photographer and silk-screener.
He began using wood, stone, and metal, but he's more interested in carving in gold, silver, and argillite. His style is distinctive and reflects the
Haida culture; because of that, collectors seek him out. He's been hereditary chief of the Dadens since 1991 and lives in Vancouver.

ELSIE TAYLOR GOINS

Eastern Cherokee

EDUCATION: B.S., history and geography; M.S., education.

ABOUT THE ARTIST: Goins not only is active in Native arts like jewelry
making and beading, but she has been doing genealogical research for
most of her life. She has taught high school history and worked for
the Department of Defense with the U.S. Navy in Washington, D.C. Active in many organizations like the Cherokee Historical Association and
the Eastern Cherokee, Southern Iroquois and United Tribes of South
Carolina, Inc., she has been featured in the 1982 publication *Ohoyo One
Thousand: A Resource Guide to American Indian/Alaska Native Women.*

Selection of Jewelry by Elsie Taylor Goins. Beads and Pins Rosette, 22", 1960; Bone, Shell and Brass beads Necklace, 36", 1978; Beaded Earrings: Turquoise Nuggets, 1984, Seedbeads, 1984, Coral, 1984. Courtesy of Eastern Cherokee, Southern Iroquois and United Tribes of South Carolina.

LARRY GOLSH

Pala Mission/Cherokee (1942–) Phoenix, Arizona
Jeweler, painter, sculptor

EDUCATION: Worked with Pierre Touraine from 1972 to 1983 and was the first Native American to study at the Gemological Institute of America. He also observed Charles Loloma at work, learning how to set diamonds from him. Majored in fine arts at Arizona State University, where he studied with Ben Goo, a renowned sculptor. Manfred Susunkewa, a Hopi silversmith and Kachina carver, taught Golsh how to work with silver. Also apprenticed with Charles Loloma, a master jewelry maker.

AWARDS: National Endowment for the Arts grants (two); Arizona Commission on Arts and Humanities grant; numerous awards for jewelry creations. Judges jewelers at the Heard Museum, Scottsdale National Indian Art Show, and Santa Fe Indian Market.

REPRESENTATION: Lovena Ohl Gallery, Scottsdale, Arizona; Galeria Capistrano, San Juan Capistrano, California; Squash Blossom Gallery, Vail, Aspen, and Denver, Colorado; Glen Green Galleries, Santa Fe, New Mexico; Faust Gallery, Scottsdale, Arizona.

ABOUT THE ARTIST: Golsh works with numerous sketches to create his jewelry, often making facsimiles of the final product in wood, silver, or plaster before the work is finished. He uses exotic and unusual stones, is innovative, and uses all his art training when creating jewelry. The artist was featured in a 1984 PBS television special entitled *Larry Golsh— American Indian Artist.*

SHAL GOSHORN
(a.k.a. Noon da Da Lon a ga el, "Yellow Moon")

Cherokee (1957–) Baltimore, Maryland
Jeweler, photographer, painter

EDUCATION: Majored in silversmithing at the Cleveland Institute of Art in Ohio, changed her major to photography in her third year, then transferred to Atlanta College of Art in Georgia, graduating with a B.F.A. double major in painting and photography (1980).

AWARDS: Her work has been commissioned by many public and private institutions and has been awarded many prizes.

ABOUT THE ARTIST: Goshorn has done cover art and photographic illustrations for many publications, her work is held in many collections, such as the Indian Arts and Crafts Board and Prudential Insurance, and her photographs are currently being assembled for a book that will document contemporary Native life.

RUBY HALEY

Hopi (ca. 1960–) Gallup, New Mexico
EDUCATION: Self-taught.
REPRESENTATION: Cristof's Art Gallery, Santa Fe, New Mexico.
ABOUT THE ARTIST: Haley's craftsmanship is meticulous. She works exclusively with sterling silver and usually creates traditional squash blossom necklaces. Haley's family members work with her on some of her jewelry.

RON HENRY

Navajo (1961–) Coyote Canyon, New Mexico
EDUCATION: Learned his arts from his mother, Louise, a noted weaver and jewelry designer, and his brother Ernie, also a jeweler.
REPRESENTATION: Tribe Azure, Tucson, Arizona.
ABOUT THE ARTIST: Henry employs bold and vigorous techniques to create his contemporary jewelry. From a jewelry-making family, he learned the art and eventually went into business with other family members to pro-

Portrait of Ruby Haley. Courtesy of Cristof's, Santa Fe, NM.

duce a line of Native American jewelry from his sales outlet, Chi-Nah-Bah. At the young age of 21, he became a successful jeweler.

WATSON HONANIE

Hopi (1953–) Arizona
Jeweler—often works with gold

AWARDS: Best of Classification in all jewelry categories at the Santa Fe Indian Market (1991).

REPRESENTATION: Tribal Expressions, Arlington Heights, Illinois; Monongye's Gallery, Old Oraibi, Arizona; McGee's Indian Art Gallery, Keams Canyon, Arizona; Many Hands, Sedona, Arizona; Tanner Chaney Gallery, Albuquerque, New Mexico; Silver and Sand Trading Company, Taos, New Mexico; October Art Ltd., New York; Red Rock Trading Company, Alexandria, Virginia.

Inlaid stones in silver bracelet by
Ron Henry. Courtesy Tribe Azure
Jewelry and Art, Tucson, AZ.

Carved silver bracelet by Ron
Henry. Courtesy Tribe Azure
Jewelry and Art, Tucson, AZ.

Openwork silver bracelet with
inlaid lapis lazuli by Ron Henry.
Courtesy Tribe Azure Jewelry and
Art, Tucson, AZ.

Selection of gold and silver
jewelry by Watson Honanie.
Courtesy of Tribal Expressions,
American Indian Art Gallery,
Arlington Heights, IL.
www.tribalexpressions.com.

ABOUT THE ARTIST: Honanie has popularized his overlay gold style and was the first to combine silver and gold in his designs. Now he very rarely works in just one metal. He often carves Hopi Kachinas or scenes of Hopi life into his overlay jewelry.

SHERIAN HONHONGVA

Hopi (1960–) Arizona
Jeweler

EDUCATION: Honhongva apprenticed with her uncle, Charles Loloma, and studied with her sister, Verma Nequatewa.

REPRESENTATION: Lovena Ohl Gallery, Scottsdale, Arizona; Tribal Expressions, Arlington Heights, Illinois.

ABOUT THE ARTIST: Honhongva and her sister began exhibiting their own jewelry in 1989 under the name Sonwai, which in Hopi means "beautiful." They worked with Loloma for 23 years, perfecting a skill that is distinctive and of high quality.

DAN JACKSON

Navajo (ca. 1944–) Jeddito, Arizona

EDUCATION: Learned silversmithing from his father.

REPRESENTATION: Cristof's Art Gallery, Santa Fe, New Mexico.

ABOUT THE ARTIST: Jackson comes from an artistic family: his father, who was 106 when he died, taught him silversmithing, and his mother, Bernice Charlie, was a weaver. Jackson created the "rug" pattern using sterling silver overlay in about 1987. He creates bolos, buckles, bracelets, and concho belts.

THOMAS JIM

Navajo (1955–) Arizona
Jeweler

EDUCATION: Self-educated.

REPRESENTATION: Lovena Ohl Gallery, Scottsdale, Arizona; Waddell Trading Company, Tempe, Arizona; Packard's Indian Trading Co., Inc., Santa Fe, New Mexico; Gilcrease Museum Gift Shop, Tulsa, Oklahoma; Elk Ridge Art Company, Golden, Colorado.

ABOUT THE ARTIST: Jim's work is often made of silver stamped beads that

Portrait of Dan Jackson. Courtesy of Cristof's, Santa Fe, NM.

he chisels, stamps, and files with decorations. He began working for John Yellowhorse, the silversmith at Rocking Horse Ranch, in 1982, and did quite a bit of his work there.

ROGER JOHN

Navajo; Gallup, New Mexico
Jeweler, silversmith

EDUCATION: Self-taught; began making jewelry at age nine.

REPRESENTATION: Native Artists United, Thoreau, New Mexico.

ABOUT THE ARTIST: John makes mostly silver overlay pieces. His work is thematic, often interpreting the Christ journey. He mainly makes bracelets, pendants, bolo ties, buckles, and belts. Periodically, he makes special orders with semiprecious stones. Since the early 1990s he has been self-employed as a jeweler-silversmith.

JOE JOJOLLA

Isleta (1945–) Isleta Pueblo, New Mexico
Jeweler, silversmith, photographer

EDUCATION: Self-taught silversmith. Santa Monica City College; associate degree, undesignated, New Mexico State University; B.S., liberal arts, Regents College, New York.

REPRESENTATION: Jojola represents himself, is a member of the IACA (since 1980), and usually works on order.

ABOUT THE ARTIST: Jojola started silversmithing as a young man, continuing his craft while stationed in Germany with the army. His work has been featured by the Indian Arts and Crafts Association. He makes custom-ordered jewelry, belt buckles, rings, necklaces, and watchbands for his clients, using both old and modern tools. To help his customers with decisions, Jojola will provide a photo package (for a fee) and also will register the work. He now works as a photographer for a modeling firm in New Mexico.

BENNETT KAGENVEAMA

Hopi (1964–) Arizona
Jeweler

EDUCATION: Self-taught.

REPRESENTATION: Waddell Trading Company, Tempe, Arizona; Indian Craft Shop, Washington, D.C.

ABOUT THE ARTIST: Kagenveama often creates silver overlay pieces decorated with Kachinas and other Hopi motifs.

RODERICK KASKALLA AND LELA ROMERO

Kaskalla: *Zuni* (1955–) Zuni Pueblo, New Mexico
Romero: *Nambe/Cherokee*
Jewelers

EDUCATION: Kaskalla learned silversmithing by watching his aunts, Rose Hustito and Perlita Boone. His grandmother Mabel Lonjose introduced him to channel inlay work. He also took some modern art courses at Fort Lewis College.

AWARDS: One of his bracelets is on permanent exhibit at the Albuquerque International Airport.

ABOUT THE ARTIST: Kaskalla creates abstract, clean-edged patterns for his jewelry. His work follows the Zuni roots, using colors to indicate the six directions of that culture (north, west, east, south, zenith, and nadir). His wife, Lela Romero, often assists him.

JIMMIE KING, JR.

EDUCATION: Learned from his mentor, Rena, a silversmith.

REPRESENTATION: Cristof's Art Gallery, Santa Fe, New Mexico.

ABOUT THE ARTIST: King's inlaid gold and silver bracelets are made from three sheets of metal (a flat interior one, a thicker middle one, and a domed outside sheet). He welds them together, then shapes them around a car axle with a rawhide mallet. He is a man of strong beliefs and differences. He works with traditional Zuni stonecutting, Navajo and Zuni silversmithing, and his own designs. His trademark resembles a bow knot with six dots over it. His medicine men mentors (Tom Yellowtail and Hugh Little Owl) told him the significance of the six dots is that they represent east, south, west, north, Father Sky, and Mother Earth.

Portrait of Jimmie King, Jr. Courtesy of Cristof's, Santa Fe, NM.

CLARENCE LEE

Navajo (1952–) Arizona
Jeweler, painter

AWARDS: Best of Show, Eight Northern Indian Pueblos Artist and Craftsman Show (1982, 1983); Best of Classification, Indian Market (1983); Grand Award, Red Earth Awards Ceremony, Oklahoma (1994); as well as many others.

REPRESENTATION: Eagle Plume Gallery, Allenspark, Colorado; Mudhead Gallery, Denver and Beaver Creek, Colorado; Canyon Country Originals, Tucson, Arizona.

ABOUT THE ARTIST: Lee makes jewelry that tells a story about Navajo life—past and present. He makes his own dies and stamps and uses an appliqué technique where each piece of the work is cut from silver, gold, or copper, then soldered piece by piece onto the base. His work is often whimsical, incorporating Navajo home scenes, horses, dogs, goats, and people.

JAMES LITTLE

Navajo (1947–) Arizona
Jeweler

EDUCATION: Navajo Community College (1970–72), studied jewelry under Kenneth Begay.

REPRESENTATION: Lovena Ohl Gallery, Scottsdale, Arizona; Galeria Capistrano, San Juan Capistrano, California; Squash Blossom Gallery, Aspen, Vail, and Denver, Colorado; Galeria Capistrano, Santa Fe, New Mexico; Four Winds Gallery, Pittsburgh, Pennsylvania.

ABOUT THE ARTIST: Little is a minimalist, choosing to set off one stone rather than to surround it with a complex design. Though his designs are modern, they do reflect Navajo themes often suggested by his mother's rug patterns.

JAKE LIVINGSTON

Zuni/Navajo (1947–)
Jeweler

EDUCATION: Livingston credits Gibson Nez with teaching him the finer points of jewelry, but Livingston's father, Jacob Halso Su, taught him how to work with silver.

AWARDS: 1988 IACA Artist of the Year; top awards at Santa Fe Indian Market, the Heard Museum Show, and the Museum of Northern Arizona, as well as many others.

REPRESENTATION: Elk Ridge Art Company, Golden, Colorado.

ABOUT THE ARTIST: Livingston won three Purple Hearts in the Marine Corps (Vietnam) and did not begin selling his work until three years after he came home (1972). His first award was for a reversible concho belt, which won Best of Show at the 1974 Gallup Ceremonial. Livingston works with both silver and gold, as well as semiprecious stones.

JAN LOCO

Warm Springs Apache (1949–) Texas
Jeweler

REPRESENTATION: White River Trader, Indianapolis, Indiana; Dewey Galleries, Ltd., Santa Fe, New Mexico; Red Rock Trading Company, Alexandria, Virginia.

ABOUT THE ARTIST: Loco didn't know she was an Apache until her adoptive parents revealed that fact when she became an adult. Once she discovered her heritage, she moved to Santa Fe, New Mexico, met Allan Houser, and, with his help, reconstructed her past. She began making jewelry in 1988, working in copper and silver. She always makes her pins in multiples of four, a number sacred to the Apache.

PHIL LORETTO

Jemez (1951–) New Mexico
Jeweler, sculptor, painter, poet

EDUCATION: Institute of American Indian Arts (1968–69); studied under Paolo Soleri, Arizona State University (1969); B.A., painting, Fort Lewis College (1976). Learned how to create jewelry from his father-in-law, Chee Keams, a Navajo silversmith.

REPRESENTATION: Elaine Horwitch Gallery, Santa Fe, New Mexico; Packard's Indian Trading Co., Inc., Santa Fe; Wheelwright Museum of the American Indian/Case Trading Post, Santa Fe.

ABOUT THE ARTIST: Because Loretto is politically active, quite a bit of his work reflects his interests. One of his concha belts describes Columbus's arrival in the "new world." Each piece is individually stamped and hammered.

JULIAN LOVATO

Santo Domingo (1925–) Santo Domingo Pueblo, New Mexico
Jeweler

EDUCATION: Lovato came from a family of jewelers and learned from his father and grandfather. He also picked up some techniques from his mentor, Frank Patania, an Italian silversmith and owner of the Thunderbird Shop in Santa Fe, New Mexico. Patania passed his thunderbird hallmark on to Lovato.

AWARDS: Entered his first Gallup Intertribal Ceremonial in 1977 and won three first prizes.

REPRESENTATION: Tanner Chaney Gallery, Albuquerque, New Mexico; Santa Fe East, Santa Fe, New Mexico; Brooks Indian Shop, Taos, New Mexico; Thunderbird Shop, Santa Fe, New Mexico, and Tucson, Arizona.

ABOUT THE ARTIST: Lovato's jewelry has a sculptural quality, obviously an influence of Patania. His pieces have a spare, exact look that makes the stones appear to be floating.

RAY LOVATO

Santo Domingo (1946–) Santo Domingo Pueblo, New Mexico
Jeweler

EDUCATION: Learned the art from his parents, Ike and Tonita Lovato.

REPRESENTATION: Notah-Dineh Trading Co., Cortez, Colorado; Mudhead Gallery, Denver and Beaver Creek, Colorado; Squash Blossom Gallery, Aspen, Vail, and Denver, Colorado; Dewey Galleries, Ltd., Santa Fe, New Mexico; www.e-pueblo.com.

ABOUT THE ARTIST: Lovato uses only natural turquoise for his pieces and is recognized for his corn necklaces, where the turquoise he uses is shaped like corn kernels.

DUANE MAKTIMA

Laguna/Hopi (1954–) Holbrook, Arizona
Jeweler, carver

EDUCATION: Learned how to carve Kachinas from his grandfather. Art internship with Jacob Brookins, Northern Arizona University; B.F.A., metalsmithing, Northern Arizona University (1982); fellowship, Southwestern Association on Indian Affairs (1982).

Earrings with inlaid stones by Duane Maktima. Courtesy of Tribal Expressions, American Indian Art Gallery, Arlington Heights, IL. www.tribalexpressions.com.

Pendant with rosarita and ivory by Duane Maktima. Courtesy of Tribal Expressions, American Indian Art Gallery, Arlington Heights, IL. www.tribalexpressions.com.

REPRESENTATION: Tribal Expressions, Arlington Heights, Illinois; Gallery 10, Inc., Scottsdale and Carefree, Arizona, and Santa Fe, New Mexico; Many Goats, Tucson, Arizona; Merrill B. Domas American Indian Art, New Orleans, Louisiana; Wadle Galleries Ltd., Santa Fe; Four Winds Gallery, Pittsburgh, Pennsylvania; Red Rock Trading Company, Alexandria, Virginia; Duane Maktima Studio/Gallery, Glorieta, New Mexico.

ABOUT THE ARTIST: Ancient artifacts on display at the Museum of Northern Arizona inspired Maktima and made him wonder what they meant. He learned more about his cultures and returned to Northern Arizona University to study prehistoric and historical jewelry designs. He uses that knowledge to create unusual color combinations and abstract designs, signing his pieces with his initials and a stylized parrot, the insignia of the Laguna clan to which he belongs. He creates bolos, bracelets, buckles, cuffs, necklaces, pins, rings, and custom-designed jewelry.

BYRON MCCURTAIN

Kiowa (February 14, 1958–) Lawton, Oklahoma

EDUCATION: Institute of American Indian Arts, Santa Fe, New Mexico.

Opal pendant by Byron McCurtain. Yowah, black and blue opal, and red coral stones make this a stunning piece. Courtesy of Tribal Expressions, American Indian Art Gallery, Arlington Heights, IL. www.tribalexpressions.com.

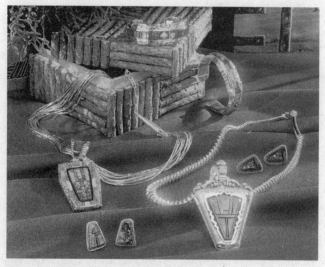

Selection of Byron McCurtain jewelry on red background. Courtesy of Tribal Expressions, American Indian Art Gallery, Arlington Heights, IL. www.tribalexpressions.com.

REPRESENTATION: Tribal Expressions, Arlington Heights, Illinois.

ABOUT THE ARTIST: When McCurtain met Red Streak Water (Navajo), he was introduced to the art of jewelry. Through the years, McCurtain soaked up all he could about the business, and upon his entrance to the Institute of American Indian Arts (IAIA), he changed his field to painting. By the age of 24, he finished a two-dimensional degree in photography instead of painting. Shortly afterward, he landed a job in a lapidary and learned more about jewelry when Gibson Nez took him under his wing. Two years later, McCurtain went back to IAIA, this time as a jeweler. Since that time, he has become a jeweler par excellence and his work is collected internationally.

JESSE LEE MONONGYE

Navajo/Hopi (1952–) Arizona
Jeweler

EDUCATION: Apprenticed with his father, Preston Monongye.

AWARDS: Selected by the Heard Museum as artist-in-residence (1986–87); has won many awards for his jewelry.

REPRESENTATION: Margaret Kilgore Gallery, Scottsdale, Arizona; Garlands Indian Jewelry Shop, Sedona, Arizona; Galeria Capistrano, San Juan Capistrano, California; Galeria Capistrano, Santa Fe, New Mexico; Mosi Lakai-Bi'Kisi, Santa Fe, New Mexico.

ABOUT THE ARTIST: Jesse didn't take jewelry seriously until his mother came to him in a dream and told him he'd be a famous artist. He did not know his father until they met in 1974. Once they made contact, Jesse began exploring the Hopi side of his heritage and added it to the designs he created for his jewelry. He combines both Hopi and Navajo motifs in his work and is considered an exceptional lapidary artist. His designs are considered intricate and often represent the heavens (he uses the galaxies and stars in a lot of his work).

PRESTON MONONGYE
(a.k.a. Snow Chief)

Hopi/Mission (1929–87) Arizona
Jeweler, painter, etcher, lithographer

EDUCATION: Self-taught. Apprenticed to his uncle Gene Pooyouma, at Hopi, beginning in 1936; Haskell Indian Junior College; law courses, Occidental College, Los Angeles, mid-1950s.

AWARDS: Numerous awards at fairs and juried competitions, including Intertribal Indian Ceremonial, Gallup, New Mexico (1966, 1970–77); Museum of Northern Arizona Annual Hopi Show, Flagstaff, Arizona; New Mexico and Arizona State Fairs; Santa Monica All Indian Ceremonial Show, Santa Monica, California; and Heard Museum Guild Indian Fair and Market.

REPRESENTATION: Christopher's Enterprises, Inc., Albuquerque, New Mexico; Tanner's Indian Arts, Gallup, New Mexico.

ABOUT THE ARTIST: Born to a Hopi father and California Mission mother, Monongye followed Hopi traditions as a child and became a traditional jeweler, influencing the younger generation with his casting procedures. He often re-created Kachinas with explicit details and authenticity, painting them after World War II until the 1960s, when he turned his interests to creating jewelry. One of the first to use gold in his jewelry, Monongye passed on his knowledge to his son Jesse, as well as other young jewelers. During the latter part of his life, his interest turned once again to painting, as well as etching and lithography.

ARNOLD MORRIS

Navajo; Rehoboth, New Mexico

EDUCATION: A.A., Institute of American Indian Arts, Santa Fe, New Mexico.

REPRESENTATION: Native Artists United, Thoreau, New Mexico.

ABOUT THE ARTIST: Morris has been creating silver jewelry with a Navajo rug design since about 1990. He began to be interested in art when at the Institute of American Indian Arts, then learned how to silversmith by watching one of his friends.

PHIL NAVASYA

Hopi; Arizona

Jeweler

REPRESENTATION: American Indian Contemporary Arts, San Francisco, California.

ABOUT THE ARTIST: Navasya's rings are made in the shape of spaceships. His abstract jewelry reflects his interpretation of Hopi life.

VERMA NEQUATEWA

(a.k.a. Sonwei)

Hopi (1949–) Arizona

Jeweler

EDUCATION: Apprenticed with her uncle, Charles Loloma.

REPRESENTATION: Lovena Ohl Gallery, Scottsdale, Arizona; Dewey Galleries, Santa Fe, New Mexico.

ABOUT THE ARTIST: With her sister, Sherian Honhongva, Verma learned how to create unusual jewelry from the master jeweler Charles Loloma and worked with him for 23 years. The sisters started exhibiting their own jewelry in 1989 under the name Sonwai, which means "beautiful" in Hopi. They use only top-quality stones and believe that quality is all that matters. Their studio is at the Third Mesa in Arizona.

AL NEZ

Navajo (1959–) Tuba City, Arizona

Jeweler

EDUCATION: Self-taught.

REPRESENTATION: Lovena Ohl Gallery, Scottsdale, Arizona; Waddell Trading Company, Tempe, Arizona; Sherwoods, Beverly Hills, California; Eagle Plume Gallery, Allenspark, Colorado; Mudhead Gallery, Denver and Beaver Creek, Colorado; Indian Craft Shop, Washington, D.C.; Indian Post, Allentown, Pennsylvania; Sedona Indian Jewelry.

ABOUT THE ARTIST: Nez uses the style Kenneth Begay made popular in the 1940s, precisely chiseling lines around a stone. He uses silver, gold, and various semiprecious stones in his work.

GIBSON NEZ

Navajo/Apache (1944–) Jicarilla Apache Reservation, New Mexico
Jeweler, silversmith

EDUCATION: Self-taught.

AWARDS: Best of Show at the Heard Museum and at the 1994 Santa Fe Indian Market, and has won more than 700 ribbons since 1990, as well as the Smithsonian Medal of Honor.

REPRESENTATION: Hogan in the Hilton, Santa Fe, New Mexico; Moondancer Gallery, Redondo Beach, California; Gallery of the American West, Sacramento, California; Galeria Capistrano, San Juan Capistrano, California; Mudhead Gallery, Denver and Beaver Creek, Colorado; Tanner Chaney Gallery, Albuquerque, New Mexico; Indian Post, Allentown, Pennsylvania.

ABOUT THE ARTIST: Nez, a member of the Indian Cowboy Association Hall of Fame, is also credited with helping many of today's up-and-coming jewelers. Nez's jewelry is popular with many celebrities. His large, stunning works are produced in both silver and gold, accented with turquoise, coral, and lapis lazuli. He exhibits at many Indian markets and travels to promote his jewelry. Recently he has started making silver pottery and won Best of Show at the 1994 Santa Fe Indian Market for that work.

BEN NIGHTHORSE

(a.k.a. Ben Nighthorse Campbell)

Northern Cheyenne (1933–) Auburn, California
Jeweler—gold, sterling

EDUCATION: Learned the art of making jewelry from his father, Albert. B.A., San Jose University; Meiji University, Tokyo.

Selection of jewelry by Ben Nighthorse Campbell. Courtesy of Toh-Atin Gallery, Durango, CO.

AWARDS: More than 200 first place awards, including those received at the Santa Fe Indian Market, Gallup Intertribal Ceremonial California State Fair Art Show, Indian Arts and Crafts Association, and G'Dam Tash. Nighthorse is now retired from juried competition.

REPRESENTATION: Squash Blossom Gallery, Vail, Denver, and Aspen, Colorado; Toh-Atin, Durango, Colorado; Fortunoff's, New York City; Interior Craft Shop, Washington, D.C.; Gallery of the American West, Sacramento, California; Canyon Country Originals, Tucson, Arizona.

ABOUT THE ARTIST: This jeweler works with as many as five different metals, and his work is so intricate, there are often as many as 38 steps in creating a piece of jewelry. Sometimes he will incorporate petroglyphs into his jewelry designs. Nighthorse has sold his work to many luminaries, such as Presidents Bush, Reagan, Ford, Carter, and Nixon, as well as movie stars. His contemporary jewelry is admired by his peers, and Nighthorse is considered one of the best in the business. In addition to being a talented artist, Nighthorse acts as a U.S. congressman from Colorado's third district.

ANGIE REANO OWEN

Santo Domingo (1946–   ) Santo Domingo Pueblo, New Mexico
Jeweler

EDUCATION: Worked with her parents, Joe I. Reano and Clara Lovato Reano, to make jewelry. As an adult, Owen researched ancient mosaic work and taught herself the tradition of creating mosaic "in the round" work, originally done by the Hohokam.

AWARDS: Numerous awards and exhibits at the American Craft Museum, the Millicent Rogers Museum, and the Albuquerque International Airport. Dubin Fellow, Indian Arts Research Center (1995).

REPRESENTATION: Gallery 10, Inc., Carefree and Scottsdale, Arizona, and Santa Fe, New Mexico; American Indian Contemporary Arts, San Francisco; Squash Blossom Gallery, Vail, Aspen, and Denver, Colorado; Indian Craft Shop, Washington, D.C.; Dewey Galleries, Ltd., Santa Fe; Packard's Indian Trading Co., Inc., Santa Fe; Wheelwright Museum of the American Indian/Case Trading Post, Santa Fe; Quintana Galleries, Portland, Oregon; Indian Post, Allentown, Pennsylvania; Texas Art Gallery, Dallas.

ABOUT THE ARTIST: Owen slices the stones and shells she uses into smaller pieces, then glues them into a mosaic design. Once the design is completely dry, she grinds it down, then buffs and polishes it.

NORBERT PESHLAKAI

Navajo; Fort Defiance, Arizona
Jeweler, silversmith

EDUCATION: Studied painting and jewelry making, Haskell Junior College for Native Americans, Kansas.

ABOUT THE ARTIST: Peshlakai creates silver jewelry and miniature silver pots. He often stamps his designs on his pieces and is influenced by the Crystal textiles woven by his mother. He is a fourth-generation silversmith; in fact, the word *peshlakai* means "silver" in Navajo.

HENRI PETER

REPRESENTATION: Tribe Azure Jewelry and Art Gallery, Tucson, Arizona.

ABOUT THE ARTIST: Peter lives with his wife in the foothills of the Andes and continues to produce Native American art and jewelry. He has traveled the world and uses his cultural knowledge to produce truly multicultural work.

Cuff by Henri Peter. Inlaid with various stones and incorporates lightning and other designs. Courtesy of Tribe Azure Jewelry and Art, Tucson, AZ.

MCKEE PLATERO

Navajo (1957–) New Mexico
Jeweler

REPRESENTATION: Teal McKibben, Santa Fe, New Mexico; Four Winds Gallery, Australia.

ABOUT THE ARTIST: Platero creates silver stamped work, as well as gold, red brass, and iron pieces. He does his own lapidary work. His inspiration comes from nature, as well as worldly events. Platero often creates work related to the political strife of the day. He is considered one of the most technically proficient contemporary silversmiths.

VERONICA POBLANO

Zuni (1951–) Zuni, New Mexico
Jeweler

EDUCATION: Encouraged by Joe Tanner of Tanner's Gallery in Gallup, New Mexico.

AWARDS: Best of Division, Red Earth Awards Ceremony (1994); SWAIA fellowship and "master artist" award (1996).

REPRESENTATION: Tribal Expressions, Arlington Heights, Illinois; Galeria Poblano, Zuni, New Mexico.

ABOUT THE ARTIST: Poblano started carving stone in 1965 and began making jewelry after that; however, it wasn't until she moved to California in the late 1980s. When she moved back to Zuni in 1992, her career went into full gear. She purchases only the best materials and is known for her quality work in both silver and gold. She often sells to notable Hollywood personalities, including Kevin Costner and Robin Williams.

Selection of necklaces by Veronica Poblano. Courtesy of Tribal Expressions, American Indian Art Gallery, Arlington Heights, IL. www.tribalexpressions.com.

PHIL POSEYESVA

Hopi (1958–) Arizona
Jeweler

EDUCATION: He was influenced by Charles Loloma and began combining traditional work with contemporary.

REPRESENTATION: Lovena Ohl Gallery, Scottsdale, Arizona; Waddell Trading Company, Tempe, Arizona; Ansel Adams Gallery, Yosemite National Park, California; Mudhead Gallery, Beaver Creek and Denver, Colorado; Southwest Expressions, Chicago; Adobe East Gallery, Millburn, New Jersey; Packard's Indian Trading Co., Inc., Santa Fe, New Mexico; The Turquoise Lady, Houston, Texas.

ABOUT THE ARTIST: Poseyesva combines traditional Hopi overlay styles with asymmetry and lapidary touches. He uses both gold and silver in his work, draws his designs freehand, and often places his stones slightly off-center, accentuating his detailed overlay designs.

ANDRES QUANDELACY

Zuni; New Mexico
Jeweler, carver

EDUCATION: Learned some of his carving skills from his mother, Ellen Quandelacy, as well as other members of his well-known family.

REPRESENTATION: Indian Craft Shop, Washington, D.C.; Keshi—The Zuni Connection, Santa Fe, New Mexico; Wadle Galleries, Ltd., Santa Fe; Grey Dog Trading, Tucson, Arizona; Zuni Fetishes Direct, Gallup, New Mexico; Sedonawolf, Arizona.

ABOUT THE ARTIST: Quandelacy carves fetish necklaces and standing fetishes. His bears are standing bears.

ELLEN QUANDELACY

Zuni (1924–) New Mexico
Jeweler, carver

EDUCATION: Learned from her father and her husband how to make fetish necklaces and tabletop fetishes.

REPRESENTATION: Wadle Galleries, Ltd., Santa Fe, New Mexico; Indian Craft Shop, Washington, D.C.; Keshi—The Zuni Connection, Santa Fe; Quintana Galleries, Portland, Oregon; Red Rock Trading Company, Alexandria, Virginia; Grey Dog Trading, Tucson, Arizona.

ABOUT THE ARTIST: Quandelacy is the matriarch of a large Zuni family who have become noted for their fetish necklaces and tabletop fetishes. She began making jewelry at the age of 46, creating channel inlay silver bracelets and necklaces (signed "E.Q. Zuni"). In the 1980s she had a stroke and began carving animals from stone, which are very collectible today.

FAYE QUANDELACY

Zuni (1958–) New Mexico
Jeweler, carver, potter, sculptor

EDUCATION: Institute of American Indian Arts, Santa Fe, New Mexico.

REPRESENTATION: Indian Craft Shop, Washington, D.C.; Keshi—The Zuni Connection, Santa Fe, New Mexico; Wadle Galleries, Ltd., Santa Fe; Red Rock Trading Company, Alexandria, Virginia.

ABOUT THE ARTIST: Her Corn Maidens, decorated with crosses, dragonflies, and stars, are the most recognizable of her carvings. Her mother is Ellen Quandelacy.

GEORGIA QUANDELACY

Zuni (1957–) New Mexico
Jeweler, carver

EDUCATION: Learned some of her carving skill from her mother, Ellen Quandelacy.

REPRESENTATION: Indian Craft Shop, Washington, D.C.; Keshi—The Zuni Connection, Santa Fe, New Mexico; Wadle Galleries, Ltd., Santa Fe.

ABOUT THE ARTIST: Quandelacy's bears are carved of jet, and each has an inlaid sun design on the side.

STEWART QUANDELACY

Zuni; New Mexico
Jeweler, carver

EDUCATION: Learned some of his skills from his mother, Ellen Quandelacy.

REPRESENTATION: Indian Craft Shop, Washington, D.C.; Keshi—The Zuni Connection, Santa Fe, New Mexico; Wadle Galleries, Ltd., Santa Fe; Grey Dog Galleries, Tucson, Arizona.

ABOUT THE ARTIST: Quandelacy carves fetish necklaces, as well as standing fetishes. His bears are medicine bears, with a heartline and arched back, the best known of the Quandelacy family carved bears. He is the older brother to Andres, Avery, Sandra, and Faye.

CHARLENE CHARLYN™ REANO

Santo Domingo (1966–) Santo Domingo Pueblo, New Mexico
Jeweler

EDUCATION: Learned her craft from her parents, Joe B. and Terry Reano.

REPRESENTATION: Hozhoni Gallery, Naperville, Illinois.

ABOUT THE ARTIST: This artist uses the trademark symbol for her name since she is not the only artist with her birth name. One of her trademarked techniques is to use several different metals "married" together. She uses tufas to create new and innovative molds for her jewelry. Her husband, Shane Hendren (Navajo), often assists her on certain pieces, and his hallmark will appear next to hers when they have collaborated.

CHARLOTTE AND PERCY REANO

Santo Domingo (Charlotte: 1950–) (Percy: 1951–) New Mexico
Jewelers—mosaic, beadwork

EDUCATION: Percy learned how to make jewelry as a boy.

ABOUT THE ARTISTS: The couple works together with Percy cutting the material and doing the final grinding of the beads, while Charlotte drills and strings them. They use power-driven tools.

FRANK AND CHARLENE SANCHEZ REANO

Frank: *Santo Domingo* (1962–)

Charlene: *San Felipe* (1960–)

Jewelers—mosaic

EDUCATION: Charlene studied art at New Mexico Highlands University. She and Frank worked with Angie Reano Owen (Frank's sister) to learn different techniques.

REPRESENTATION: Margaret Kilgore Gallery, Scottsdale, Arizona; American Indian Contemporary Arts, San Francisco.

ABOUT THE ARTISTS: The Reanos have a unique earring style, cutting a shell into two halves and then cutting a "kiva step" design inside each half. Charlene designs, cuts, and places the stones; Frank grinds the stones.

JOE B. AND TERRY REANO

Santo Domingo; New Mexico

Jewelers—turquoise

EDUCATION: Self-taught.

REPRESENTATION: Lovena Ohl Gallery, Scottsdale, Arizona.

ABOUT THE ARTISTS: Joe and Terry, parents to Charlene (Charlyn™) Reano, another prominent jeweler (no relation to Charlotte and Percy Reano), make their necklaces by hand. They use only natural turquoise.

HOWARD SICE

Hopi-Laguna (May 25, 1948–) Winslow, Arizona

Jeweler, engraver, sculptor

EDUCATION: Self-taught.

AWARDS: Numerous awards for his engraving and sculpting of precious and semiprecious metals, including first place at the Heard Museum in Phoenix, Arizona, and Best of Show at the Northern Arizona Museum Hopi Show.

REPRESENTATION: Long Ago & Far Away Gallery, Manchester, Vermont; Silver Bear Jewelry, St. Louis, Missouri.

ABOUT THE ARTIST: Sice creates silver and gold jewelry, as well as engraved miniature Hopi pots. His bowls have won him national acclaim and are highly sought-after collectibles. In his jewelry, he uses exotic and rare earth metals, silver, gold, and stone work and imitates traditional South-west and Pueblo imagery in his contemporary designs.

SMOKEY

Zuni (1956–) New Mexico
Jeweler, silversmith

EDUCATION: Learned his needlepoint technique from his mother, and his lapidary and silversmithing from the production shop in his father-in-law's trading post. He was inspired by Edith Tsabetsaye to experiment with his style.

AWARDS: First place in needlepoint, Indian Market, Santa Fe, New Mexico (1990).

ABOUT THE ARTIST: He uses Sleeping Beauty turquoise as his primary stone. His experimental designs are modern, not traditional, thus he finds it hard to sell them.

CHARLES SUPPLEE

Hopi/French (1959–) Arizona
Jeweler

EDUCATION: Worked with Pierre Touraine from 1982 to 1984.

REPRESENTATION: Lovena Ohl Gallery, Scottsdale, Arizona; Eagle Plume Gallery, Allenspark, Colorado; Mudhead Gallery, Beaver Creek and Denver, Colorado; Santa Fe East, Santa Fe, New Mexico; Elk Ridge Art Gallery, Golden, Colorado.

ABOUT THE ARTIST: Supplee has been commended for his superior inlay work and elegance. He incorporates some of his early memories of Navajo jewelry (he grew up in Ganado, Arizona, where his father worked as a schoolteacher on the Navajo reservation) with what he learned with Touraine, then bends the idea so that his creation became distinctly his own. He has also collaborated with Al Qoyawayma, a Hopi artist-potter, on ceramic and metal sculptures.

ROY TALAHAFTEWA

Hopi (August 25, 1955–) Shungopovi, Arizona
Jeweler

EDUCATION: Took art classes in elementary school and attended the Institute of American Indian Arts, Santa Fe, while in high school. Sculptor Allan Houser was an influence on Talahaftewa's work.

Silver carved belk buckle with Elk design by Roy Talahaftewa. Courtesy of Tribal Expressions, American Indian Art Gallery, Arlington Heights, IL. www.tribalexpressions.com.

AWARDS: Won his first prize at the age of eight for a painting he'd entered in a Museum of Northern Arizona contest. Best of Show, Indian Market (1986); Best of Jewelry and Best of Division, Indian Market (1990).

REPRESENTATION: Many Hands, Sedona, Arizona; Ansel Adams Gallery, Yosemite National Park, California; Indian Craft Shop, Washington, D.C.; Southwest Trading Company, St. Charles, Illinois; Tribal Expressions, Arlington Heights, Illinois.

Kachina necklace and bracelet with inlaid stones by Roy Talahaftewa. Courtesy of Tribal Expressions, American Indian Art Gallery, Arlington Heights, IL. www.tribalexpressions.com.

ABOUT THE ARTIST: After years of encouragement from his mom, Tala-haftewa started making jewelry full-time in 1977. He creates concha belts with realistic silver-stamped Kachinas on them, as well as pendants and necklaces, and other jewelry. At first he worked with silver only, but he now incorporates some stones into his designs and works with gold as well.

HERBERT TAYLOR

Navajo (1951–) Indian Wells, Arizona
Jeweler—gold and silver

EDUCATION: Self-taught.

AWARDS: Best of Show, Heard Museum, Phoenix, Arizona (1992); Best of Show, Southwest Museum, Los Angeles (1992). Several first place ribbons from the Santa Fe Indian Market, including three in 1994.

REPRESENTATION: Cristof's Art Gallery of Santa Fe, Santa Fe, New Mexico; Blue-Eyed Bear, Sedona, Arizona; Desert Son, Tucson, Arizona; Tribal Expressions, Arlington Heights, Illinois.

ABOUT THE ARTIST: Taylor's whole family is in the jewelry business. He learned some of his early skills from watching his father make jewelry, then continued to learn on his own. He creates silver concho belts, as well as jewelry, makes his own tools, and sketches out his designs before stamping the silver. He is a versatile jeweler, always looking for different ways to approach the art, though he considers himself a traditional jeweler. Taylor's work has been shown all over the United States at museum shows and markets.

BOBBIE TEWA

San Juan/Hopi (1948–) San Juan Pueblo, New Mexico
Jeweler

EDUCATION: Took an eight-week silversmithing course sponsored by the federal Manpower Program.

AWARDS: Two Best of Division awards, Indian Market (1982).

REPRESENTATION: Squash Blossom Gallery, Aspen, Vail, and Denver, Colorado; Mosi Lakai-Bi'Kisi, Santa Fe, New Mexico; Santa Fe East, Santa Fe, New Mexico; Four Winds Gallery, Pittsburgh, Pennsylvania; Pot Carrier American Indian Arts, Vashon Island, Washington.

ABOUT THE ARTIST: Tewa was encouraged to enter her first Indian Market by friend and mentor, the late Harvey Chavarria. Tewa's pieces sold immediately. The artist combines traditional Hopi motifs with Pueblo pottery designs, creating goblets as well as jewelry.

KELVIN THOMPSON

Ojibway (November 5, 1958–) Ebbenflow, Manitoba, Canada
Jeweler, carver

EDUCATION: Influenced by Northwest Coast artists, such as Barry Wilson and Derek Wilson, and has had an apprenticeship with Henry Robertson.

REPRESENTATION: Coastal Peoples, Vancouver, British Columbia, Canada.

ABOUT THE ARTIST: Thompson, who has been carving since 1978, is equally at home as a jeweler, working with silver and gold. Kelvin's designs, whether in gold, silver, ivory, or wood, reflect his attention to detail and superb craftsmanship. He is very aware of his Native culture and hopes that through his artwork he is able to help preserve and pass on the Northwest Coast Native culture.

RAY TRACEY

Navajo (1953–) Navajo Reservation near Ganado, Arizona
Jeweler—14-karat gold and sterling silver, inlaid precious and semiprecious stones

EDUCATION: University of Utah, Brigham Young University, and Trenton School of Jewelry.

AWARDS: Best in Division, Santa Fe Indian Market (1991); first place, Santa Fe Indian Market (1992, 1993); *Niche* Magazine Awards (1993).

REPRESENTATION: Ray Tracey Galleries, Santa Fe, New Mexico, and Scottsdale, Arizona; Southwest Studio Connection, Southampton, New York; Squash Blossom Gallery, Denver, Vail, and Aspen, Colorado; Margaret Kilgore Gallery, Scottsdale.

ABOUT THE ARTIST: Tracey started making jewelry at the age of nine, left the business for a while to pursue a career in acting, then returned to his first love in 1977 and made a success out of creating jewelry known for its unusual colors and shapes. Tracey employs Native American artisans to produce his jewelry in Gallup, New Mexico. His hand inlaid pieces are designed with such stones as sugilite, lapis, turquoise, and coral. He also uses opals, diamonds, 14-karat gold, and platinum with 18-karat and 24-karat gold. He rarely uses more than two or three colors in the same piece. Many pieces feature eagle feathers because, according to Tracey, "the eagle is sacred to most Indian tribes . . . considered to be the messenger for the Great Spirit."

EDITH TSABETSAYE

Zuni (1940–   ) New Mexico
Jeweler, silversmith

AWARDS: Best of Show, Indian Market, Santa Fe, New Mexico (1980). Ribbons at 1998 Gallup Ceremonials and 1999 Santa Fe Indian Market, as well as many others.

REPRESENTATION: Many Goats, Tucson, Arizona; Tanner Chaney Gallery, Albuquerque, New Mexico; Turquoise Village, Zuni Pueblo, New Mexico; Joe Milo's Trading Company, Vanderwagen, New Mexico; Gallery of the American West, Old Sacramento, California.

ABOUT THE ARTIST: Tsabetsaye is a master at needlepoint designs in jewelry and has inspired younger jewelers to continue in her footsteps. She sometimes uses more than 1,000 stones for concha belts, but is not producing as much as she used to because of arthritis in her hands.

RICHARD TSOSIE

Navajo (1953–   ) Arizona
Jeweler, artist, sculptor

EDUCATION: Self-taught.

REPRESENTATION: Lovena Ohl Gallery, Scottsdale, Arizona; October Art Ltd., New York; Garlands Indian Jewelry Shop, Sedona, Arizona; Many Hands, Sedona; Sedonawolf Gallery, Sedona.

ABOUT THE ARTIST: The photographer Jerry Jacka first brought Tsosie and his work to the public. The artist not only makes jewelry, but is also a fine sculptor. Tsosie uses the technique of reticulation to decorate his contemporary jewelry. He works mostly with silver. His work has been highlighted in many volumes on Native American artists.

LLOYD WADHAMS, JR.

Kwaguilth (1967–   ) Alert Bay, British Columbia, Canada

EDUCATION: Followed in the footsteps of his family, who were Northwest Coast carvers.

REPRESENTATION: Coastal Peoples, Vancouver, British Columbia, Canada.

ABOUT THE ARTIST: Wadhams started creating Native art as a teenager, working with cedar at first, then progressing to carving silver and gold jewelry. He is a traditional artist, but his work is distinctive. As a result, many collectors admire and purchase his work.

ALAN WALLACE

Washoe/Taos; Taos Pueblo, New Mexico
Jeweler, artist

EDUCATION: Largely self-taught.

AWARDS: Wallace has won many awards for his mosaic work.

REPRESENTATION: Blackhawk Gallery, Saratoga, Wyoming; Gallery of the American West, Old Sacramento, California.

ABOUT THE ARTIST: Wallace creates necklaces, rings, and bracelets with finely worked mosaic designs and scenes. Some of his pieces reflect pueblo life; for example, an image of a Kachina may find its way into Wallace's larger bracelets. He works with many semiprecious stones, as well as both silver and gold.

DEREK WILSON

Kwaguilth (1950–) Kemano, British Columbia, Canada

EDUCATION: Learned about carving from his uncle, Henry Robertson. Self-taught as a jewelry designer. Formal training in stone setting at Vancouver Community College (1994).

REPRESENTATION: Coastal Peoples, Vancouver, British Columbia, Canada.

ABOUT THE ARTIST: Wilson, who takes the killer whale as his family crest symbol, comes from a long line of artisans. He's a hereditary chief of the Haisla Nation. His attention to detail, as well as his fine intricacy and design innovation, has aided in establishing him as an accomplished Northwest Coast Native artist. Though he follows traditional style, he puts a contemporary spin on his designs.

LEE YAZZIE

Navajo (1946–) south of Gallup, New Mexico
Jeweler

EDUCATION: Learned about his craft by watching his parents, both silversmiths, and, later, by taking a course at Fort Wingate Boarding School, Fort Wingate, New Mexico.

AWARDS: Three Best of Show Awards, Gallup Intertribal Ceremonial (between 1969 and 1990); two first place ribbons, Gallup Intertribal Ceremonial (2000).

REPRESENTATION: Lovena Ohl Gallery, Scottsdale, Arizona; Waddell

Trading Company, Tempe, Arizona; Eagle Plume Gallery, Allenspark, Colorado; Indian Craft Shop, Washington, D.C.; Tanner's Indian Arts, Gallup, New Mexico; Sedona Wolf Gallery, Sedona, Arizona.

ABOUT THE ARTIST: Yazzie, a world-renowned jeweler, worked with Preston Monongye in the 1970s, doing some of his lapidary work. He also worked at Tanner's Indian Arts and Crafts Center, Gallup, New Mexico, and learned how to cut good stones there. The design for which he is best known is his corn bracelet. He shapes and polishes each "kernel" before placing them in the construction of the bracelet itself. Other members of his family (brother Raymond and sister Mary Marie Lincoln) are also Native American artisans of repute.

LEO YAZZIE

Navajo (1940–) Black Mesa, Arizona
Jeweler

EDUCATION: Studied sociology at Northern Arizona University and took a class on metalsmithing while there.

REPRESENTATION: Gallery 10, Inc., Carefree and Scottsdale, Arizona, and Santa Fe, New Mexico; Beckwith Gallery, Wellesley, Massachusetts; Quintana Galleries, Portland, Oregon; Hoel's Indian Shop.

ABOUT THE ARTIST: Yazzie's interest in creating jewelry was fed during the time he was attending Northern Arizona University. It's been more than 20 years since then and he continues to make jewelry. He incorporates traditional rug-weaving designs into his jewelry and juxtaposes traditional Navajo textile patterns with lapis stones.

ALBENITA YUNIE

Zuni (1944–) New Mexico
Jeweler, carver

EDUCATION: Learned some of her technique from her famous mother, Ellen Quandelacy.

REPRESENTATION: Wadle Galleries, Santa Fe, New Mexico; Penfield Gallery, Albuquerque, New Mexico.

ABOUT THE ARTIST: Albenita comes from the Quandelacy family, a group of carvers who each have their own distinctive style. Hers is that she creates fetish bears in all colors.

Prices

Allen Adkins. Men's ring. Eagle Profile design. 14-karat gold, 3/8" width

7-point diamond in bezel setting. $795–$1,000 (depending on size of diamond).

Norman Bentley. Men's ring. Split Raven design. 14-karat gold, 11mm width. $1,000–$1,200.

————. Men's ring. Frog Frontal design. 14-karat gold and silver, 11mm width. $500–$550.

Gail Bird and Yazzie Johnson. Keshi pearl necklace in twisted rope design with abalone clasps. $3,600–$3,800.

————. Coin pearl rope with Yowah opal satellite and 18-karat gold clasps. $6,400.

"CA W'in" Jimmy Calabaza. Turquoise and silver necklace. 30" long, beads approximately 2½" in diameter. $350–$400.

Irene and Carl Clark. Pendant with mosaic inlay/opal/turquoise 11-point VSI diamond set in 14-karat gold. $7,200–$7,500.

Dennis and Nancy Edaakie. Pin, roadrunner design. 2½" in diameter, inlaid with pen shell, abalone, mother-of-pearl, coral, and serpentine. Signed on the back "Dennis E." Attachment to convert pin to be worn as a pendant. $650–$700.

Christina Eustace. Raincloud necklace. Sterling silver, coral, sugilite, lapis, mother-of-pearl, opal, and spiny oyster. Has an 18" opening; the center pendant extends another 1¾". $1,800–$2,000.

Carmen Goertzen. Engagement set. Eagles facing and killer whale. 14-karat gold, ⅜" total width 24-point diamond in bezel setting. $1,000–$1,600.

Watson Honanie. Gold and silver belt buckle. Incorporates a 14-karat gold bear in a gold forest. The construction of this buckle required a bottom layer of silver that was finely incised to give it texture. Upon that was placed the gold bear and forest scene. Then an incised silver shadow box was created in which a center bear walks. Upon that are overlaid walking bears and water symbols. Total of four layers of metal. 3¾" long × 2½" wide for a 1½" belt or less. $1,495–$1,600.

Sherian Honhongva. Pins. Turquoise, red coral, and lapis are separated by slivers of sterling silver in the maiden pin. The snake pin includes turquoise, ivory, and red coral. $1,750–$1,900.

Thomas Jim. Man's sterling silver and turquoise bracelet. 2½" in diameter. $300.

Clarence Lee. Pin. Hopi maiden. Sterling silver. 2¾" high. $95–$125.

James Little. Ring in 14-karat white gold with 2.37ct diamonds white and canary. Cross design with a diamond shape in the center of the design. $6,500–$6,800.

———. Cuff. 14-karat gold and turquoise. $5,500.

Ray Lovato. Necklace. Hand-cut beads from natural New Landers spider-web turquoise. The necklace measures 18" in length and the beads are graduated in size from $\frac{1}{4}$" in diameter to $\frac{1}{8}$" in diameter. $450–$500.

Al Nez. Gold tufa cast earrings. $\frac{7}{8}$" × $\frac{5}{8}$"with four lapis lazuli gems. $875–$925.

———. Necklace. Contains six tufa cast Kachina faces. Entirely handmade in 14-karat gold with a Florentine finish. The gem turquoise is from the Lone Mountain mine in south-central Nevada. Rainbows and sun faces. 36" long and is easily adjustable as the hook can be fastened on any link. $5,600–$6,000.

Ben Nighthorse. Bracelet. Designed as an ode to the Ancients. The "sky" is filled with Anasazi rock art figures, spirits of the Ancients. The Rocky Mountains are symbols of power and strength through the eons. The mountains are inlays of turquoise and coral. (Also available in gold.) $1,100–$1,400 in sterling silver.

———. Rings. Relief designs on these rings are similar to, and a companion of, the Ben Nighthorse Rock Art Bracelets. Motif inspired by the prehistoric rock art designs found on canyon walls throughout the Four Corners area, especially on rock cliffs of Mesa Verde, Chaco Canyon, and Canyon de Chelly. $150–$200 in sterling silver. $750–$800 in 18-karat gold through size 9$\frac{1}{2}$". $850–$900 in 18-karat gold size 10 and up.

Norbert Peshlakai. Butterfly pin. Sterling silver and agate. $595–$625.

Phil Poseyesva. Belt buckle. Sterling silver with Kokopelli designs. $515–$550.

Andres Quandelacy. Necklace. Mother-of-pearl and coral mountain lion fetish. 22$\frac{1}{2}$" long. $290–$310.

Georgia Quandelacy. Bear fetish. Jet wolf with coral heartline 1$\frac{1}{8}$" high, 2" long. $60–$75.

Stewart Quandelacy. Fetish. Denim lapis medicine bear with coral heartline 2$\frac{3}{8}$" high, 2$\frac{3}{4}$" long. $300–$350.

Charlene Reano. Necklace. Sterling silver and sugilite. 16". $510–$525.

———. Earrings. Sterling silver and 14-karat gold. 1" × $\frac{3}{4}$". $135–$150.

Roy Talahaftewa. Necklace. Tufa cast pendant inlaid with lapis, turquoise, red coral, and sugilite. Handmade bezel holds turquoise stone, accompanied with a handmade chain. 3" × 2". $725–$775.

————. Necklace. 14-karat and lapis, 19" long, includes a 3" × 1¼" tufa cast 14-karat pendant inlaid with red and pink coral, turquoise, and black jade. Handmade 14-karat cone and hook clasp. $3,900–$4,100.

Kelvin Thompson. Bear bracelet. Hand-carved sterling silver. 1⅜" × 6¼". $500–$600.

Richard Tsosie. Silver bracelet. Emerging eagles. Both overlay and granulation techniques are present in this free-form silver bracelet. The center of the bracelet is a garnet gem in a Tiffany-style setting in a large sugilite gemstone. From there two eagles emerge and seem to take flight. For a 6" to 6¼" wrist. $650–$700.

CHAPTER 7

Leather

The leather items that Native Americans make include everything from clothing to decorated drums, rattles, breastplates, moccasins, and many other items. Since items of clothing are not always signed, it is not certain who created these pieces, thus the list of artists in this category is shorter than others but no less significant. Because Native American clothing was often decorated with quills or beadwork, we have included that information here as well.

Clothing Decoration: Quillwork

The Plains Indians used quills in decoration, and their artistry with this technique reached its peak after horses became a part of their lifestyle. Skill at the craft was a subject of pride, and there were very established levels of expertise among the women in the tribes. The most creative of the quillwork artists perfected dyes, designs, and stitches that the other women willingly copied. It was an honor for a woman of great skill to pass her secrets along to another. The patterns used were mostly geometric designs before 1880. After that, some tribes began using floral designs.

When trade beads became more widely used in the early 1880s, the art of quillwork was threatened. Today the Sioux tribe produces most of the available quillwork.

Sewing the quills of a porcupine onto a soft hide was an ancient Blackfoot method of decorating clothing, a method that other tribes shared as well. Before the quills were sewn onto the fabric, the quill-worker soaked them in her mouth to soften them. She then sewed the quills in such a way that they would form patterns and designs.

Quills could be used in their natural colors or dyed; most Native American quill artists used red, yellow, and green dyes. The dyes were derived from plants that were moistened, covered by the quills, then wrapped until dry. When dry, the plant color would have permanently soaked into the quills. At other times, the quillworker would boil the quills with an appropriate dye material and a mordant. Of course, the quillworker's palette of colors expanded greatly when aniline dyes became available.

Tools used in quill decorating include a piece of hide upon which to work, an awl, a smooth object used to flatten the quills once they are sewn down, and strands of rolled sinew. Quillworkers kept their quills in special bags fashioned out of buffalo bladders. A slit was made in the bag, through which the quills were inserted. The bag was usually stiff enough so that the quills inside would be kept straight. Quillworkers preferred to work with thin quills because they didn't split as easily as the larger, older ones.

Blackfoot quillworkers go through a traditional initiation and have to follow rules as they practice their art. They cannot eat porcupine meat or allow anyone to pass in front of them while they quill. An older woman will initiate a younger woman into the art. Unfortunately, because of the advent of beadwork and the lack of knowledge of the art of quillwork among the older women, there are few quillworkers left among the Blackfoot women today.

Clothing Decoration: Trade Beads

Beads first came to North America when the Spanish started trading and Jamestown, Virginia, opened the first glass factory in 1622. Glass trade beads were spread all over the country by explorers, and several became so popular that they garnered names. The "Russian Blue" bead became the most popular bead and was soon dubbed the "Chief" bead. Other popular beads included the "Hudson Bay" bead, a red bead with a translucent center, used in Canadian trade; the "Vaseline" or "Cave Agate" bead, a faceted and transparent bead with a hole through its center, made in a variety of colors; and the "Hubbell" bead, made in Czechoslovakia between 1915 and 1920 and sold by the Hubbell Trading Post in Ganado, Arizona, located on the Navajo reservation.

Different patterns are used in beading techniques, such as weft and warp combinations; the bias-diagonal stitches that are very difficult to perfect and most often used throughout the Great Lakes region; oblique weaving; concentric circling; bead wrapping; spot or overlay stitching; spiral stitching found in Native American coiled basketry, a stitch that was used by the Midwestern Musquakiis; the spoked pattern, used by

Oklahoman tribes; scalloped bead winding, used by the Utes and Comanches; and the lazy stitch, used by most Indians west of the Mississippi, the most commonly used stitch.

Plains Indian beadwork started shortly after European beads were introduced to Indian culture. Plains women immediately used them as decorative accents on leather clothing, fashioning the beads into geometric patterns, animals, or human figures. After 1910 Plains beadwork declined sharply in quality; the supposition is that this was due to a transition from beading for themselves to beading for the tourist trade. Some experts say just the opposite, arguing that quillwork was at its peak between 1880 and World War I, simply because the tribes were confined to reservations, thus creating more time to perfect their work for the tourist trade. The tribes beaded everything they could, from doctors' bags to bottles, as well as the traditional items. Since buffalo hides and deerskin were not so readily available, beaders began applying beads to wool and canvas cloth.

Because of the interaction between Plains tribes, their work resembles each other's. Cheyenne and Arapaho artwork is quite similar, while Kiowa, Comanche, and Plains Apache beadwork is sparse on their clothing (they worked on borders and figures instead). When sewing on their beads, Sioux beaders used the lazy stitch, which leaves the beadwork in loose rows, with a bumpy appearance. Blackfoot beading was done with the appliqué stitch, requiring the simultaneous use of two threads, one holding the beads, the other stitching them down.

Bead colors that were popular with the Blackfoot tribe include blue, "greasy" yellow, "Cheyenne" pink, green, and rose. Italian seed beads are common and are a good quality glass with soft, subtle colors. New beads, however, arrived with each ship to the New World, and Indian beadwork incorporated Russian cobalt and Czechoslovakian glass beads as well. The geometric beadwork of the Blackfoot consists of large figures made up of other smaller ones (e.g., squares, triangles, rectangles). The feather design and mountain design are commonly used, but there are no tribal meanings to a beadmaker's designs.

Some trade beads may have reached the Blackfoot as early as the beginning of the 1700s, through trade with other tribes who had direct contact with merchants. Pony beads were widely used on Blackfoot garments beginning around 1830. The most common color combination was white and sky blue. Beads were used to trade for a good buffalo robe or horse. During the 1870s, when seed beads were introduced, Blackfoot beadworkers turned to the style of beadwork most common today. Once the smaller beads were available, whole articles of clothing were beaded instead of just the edges, and flower and leaf designs became popular.

Quite a few of today's beaders follow the old traditions and bead on leather; however, a fair number bead on other types of material and use techniques particular to their own needs. Because a lot of beaders do not sign their work, biographies of the major beaders are rare, thus there are fewer listings in this chapter.

The Artists

ARTHUR D. AMIOTTE

Oglala Sioux (1942–) Pine Ridge, South Dakota
Leatherworker; painter—petroglyphs, miscellaneous media

EDUCATION: B.S., education (double major: art education and commercial art), Northern State College (1964); University of Oklahoma (1966); Pennsylvania State University (summers 1967, 1968, 1971); University of South Dakota (1969); Master of Interdisciplinary Studies (anthropology, religion, and art), University of Montana (1983).

AWARDS: Amiotte's many awards, appointments, publications, films, and lectures number in the hundreds and include an Honorary Doctorate of Lakota Studies given by the Ogala Lakota College in Kyle, South Dakota (1988) and an award for "Outstanding Contribution to South Dakota History" given by the Dakota History Conference and Center for Western Studies at Augustana College (May 1992).

REPRESENTATION: The Heritage Center, Inc., Pine Ridge, South Dakota.

ABOUT THE ARTIST: Amiotte's work has been exhibited extensively throughout the last 30 years throughout the United States. His commissions and published art have become book covers, Governor's Awards (South Dakota) posters for Oglala Lakota College, and limited editions. He lectures all over the country about Plains art and traditional, as well as contemporary, Indian artists. He also teaches and writes quite extensively about the Native American experience and the arts.

LESLIE BITSIE

Navajo
Beadworker

EDUCATION: Self-taught.
REPRESENTATION: Eastern Cowboys, Scottsdale, Arizona.
ABOUT THE ARTIST: Adept at working with leather and beads, Bitsie pro-

duces quite a few pipe bags and medicine bags out of buckskin with glass beadwork.

BLACK EAGLE

Shoshone/Yokut; Elko, Nevada

Leatherworker, beadworker, weapons maker, woodworker, painter, drawer, jeweler, musician

EDUCATION: Self-taught, deriving inspiration from experience, research, and heritage, such as memories of his grandmother and other ancestors.

AWARDS: Best of Division, drawing/printmaking, Red Earth Awards Ceremony (1994); Best of Class/Best of Division, Heard Museum Indian Fair

Ermine-trimmed war shirt by Black Eagle. Made of five full hides of Shoshone brain-tanned and smoked deerskin, sewn together with bison sinew. Waxed linen thread used to sew the intricate design composed of over 8500 seed beads (colors include cobalt, porcelain, greasy yellow, grassy green, and red white-hearts). One hundred forty-one genuine human hair scalp locks hanging on the sleeves and body of the shirt, all wrapped in red wool trade cloth and sealed with hide glue. Hand-faceted Russian Blue and Greasy Red trade beads dating from 1750-1890 used at the top of the hair locks. Beaded three band red wool trade cloth decorates the front collar. Red pigments from Mother Earth were hand-painted and literally touched onto the war shirt by Black Eagle, a way of signing it, signifying enemies killed at close range in hand-to-hand combat. Dragonflies painted on near the collar transfer the dragonflies' talent for being hard to kill. Designed, handmade, and signed by Black Eagle, 1999. Courtesy of Black Eagle.

Bow and arrows set. Consists of an ash wood bow, a bow case, attached quiver, four arrows, a Strike-a-Light in a pouch, a Medicine Pouch, an awl in a pouch, and an extra bowstring. Arrows have bone points, wild rose shafts, turkey feather fletching, pigments from Mother Earth, and bison sinew ties. Awl is made from a highly polished deer antler. Courtesy of Black Eagle.

Portrait of Black Eagle, Shoshone-Yokus artist. Courtesy of MB Black Eagle.

and Market (1994); Best of Class, textiles and attire, Eitejorg Museum Indian Market, Indianapolis, Indiana (1994); and many other awards.

ABOUT THE ARTIST: Black Eagle is unique in that he started winning awards for his creations immediately upon beginning his professional art career (in 1991). He "takes great pride in using genuine materials in his art . . . real bison and deer sinews, rawhides and ground pigments from Mother Earth . . . Shoshone brain-tanned smoked deerskin and pre-1900 antique beads. . . ." He creates warrior tools, cradleboards, leather outfits, jewelry, and many other items in the traditional fashion. His website is www.warriorart.com.

DAVID BRUSH

Menominee/Sioux
Beadworker, featherworker, leatherworker

EDUCATION: Self-taught.

REPRESENTATION: Eastern Cowboys, Scottsdale, Arizona.

ABOUT THE ARTIST: Brush often works with feathers, beads, and leather, creating one-of-a kind knife sheaths and other Plains Indian items.

Intricately designed beaded front knife sheath by David Brush. Courtesy of Jay Sadow and The Eastern Cowboys, Scottsdale, AZ.

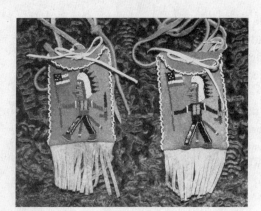

Menominee Artist David Brush stops his Pow Wow dancing performances long enough to hand make patriotic items like these medicine pouches. Courtesy of Jay Sadow and the Eastern Cowboys, Scottsdale, AZ.

JEROME CLARKE

Sioux
Leatherworker, beadworker

REPRESENTATION: Eastern Cowboys, Scottsdale, Arizona.

ABOUT THE ARTIST: Clarke works with leather, often making ceremonial shields.

RICKY M. HILL

Mohawk/Tuscarora (1958–2001) New York
Leatherworker

EDUCATION: Self-taught.

REPRESENTATION: www.IroqArt.com.

ABOUT THE ARTIST: Hill grew up in New York state, but lived in Scottsdale, Arizona up until his death. He created breastplates, chokers, drums, shields, pouches, and other leather items. He did not sell ceremonial items because of his religious beliefs. In addition to leatherworking, Hill acted and modeled. After a courageous battle with lymphoma, he passed away in 2001.

VELMA JOCKO

(a.k.a. Kahontawakon)

Mohawk (1927–) Hogansburg, New York
Leatherworker; beadworker; artist—pencil, watercolors

EDUCATION: Learned the basics of leatherwork and beadwork from her father.

AWARDS: Awards include a blue ribbon for a purse exhibited at the New York State Fair in 1978.

Beaded leather work gloves by
Melody Lightfeather. Courtesy of
Jay Sadow and the Eastern
Cowboys, Scottsdale, AZ.

REPRESENTATION: Kanesatake Indian Arts & Crafts, Oka, Quebec, Canada.

ABOUT THE ARTIST: Jocko makes a variety of items, often using designs inspired by nature or traditional Iroquois patterns. She uses a raised beadwork technique and decorates vests, pocketbooks, pouches, and moccasins. She is also an artist, drawing or painting nature scenes. Jocko often exhibits at the New York State Fair and takes individual orders to work on at home.

MELODY LIGHTFEATHER
(a.k.a. Melody Lightfeather Watson)
Pima (1952–2001)
Beadworker, painter

REPRESENTATION: Eastern Cowboys, Scottsdale, Arizona.

ABOUT THE ARTIST: An internationally acclaimed artist whose work appeared in the White House and the Smithsonian Institution, Lightfeather did beadwork, as well as paintings. She was killed in an automobile accident in Albuquerque, New Mexico, in 2001.

LAVERN LITTLE
Yankton Sioux
Leatherworker, painter

EDUCATION: Self-taught.

REPRESENTATION: Eastern Cowboys, Scottsdale, Arizona.

ABOUT THE ARTIST: Little creates leather pieces, bow-and-arrow sets, pipe sets, and other Sioux ceremonial pieces. He paints on deerhide, uses natural accents in his work, and creates strong medicine items. His work is sold throughout the world and respected by his customers.

Northern Plains Indian buckskin quiver, lined with felt, dressed with glass beadwork, by Lavern Little, ca. 2001. Courtesy of Jay Sadow and the Eastern Cowboys, Scottsdale, AZ.

Ceremonial shield by Lavern Little. Entirely handcrafted, painted in the Plains Indian Warbonnet design of the Sioux Nation. Courtesy of Jay Sadow and the Eastern Cowboys, Scottsdale, AZ.

ALICE NEW HOLY BLUE LEGS

Lakota; North Dakota

Porcupine-quill artist

EDUCATION: Alice is a descendant of a long line of quillworkers.

AWARDS: National Heritage Fellow, Folk Arts Program of the National Endowment for the Arts (1985).

ABOUT THE ARTIST: Alice, a skilled quill worker, has taught other family members, as well as non-family, to work with quills. Her work is held by private collections and museums, such as the Museum of New Mexico, Santa Fe. She was part of a video called *Lakota Quillwork: Art and Legend*.

BJ QUINTANA

Albuquerque, New Mexico

Leatherworker, drum maker, painter, photographer, sculptor

EDUCATION: San Juan College; University of Albuquerque. Influenced by artist Joel-Peter Witkin.

REPRESENTATION: Native American Collections, Inc., Denver, Colorado.

ABOUT THE ARTIST: Of Native American descent, Quintana was adopted as an infant by a white couple. Her original foray into the art world was as a photographer. After her parents' deaths, she moved to Taos in 1986. There she began working as a painter and sculptor. Her painting explores the world of abstract expressionism, and her leatherwork (particularly her drums) expresses her Native American heritage.

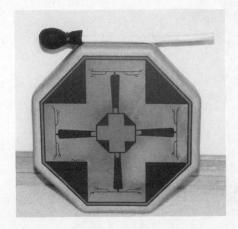

Deer Dance Drum by BJ Quintana.
14" wide. Courtesy of Jill Giller,
Native American Collections,
www.nativepots.com. Photo by Bill
Bonebrake.

Biting Bear Drum by BJ Quintana.
14" wide. Courtesy of Jill Giller,
Native American Collections,
www.nativepots.com. Photo by Bill
Bonebrake.

DEBORAH MAGEE SHERER

Blackfoot; Blackfoot Indian Reservation, Montana
Quillworker, leatherworker

EDUCATION: B.A., art history, Montana State University; master's degree, education, University of Montana. Brief internship at Smithsonian Institution. Was taught quillwork by a member of her tribe.

AWARDS: Juried shows include Indian Art Northwest and the Heard Museum (second place and a Best of Division award). Featured artist for the Native American Art Show 2000 in Great Falls, Montana.

ABOUT THE ARTIST: Sherer uses authentic, traditional materials in all her

Leather beaded bag by Liz Welch.
Courtesy of Jay Sadow of the
Eastern Cowboys, Scottsdale, AZ.

craftwork, but also explores more modern, diverse ways of using those materials and techniques. Currently, she lives in Browning, Montana, with her husband and three sons.

SOPHIE THOMAS

Okanagan (1893–) Stony Creek Reserve, Victoria, British Columbia, Canada
Leatherworker

EDUCATION: Self-taught.

ABOUT THE ARTIST: Thomas stretches, dries, scrapes, washes, restretches, and softens the hides she uses herself. It is a long project and has to be perfectly timed so that the hide will turn the right color. In 2001 a film about Thomas and her talent as an herbalist–medicine woman was released in Canada. Entitled *The Warmth of Love, the Four Seasons of Sophie Thomas*, it was created by pop icon Terry Jacks as a video about the environment and designed to educate the public about what is happening with the environment.

Prices

Black Eagle. Single Lightning Strike Warrior Breastplate with Antique Missouri River Blue Beads. $4,800.

———. Breastplate with Green Hearts. $3,500.

———. Double Lightning Strike Breastplate. $2,600.

———. Brown Diamond Breastplate. $2,400.

———. Blue Four Winds Breastplate. $2,400.

———. Black Diamond Breastplate. $2,400.

———. Large Cranberry Heart Breastplate. $2,500.

———. Large Amber (color) Breastplate. $2,500.

———. Rawhide rattles: "Recalling the Bison Hunt," $650; "Medicine Eagle," $550; "Turtle Medicine with Feathers," $550.

———. Miniature Dreamer Bird Shield with weapons collection, $2,200; "The Day War Pony Was Honored" Miniature Horse Shield, $1,300; Miniature Dreamer Bird Shield framed with barnwood, $1,400; Miniature Wolf Shield, $1,300; Miniature Bison Shield, $850; Miniature Dreamer Bird Shield, $850.

CHAPTER 8

Pottery

One of the most popular Native American arts is pottery. The art of pottery making combines Native Americans' love of the earth with their need to express themselves and produces a utilitarian bowl, pot, or dish. New potters, whose work combines the old techniques with new ideas, often win awards at annual crafts markets and exhibitions. There are new pottery artists emerging all the time, usually from some of the families that have been producing Native American pots for generations. Like other Native American arts, pottery-making techniques and secrets are passed down by the family members, thus some of the surnames you see in this chapter will be repeated.

The greatest number of Native potters come from the Southwest, where the natural conditions are such that clay is readily available and the tribes have produced pottery for the tourist trade for hundreds of years. Most modern potters from New Mexico and Arizona still hand-throw pottery without the benefit of a wheel. Some use a yucca-leaf brush with one end chewed into fibers to decorate. Acoma, San Ildefonso, Zuni, and Hopi mesas still paint deer, birds, flowers, geometric designs, and identifiable symbols of their villages onto their pots. New techniques, like selective firing where the black carbon is burned away to reveal red clay, are also used by some potters.

The major pottery-making tribes and their distinctive characteristics are noted in the following chart.

TRIBE	CHARACTERISTICS
Acoma	Acoma pottery usually features a white background with fine-lined geometric designs. The Acoma typically decorate pots with birds and often make corrugated white pottery.
Cochiti	The Cochiti Pueblo potters are well-known for creating storyteller figures. First made famous through the work of potter Helen Cordero, storytellers have become an integral part of

Pueblo pottery. The figures, originally modeled after Cordero's grandfather and his storytelling techniques, are folk art in the purest Native American form. Cordero began making her storytellers in the 1950s, combining the ancient seated figure (originally created in the late 1800s to "tease" the white man) with outstretched legs, head thrown back, and mouth wide open, with tiny figures seated or climbing on the figure, their faces showing either rapture or fear (depending on the story being told by the seated figure). Cordero, 45 years old at the time, didn't realize what kind of impact her figures would make on the art of pottery. She won instant fame, even to the point of being featured on the cover of *National Geographic* in November 1982. When other Cochiti potters saw the popularity of Cordero's figures, they began making storytellers as well, and now a number of artisans from other pueblos, such as Jemez, Acoma, Nambe, Isleta, and San Felipe, are also making storytellers in recognizable styles.

Hopi	Earliest pieces were black-on-white, gray, and sometimes orange. Yellow pieces were made during the 14th and 15th centuries. After the Spanish built missions in the Hopi area in 1625, potters developed additional shapes and designs that were eventually called Polacca Yellow Ware. By the end of the 19th century, trading became an important part of the Hopis' economic system, and the Hopi-Tewa potter Nampeyo began copying some of the prehistoric designs. By combining new and old shapes and patterns, she created her own style. During the 1800s the Hopi slip method was similar to that of the Zuni and Acoma potters. The descendants of Paqua Naha (Frog Woman) utilize a rare fine, white firing clay as their slip. Hopi pottery has practical uses: cooking, carrying, and storing water, and serving and storing food. A water jar (*kuysivu*) and the dipper (*kuyapi*) are commonly made and decorated by Hopi potters, as are shallow, open serving bowls and shoe pots (pottery used to keep food warm). Pots—both old and new—are often decorated with macaws, large wild parrots that never lived anywhere near Hopiland. Today's pottery making is based on the First Mesa, with some men joining in what has traditionally been a female occupation (e.g., Tom Polacca, Fannie Nampeyo's son; then Polacca's sons, Gary Nampeyo Polacca and Loren Hamilton Nampeyo).
San Ildefonso	The northernmost village in the pueblos, this tribe uses the Rain Bird design, and its pottery is also noted for its distinct black-on-white wares, as well as redware. San Ildefonso potters have made pottery in essentially the same fashion for more than 700 years. Instead of following the trends in design technique adopted by other potters, these potters kept to their richly for-

mal heritage. The famous potter Maria Martinez and her family began the black-on-black style that is recognizably San Ildefonso.

Santa Clara	Santa Clara potters use clay, tempering materials, and red paint for their creations, gathering the clay from a place called Na Pi'l we, about 1 mile west of the pueblo, as well as from other locations, producing a variety of colors in the finished pieces. The tempering material comes from a place about 7 miles northwest of the village called Makawa oky. Santa Clara pottery families, both contemporary and historical, are well-known in today's Indian collectibles market.
Taos	Pottery made in this pueblo traditionally incorporates flecks of mica in the clay.
Tesuque	These potters seem to better comprehend the changes in pottery making and concentrate on small decorative details, incorporating designs like the Rain Bird into a secondary design. Tesuque pottery reached its peak at the end of the 19th century and rapidly declined after that.
Zuni	The Rain Bird design is one of the most frequently used and easily recognized of all Zuni pottery designs. Their pottery underwent a change in glaze types by about 1700, when the potters favored a dull and flat look to their pots. The Rain Bird design first came into evidence at this time and is divisible into several distinct features. The center of the design is a single coil, representing the bird's head and beak, and below this coil is its crest. On either side of this design is a stepped outline that encloses two solid figures: the body and the wings. Through the study of Pueblo pottery design, one can discern many minute changes in this design, yet the basics are the same whether one calls the design a bird, a chicken, a turkey, or its rightful name, the Rain Bird.

The Artists

KAREN ABEITA

Hopi (September 23, 1960–)
Potter

EDUCATION: Studied in Albuquerque, New Mexico, to become an optical technician in late 1970s–early 1980s. Learned pottery-making skills from contemporaries such as Fawn Garcia and Mark Tahbo.
AWARDS: SWAIA Fellow (2000).

REPRESENTATION: Robert F. Nichols Gallery, Canyon Road, Santa Fe, New Mexico; Native American Collections, Denver, Colorado.

ABOUT THE ARTIST: Abeita comes from a long line of potters. Her grandmother's first cousins, Sadie Adams, Joy Navasie, and Beth Sakeva, are well known in the business. However, Abeita's pottery is traditional, made from Native materials she and her husband gather, and often decorated in the prehistoric Sikyatki style. Because Karen works very hard on her firing techniques, her work has a warm glow to it.

TAMRA L. ABEITA

Acoma; Acoma Pueblo, New Mexico
Potter

ABOUT THE ARTIST: The artist is young, but up-and-coming. She creates handmade Acoma pottery, horsehair-fired pottery, and wooden horses.

ELIZABETH ABEYTA
(a.k.a. Nah-Glee-eh-bah)

Navajo (1956–)
Potter, clayworker, sculptor

EDUCATION: Attended Navajo Community College, Tsaile, Arizona (1974); Institute of American Indian Arts, Santa Fe (1976–78). Studied ceramics at San Francisco Art Institute (1980); University of Wyoming.

AWARDS: First place, sculpture, Navajo Show, Museum of Northern Arizona, Flagstaff (1985); second place, sculpture, SWAIA, Indian Market (1989); first place, sculpture, SWAIA, Indian Market (1990); second place, sculpture, SWAIA, Indian Market (1992).

REPRESENTATION: Agape Southwest Pueblo Pottery, Albuquerque, New Mexico.

ABOUT THE ARTIST: Abeyta makes clay figurines that are ethereal and free-flowing, airbrushed to look like sandstone. She began her artistic career at the suggestion of her father, noted artist Narciso Abeyta. Her pottery figures are traditional but finished in a contemporary way. They often reflect the faces of the Navajo way of life and people, such as singers, dancers, mudheads, and Kachinas.

BLANCHE ANTONIO

Acoma (1927–) New Mexico
Potter

EDUCATION: Learned how to pot from her mother, Juana Pasqual, and grandmother Juana Concho.

ABOUT THE ARTIST: Other members of her family who also create pottery include her clan grandmother, Marie Z. Chino, her sister, Mary Lukee, her sister-in-law Romolda Pasqual, and her nieces Bonnie Leno and Kimberly Pasqual. Antonio creates bowls, jars, wedding vases, figurines, and storytellers in the traditional colors and designs of the Acoma Pueblo potters. She made her first storyteller in the late 1970s.

HILDA ANTONIO

Acoma (1938–) New Mexico
Potter—storytellers

EDUCATION: Learned how to pot from mother, Eva B. Histia.

AWARDS: Has regularly won prizes for her storytellers and storyteller owls at the Indian Market since the mid-1970s.

REPRESENTATION: Turquoise Village, Zuni, New Mexico; Pueblo Pottery Gallery, San Fidel, New Mexico.

ABOUT THE ARTIST: Antonio comes from a line of well-known potters, including her aunts, Lucy Lewis and Elizabeth Woncada, her grandmother Helice Valdo, her daughter, Mary A. Garcia, and her sister, Rose Torivio. Hilda created her first storyteller in the late 1950s, one of the first to do so.

MARTHA AQUERO

Cochiti (1944–) Cochiti Pueblo, New Mexico
Potter

EDUCATION: Learned from her mother, Damacia Cordero.

AWARDS: First and second place, Santa Fe Indian Market.

REPRESENTATION: Sacred Hoop Trading, Minneapolis, Minnesota.

ABOUT THE ARTIST: Aquero has been making storytellers and figurines since the 1960s in the same style as her mother did. Aquero signs her pieces "Martha Arquero-Cochiti."

DELORES ARAGON

Acoma (1969–) New Mexico
Potter

EDUCATION: Learned potting skills from her mother, Marie Juanico, mother-in-law, Wanda Aragon, and husband, Marvia Aragon, Jr.

AWARDS: Second place, Acoma jars, SWAIA (2000).

REPRESENTATION: Robert Nichols Gallery, Canyon Road, Santa Fe, New Mexico; Pueblo Pottery Gallery, San Fidel, New Mexico.

ABOUT THE ARTIST: Began creating small clay animals at the age of five. Aragon is now teaching her young son, Marvis III, how to make pottery. She works in miniature, does fine-line work, and has combined modern elements with ancient in decorating her pots.

JOHN ARAGON

Acoma; Acoma Pueblo, New Mexico
Potter

EDUCATION: Encouraged by his mother and grandmother (Lupe Aragon), John began potting at a young age.

REPRESENTATION: www.FinePuebloPottery.com; Kleywood Southwest, San Antonio, Texas.

ABOUT THE ARTIST: Because the pottery he creates is in demand, Aragon now pots year-round rather than only during the summer months, as did his grandmother. He uses the parrot design only on water jars and uses other designs for other pots, depending on the pot's shape and style. He is famous for the Mimbres designs he creates on his pots completely by hand.

WANDA ARAGON

Acoma (1948–) New Mexico
Potter

EDUCATION: Learned how to pot from her mother, Frances Torivio Pino.

AWARDS: Seed pot received second place at the Merrillville, Indiana, Art Expo 2000; water jar with parrot design received third place at the 2001 Eiteljorg Museum Indian Market; and many other awards.

REPRESENTATION: Andrea Fisher Fine Pottery, Santa Fe, New Mexico; Penfield Gallery, Albuquerque, New Mexico; Bear Creek Gallery at River Crossing, Indianapolis, Indiana.

ABOUT THE ARTIST: Wanda Aragon, Delores Aragon's mother-in-law, has taught other members of her family the time-honored traditional techniques by which she works. Other members of her family are potters, including her sister, Lillian Salvador, her mother-in-law, Daisy Aragon, her sister-in-law Rose Torivio, and her aunts. In addition to traditional pots in the Acoma style, Aragon also creates miniatures. One of the first things this artist created were pottery owls during the 1960s. Aragon made her first storyteller in the early 1970s. She also makes nativities and bird and animal figurines, all painted in the Acoma style, with traditional pottery designs.

ESTHER ARCHULETA

Santa Clara; New Mexico
Potter

EDUCATION: Learned the pottery-making tradition from her famous mother, Margaret Tafoya.

REPRESENTATION: Four Winds Gallery, Pittsburgh, Pennsylvania.

ABOUT THE ARTIST: Archuleta creates red clay pots in the traditional Santa Clara style.

MARY E. ARCHULETA

Santa Clara/San Juan; New Mexico
Pottery

EDUCATION: Learned from her mother, Margaret Tafoya.

REPRESENTATION: Four Winds Gallery, Pittsburgh, Pennsylvania; Andrea Fisher Fine Pottery, Santa Fe, New Mexico.

ABOUT THE ARTIST: Archuleta creates both the Santa Clara style pottery (she was raised there) and the San Juan style (she married into the tribe). Sometimes the two styles blend together to create a new and distinct style

JOSEPHINE ARQUERO

Cochiti (1928–) New Mexico
Potter—storytellers

EDUCATION: Learned the art of pottery-making from mother, Damacia Cordero.

AWARDS: Won an award in 1971 for a storyteller, and has won many more since that time.

REPRESENTATION: Adobe Gallery, Albuquerque, New Mexico.

ABOUT THE ARTIST: Arquero comes from a long line of potters, including her sisters, Martha and Gloria Arquero, and Marie Lewake. She made her first storyteller in 1969 and has also created human and animal figures.

MARTHA ARQUERO

Cochiti (1945–) New Mexico
Potter—storytellers

EDUCATION: Learned the art of potting from her mother, Damacia Cordero.

AWARDS: Her frog and human storytellers have won awards at such places as the Indian Market and the New Mexico State Fair.

REPRESENTATION: Kennedy Indian Arts, Bluff, Utah.

ABOUT THE ARTIST: Arquero created her first storyteller in 1975. Her whole family has been involved in pottery-making; most of them make storytellers like the ones created by their mother, Damacia Cordero. Arquero has created human and animal figures, as well as a kangaroo storyteller with a baby in its pouch (1982). In recent years she has expanded her repertoire and has added a Santa and Mrs. Santa Claus to her collection. She gathers her clay and paints from hills near her home, makes her black from wild plants, then fires the pieces with a hot fire consisting of cowchips and plenty of wood.

LINDA "JO'POVI" ASKAN

Santa Clara (1952–) Santa Clara Pueblo, New Mexico
Potter

EDUCATION: Learned how to pot from her grandmother Adelaide (Lala) Sisneros and her mother, Marie Sisneros Askan. Attended the Institute of American Indian Arts.

REPRESENTATION: Cristof's Art Gallery, Santa Fe, New Mexico.

ABOUT THE ARTIST: Askan worked as a respiratory therapy technician before becoming a full-time potter. She digs her own clay, then coils the shapes and fires them outdoors in a dung fire, as did her ancestors. Her pottery is the traditional red and black, depending on the clay slip and her firing methods. She has taught her daughters the art of pottery making. Other members of her family are also potters.

HARRISON BEGAY

(*see* biography in the "Art" chapter pg. 14–15)

CECILIA BENALLY

Navajo; Rehoboth, New Mexico
Potter

EDUCATION: Self-taught.

REPRESENTATION: Native Artists United, Thoreau, New Mexico.

Portrait of potter Linda "Jo'Povi" Askan. Courtesy of Cristof's, Santa Fe, NM.

ABOUT THE ARTIST: Benally and her husband, Anthony, make Navajo etched pottery and have been doing so since about 1995. They both come from artistic families with relatives who make rugs, pottery, jewelry, and silver items, so their talent comes naturally. She says, "Our pottery usually ranges from three inches tall, taking about thirty minutes to make, to large fifteen inch pieces that take nearly a day to make. We make some special larger pieces that often take over a day and a half to complete. We often add special designs to our work such as the Kokopelli figure, humming-birds, feathers and other geometric designs."

BLUE CORN

San Ildefonso (ca. 1923–May 3,1999) San Ildefonso, New Mexico
Potter

EDUCATION: Began making pottery at the age of three at her grandmother's knee.

REPRESENTATION: Adobe Gallery, Albuquerque, New Mexico; Andrea Fisher Pottery, Santa Fe, New Mexico.

ABOUT THE ARTIST: Blue Corn originally made only black pottery, but then she decided to do a polychrome. Though she learned how to pot at a young age, she did not formally begin making pottery until after World War II. She made her pots in the traditional way, following the same black-on-black style that Maria Martinez had made famous. As other potters, Blue Corn believed her mood influenced the pot and vice versa. Her pots are white-on-white, a hard to polish slip that's the base for her polychrome; she also made black and red pots.

AUTUMN BORTS

Santa Clara
Potter

EDUCATION: Learned her art from her mother, Linda Cain, and grandmother Mary Cain.

REPRESENTATION: King Galleries, Phoenix, Arizona; Blue Rain Gallery, Taos, New Mexico.

ABOUT THE ARTIST: Borts finds her inspiration in nature and often incorporates dragonflies, butterflies, and hummingbirds into her pottery. She uses multicolored slips, sometimes utilizing four or five different colors in her designs.

MARY CAIN
(a.k.a. Blue Rain)

Santa Clara; New Mexico
Potter

EDUCATION: Learned the Tafoya pottery tradition from her grandmother Sarafina Tafoya (Autumn Leaf), her grandfather Geronimo Tafoya (Chief White Flower), and her mother, Christina Naranjo.

REPRESENTATION: Andrea Fisher Fine Pottery, Santa Fe, New Mexico.

ABOUT THE ARTIST: Cain worked with her mother during the 1970s, and the pieces they made together are signed by both of them. Cain's daughter, Linda, and many other members of this famous pottery-making family are engaged in the business. Cain makes black polished pots. She creates traditional Santa Clara pottery in both red and black.

JOE AND BARBARA CERNO

Acoma; Acoma Pueblo, New Mexico
Potters

EDUCATION: Self-taught.

REPRESENTATION: Pueblo Arts, Scottsdale, Arizona; Blue Rain Gallery, Taos, New Mexico; Wright's Gallery of Native American Art, Albuquerque, New Mexico; Pueblo Pottery Gallery, San Fidel, New Mexico; Kennedy Gallery, Bluff, Utah.

ABOUT THE ARTISTS: This talented couple makes kiln-fired polychrome pottery. Their seed jars are often decorated with Mimbres motifs, and they create very large pottery vessels influenced by Acoma, Mimbres, and Zuni designs. They are one of the few couples still making ollas with classic decorations.

KAREN KAHE CHARLEY

Hopi; Arizona
Potter

EDUCATION: Taught to pot by her mother, Marcella Kahe.

AWARDS: Best Pottery, Museum of Northern Arizona Hopi Show (2001).

REPRESENTATION: Pueblo Arts, Scottsdale, Arizona; www.AncientNations.com.

ABOUT THE ARTIST: Charley did not begin creating pottery pieces until 1983. She uses the orange-red color that her family has kept a secret and which other Hopi potters have not yet imitated. She has shown her work at the Tulsa Indian Arts Festival in Oklahoma, the Santa Fe Indian Market in New Mexico, and Pueblo Grande in Phoenix, Arizona.

CARRIE CHINO CHARLIE

Acoma; Acoma Pueblo, New Mexico
Potter

EDUCATION: Inspired by the large seed jars Grace Chino (her aunt) has created.

REPRESENTATION: Andrea Fisher Fine Pottery, Santa Fe, New Mexico.

ABOUT THE ARTIST: Charlie, the daughter of Marie Z. Chino, is considered one of the best Acoma potters. She produces traditional ceramics made with native clay and painted with natural pigments; however, she fires her work in an electric kiln. She considers her work to be a blend of traditional and modern styles.

STELLA CHAVARRIA

Santa Clara (January 23, 1939–) New Mexico
Potter

EDUCATION: Learned her skills from the many illustrious potters in her family, the Tafoyas and Naranjos.

REPRESENTATION: Faru Gallery, St. Louis, Missouri; Pueblo Pottery Gallery, San Fidel, New Mexico.

ABOUT THE ARTIST: Daughter of Teresita Naranjo, Chavarria has learned the trade from some of the best potters in the business, her family, and is expected to become as well known as they are. She pencils in her decoration before carving it into the leather-hard clay with an old kitchen paring knife. She signs her work "Stella Chavarria, Santa Clara."

EVELYN CHEROMIAH

Laguna; Laguna Pueblo, New Mexico
Potter

EDUCATION: Self-taught.

REPRESENTATION: Tribal Expressions, Arlington Heights, Illinois; Faust Gallery, Scottsdale, Arizona; Andrea Fisher Fine Pottery, Santa Fe, New Mexico.

ABOUT THE ARTIST: When creating new pottery, Cheromiah asks her ancestors (deceased potters) for help. In her long years as a potter, she has seen the change in the way Laguna pottery was created—changes made during the advent of the tourist season, the invasion of the railroad and all it carried into the once-quiet reservations. Cheromiah was responsible for reviving the art of making large ollas at the Laguna Pueblo.

LEE ANN CHEROMIAH

Laguna; Laguna Pueblo, New Mexico
Potter

EDUCATION: Learned most of her craft from her mother, Evelyn.

REPRESENTATION: Tribal Expressions, Arlington Heights, Illinois.

ABOUT THE ARTIST: Cheromiah believes that the spirit of the clay works in conjunction with the potter's spirit, and if they agree, then the design works; if not, the pot won't come out right. The artist makes older styles of pottery. In an article called "Talking to the Clay" (*Canku Ota*, May 20, 2000, issue 10), Cheromiah explains the process of making her pottery and how she talks to the clay from the moment she gathers it throughout the process of making a pot and right up to the point where she sends the pot off into someone else's home.

GILBERT CHINO

Acoma; Acoma Pueblo, New Mexico
Potter

EDUCATION: Self-taught.

REPRESENTATION: Pueblo Pottery Gallery, San Fidel, New Mexico.

ABOUT THE ARTIST: Chino believes that today's potters are wage earners, some even manufacturing their pottery (using molds and machines rather than throwing the pots by hand), which makes the pot lose much of its value. Others, he says, put their spirit into pottery making, keeping it an art.

GRACE CHINO

Acoma; Acoma Pueblo, New Mexico
Potter

EDUCATION: Her mother, Marie Chino, taught her much of what she knows about pottery.

REPRESENTATION: Andrea Fisher Fine Pottery, Santa Fe, New Mexico; Penfield Gallery, Albuquerque, New Mexico.

ABOUT THE ARTIST: Grace was responsible for teaching many Chino family members, including her niece, Carrie Chino Charlie. Grace lets each pot "decide" which design she will use and does not believe in a "design trademark" as do many other potters of her generation.

MARIE Z. CHINO

Acoma (1907–82) Acoma Pueblo, New Mexico
Potter

EDUCATION: Self-educated.

REPRESENTATION: Pueblo Pottery Gallery, San Fidel, New Mexico.

ABOUT THE ARTIST: The matriarch of the Chino family of potters, Marie was partially responsible for the resurgence of interest in making pottery at the Acoma Pueblo. She worked with Lucy Lewis and perfected fine-line decorations. Her style of stepped designs was well known, and her daughter Grace continued the style after Marie's death.

SHIRLEY CHINO

Acoma; Acoma Pueblo
Potter

EDUCATION: Learned how to pot from family members.

REPRESENTATION: Eastern Cowboys, Scottsdale, Arizona.

ABOUT THE ARTIST: Chino creates pots in the Acoma style and is known for her nativity sets.

ALICE CLING

Navajo (1946–) Black Mesa, Arizona
Potter

EDUCATION: Learned how to pot from her mother, Rose Williams.

AWARDS: Cling has won many awards at fairs in Santa Fe, New Mexico, Flagstaff, Arizona, and other places across the country.

REPRESENTATION: Cristof's Art Gallery, Santa Fe, New Mexico.

ABOUT THE ARTIST: Cling, her mother, and aunt, Grace Barlow, have inspired many Navajo potters to make commercial art pottery. Cling's four children make pottery with her, digging the clay from a special place near Black Mesa. By screening it to rid it of impurities and mixing with sand for temper and with water to make it workable, she achieves the coloration that is obviously hers, a softly burnished and lightly pitch-coated

Pot by Shirley Chino, an Acoma potter who produces a wide variety of moderately priced pieces. She is known for her nativity sets. Courtesy of Jay Sadow and The Eastern Cowboys, Scottsdale, AZ.

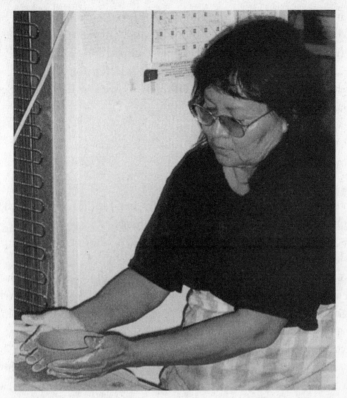

Portrait of Alice Cling working on a pot. Courtesy of Cristof's, Santa Fe, NM

surface. Her pots are usually undecorated, because she believes in letting the pigmentation of the pot serve as the pot's decoration.

KARITA COFFEY

Comanche (1947–) Oklahoma
Potter, ceramist

EDUCATION: Institute of American Indian Arts, Santa Fe, New Mexico (1965); B.F.A., University of Oklahoma (1971); teacher's certification in art and master's degree in education, University of Oklahoma.

AWARDS: Coffey's many awards and recognitions include being included in *Who's Who in American Indian Art* and the *Dictionary of International Biographies*, and she was appointed to the Native American Council of Regents of the Institute of American Indian Arts.

ABOUT THE ARTIST: Coffey makes ceramic forms that interpret the Plains

Indian culture, from the traditional forms to the contemporary. She creates different types of pots, such as sculpted tall moccasins made of clay. She has shown her work in national competitions all over the United States, and some of her works were also selected for a traveling exhibit called "Arts of Indian America," which showed in Germany, Scotland, England, and Turkey.

CAROLYN CONCHO

Acoma; Acoma Pueblo, New Mexico
Potter

EDUCATION: Inspired to make pottery by her famous grandmother, Delores S. Sanchez, and mother, Katherine Sanchez Lewis.

AWARDS: Many awards at the Santa Fe Indian Market and Gallup Intertribal.

REPRESENTATION: Penfield Gallery, Albuquerque, New Mexico; Native American Collections, Denver, Colorado; Tribal Expressions, Arlington Heights, Illinois; Reflections of Culture, Fort Atkinson, Wisconsin.

ABOUT THE ARTIST: Concho creates commercial Acoma ware that is slip-cast ceramic. She has made figurines (e.g., statues of the Virgin Mary), as well as traditional pottery like seed pots, bowls, and plates. Concho comes from the Lewis family of potters (Rebecca Lucario, Diane Lewis, and sister-in-law Sharon Lewis).

BUFFY CORDERO
(a.k.a. Buffy Cordero-Suina)

Cochiti (1969–) Cochiti Pueblo, New Mexico
Potter—storytellers

EDUCATION: Learned the trade from her grandmother Helen Cordero, as well as from a teacher at school.

REPRESENTATION: Adobe Gallery, Albuquerque, New Mexico.

ABOUT THE ARTIST: Cordero began making storytellers in about 1980 and has learned much about the art from the members of her family, most of whom are potters. She has been featured in "The Legacy of Generations: Pottery by American Indian Women," an exhibit at the National Museum of Women in the Arts.

DAMACIA CORDERO

Cochiti (1905–) Cochiti Pueblo, New Mexico
Potter—storytellers

EDUCATION: Learned from mother, Lucinda Suina.

REPRESENTATION: Adobe Gallery, Albuquerque, New Mexico.

ABOUT THE ARTIST: Cordero has kept pottery making in her family, passing on what she learned from her mother to her own daughters, Josephine Arquero, Martha Arquero, Gloria Arquero, and Marie Lewake. Cordero began creating pottery in the 1920s. Her early storytellers, made in the mid- to late 1950s and 1960s, are held by the Museum of New Mexico. These early pieces depict "singing" storytellers—figures of mothers singing to their children. One of the first shows to exhibit her work was "What Is Folk Art?," which was held in 1973 by the Museum of International Folk Art in Santa Fe.

GEORGE CORDERO

Cochiti (1944–) Cochiti Pueblo, New Mexico
Potter—storytellers

EDUCATION: Learned the trade from his mother, master storyteller creator Helen Cordero.

REPRESENTATION: Adobe Gallery, Albuquerque, New Mexico.

ABOUT THE ARTIST: He began making storytellers in 1982 and has shared what he's learned with his daughter, Buffy, his nephews Tim Cordero and Kevin Peshlakai, and his sister, Antonita Suina.

HELEN CORDERO

Cochiti (1915–94) Cochiti Pueblo, New Mexico
Potter—storytellers

EDUCATION: Learned how to make pottery from her cousin-in-law, Juanita Arquero.

AWARDS: Many throughout the years. Her first storytellers won first, second, and third prizes in 1964 at the New Mexico State Fair, and first prize in 1965 at the SWAIA's Santa Fe Indian Market.

REPRESENTATION: Adobe Gallery, Albuquerque, New Mexico.

ABOUT THE ARTIST: Cordero is the premier storyteller creator in the Southwest and has passed on her skill and technique to other family members, such as her son, George, her daughter, Tony (Antonita Suina), her grandchildren, Tim Cordero and Buffy Cordero, and her great-nephew Kevin Peshalakai. She created her first storytellers as a tribute to her grandfather Santiago Quintana. Cordero's work has been internationally exhibited and was recognized in *National Geographic* in November 1982.

TIM CORDERO

Cochiti (1963–) Cochiti Pueblo, New Mexico
Potter—storytellers

EDUCATION: Taught the traditional storytelling pottery art by his grandmother Helen Cordero.

REPRESENTATION: Adobe Gallery, Albuquerque, New Mexico.

ABOUT THE ARTIST: Cordero comes from a long line of famous potters. He made his first storyteller in 1980 while living in Cochiti with his grandmother. Like his grandmother's figures, most of Tim's adult storytellers' eyes are closed and their mouths are open. Since he (as a Cochiti) is traditionally not allowed to make clown and Kachina figures, he incorporates them into his storyteller figures.

POPOVI DA

(a.k.a. Red Fox)

San Ildefonso (1923–71) San Ildefonso Pueblo, New Mexico
Potter, silversmith

EDUCATION: Taught by his mother and father, Maria and Julian Martinez, as well as by instructors at the Santa Fe Indian School.

REPRESENTATION: Adobe Gallery, Albuquerque, New Mexico.

ABOUT THE ARTIST: The eldest son of the famous Maria and Julian Martinez, Da opened his own studio in San Ildefonso in 1948. He decorated his mother's pottery from 1953 to 1971. He also accumulated a collection of her work, which was on display at the Popovi Da Studio of Indian Art at San Ildefonso. In addition to being a potter, Da also made silver jewelry and was regarded by Santa Fe art patrons as a talented, innovative artist.

TONY DA

San Ildefonso (1940–) San Ildefonso, New Mexico
Potter, artist

EDUCATION: No formal training. Learned his traditional style from his grandmother Maria Martinez, as well as from other members of his well-known family.

REPRESENTATION: Adobe Gallery, Albuquerque, New Mexico.

ABOUT THE ARTIST: Da was one of the foremost male traditional potters before an automobile accident. He no longer pots, though he does paint. Da is considered by many to be a great innovator, and his work is still copied by today's up-and-coming potters. He uses traditional abstract designs in his work and usually chooses earth and water tones, the same colors used in Pueblo pottery. He would sign his pottery with his hallmark, a stylized "DA."

TONY DALLAS

Hopi (1956–) Arizona
Potter—storytellers

EDUCATION: Learned his trade from mother-in-law, Lucy Suina, who introduced him to pottery in 1982.

REPRESENTATION: Adobe Gallery, Albuquerque, New Mexico; Penfield Gallery, Albuquerque; Firecloud Arts, Pacifica, California; Serendipity Trading Co., Estes Park, Colorado.

ABOUT THE ARTIST: After being taught by his mother-in-law, Dallas started creating mudhead storytellers, which usually hold a bowl and have little mudheads crawling all over the larger storyteller. Since it is tradition that only Cochitis are allowed to make and sell storytellers, Dallas is unique to the craft.

RAYMOND LEE DESCHENE

Dineh (1971–) Winslow, Arizona
Potter

EDUCATION: Studied commercial arts.

REPRESENTATION: Native Reflections, Salt Lake City, Utah.

ABOUT THE ARTIST: Deschene uses an etching and airbrush technique to decorate his pottery with wildlife. Married with two children, this artist is also a singer-drummer with Indian Creek, a powwow drum group (which has a recording on the market).

DESIDER

San Ildefonso; New Mexico
Potter

EDUCATION: Learned how to pot, along with other members of her family, including Maria Martinez, her sister.

ABOUT THE ARTIST: As did her famous sister, Desider also potted and created valuable works that are in prized collections today.

JUANITA DUBRAY

Taos; Taos Pueblo, New Mexico
Potter

EDUCATION: Learned from people in the pueblo.

ABOUT THE ARTIST: DuBray began making micaceous pottery during the 1980s. At first her designs were plain, but they gradually became adorned with unique corn motifs, the symbol "of the gift of life," DuBray says. This potter often teaches classes on her art throughout the Southwest.

DEBRA TRUJILLO DUWYENIE

Santa Clara; Espanola, New Mexico
Potter

EDUCATION: Learned how to pot from her mother, Genevieve Gutierrez.

REPRESENTATION: Tribal Expressions, Arlington Heights, Illinois; King Galleries, Scottsdale, Arizona.

ABOUT THE ARTIST: Duwyenie has been potting regularly since 1979, having been brought up in the tradition. She is known for her small polished seed pots, often decorated with turtles, hummingbirds, rabbits, or sunfaces. After leaving her position as assistant to the dean of the Institute of American Indian Arts, Duwyenie started marketing to galleries and attending shows. She often creates multiple turtle designs on her pots, as well as incorporating classic Pueblo designs with feathers, mountains, clouds, and clan symbols.

VIRGINIA EBELACKER

Santa Clara; New Mexico
Potter

Selection of decorated miniature pots by Debra Trujillo Duwyenie. Courtesy of Tribal Expressions, Arlington Heights, IL.

EDUCATION: Taught by her mother, the well-known potter Margaret Tafoya.

AWARDS: Many awards and blue ribbons at SWAIA.

REPRESENTATION: Gallery Adobe East, DelRay Beach, Florida; Andrea Fisher Fine Pottery, Santa Fe, New Mexico.

ABOUT THE ARTIST: Ebelacker is well known for her very large highly polished black and sienna storage jars and wedding vases. Her pieces often measured 16 inches in diameter or more. Ebelacker's work has become collectible and will be more so with the passage of time. Her pottery is becoming more rare.

GRACE MEDICINE FLOWER
(a.k.a. Wopovi, "Medicine Flower")

Santa Clara (1938–) Santa Clara Pueblo, New Mexico
Potter

EDUCATION: Learned the trade from her famous father, Camilio Tafoya, one of the first male potters in the pueblo, and from her mother.

REPRESENTATION: Canyon Country Originals, Tucson, Arizona.

ABOUT THE ARTIST: She uses an incised style of decoration on her miniature pottery, often embellishing it with feathers, flowers, or butterflies. Her brother, Joseph Lonewolf, also uses this style. She works in both black and red and is one branch of the family who popularized the sgraffito style. Her tools were made by her father, and she bakes the clay the traditional way.

JODY FOLWELL

Santa Clara (1942–) Santa Clara, New Mexico
Potter

EDUCATION: Learned a lot of her technique from her famous family, the Naranjos.

REPRESENTATION: Gallery 10 (Lee Cohen), New York; Andrea Fisher Fine Pottery, Santa Fe, New Mexico; Grey Dog Trading, Tucson, Arizona.

ABOUT THE ARTIST: Folwell feels that her pottery pieces are spiritual creations, as if they molded themselves. She also believes that the people who pick up a piece of pottery will feel the spiritual power. She has taken many traditional Santa Clara styles and made them abstract. She often gets inspiration from ancient ruins like those at Chaco Canyon, New Mexico. Lee Cohen, the owner of Gallery 10, once called Folwell the first "impressionist potter." She often brings her political and spiritual beliefs into her work.

B. J. FRAGUA
(a.k.a. Betty-Jean Fragua)

Jemez
Potter

EDUCATION: Learned how to pot from her mother, Juanita.

REPRESENTATION: Tribal Expressions, Arlington Heights, Illinois.

ABOUT THE ARTIST: Fragua comes from a family of potters and learned the basics from her mother before developing her own distinctive style. Her pots are often white backgrounds with beige or brown banded designs. She creates lidded pots, as well as vases.

GLENDORA FRAGUA

Jemez; New Mexico
Potter

Corn Maiden pot by BJ Fragua. Painted recessed sections of this pot combined with traditional Pueblo designs. $1500. Courtesy of Tribal Expressions, Arlington Heights, IL.

Lidded pot by BJ Fragua. A simple cloud design was painted into the recessed area of this pot. 8" × 6½". $250. Courtesy of Tribal Expressions, Arlington Heights, IL.

Kiva Pot by Glendora
Fragua. Carved and painted.
5" × 2½". Courtesy of Tribal
Expressions, Arlington
Heights, IL.

Lidded turtle vase by
Glendora Fragua. Carved
and inlaid with red coral.
7" × 4". $1000. Courtesy of
Tribal Expressions,
Arlington Heights, IL.

EDUCATION: Learned how to pot from her mother, Juanita.

REPRESENTATION: Tribal Expressions, Arlington Heights, Illinois.

ABOUT THE ARTIST: Fragua comes from a family of potters and learned the basics from her mother before developing her own distinctive style. She often incorporates turtle designs in her work.

JUANITA C. FRAGUA

Jemez; New Mexico
Potter

EDUCATION: Fragua often studies the old pots to get design ideas, but credits Al Momaday (N. Scott Momaday's father) for teaching her how to draw.

REPRESENTATION: Jewels of Clay, Scottsdale, Arizona; Penfield Gallery, Albuquerque, New Mexico.

ABOUT THE ARTIST: A member of the Corn clan, Fragua often uses corn designs on her pottery. She has been making pottery for approximately 25 years. Her pieces are painted with soft gray-blues, tans, and chalky whites. She introduced melon bowls to the Jemez Pueblo and is best known for those pieces. Fragua's children are following in their mother's footsteps and becoming well-known potters in their own rights.

CANDELARIA GACHUPIN

Zia (1908–) New Mexico
Potter

EDUCATION: Learned her skills from her family (she's a fifth-generation potter).

REPRESENTATION: Pueblo Arts, Scottsdale, Arizona.

ABOUT THE ARTIST: Gachupin passed her pottery-making knowledge on to her daughter Dora Tse Pe Pena. She often told her children that if a pot is ruined in the process of creation, it just wasn't meant to be.

DELORES LEWIS GARCIA

Acoma; Acoma Pueblo, New Mexico
Potter

EDUCATION: Taught by her mother, famous potter Lucy Lewis.

REPRESENTATION: Andrea Fisher Fine Pottery, Santa Fe, New Mexico; Adobe Gallery, Albuquerque, New Mexico; King Galleries, Scottsdale, Arizona.

ABOUT THE ARTIST: Garcia is a traditional potter who says that the deer design, which has a spiritual and symbolic connection to the tribe, is an important symbol to their pottery. She also believes that you can't copy another's pottery because it will never be the same. Garcia was one of the subjects of a video produced in 1990 by John Anthony entitled *Daughters of the Anasazi*.

GOLDENROD GARCIA

Santa Clara (1942–) New Mexico
Potter

EDUCATION: Learned the trade from her mother, Petra Gutierrez, as well as other members of her family.

ABOUT THE ARTIST: Actively potting since 1972, Garcia comes from a large family of potters—her mother and all of her sisters. She creates sgraffito blackware and redware pots decorated with animals and traditional Native symbols.

JOANNE CHINO GARCIA

Acoma; Acoma Pueblo, New Mexico
Potter

EDUCATION: The granddaughter of the late Marie Z. Chino and daughter 'of Carrie Chino Charlie, Garcia learned how to pot from the experts in her family.

REPRESENTATION: Penfield Gallery, Albuquerque, New Mexico.

ABOUT THE ARTIST: Garcia considers seed jars created by Grace Chino, her aunt, some of the most beautiful made.

TAMMY GARCIA

Santa Clara; Santa Clara Pueblo, New Mexico
Potter

EDUCATION: Learned from family members.

REPRESENTATION: King Galleries, Scottsdale, Arizona; Blue Rain Gallery.

ABOUT THE ARTIST: Garcia comes from a long line of artists and believes, as most potters do, that the clay has a life of its own and can decide whether or not it wants to cooperate. She respects the clay and appreciates her own ability to work with it. In addition to pottery, she also sculpts. Her tendency is to use the entire surface of the pot, to decorate all of it rather than one simple band.

CORDI AND GLEN GOMEZ

Pojoaque; Pojoaque Pueblo, New Mexico
Potters

EDUCATION: Cordi learned how to pot from her mother. Cordi has passed on her skills to her son, Glen.

ABOUT THE ARTISTS: This mother-and-son team produces small- to medium-sized micaceous pots. Glen's innovative designs include subtle diagonal textures on the exterior of his pots. Cordi makes Indian bread and molding pots. She works out of her kitchen in the Pojoaque Pueblo.

BARBARA GONZALES

San Ildefonso; San Ildefonso Pueblo, New Mexico
Potter

EDUCATION: Learned how to pot with other members of her family, including Maria Martinez, her great-grandmother.

REPRESENTATION: Penfield Gallery, Albuquerque, New Mexico.

ABOUT THE ARTIST: Gonzales learned her trade from her illustrious family and has created works that are valued by collectors all over the world. In the 1950s and 1960s, Gonzales revived the painted polychrome designs that Popovi Da, Maria Martinez's son, had used.

JOHN GONZALES

San Ildefonso (1955–) San Ildefonso Pueblo, New Mexico
Potter

EDUCATION: B.A., Stanford University (1980); master's degree, city planning, M.I.T. (1982). Learned pottery from his father, Lorenzo.

AWARDS: Quail Run Fellowship, SWAIA, Santa Fe, New Mexico (1994); first, sgraffito with stone or metal, Santa Fe Indian Market (1994); Up and Coming Pottery Artist, ENIPC Arts and Crafts Show (1994); third place, sgraffito with stone or metal, Santa Fe Indian Market (1996); Honorable Mention, sgraffito, all other, Santa Fe Indian Market (1998); first place, sgraffito with stones, Santa Fe Indian Market (2000). Inducted into the Stanford University American Indian Hall of Fame (October 1998).

REPRESENTATION: John Gonzales Pottery, Santa Fe, New Mexico.

ABOUT THE ARTIST: Gonzales has had a varied career and is politically involved with his tribe now, acting as governor. He started creating pottery in the 1990s and quickly became known for his sgraffito work. Currently, he's concentrating more on his leadership with the pueblo, though he still maintains a Web site (www.sanildefonso.com) with examples of his and other potters' work.

ROSE GONZALES

San Ildefonso (1900–89) San Ildefonso Pueblo, New Mexico
Potter

EDUCATION: Learned how to make pottery from her mother-in-law, Ramona Sanchez Gonzalez.

ABOUT THE ARTIST: An innovator in the art of pottery, Gonzales came from San Juan when she married a man from the San Ildefonso tribe in 1920. She was inspired to create pottery in the 1930s after seeing some old carved pottery shards. Her pottery has a distinctive rounded edge. Unlike other potters from San Ildefonso who painted their designs into the pots, she made the first carved and modern pottery at the pueblo and is considered an innovative and important potter. Gonzales taught her son Tse-Pe and his wife, Dora, as well as teaching classes on pottery making at the pueblo.

LOIS GUTIERREZ DE LA CRUZ

Santa Clara; New Mexico
Potter

EDUCATION: Learned how to pot from her mother, Petra Montoya Gutierrez.

REPRESENTATION: Modo Gallery, Hudson, New York; Kleywood Southwest, San Antonio, Texas.

ABOUT THE ARTIST: Gutierrez's husband, Derek de la Cruz, helps her gather clay. When she began potting, they were partners; now she signs the pottery herself. She uses smoothing stones passed down through her family and uses a symbol of the four sacred Tewa mountains on the rim of her pots. Her pottery is polychrome, a distinct buff color, and she often decorates her pieces with lizards, hummingbirds, or humpbacked flute players.

MARGARET AND LUTHER GUTIERREZ

Santa Clara (Margaret: 1936–) (Luther: –1987) New Mexico
Potters

EDUCATION: Learned from Lela and Van Gutierrez, responsible for modifying a polychrome method that is distinctly their own.

REPRESENTATION: Adobe Gallery, Albuquerque, New Mexico.

ABOUT THE ARTISTS: This couple (brother and sister) is carrying on the work of their parents (Lela and Van). Their mother worked with Luther from 1960 until her death in 1969. Luther and Margaret worked together until 1984. Using a red base and a tan background, they painted their designs in pastels. Their clay sources are secret. They were recognized during the 1960s–70s for their polychrome pottery.

PETRA GUTIERREZ

Santa Clara; New Mexico
Potter

EDUCATION: Self-taught.

ABOUT THE ARTIST: Gutierrez's whole family is involved with pottery: daughters, Minnie Vigil, Goldenrod Garcia, Thelma Talachy, and Lois Gutierrez, and daughter-in-law Virginia Gutierrez. Her daughters are half Santa Clara and half Pojoaque.

STEPHANIE GUTIERREZ

Santa Clara; New Mexico
Potter

EDUCATION: Learned the distinctive Gutierrez style from her grandfather Luther Gutierrez.

ABOUT THE ARTIST: Gutierrez is the fourth generation of her potting family. She carries on the tradition of polishing her pots with a rag instead of a stone, giving the pottery a silky feel.

VIRGINIA GUTIERREZ

Nambe/Pojoaque; Arizona
Potter

EDUCATION: Virginia's aunt, the last working Nambe potter, taught her how to work the clay.

REPRESENTATION: Andrea Fisher Fine Pottery, Santa Fe, New Mexico.

ABOUT THE ARTIST: Gutierrez married into the Santa Clara Pueblo, but her design is distinctive: part Nambe (where she learned) and part her own. Her artwork is complex, created on clays from Nambe and Pojoaque, sand from Nambe, and paints from northern New Mexico. She does not polish her pottery and frequently creates seed jars.

NATHAN HART

Cheyenne
Potter

Pots by Nathan Hart and Harrison Begay. Courtesy of Tribal Expressions, Arlington Heights, IL.

EDUCATION: B.S., Bethel College, North Newton, Kansas.

REPRESENTATION: King Galleries, Scottsdale, Arizona.

ABOUT THE ARTIST: Hart's bowls and other pieces resemble pottery, thus he is grouped with pottery artists even though his "pots" are actually made of wood. He is a content development and exhibit design consultant to Ralph Appelbaum Associates, New York City, for their work on the exhibit and interpretive design for the Cultural Center and Museum of the Native American Cultural and Education Authority in Oklahoma City, Oklahoma. Before devoting his time to his art, Hart was the executive vice president for Raven Asset Management, a Native-owned investment advisory firm headquartered in Juneau, Alaska.

DAISY HOOEE

Hopi-Tewa (1910–1994) Arizona
Potter

EDUCATION: Hooee's grandmother Nampeyo taught her how to paint freehand. Hooee studied ceramics in Paris for two years in the 1920s.

REPRESENTATION: Canyon Country Originals, Tucson, Arizona.

ABOUT THE ARTIST: Hooee painted the same way her grandmother taught her, in the early 1900s. Though born a Hopi, Hooee married a Zuni man and went to live in the Zuni Pueblo, where she was responsible for reviving Zuni pottery in the 1940s. As a craftsperson, Hooee taught young pottery artists and urged them to use the old ways instead of the commercial clay. She worked with students in the Zuni high school during the 1960s–70s. Her work is signed "Nampeyo" to honor her grandmother.

RONDINA HUMA

Hopi/Tewa; Arizona
Potter

AWARDS: Many awards, including Best of Show at Santa Fe Indian Market (1996).

REPRESENTATION: Pueblo Arts, Scottsdale, Arizona; 4Peaks Gallery.com; Andrea Fisher Fine Pottery, Santa Fe, New Mexico.

ABOUT THE ARTIST: Huma believes, as do other potters, that firing problems can mean something bad will happen within the family. She is well known for her intricate Sikyatki designs. Her work is highly collectible and priced dearly.

HARRISON JUAN

Dineh (March 1, 1953–   ) Lake Valley, New Mexico
Potter, painter—airbrush work, watercolors, oils, acrylics, sand; sculptor, carver—stone, wood, and etchings.

EDUCATION: A.A., elementary education and recreation.

AWARDS: Juan's awards include first place honors in Woodburning Art and Pencil Sketch, Oil/Acrylic (mixed) and Painting at the Indian Arts Festival in Farmington, New Mexico (1994).

REPRESENTATION: Native Reflections, Salt Lake City, Utah; Indian Summer Native American Art, Salt Lake City, Utah.

ABOUT THE ARTIST: Juan is of the Mountain clan and the Folding Arm People. He has been commissioned to do murals at La Vida Mission in New Mexico. A versatile artist, Juan does shows in New Mexico and has sold his work to collectors all over the United States.

MARIE JUANICO

Acoma; Acoma Pueblo, New Mexico
Potter

EDUCATION: Learned from her mother, Delores Sanchez.

REPRESENTATION: Robert F. Nichols Gallery, Canyon Road, Santa Fe, New Mexico; Adobe Gallery, Albuquerque, New Mexico.

ABOUT THE ARTIST: Juanico began making pottery at the age of four. Today she incorporates both traditional and complex Mimbres designs into her work, passing on what she has learned to her daughter (Delores Aragon). Juanico digs and mixes her own clay, makes her own colors, and creates her pots by hand. She strongly believes that Acoma potters should return to original, traditional techniques and use their ancient language (Tewa).

MARCELLA KAHE

Hopi; Arizona
Potter

EDUCATION: Self-taught.

REPRESENTATION: Andrea Fisher Fine Pottery, Santa Fe, New Mexico.

ABOUT THE ARTIST: Kahe is the mother of Karen Kahe Charley and has taught her daughter about the art of potting. Kahe has shown her work at most of the Southwestern markets and is a highly respected master potter.

JUANA LENO

Acoma (1917–2000) New Mexico
Potter

REPRESENTATION: Adobe Gallery, Albuquerque, New Mexico; Andrea Fisher Fine Pottery, Santa Fe, New Mexico.

ABOUT THE ARTIST: When Leno and her family knead the clay for her pottery, they leave their sneakers on. Most potters do their kneading barefoot. Considered a matriarch of Acoma potters, she was one of the last Acoma potters to do outdoor firings. She signed her work "Mrs. Juana Leno." Her daughter, Rose, continues to create pottery in the Leno tradition.

IVAN AND RITA LEWIS

Ivan: *Acoma* (1919–) New Mexico
Rita: *Cochiti* (1920–) New Mexico
Potters—storytellers

EDUCATION: Both members of this husband-and-wife team are self-taught potters. Ivan observed his mother, Lucy Lewis, while Rita observed her mother, Ascencion Banada.

AWARDS: Rita started making storytellers in 1973 with Ivan, and they have been steadily winning awards at the Indian Market in Santa Fe, New Mexico, ever since.

ABOUT THE ARTISTS: This pair comes from a long line of potters on both sides of the family. In the 1980s Ivan became known for his reproductions of 19th-century Cochiti caricatures. Rita assisted him in copying the designs, but she has her own ideas about the contemporary storyteller designs. Their daughter, Patricia, and daughter-in-law, Mary, have also made storyteller figures.

LUCY M. LEWIS

Acoma (ca. 1890/99–1992) Acoma Pueblo, New Mexico
Potter

EDUCATION: Self-taught; influenced by polychrome pottery she saw in the kiva. Studied Mimbres and Anasazi pottery at the Museum of New Mexico.

AWARDS: Lewis's awards are many, and they include honors from the governor of New Mexico (1983); the American Craft Council Gold Medal (1985); a citation from the College Art Association Women's Caucus

(1992); as well as being invited to the Nixon White House, being a guest on television programs, and having her work held by many museums.

REPRESENTATION: Adobe Gallery, Albuquerque, New Mexico.

ABOUT THE ARTIST: Lewis, the best known of the Acoma potters (other than Maria Martinez), exhibited her pottery in solo shows and at Indian markets, taught and demonstrated traditional pottery at the Idyllwild School of Music and the Arts in California, and made inroads for the many Acoma potters who've followed her. Her children, Emma, Dolores, Ivan, and Andrew, are continuing her tradition by making pottery from the secret place where Lewis always gathered her clay. Her style was white-painted decoration on black pottery.

HAROLD LITTLEBIRD

Santo Domingo/Laguna (1951–)
Potter—stoneware, ceramics; poet

ABOUT THE ARTIST: Littlebird's work is reminiscent of pre-Columbian vessels, but he uses pastels rather than earth tones. The process he uses is called "sealed earth," or "terrasigilatta." He calls his work "skyscapes." He travels and does storytelling for schools and other organizations.

JOSEPH LONEWOLF

Santa Clara (January 26, 1932–) New Mexico
Potter

EDUCATION: Learned the trade from his famous father, Camilio Tafoya, and from his mother, Agapita Silva. Lonewolf has begun passing on his art to his own children.

REPRESENTATION: Mesa Verde Pottery, Cortez, Colorado; Andrea Fisher Fine Pottery, Santa Fe, New Mexico.

ABOUT THE ARTIST: Lonewolf started his pottery-making career in 1971 when he experienced a back injury. An innovative potter, he uses an incised style of decoration on his pots, which are, for the most part, miniatures. He doesn't use any contemporary tools, preferring to create his work the traditional way. His pottery is often decorated with wildlife and ancient symbolism, and his pieces are often called "pottery jewels." Though pottery is his first love, Lonewolf also learned beadwork, drawing, painting, clay work, and woodwork from family members. His sister, Grace Medicine Flower, also uses the same type of incised decoration on her pots.

ROSEMARY "APPLE BLOSSOM" LONEWOLF

Santa Clara; New Mexico
Potter

EDUCATION: Learned the pottery-making tradition from her father, Joseph Lonewolf.
AWARDS: Visual Arts Fellowship, Arizona Commission on the Arts (1994).
REPRESENTATION: Modo Gallery, Hudson, New York.
ABOUT THE ARTIST: Like the other potters in her family, Lonewolf makes miniature pieces with incised decorations. She uses traditional designs in her pottery and hand mines and mixes the clay she uses. She explores both traditional and contemporary themes in her work, often incorporating her mixed heritage (Pueblo Indian/Scotch/Irish) into those themes.

CAROLINE LUCARIO

Acoma (September 3, 1946–)
Potter

EDUCATION: Learned from her mother and taught herself.
REPRESENTATION: Native Artists United, Thoreau, New Mexico.
ABOUT THE ARTIST: Began potting in the late 1980s after watching her mother and others create admirable pots. Taking a hint from her mother, Lucario began making pots in the same tradition that her mother and grandmother did. She is a true recycler, creating new pots from the shards of old ones. Lucario takes her pots to Old Acoma to sell, in the same manner as her mother did.

JUANITA MANYGOATS

Hunkpapa Sioux; Standing Rock Reservation, North Dakota
Potter, beader

EDUCATION: Her aunt, Alice Blackhorse, inspired this artist.
REPRESENTATION: Native Artists United, Thoreau, New Mexico.
ABOUT THE ARTIST: Manygoats started doing beadwork at the age of 13, and she now creates beaded necklaces, barrettes, bolo ties, chokers, and earrings. She uses the old style of beading patterns, but she creates her own designs. Manygoats takes her work to her customers, enjoying the interaction of being in business for herself.

MARY MARTIN

Cochiti (1927–   ) New Mexico
Potter—storytellers

EDUCATION: Learned the art of pottery from her friend Dorothy Trujillo.

ABOUT THE ARTIST: Martin's family has potted for generations; for example, some of the artists include her grandmother Seferina Suina, her
cousins, Seferina Ortiz and Ada Suina, and her daughters, Gladys Martin
and Adrienne Martin. Martin has also passed on her experience to Kathy
Trujillo. Martin made her first storyteller in 1974 and has since made a variety of storytellers, nativities, and drummers.

JULIAN MARTINEZ

San Ildefonso (1879–1943) San Ildefonso Pueblo, New Mexico
Potter, painter

EDUCATION: He worked alongside his famous wife, Maria Martinez.

REPRESENTATION: Adobe Gallery, Albuquerque, New Mexico; Blue Deer
Gallery, Dallas/Fort Worth, Texas.

ABOUT THE ARTIST: Martinez worked as a painter, influencing other Pueblo
artists with his simplistic style, but he's best known as partner to his famous
potter wife, Maria. In 1919 Martinez perfected the technique of painting
pots with a matte black design that became his and his wife's trademark.
He also discovered the *puname* and *avanyu* designs that became distinctive
of San Ildefonso pottery. When he worked with Maria, she polished the
pottery, while he painted the designs. After he died in 1943, other members
of Maria's family took over the jobs that he had originally done.

MARIA MONTOYA MARTINEZ

San Ildefonso (1881/87–1980) San Ildefonso Pueblo, New Mexico
Potter—black-on-black

EDUCATION: Taught by her aunt Nicolasa how to make cookware and
everyday ceremonial vessels.

AWARDS: Numerous, including two honorary doctorates: New Mexico State
University (1971); Columbia College (1977).

REPRESENTATION: Adobe Gallery, Albuquerque, New Mexico; Freeport
Art Museum and Cultural Center, Freeport, Illinois.

ABOUT THE ARTIST: Maria worked with her husband, Julian, as well as
working with and/or teaching her son Popovi Da, her sister, Clara, her
daughter-in-law (her son Adam's wife) Santana, her grandson, Tony Da,

her sisters Maximiliana and Desider, as well as her great-granddaughter, Barbara Gonzales. With her husband she perfected the black-on-black process/design that has become her signature. Most consider Maria the greatest Native American potter of all times. She showed her pottery all over the world and met presidents, movie stars, and international celebrities, from 1904 to her death. Her work is held by both national and international museums.

SANTANA AND ADAM MARTINEZ

San Ildefonso (Santana: 1909–February 4, 2002) (Adam: 1904–January 21, 2000) San Ildefonso Pueblo, New Mexico
Potters

EDUCATION: Santana learned how to decorate pottery by working with her famous mother-in-law, Maria Martinez.

ABOUT THE ARTISTS: Santana found mixing the clay and temper the hardest step of making pottery. She decorated pots for Maria Martinez after Julian, Maria's husband, died in 1943. Adam and Santana worked together to produce pots after Maria died. Examples of their pottery can be found in museums throughout the world, including the Smithsonian.

MAXIMILIANA

San Ildefonso; San Ildefonso Pueblo, New Mexico
Potter

EDUCATION: Learned how to pot from members of her family, including Maria Martinez, her younger sister.

ABOUT THE ARTIST: A formidable potter in her own right, Maximiliana created valuable works that are held by museums and galleries throughout the United States.

CHRISTINE NOFCHISSEY MCHORSE

Navajo (December 21, 1948–) Morenci, Arizona
Potter

EDUCATION: McHorse was influenced by her husband, Joel McHorse (Taos), who learned pottery from his grandmother Lena Archuleta. Institute of American Indian Arts (1963–67).

AWARDS: Best of Class Award, Santa Fe Indian Market (1994); Challenge Award, Santa Fe Indian Market (1996). Many shows and museum holdings, including Museum of Indian Arts and Culture, Santa Fe, New Mexico, and Denver Museum of Natural History, Denver, Colorado.

REPRESENTATION: Jerome Evans Gallery, Lake Tahoe, Nevada; Nofchissey-McHorse Studio, Santa Fe, New Mexico.

ABOUT THE ARTIST: McHorse creates micaceous pottery that combines the influences of several tribes' cultures. Some of her pieces are quite large (25 inches tall) and sound like glass when tapped. She designs her work specially to highlight the beauty of the micaceous clay.

LUCY LEUPPE MCKELVEY

Navajo
Potter

EDUCATION: Learned how to pot while in college in 1973.

AWARDS: Has been showing at the Santa Fe Indian Market since 1975 and has won numerous awards for her work.

REPRESENTATION: Elk Ridge Art Gallery, Golden, Colorado; Kleywood Southwest, San Antonio, Texas.

ABOUT THE ARTIST: This potter uses rug designs, wedding baskets, and supernatural spirits in her pottery. She has caused collectors to take a new look at traditional Navajo pottery. She and her daughters (Cecilia, Celeste, and Celinda) use sandpaintings and Anasazi designs on their pots. The girls put themselves through college by selling their pottery.

ELIZABETH MEDINA

Zia; Arizona
Potter

EDUCATION: Learned some of her skill from working with her mother.

AWARDS: Many awards and honors at the Santa Fe Indian Market.

REPRESENTATION: Elk Ridge Art Gallery, Golden, Colorado.

ABOUT THE ARTIST: Medina makes sure to fire her pots carefully in order to get the right color and no smudges on her decorated pots. She decorates her pots the traditional family way, on a beige slip. Her husband, Marcellus, paints her traditional pots with highly detailed visions of Indian dancers.

EMMA MITCHELL

Acoma; New Mexico
Potter

EDUCATION: Learned from other family members.

ABOUT THE ARTIST: Mitchell, her mother, and her sister all use Argentine corned beef tins as scrapers and trimmers. When Mitchell has a few pots ready, she lines them up and decides which design to use. She was one of the potters represented in a video entitled *Daughters of the Anasazi* (produced and directed by John Anthony).

EUDORA MONTOYA

Santa Ana; New Mexico
Potter

EDUCATION: Learned how to pot with her sisters after their mother died.
REPRESENTATION: Andrea Fisher Fine Pottery, Santa Fe, New Mexico.
ABOUT THE ARTIST: Montoya is responsible for keeping Santa Ana pottery alive. She makes bowls and water jars the old way, using the ancient designs, collects her red and gray clay, as well as her fine sand, from Santa Ana, but buys her white slip from the Zia Pueblo. She has begun teaching some of the other women in the village so that they may continue the Santa Ana pottery tradition.

SYLVIA NAHA

Hopi (1951–August 1999)
Potter

EDUCATION: Naha learned from her mother, Helen (Feather Woman).
AWARDS: Many awards and has been mentioned in quite a few books on pottery.
REPRESENTATION: Gallery of the American West, Old Sacramento, California.
ABOUT THE ARTIST: Naha is the daughter of Helen and Archie Naha and granddaughter of Paqua Naha. (Helen was called Feather Woman, and Paqua Naha is the original Frog Woman.) Sylvia used Mimbres designs in her work and signed her name with a feather and an "S"—her children also use the same signature: a feather and the first letter of their name.

BESSIE NAMOKI

Hopi; Arizona
Potter

EDUCATION: Learned some of her skills from her mother.
ABOUT THE ARTIST: Namoki uses a polishing stone that her mother had

used before her. She makes her pottery the old way, shaping the clay by hand and painting with a yucca brush.

NAMPEYO
(a.k.a. Snake Girl)
Hopi/Tewa (1859/60–1942) New Mexico
Potter

EDUCATION: Self-taught.

ABOUT THE ARTIST: Nampeyo studied pottery from an early age. During her 20s, she searched archaeological remains and used the shards of Anasazi pottery as a tool for learning her own way of decorating. Using those shards, she searched for a new way of making, mixing, and molding clay. Her exploration brought forth a totally different look in Hopi pottery than what had existed before. She became known as the foremost Hopi pottery and was at the height of her fame from approximately 1901 to 1910. Her granddaughter, Daisy Hooee, signed her work "Nampeyo" in honor of her grandmother.

CHRISTINA NARANJO
Santa Clara (1891–1980) New Mexico
Potter

EDUCATION: Learned the Tafoya potting tradition from her mother, Sarafina Tafoya. Her whole family learned how to pot (sister is Margaret Tafoya and brother is Camilio Tafoya).

REPRESENTATION: Blue Rain Gallery, Taos, New Mexico; Adobe Gallery, Albuquerque, New Mexico.

ABOUT THE ARTIST: Naranjo worked with her daughter, Mary Cain (in the 1970s), and taught other members of her family (including her daughter Teresita, and her granddaughters, Linda, Stella Chavarria and Sharon Naranjo Garcia) the Tafoya potting tradition. She often signed her work "Tina Naranjo."

GERI NARANJO
Santa Clara (August 6, 1952–) Santa Clara, New Mexico
Potter

EDUCATION: Learned from her mother, Ursulita S. Naranjo.

AWARDS: Best of Miniature Pottery awards at Santa Fe, and many others at other fairs including the New Mexico State Fair and the Gallup Intertribal Ceremonial.

REPRESENTATION: Cristof's, Santa Fe, New Mexico.

ABOUT THE ARTIST: Naranjo's family has been working pottery for generations, and she began working with clay herself at a very young age. She digs her clay near the pueblo, forms her pottery by hand, and polishes the pieces in the traditional way, with a river stone. She etches her designs into the pieces in a style called Sgraffiti, then fires the pots in an outdoor oven, smothering the pieces at the right time to create black pottery.

JODY NARANJO

Santa Clara

Potter

EDUCATION: Learned from her family members, most of whom are celebrated potters.

AWARDS: Fellowship, SWAIA; first place, contemporary scraffito, Santa Fe Indian Market.

REPRESENTATION: Tribal Expressions, Arlington Heights, Illinois.

ABOUT THE ARTIST: An innovative and talented member of the new generation of potters, Naranjo combines traditional and contemporary designs on her pots. She mixes her clay and fires the pots in the traditional way. Her designs are carved into her pottery with an Exacto knife and often represent Naranjo's memories of events in her life.

Navajo Waterbirds pot by Jody Naranjo. 18 water birds encircle this 5" × 5" pot. $1250. Courtesy of Tribal Expressions, Arlington Heights, IL.

"Motherhood" pot by Jody Naranjo. Courtesy of Tribal Expressions, Arlington Heights, IL.

LOUIS AND VIRGINIA NARANJO

Cochiti (Louis: 1932–) (Virginia: 1932–) New Mexico
Potters—storytellers

EDUCATION: Louis taught himself the art of pottery by watching his mother, Frances Suina; Virginia also learned by watching Suina.

AWARDS: In 1973 Virginia won an award for one of her turtle storytellers. Together, the Naranjos have won many awards for their pottery.

REPRESENTATION: Adobe Gallery, Albuquerque, New Mexico; Andrea Fisher Fine Pottery, Santa Fe, New Mexico; Blue Rain Gallery, Taos, New Mexico

ABOUT THE ARTISTS: This husband-and-wife team, who made their first storyteller in 1974, are known for their nativity and storyteller figures. Their storytellers are unique because they feature animals. Louis was the first potter who made bear storytellers.

MONICA NARANJO

Santa Clara (1976–) Santa Clara Pueblo, New Mexico
Potter

EDUCATION: Learned pottery making from her mother, Geri Naranjo.

AWARDS: Best of Miniature Pottery Division, Santa Fe Indian Market; awards at prestigious juried shows.

REPRESENTATION: Cristof's Art Gallery, Santa Fe, New Mexico.

ABOUT THE ARTIST: Naranjo has been working with clay since she was very young. Like her mother, she forms her clay by hand and polishes it in a technique called Sgraffiti.
 She and her mother both use traditional designs such as *avanyu* and share their tools as well as their polishing rocks.

ROSE NARANJO

Santa Clara/Laguna (1917–) New Mexico
Potter

EDUCATION: Self-taught.

AWARDS: Named one of Santa Fe's Living Treasures in 1994.

ABOUT THE ARTIST: Naranjo raised 10 children and taught them all to pot, while also making sure they all went to college. Some of those children went on to become established artists in their own right, such as Michael Naranjo, Teresita Naranjo, Rina Swentzell, Jody Folwell, and Nora

Naranjo-Morse. She is considered one of the matriarchs of Santa Clara. Naranjo feels the day she fires her pots is "Judgement Day," the time when she can see whether her work will come out the way she wishes. She likes to make wedding vases.

TERESITA NARANJO
Santa Clara (1919–99) New Mexico
Potter

EDUCATION: Learned the Tafoya pottery tradition from her mother, Christina Naranjo.

REPRESENTATION: Andrea Fisher Fine Pottery, Santa Fe, New Mexico; Adobe Gallery, Albuquerque, New Mexico; Gallery Adobe East, Delray Beach, Florida.

ABOUT THE ARTIST: Naranjo started making a living from her pottery in 1957. She created carved and polished black pottery and was in great demand at shows and galleries. Her daughter, Stella Chavarria, continues the family pottery tradition.

NORA NARANJO-MORSE
Santa Clara/Tewa (October 27, 1953–) Santa Clara Pueblo, New Mexico
Artist, sculptor, silversmith, poet

EDUCATION: Bachelor of University Studies degree, College of Santa Fe (1980); silversmithing program, Institute of American Indian Arts, Santa Fe (1991). Learned how to work clay from Jody Folwell.

AWARDS: Starting in 1979 with a third place award in clay sculpture at the SWAIA Indian Market in Santa Fe, Naranjo-Morse has won awards for her clay sculptures, forms, and scenes, as well as for ceramic sculpture, and has had her poems published in many anthologies and books. Dublin Fellow, Indian Arts Research Center (2000).

REPRESENTATION: American Indian Contemporary Arts, San Francisco.

ABOUT THE ARTIST: Naranjo-Morse is the youngest child of Rose Naranjo, a well-known Santa Clara/Laguna potter. Her eight siblings have been potters, at one point or another. This well-versed artist has a wide range of abilities and interests. She has acted as artist-in-residence at the Santa Fe Indian School, teaching pottery techniques; has held workshops in basic silk-screening and the culture of the Native Americans; has toured Europe to teach pottery; has given poetry readings throughout the United States; and has held one-woman as well as group exhibits.

CHARMAE SHIELDS NATSEWAY

Acoma (August 1, 1958–) Acoma, New Mexico
Potter

EDUCATION: Learned pottery from her family.

AWARDS: Many awards from fairs throughout the country.

REPRESENTATION: Cristof's Art Gallery, Santa Fe, New Mexico.

ABOUT THE ARTIST: Natseway creates unusual and original designs and
    shapes when potting. Her seed pots have been made in a flat, circular
    form, and she's also made cube and pyramid designed pots. She started
    potting in 1976, after being taught by her mother. She gets her inspira-
    tion from prehistoric pottery, but then takes her own ideas and incorpo-
    rates them into her work. She is married to another potter, Thomas
    Natseway.

THOMAS G. NATSEWAY

Laguna (April 19, 1953–) Laguna Pueblo, New Mexico
Potter

EDUCATION: Taught by Ethel Shields and her daughter Charmae Shields
    Natseway (now his wife).

Portrait of Charmae Natseway with one of her pots.
Courtesy of Cristof's, Santa Fe, NM.

AWARDS: Approximately 18 second place awards, 16 first place awards, Best of Miniature Pottery Division (1995), and 3 Miniature Pottery Awards during the years at Santa Fe Indian Market.

REPRESENTATION: Cristof's Art Gallery, Santa Fe, New Mexico.

ABOUT THE ARTIST: Natseway started making pottery in 1979 and creates miniatures from clay dug a distance away from the Acoma Pueblo. He uses Charmae's old brushes and tools, painting his pots without glasses or magnification. His designs reflect his study of prehistoric pottery.

JOY NAVASIE
(a.k.a. Frog Woman)

Hopi (January 3, 1916–) Arizona
Potter

EDUCATION: Learned how to pot from her mother, Paqua Naha (also called Frog Woman).

Portrait of Thomas Natseway. Courtesy of Santa Fe, NM.

AWARDS: Many awards, including Santa Fe Indian Market, Gallup Inter-tribal Ceremonial, and others.

REPRESENTATION: Pueblo Pottery Gallery, San Fidel, New Mexico; Pen-field Gallery, Albuquerque, New Mexico.

ABOUT THE ARTIST: Navasie is the most famous of the Navasie potters and uses the same name (Frog Woman) as her mother, Paqua Naha. She uses Sikyatki decorations on her pots, painting them on almost pure white slip, and doesn't use any commercial tools, dyes, or clay.

MARIANNE NAVASIE

Hopi (1951–)
Potter

EDUCATION: Learned how to pot from her mother, Joy Navasie (Frog Woman).

REPRESENTATION: Cristof's Art Gallery, Santa Fe, New Mexico.

ABOUT THE ARTIST: Navasie, who began potting in her mid-20s, sticks to traditional designs. She signs her pots with the family frog, the tadpole, and her initial "M."

FELIPE ORTEGA

Jicarilla Apache; La Madera, New Mexico
Potter

EDUCATION: Jesucita Martinez of Petaca taught Ortega to make micaceous bean pots.

ABOUT THE ARTIST: Ortega continued Martinez's traditional pots and, after her death, was the only Jicarilla making them. He has since taught others the art in order to keep the tradition alive and is considered a master teacher. He creates micaceous pottery in the old tradition, though he orig-inally started potting bean pots.

SEFERINA ORTIZ

Cochiti (1931–) Arizona
Potter—storytellers

EDUCATION: Learned how to pot from mother, Laurencita Herrera.

REPRESENTATION: Adobe Gallery, Albuquerque, New Mexico; Andrea Fisher Fine Pottery, Santa Fe, New Mexico.

ABOUT THE ARTIST: Ortiz's pottery-making family includes her grandmothers, Reyes Romero and Seferina Suina, and her great-aunt Este-phanita Herrera. She also has passed on her skills to her own children: Joyce Ortiz Lewis, Janice Ortiz, Juanita I. Ortiz, and Virgil Ortiz. Her technique doesn't consist of special tools or techniques, she just creates as she "go[es] along and see[s] what comes out." She began making small dolls and animals in the early 1960s and created her first storyteller in 1962. Ortiz's work was heralded, along with other storyteller makers, in the 1973 Museum of International Folk Art in Santa Fe's show "What Is Folk Art?"

CLYDE LELAND OTIPOBY
Comanche (1940–) Clinton, Oklahoma
Artist, illustrator, potter, sculptor

EDUCATION: Arkansas City Junior College, Kansas; Oklahoma State University (1966–68).

ABOUT THE ARTIST: Otipoby worked as an illustrator in the Air Force for four years and has taught art at the Lincoln Elementary School in Ponca City, Oklahoma. His work has been exhibited throughout the Southwest.

PAHPONEE
(a.k.a. Snow Woman)
Kickapoo/Potawatomi
Potter

EDUCATION: Self-taught.

REPRESENTATION: Tribal Expressions, Arlington Heights, Illinois.

ABOUT THE ARTIST: Pahponee is active in tribal traditions, as well as in her art. She often incorporates Native prayers or symbols in her work. Some-times she does not use glazes in her work but simply creates her designs through the firing process.

GLADYS PAQUIN
(a.k.a. Sratyu'we)
Laguna/Zuni; New Mexico
Potter

EDUCATION: Self-taught.

AWARDS: Many, including recognition for her traditional pots at the Santa Fe Indian Market.

Vase by Pahponee. Tall, balanced, and beautifully colored, this large vessel has thick walls and is embellished with surface carvings depicting Paphonee as a dancer together with two-leggeds, four-leggeds, wingeds, swimmers, crawlers, whirl wind, star nations, Grandmother moon, and Grandfather sun. 11" × 20" gourd shaped, a lovely pot for $3,500. Courtesy of Tribal Expressions, Arlington Heights, IL.

REPRESENTATION: Penfield Gallery, Albuquerque, New Mexico.

ABOUT THE ARTIST: Paquin began potting during the 1980s, reviving interest in Laguna pottery (an art that almost died during the 1950s–60s). She began copying the old Laguna decorations and loves using parrots in her work. Paquin feels she puts a lot of herself in the pot and has to tell it how to be. Each of her pots is a little different. She signs them with her Santa Ana name, Sratyu'we.

KEVIN PESHALAKAI

Cochiti (1963–) Cochiti Pueblo, New Mexico
Potter—storytellers

EDUCATION: Learned trade from his grandmother Helen Cordero and other members of the Cordero family.

REPRESENTATION: Adobe Gallery, Albuquerque, New Mexico.

ABOUT THE ARTIST: He made his first storyteller in 1981.

TOM POLACCA

Tewa/Hopi (1935–) Arizona
Potter

EDUCATION: Learned how to pot from members of his famous family (including his mother, Fannie Nampeyo).

ABOUT THE ARTIST: Polacca, Fannie Nampeyo's son, couldn't show his pots at first because, traditionally, potters are female. His sgraffito style is a little different in that he doesn't paint his design into the pot—instead, he carves it into the piece with a knife, then paints it in shades of red, brown, yellow, and orange, giving it a sunset-like tone.

AL QOYAWAYMA
(a.k.a. Gray Fox Walking at Dawn)
Hopi (February 26, 1938–) Los Angeles, California
Potter

EDUCATION: Studied with his aunt, Hopi potter Elizabeth White. Worked with ceramics in high school, then graduated in 1961 from California State Polytechnic University, San Luis Obispo, with a B.S. in mechanical engineering.

REPRESENTATION: Gallery 10, Inc. Santa Fe, New Mexico; Blue Rain Gallery, Taos, New Mexico; Native Pots, Denver, Colorado.

ABOUT THE ARTIST: Though he had learned how to work with clay as a child, Qoyawayma has spent much of his life as a manager of environmental services and founded the American Indian Science and Engineering Society. As an artist, Qoyawayma believes that "most pottery today reflects the past." His pottery is embellished with sculpted figures (sometimes Kachinas) and is often done in an elegant bone-white color. His pieces could be considered a blend of pottery and sculpture, a style that is unique and completely his own. Though he has been inspired by the ancient pottery, he brings his own talents to it. He has also served as consultant to the Smithsonian Institute, which is trying to identify the original clay sources used by ancient Hopi potters. Qoyawayma's work is held by many museums throughout the country.

MARGARET QUINTANA

Cheyenne/Arapaho; Watonga, Oklahoma
Potter—storytellers

REPRESENTATION: Brooks Indian Shop, Albuquerque, New Mexico; Wadle Galleries, Santa Fe, New Mexico.

ABOUT THE ARTIST: Quintana works with micaceous clay to create her Cochiti-style storytellers. Her husband, Paul, is Cochiti, and she learned how to pot in the 1980s after moving to the pueblo with him. Her work is held by museums such as the Millicent Rogers.

DEXTRA NAMPEYO QUOTSKUYVA

Hopi-Tewa (September 7, 1928–) Polacca, First Mesa, Arizona
Potter

EDUCATION: Learned how to pot from her mother, Rachel Namingha, who learned from her grandmother Nampeyo. Quotskuyva is a fourth-generation potter.

AWARDS: Her many awards include being designated one of Arizona's Indian Living Treasures in 1994.

REPRESENTATION: Pueblo Pottery Gallery, San Fidel, New Mexico; King Galleries, Scottsdale, Arizona.

ABOUT THE ARTIST: Quotskuyva did not throw her first pot until 1967, when she was 39 years old. When creating her work, she uses the same tools her great-grandmother Nampeyo did: organic and mineral paints, yucca leaf brushes, and polishing stones. Quotskuyva is recognized as one of the best potters in the Southwest.

STEPHANIE C. RHODES
(a.k.a. Snow Flake Flower)

Cochiti (1932–) Cochiti Pueblo, New Mexico
Potter—storytellers

EDUCATION: Learned some of her technique from Mary Martin, though mostly self-taught.

AWARDS: Some of the first awards Rhoades won for her storytellers were in 1982 and 1983 at the New Mexico State Fair and the Indian Market, respectively.

REPRESENTATION: Wrights Gallery, Albuquerque, New Mexico.

ABOUT THE ARTIST: Potters in her family include her grandmother Estephanita Herrera, and her sister, Ada Suina, and she has passed on her knowledge to her children, Jonathan Loretto and Morningstar Rhoades. Rhodes made her first storyteller in 1979. When Rhodes's daughter went into a coma and remained there for 16 years, the artist attached a prayer to each storyteller she created. Her daughter woke from the coma in 2001. She signs her name "Snow Flake Flower" to her works.

ROSE PECOS AND SUN RHODES

Jemez; New Mexico
Potters—storytellers

EDUCATION: Self-taught.

REPRESENTATION: Wright's Gallery, Albuquerque, New Mexico.

ABOUT THE ARTISTS: Husband-and-wife team who make storytellers in the Navajo style. The children who gather around the storyteller are often more realistically portrayed than the storyteller him/herself. The figures are dressed in Navajo style, often holding Navajo baskets or cradleboards.

EDNA ROMERO

Taos (1937–) Taos Pueblo, New Mexico
Potter

EDUCATION: Learned from other potters in the area.

AWARDS: Romero has won awards for her pots at Indian markets.

REPRESENTATION: Pueblo Pottery Gallery, San Fidel, New Mexico.

ABOUT THE ARTIST: Romero began making pots during the late 1980s. Her micaceous style is graceful, yet strong. She digs her clay from a mountain near Taos to make pots that can be used for cooking. Her husband helps her gather the wood she needs for firing the pots and her children and grandchildren often help with the polishing.

MARIA PRISCILLA ROMERO

Cochiti (1936–) Cochiti Pueblo, New Mexico
Potter—storytellers

EDUCATION: Learned the art of pottery from her mother, Maggie Chalan, and her mother-in-law, Teresita Romero.

REPRESENTATION: Smithsonian Institute, Washington, D.C.; Heard Museum, Phoenix, Arizona; Museum of Man in San Diego, California.

ABOUT THE ARTIST: Since making her first storyteller in 1979, Romero has passed on what she has learned about pottery making to her daughter, Mary Eunice Ware. Romero is known for her small storyteller frogs, as well as storyteller cats and bears.

VIRGINIA ROMERO

Taos; New Mexico
Potter

EDUCATION: Self-taught.

REPRESENTATION: Blue Rain Gallery, Taos, New Mexico; Andrea Fisher Fine Pottery, Santa Fe, New Mexico; Kleywood Southwest, San Antonio, Texas.

ABOUT THE ARTIST: Romero has not lost a pot since she began in 1919. According to the potter, the reason is that she uses wood in her firing process instead of manure. She doesn't add anything to her Taos clay, just shapes her pots, smooths them (skipping the polishing process), and files them.

MARIA "LILLY" SALVADOR

Acoma; Acoma, New Mexico
Potter, jeweler, weaver

EDUCATION: Grants High School; New Mexico State, New Mexico. Also learned the basics of pottery from her mother, Frances Torivio.

AWARDS: First, second, and third prizes, Santa Fe Indian Market (1994); first prize, Acoma pots, Santa Fe (2001); Pasadena Craftsmen Show, Pasadena California.

REPRESENTATION: Lilly's Pottery Gallery, Acoma Pueblo, New Mexico.

ABOUT THE ARTIST: Salvador's work is on permanent collection at several museums. She shows her work throughout the western United States and sells it from her own shop in the Acoma Pueblo. Pottery is her first love, though she is a multitalented artist. She makes Acoma pots in the traditional way, refusing to reveal her sources for her clay and the secrets of making her pottery. Salvador has been known to paint the inside of a deep jar, something that is nearly impossible. She makes slip-decorated earthenware in the traditional Acoma style. Salvador also is a silversmith, acrylic artist, weaver, and Native embroidery artist. Those items are available at her gallery, as well.

RUSSELL SANCHEZ

San Ildefonso; San Ildefonso Pueblo, New Mexico
Potter

EDUCATION: Learned how to pot from watching his great-aunt, Rose Gonzales, and her daughter-in-law, Dora Tse-Pe.

AWARDS: Many since he started entering markets and shows in 1978. Most recent: Best of Division, miniatures, SWAIA (2001).

REPRESENTATION: Gallery 10, Inc., Santa Fe, New Mexico; Native Pots, Denver, Colorado; Gallery Adobe East, Delray Beach, Florida.

ABOUT THE ARTIST: Sanchez began potting at a very young age and exhibited signs of real talent by his teens. Sanchez's work includes two-tone sienna and black jars. He often adds bear-effigy lids, inlaid stones, and green slips to the jars. In addition, he introduces different materials into the clay at various stages of the process.

EUSEBIA SHIJE

Zia; Arizona
Potter

EDUCATION: Learned some of her skill from her mother.

REPRESENTATION: Andrea Fisher Fine Pottery, Santa Fe, New Mexico; Native Pots, Denver Colorado.

ABOUT THE ARTIST: One of Zia's senior potters, Shije uses yucca fibers to paint her pots and often grinds her paints with minerals. Shije earns her living making pottery that is stone polished, then painted with a black pigment. Her trademark is the Zia bird, as it is for other Zia potters.

STELLA SHUTIVA

Acoma; New Mexico
Potter

EDUCATION: Self-taught.

REPRESENTATION: Adobe Walls Antique Mall and Trading Post, Colorado Springs, Colorado.

ABOUT THE ARTIST: Shutiva's pottery is distinctive because she textures the pieces with her corrugating tool. She was responsible for creating and popularizing the fingernail design. Shutiva taught her children how to pot, and both her daughter Jackie and her son-in-law Wilfred Garcia produce pots similar to hers.

MARY SMALL

Jemez
Potter

EDUCATION: Learned how to pot from her mother, Perfecita Toya.

AWARDS: Named IACA Artist of the Year (2002). Many awards at various shows and festivals, including Santa Fe Indian Market, Eight Northern Pueblos Indian Arts Show, the Heard Museum, Powhattan Lenape Nation Juried Indian Arts Festival in New Jersey, and many other arts and crafts venues.

REPRESENTATION: Eastern Cowboys, Scottsdale, Arizona.

ABOUT THE ARTIST: Small's pots are often large and go beyond the realm of traditional pottery. In a photo taken for public relations when she won the IACA Artist of the Year award, Small holds a very large vase, the top of which is actually sculpted with a village scene. She creates intricately figured pieces, often decorated in her trademark colors: white and a matte blue-gray made from white clay mixed with bee plant pigment. As is true for many other potters, she believes in the spiritual quality of the clay and believes you must be at peace in order to create artistic pottery from the clay.

Mary Small of Jemez Pueblo produces handmade pottery with intricate designs. Courtesy of Jay Sadow and The Eastern Cowboys, Scottsdale, AZ.

RICHARD ZANE SMITH

Wyandot
Potter

REPRESENTATION: Gallery 10, Inc., Santa Fe, New Mexico; Blue Rain Gallery, Taos, New Mexico; King Galleries, Scottsdale, Arizona; McGee's Indian Art Gallery, Keams Canyon, Arizona.

ABOUT THE ARTIST: Smith makes pots in the ancient corrugated style, then decorates them with stunning painted designs. He has used Anasazi coiling methods when he creates his corrugated pots using his signature colors of pale pink, blue, and purple. His pots look so much like baskets that collectors might not recognize them for the fine pottery they are. His work has been exhibited widely and is held in many museums, including the Philbrook and the Denver Art Museum.

JACQUIE STEVENS

Winnebago (1949–) Omaha, Nebraska
Potter

EDUCATION: Stevens created her first piece at home when she was five years old—and ate it! University of Colorado, Anthropology; Institute of American Indian Arts (1975). Mentored by Otellie Laloma.

REPRESENTATION: Gallery of Contemporary and Indigenous Art, Tucson, Arizona; Andrea Fisher Fine Pottery, Santa Fe, New Mexico.

ABOUT THE ARTIST: She makes unusual pieces and uses micaceous clay that she smokes to build her large, hand-coiled pots. Stevens was perhaps the first Native American potter to create coiled, off-round pottery, then adding other textures like reed and leather to her work.

BERNICE SUAZO-NARANJO

Taos; Taos, New Mexico
Potter

EDUCATION: Bernice's grandmother gave her the information she needed to start making pottery in 1981.

ABOUT THE ARTIST: Suazo-Naranjo respects the clay she works with, believing in the cycle of nature. Her husband, Tito, often works with her. She keeps her micaceous clay in plastic bags for three or four months to age it so that it will be plastic-like. Some of her pots are left undecorated, and others are carved with her design before she fires them.

ADA SUINA

Cochiti (1930–) Cochiti Pueblo, New Mexico
Potter—storytellers

EDUCATION: Learned the art of pottery from her cousin, Virginia Naranjo, and her mother-in-law, Aurelia Suina.

AWARDS: Has won awards for her work since she began potting in 1976.

REPRESENTATION: Armadillo Trading Company, Albuquerque, New Mexico.

ABOUT THE ARTIST: Considered one of the finest contemporary Cochiti potters, Suina creates nativities, storytellers, and drummers, with large, distinctive faces. She has begun to teach her four daughters (Caroline Grace Suina, Marie Charlotte Suina, Maria Suina, and Patty Suina) the art of pottery, and they are already winning prizes for their work. She is one of the few Cochiti potters working with the cream-colored slip that made Cochiti storytellers unique because she bought Helen Cordero's supply.

ANTONITA (TONY CORDERO) SUINA

Cochiti (1948–) Cochiti Pueblo, New Mexico
Potter—storytellers

EDUCATION: Learned trade from her mother, master storyteller creator Helen Cordero.

REPRESENTATION: Adobe Gallery, Albuquerque, New Mexico.

ABOUT THE ARTIST: Created her first storyteller in 1983. Other members of her family, such as brother, George Cordero, niece, Buffy Cordero, and nephews, Tim Cordero and Kevin Peshlakai, are also storyteller makers.

AURELIA SUINA

Cochiti (1911–) Cochiti Pueblo, New Mexico
Potter—storytellers

EDUCATION: Learned her potting skills from her mother, Victoria Montoya, and her aunt, Reycita Romero.

AWARDS: Began winning prizes for her storytellers at the 1980 Indian Market.

ABOUT THE ARTIST: Suina's family is filled with pottery artists, such as her mother and aunt, her daughter-in-law, Ada Suina, and her granddaughters, Caroline Grace Suina, Marie Charlotte Suina, Maria Suina, and Patty Suina. Aurelia, who had learned how to make figures and traditional vessels in the 1920s, started making storytellers in 1968. The identifying features of her figures are their widely spaced eyes set high on the forehead and a tiny line of a mouth. In 1973 Aurelia was one of three Cochiti potters featured in the folk art exhibit in Santa Fe, New Mexico.

FRANCES SUINA

Cochiti (1902–) Cochiti Pueblo, New Mexico
Potter—storytellers

EDUCATION: Self-taught.

ABOUT THE ARTIST: Frances's son, Louis Naranjo, daughter-in-law, Virginia Naranjo, and daughter, Sarah Suina, are all involved with pottery. Her work was included in the 1973 "What Is Folk Art?" exhibit held at the Museum of International Folk Art in Santa Fe, New Mexico. One of the distinguishing features of her work is the traditional Cochiti vessel designs that she paints on the back of her storytellers' shirts. Suina began creating traditional pottery vessels in the 1920s, made "Singing Mothers" in the 1940s and 1950s, then began making larger, seated storyteller figures in the 1960s and early 1970s.

JUDITH SUINA

Cochiti (1960–) Cochiti Pueblo, New Mexico
Potter—storytellers

EDUCATION: Taught by mother, Dorothy Trujillo.

ABOUT THE ARTIST: Suina's family is filled with pottery makers, such as sisters, Frances Pino and Cecilia Valencia, brother, Onofre Trujilio II, mother-in-law, Louise Q. Suina, sister-in-law, Vangie Suina, and aunts and great-aunts. Judith created her first storyteller in 1978.

LOUISE Q. SUINA

Cochiti (1939–) Cochiti Pueblo, New Mexico
Potter—storytellers

EDUCATION: Self-taught, though did learn some techniques from cousin, Dorothy Trujillo.

ABOUT THE ARTIST: Suina's daughter, Vangie, cousins, Helen Cordero and Seferina Ortiz, and daughter-in-law, Judith Suina, are also potters.

LUCY R. SUINA

Cochiti (1921–) Cochiti Pueblo, New Mexico
Potter—storytellers

EDUCATION: Learned art of pottery from her mother and father, Reyes T. and Vicente Romero. Shares same grandfather, Santiago Quintana, as Helen Cordero, her first cousin.

ABOUT THE ARTIST: Suina comes from a large family of potters, including her sister, Laurencita Herrera, her niece, Seferina Ortiz, her cousin, Helen Cordero, and her daughter, Evangeline Suina. She created her first storyteller in 1974 and has even helped her son-in-law, Tony Dallas, with the art of creating storytellers.

MARIE CHARLOTTE SUINA

Cochiti (1954–) Cochiti Pueblo, New Mexico
Potter—storytellers

EDUCATION: Suina's mother, Ada, taught her how to pot.

AWARDS: Suina began winning prizes for her storytellers in 1983, with her first award at the Indian Market.

ABOUT THE ARTIST: Suina comes from a large family of potters, including her grandmother Aurelia Suina, her cousins, Josephin and Martha Arquero, and her sisters, Caroline, Maria, and Patty. She created her first storyteller in 1980.

VANGIE SUINA

Cochiti (1959–) Cochiti Pueblo, New Mexico
Potter—storytellers

EDUCATION: Taught by mother, Louise Q. Suina.

AWARDS: Since her first storyteller in the early 1980s, Suina has won many awards for her work.

ABOUT THE ARTIST: Her grandmother Anita and great-aunt, Marianita Venado, were both potters. Suina began making storytellers in the early 1980s. Most of the children on her figures are holding something. She uses acrylic paints and kiln-firing in her work—the process produces a brighter, glossier, whiter polychrome finish.

CAMILIO TAFOYA

Santa Clara (d. 1995) Santa Clara Pueblo, New Mexico
Potter

EDUCATION: Learned the trade from his famous mother, Serafina, as well as other members of the Tafoya family.

REPRESENTATION: Blue Rain Gallery, Taos, New Mexico; Andrea Fisher Fine Pottery, Santa Fe, New Mexico.

ABOUT THE ARTIST: Tafoya carried on the tradition of pottery-making within his family, creating pots that were both contemporary and traditional. His children, Joseph Lonewolf and Grace Medicine Flower, have also become noted for their pots and are teaching their own families the art.

MARGARET TAFOYA

Santa Clara (1904–February 25, 2001) Santa Clara Pueblo, New Mexico
Potter

EDUCATION: Learned the trade from her family. Some of her pieces were inspired by tales she heard from her parents and grandparents.

AWARDS: National Heritage Fellow, National Endowment for the Arts Folk Arts Program (1984).

REPRESENTATION: Adobe Gallery, Albuquerque, New Mexico.

ABOUT THE ARTIST: Tafoya's trademark is polished blackware, often decorated with bear paw designs, which she considered to be good luck. She was considered a master of the art, known for making deeply carved blackware and redware vessels, which are highly valued by collectors. She believed the secret in her technique was her polishing stones that had been passed down through the generations. She never used a pottery wheel. Tafoya taught her own children, Virginia Ebelacker, Mela Youngblood, Toni Roller, and Esther Archuleta, her pottery-making skills.

MARK TAHBO

Hopi-Tewa (1958–) Arizona
Potter

EDUCATION: Learned the basics of pottery from his grandmother Grace Chappella.

REPRESENTATION: Penfield Gallery, Albuquerque, New Mexico; King Galleries, Scottsdale, Arizona; Adobe Galleries, Albuquerque.

ABOUT THE ARTIST: Tahbo uses anything that works to shape and create his pottery, often even discarded bowls and dinnerware that might serve as a *puki* (a base to support the coils of clay). His pots are nicely shaped and have thin walls, an achievement that few potters can boast.

BELEN AND ERNEST TAPIA

Santa Clara (Belen: 1941–99) New Mexico
Potters

EDUCATION: Self-taught.

ABOUT THE ARTISTS: Belen made the pottery, while Ernest did the designing. The Tapia couple regularly showed their work at the Indian Market in Santa Fe. They made traditional polished redware that was painted with white, buff, blue-grey, and matte red. She made melon jars evenly patterned with sculptured squash ribs around the entire jar. Ernest used his hands when shaping the clay because he believed working with a wheel is "not art."

ROBIN TELLER

Isleta; Isleta Pueblo, New Mexico
Potter

EDUCATION: Learned how to make storytellers from her mother, Stella.

REPRESENTATION: Tribal Expressions, Arlington Heights, Illinois.

ABOUT THE ARTIST: Teller is often inspired by the pueblo's natural beauty. Her work is detailed and intricate, respected as some of the best storytellers being made.

STELLA TELLER

Isleta; Isleta Pueblo, New Mexico
Potter

EDUCATION: Self-taught.

Mother Doll storyteller by Robin Teller. Courtesy of Tribal Expressions, Arlington Heights, IL.

AWARDS: Three-month Dobkin Fellowship, Indian Arts Research Center (2001). Many national awards from festivals and markets (like Santa Fe), and work is held by many museums throughout the country.

REPRESENTATION: Adobe Gallery, Albuquerque, New Mexico.

ABOUT THE ARTIST: Teller, who has been potting since she was eight, creates storytellers and animal figures. She has taught her four daughters

Mother Doll storyteller and Corn Maiden pot by Robin Teller. Mother: Mother holds a basket of pottery that she is giving to each child climbing on her to hear the story. Corn Maiden: 4" high with a painted corn plant and sunface on the shawl, turquoise earrings, $425. Courtesy of Tribal Expressions, Arlington Heights, IL.

how to work with clay as well. They are respected as some of the best storytellers in the business and are the only Isleta family still making them from scratch.

ROBERT TENORIO

Santo Domingo; New Mexico
Potter

EDUCATION: Learned how to pot from his mother, Juanita.

REPRESENTATION: Kleywood Southwest, San Antonio, Texas; Modo Gallery, Hudson, New York.

ABOUT THE ARTIST: This potter made contemporary stoneware before turning back to the old Santo Domingo way of creating pots. When Tenorio starts painting a pot, the design just comes to him. He doesn't plan ahead. His pots are still being used to carry food, as they did for centuries before. Tenorio uses a special white slip to get his unique color.

WAHLEYAH ANNE TIMMERMAN-BLACK

Abenaki/Susquehanna–Cherokee/Paugusset (1976–) Strong, Maine
Potter, basketmaker, beadworker, dollmaker, jeweler, painter

EDUCATION: Learned her crafts from her mother, Nowetah. Attends University of Maine, Farmington.

White Isleta Bear storyteller by Stella Teller. The bear with
5 cubs and a baby is 8 inches tall, $1100. The smaller
bear has 3 cubs and is 4.5 inches tall, $475. Courtesy of
Tribal Expressions, Arlington Heights, IL.

Storytellers by Robin and Stella Teller. Courtesy of Tribal Expressions, Arlington Heights, IL.

AWARDS: Community, state, and school awards for outstanding pottery, advanced art, and others.

REPRESENTATION: Nowetah's American Indian Museum Store, New Portland, Maine.

ABOUT THE ARTIST: Timmerman-Black designed the "Don't Drink and Drive" Maine State Christmas card (1992) and has some of her art on display at the Maine State House in Augusta. She makes coiled clay pottery, baskets, quill and bead jewelry, dreamcatchers, cornhusk dolls, and birchbark cone-shaped wigwams.

BEA TIOUX

Tesuque; Tesuque Pueblo, New Mexico
Potter, weaver, drum maker

EDUCATION: Tioux learned how to pot from her mother and great-aunt.

ABOUT THE ARTIST: Tioux produces micaceous pots with Tesuque symbols, such as those for day, night, corn, rivers, and mountains. She also produces woven items, does embroidery, makes drums, and keeps a herd of cattle.

DOROTHY TORIVIO

Acoma (August 19, 1946–) Acomita, New Mexico
Potter, weaver

EDUCATION: Taught by her mother and mother-in-law.

AWARDS: Best of Pottery Award (large brown jar), Heard Museum Guild (1984); various awards in several classes, Heard Invitational (1984); Class II Pottery, SWAIA (1994); seed bowls, SWAIA (1995); Category V Pottery, seed jar, Gallup Intertribal Ceremonial (1987); Class II Pottery, SWAIA (1998).

REPRESENTATION: Adobe Gallery, Albuquerque, New Mexico; Gallery 10, Santa Fe, New Mexico, and Scottsdale, Arizona; Quintana Galleries, Portland, Oregon.

ABOUT THE ARTIST: Torivio often repeats the same design in different sizes and shapes on her pots, which make them appear as optical illusions. She specializes in miniature pottery and seed jars. Her style is said to be like "optical art" because it "stretches and compresses with the shape of the pottery" (Gallery 10). Her materials include terra-cotta, natural sand, sediment, paints ground from stone, and rainwater. Her tools and techniques are ones that have been passed down through the generations.

MARY E. TOYA

Jemez (May 29, 1934–) Jemez Pueblo, New Mexico
Potter—storytellers

EDUCATION: Learned how to pot with her grandmother Lupe Madaline Loretto in the 1940s.

AWARDS: Toya has won prizes for almost every kind of pottery, though her specialty is storytellers.

REPRESENTATION: Goldwater's, Scottsdale, Arizona.

ABOUT THE ARTIST: Toya began creating storytellers when they started becoming popular in the 1970s. She digs her clay from pits that have been used by pottery makers for more than six centuries and collects and grinds colored stones to use as paint. Toya's claim to fame is that she made an extremely large storyteller, one that holds 115 children. Her seven daughters and two granddaughters (including Mary Ellen Toya) are following in the pottery-making tradition.

MAXINE TOYA

(a.k.a. Maxine Gauchupin Toya)
Jemez; Jemez Pueblo, New Mexico
Potter

EDUCATION: Toya learned from her mother, Marie Romero, the first Jemez to make a storyteller (in 1968).

AWARDS: Third place, Pottery B Contemporary, Heard Museum Guild (1977); first place, Storyteller Category, SWAIA (1993); second place, Category 1505, figurines, SWAIA (1993); first place, Category 1310, storytellers, SWAIA (1998); second place, Category 1312, other figures, SWAIA (1998); third place, Category 140, figures, SWAIA (1998); and many other awards.

REPRESENTATION: Heard Museum, Phoenix, Arizona; Gallery 10, Santa Fe, New Mexico, Scottsdale, Arizona, and Aspen, Colorado.

ABOUT THE ARTIST: Toya works with her sister, Laura, and their mother. She creates figures that are experimental in form, though simple in design. Toya shares her clays and skills with her fifth-grade class, as well as with her daughters.

DEL TRANCOSA

San Felipe/Cochiti (August 2, 1951–) New Mexico
Potter—storytellers

EDUCATION: Learned his art from mother-in-law, Helen Cordero.

REPRESENTATION: Adobe Gallery, Albuquerque, New Mexico.

ABOUT THE ARTIST: Trancosa made his first storyteller in 1980. His figures often remind one of Helen Cordero's.

DOROTHY TRUJILLO

(a.k.a. Dorothy Mae Trujillo, Dorothy Loretto Trujillo)

Cochiti (April 26, 1932–) Cochiti Pueblo, New Mexico
Potter—storytellers; jeweler

EDUCATION: Trujillo was taught the art of pottery by her mother, Carrie Reid Loretto, and her grandmother, Lupe Madalena Loretto.

AWARDS: Began winning awards in 1970s for her storytellers and nativities throughout the Southwest and later throughout the United States. Grand Prize at Casa Blanca Arizona.

REPRESENTATION: Adobe Gallery, Albuquerque, New Mexico.

ABOUT THE ARTIST: Trujillo's family is full of potters, such as her aunts, Loretta Cajero and Damacia Cordero, her sisters, Marie Edna Coriz, Alma Concha Loretto, Fannie Wall Loretto, Leonora (Lupe) Lucero, and Mary E. Toya, her daughters, Frances Pino, Judith Suina, and Cecilia Valencia, and her son, Onofre Trujillo II. Dorothy made her first storyteller in 1966 and has passed on her experience to others, including her friend Mary Martin.

FELIPA TRUJILLO

Cochiti (April 27, 1908–) Cochiti Pueblo, New Mexico
Potter—storytellers, figures, nativity sets

EDUCATION: Learned from her mother, Estephanita Herrera, who taught Trujillo how to make large bowls, figurines, and effigy pitchers. Trujillo learned how to make storytellers on her own.

REPRESENTATION: Adobe Gallery, Albuquerque, New Mexico.

ABOUT THE ARTIST: Trujillo's daughter, Angel Quintana, and niece, Helen Cordero, are also potters. Trujillo's first "storytellers" were actually "singing ladies," which resembled those made during the early 20th century. She began producing storytellers in earnest in the 1960s; most have her trademark baby in the cradleboard. Trujillo was one of the six potters exhibited at the "What Is Folk Art?" show at the Museum of International Folk Art in Santa Fe in 1973.

KATHY TRUJILLO

(a.k.a. Katy Trujillo)

San Ildefonso/Cochiti (1931–) San Ildefonso Pueblo, New Mexico
Potter—storytellers

EDUCATION: Learned how to pot from her parents, Rosalie and Jose A. Aguilar. Learned how to make storytellers from Dorothy Trujillo and Mary Martin.

ABOUT THE ARTIST: Trujillo's family is heavily involved in pottery. Active pottery-making members include her daughter, Evon Trujillo, her sisters, Florence A. Naranjo and Annie A. Martinez, her brothers, Alfred Aguilar and Jose V. Aguilar, Sr., her niece, Becky Martinez, and her mother-in-law, Helen Cordero. Trujillo originally made the black-on-black pottery produced in San Ildefonso, but began making figures in the 1970s when she moved to Cochiti, after marrying into the Cordero family.

MARY TRUJILLO

(a.k.a. Mary T. Trujillo, Mary Elizabeth Tapia, Mary Elizabeth Trujillo)

San Juan/Cochiti (May 26, 1937–) San Juan Pueblo, New Mexico
Potter—storytellers

EDUCATION: Learned to pot from her mother, Leondias C. Tapia. Trujillo's mother-in-law, Helen Cordero, and her neighbor, Ada Suina, taught Trujillo the art of storytellers.

AWARDS: Trujillo won her first award in 1982 at the Indian Market for her piece "Corn Husking Party." Second place, Class II Pottery, traditional painted designs, SWAIA (1983); second place, Category 1411, other figures, SWAIA (1991); third place, Category 1409, storytellers, SWAIA (1992); third place, Category 1411, other figures, SWAIA (1992); first place, Category 1412, other figures, SWAIA (1992); third place, Category 1408, storytellers, SWAIA (1992); second place, Category 1408, storytellers, SWAIA (1993).

REPRESENTATION: Adobe Gallery, Albuquerque, New Mexico.

ABOUT THE ARTIST: Trujillo's family members (e.g., her aunts, Belen Tapia, Santianita Suazo, and Martina Aquino, her great-aunt, Rose Gonzales, and her cousins, Anita Suazo and Tse-Pe) are also potters. Trujillo started making storytellers in the late 1970s–early 1980s. She uses the traditional Cochiti materials: white clay for figures, white slip, and bee plant for her black paint. Like other potters, Trujillo thinks of her ancestors (her grandfather Jose La Luz Cata, in particular) when creating her storytellers. Her storytellers have braids and wear 10-gallon hats, as did her grandfather.

ONOFRE TRUJILLO II

Cochiti (1969–) New Mexico
Potter–storytellers

EDUCATION: Dorothy Trujillo, Onofre's mother, taught him how to pot.

ABOUT THE ARTIST: Pottery-making members of Trujillo's family include his sisters, Frances Pino, Judith Suina, and Cecilia Valencia, as well as aunts and great-aunts. Trujillo created his first storyteller in 1982.

SANDRA VICTORINO

Acoma
Potter

EDUCATION: Learned a lot of her designs from her mentor, Dorothy Torivio.

REPRESENTATION: Tribal Expressions, Arlington Heights, Illinois.

ABOUT THE ARTIST: Victorino has been potting since about 1990. Her pots range from miniatures to larger pieces (her largest about 18 inches tall), and she is quite prolific, producing as many as 50 to 60 pots a year. Her designs are not necessarily marked on the pot before she begins painting. A lot of Victorino's designs were inspired by Dorothy Torivio, her mentor.

Pot by Sandra Victorino. Black and white swirl pattern. 7" × 7". $1,000. Courtesy of Tribal Expressions, Arlington Heights, IL.

Seed Pot by Sandra Victorino. 3" × 3". $175. Courtesy of Tribal Expressions, Arlington Heights, IL.

EVELYN VIGIL
(a.k.a. Evelyn Mora Vigil)

Jemez; New Mexico
Potter, basketworker

EDUCATION: Self-taught.

ABOUT THE ARTIST: During the mid- to late 1980s, Vigil was the subject of many articles about Southwestern baskets and often taught the art. Then she discovered the ancient way that the Pecos people painted their pottery, in a sense recreating an old tradition. When National Park Service officials asked her to take on the project of reconstructing the old Pecos way of making pottery, she accepted the challenge and spent many summers looking for the old pots and creating new ones in the old tradition. She now passes that skill on to the next generation of potters or to anyone else who wants to learn.

LONNIE VIGIL
(a.k.a. Kuutaan, "Rock Drawings")

Nambe (May 4, 1949–) New Mexico
Potter

EDUCATION: Learned how to pot from members of his family. Barnes

Portrait of potter Sandra Victorino. Courtesy of
Tribal Expressions, Arlington Heights, IL.

School of Commerce, Denver, Colorado (1968–69); business administration, Eastern New Mexico University, Portales (1969–73).

AWARDS: Since the early 1980s he has won major awards with his pottery, such as Best of Show at the 2001 SWAIA show for an unusually large micaceous pot. First and second place, pottery awards, SWAIA (1990); Honorable Mention, Class VII Pottery, traditional methods, Heard Museum Guild (1992); first place, traditional unslipped and unpainted pottery, SWAIA (1991); and many other awards.

REPRESENTATION: Heard Museum, Phoenix, Arizona; Cincinnati Art Museum, Cincinnati, Ohio; Horniman Museum & Garden, London; Museum of Fine Arts, Boston; Quintana Galleries, Portland, Oregon.

ABOUT THE ARTIST: Vigil left a career with the federal government to return home and begin working as a potter in the early 1980s. He first began making pots in 1983 and micaceous pots in 1990. Some are extremely large

(22 inches tall). He specializes in water jars, storage jars, and micaceous pots, and his family still uses some of his pots for cooking.

MANUEL AND VICENTA VIGIL
Tesuque; Tesuque Pueblo, New Mexico
Potters—storytellers

EDUCATION: Self-taught.
ABOUT THE ARTISTS: In 1957 Manuel was crippled by an accident, and after that time he relied almost completely on the income from his figurines to support himself and his wife, Vicenta. The created storytellers and nativities. The figures are fully clothed and have hair made of rabbit's fur. Manuel was the potter and was more often written about in newspaper articles. Vicenta worked with him.

ROBERTA A. WALLACE
Cherokee
Potter

AWARDS: Best of Division, Red Earth Awards Ceremony (1994).

MARY EUNICE WARE
Cochiti (1958–) New Mexico
Potter—storytellers

EDUCATION: Mary's mother, Maria Priscilla Romero, taught her how to pot.
ABOUT THE ARTIST: Other members of Ware's family who are potters include her grandmother Teresita Romero and her great-grandmother Cresencia Quintana. Ware created her first storyteller in 1980 and continues to make inroads in the art.

LORRAINE WILLIAMS
Navajo (1955–) Sweetwater, Arizona
Potter

EDUCATION: Learned how to pot from family members.
REPRESENTATION: Cristof's Art Gallery, Santa Fe, New Mexico.
ABOUT THE ARTIST: Williams makes the largest Navajo contemporary pots of the potters working today. She learned how to bead and make rugs early in her life, then opened up more to pottery after marrying her husband, George, and learning more about pottery from her mother-in-law, Rose Williams. Her pots are made in the traditional Navajo way with

black pitch. She wipes the pitch off with a soft rag after the pot is done. Pottery from this reservation wasn't available for sale until the 1980s. Williams first attended the Santa Fe Indian Market in 1992 and went home with a second place ribbon.

ROSE WILLIAMS

Navajo (ca. 1910/12–) Shonto area, Navajo Reservation
Potter

EDUCATION: Self-taught.

AWARDS: Best of Navajo Pottery, drum pot, Heard Museum Guild (1979); third place, Class IV Pottery, Gallup Intertribal Ceremonial (1987). Williams was designated one of Arizona's Indian Living Treasures in 1994.

REPRESENTATION: Arizona State Museum, Tucson; Museum of Northern Arizona, Flagstaff.

Portrait of Lorraine Williams with one of her large pots. Courtesy of Cristof's, Santa Fe, NM.

ABOUT THE ARTIST: Williams, a potter who has kept the Navajo tradition of making pottery alive, has passed her craft along to her 10 children and grandchildren, as well as to other potters. Alice W. Cling, another artist, is her daughter and learned pottery-making from Williams in the early 1970s. Williams is known for her very large pots, though she began creating smaller pieces during the mid-1990s.

MELA YOUNGBLOOD

Santa Clara (1931–90) Santa Clara Pueblo, New Mexico
Potter

EDUCATION: Learned the pottery-making tradition from her mother, Margaret Tafoya.

AWARDS: Award winner, Class VII Pottery, Heard Museum Guild (1979); first and third place, Class II Pottery, SWAIA (1983); first and third place, Category 1002, jars over 8 inches tall, SWAIA (1984); second place, Category 1003, bowls, SWAIA (1986); first place, Class II Pottery, Category 1003, bowls, and first place, Category 1005, wedding vases, SWAIA (1989); as well as many other awards.

REPRESENTATION: Galeria Capistrano, San Juan Capistrano, California.

ABOUT THE ARTIST: Youngblood comes from a long line of potters, including her illustrious mother, Margaret Tafoya. Youngblood was an army wife during the 1960s and began potting at a time when her husband (Walt) was serving in Vietnam. Since that time, she won many awards and passed on her ability to her children Nancy and Nathan. She presented classes and demonstrations of her work throughout the Southwest.

NANCY YOUNGBLOOD LUGO

(a.k.a. Nancy Youngblood, Nancy Karen Youngblood, Nancy Youngblood-Cutler)

Santa Clara/European (October 11, 1955–) Santa Clara, New Mexico
Potter

EDUCATION: Learned from her mother, Mela Youngblood, and from other members of her family, a branch of the Tafoya pottery-making clan.

AWARDS: First place, Category 903, melon bowls; first place, Category 1508, traditional forms, melon bowls; and second place, Category 1508, miscellaneous 6 inches or over, SWAIA (1992); Division Award, Class II Pottery; Div. B, traditional pottery, undecorated; first ad second place, Category 908; miscellaneous including canteens and plates; and Division Award,

Div. C, traditional pottery, Category 1109, miscellaneous including can-teens, SWAIA (1994); and many other awards.

REPRESENTATION: Gallery 10, Santa Fe, New Mexico, and Scottsdale, Arizona.

ABOUT THE ARTIST: Youngblood Lugo is the niece of Mary Archuleta and sister of Nathan Youngblood, as well as granddaughter of Margaret Tafoya and great-granddaughter of Sara Fina. She lived all over the United States and Europe during her childhood as a "military brat" and began making old-style black miniatures in the 1970s. All of her tools are miniature as well. When she was 14, her father (a military man of European descent) offered her $20 to make a pot and exhibit it at the Gallup Intertribal Arts Show. She did so and won second place in her class. She began exhibiting at the Indian Market in 1975 and has been there ever since, often winning awards in several different categories. She is always experimenting with different designs and often spends as much as 300 hours in the creation of one of her pieces. Youngblood Lugo has been the subject of many articles on her work with miniatures and swirling melon bowls.

NATHAN YOUNGBLOOD

Santa Clara (October 18, 1954–) Fort Carson, Colorado
Potter

EDUCATION: Learned his trade from members of his family, like his mother, Mela Youngblood, grandmother Margaret Tafoya, and sister Nancy Youngblood Lugo.

AWARDS: Second place, Class II Pottery, Div. D., traditional pottery, carved, Category 1004, and third place, Category 1001, jars, SWAIA (1989); first place, Category 908, miscellaneous, and first place, Category 1004, bowls over 8 inches in diameter, SWAIA (1992).

REPRESENTATION: Gallery 10, Santa Fe, New Mexico, and Scottsdale, Arizona; King Galleries of Scottsdale.

ABOUT THE ARTIST: A sixth-generation potter, Youngblood creates minia-ture pottery, like his sister Nancy, but he often creates larger pieces as well. He mixes his own clay and estimates it takes longer than a day of work to mix up one cubic foot. Often he has more than 100 hours invested in a pot before he sets it out to be fired at the Santa Clara Pueblo. Sometimes he holds pots out of the fire because he simply has too much time and emo-tion invested in them to take the chance that they may crack during the firing process.

CHRISTINE C. ZUNI
(a.k.a. Povi, "Flower")

San Juan; San Juan Pueblo, New Mexico
Potter

EDUCATION: Learned the pottery techniques by watching her mother, Flora A. Cata.

AWARDS: Zuni's work has won numerous blue ribbons at Native American shows in Nevada and is on display at the Heard Museum, as well as the Indian Pueblo Cultural Center in Albuquerque.

ABOUT THE ARTIST: Zuni signs her work with her Indian name, Povi, which means "flower" in the Tewa language. She has taught at the Smithsonian Institute as well as in Maryland public schools. Her pottery reflects both contemporary and traditional influences, and the majority of her work is hand-coiled, painted, and carved with traditional designs.

Values

John Aragon. Bowl. Mimbres insect bowl. $2^{3}/_{4}$" high × 7" wide. $350–$400.

Mary E. Archuleta. Pot. Redware jar. $5^{1}/_{4}$" high × 6" wide. $3,500–$3,800.

————. Bear paw pot. $5^{1}/_{4}$" high × $6^{1}/_{2}$" wide. $2,400–$2,600.

Josephine Arquero. Cochiti Pueblo female seated figurine wearing a traditional dress and a shawl thrown across her shoulders. $6^{1}/_{2}$" tall. $575–$650.

Blue Corn. Black on black feather jar. 10" × $7^{1}/_{2}$". $8,000–$8,500.

Barbara and Joseph Cerno. Mini canteen. $1^{1}/_{2}$" tall × $1^{1}/_{4}$" in diameter. $285–$300.

Stella Chavarria. Classic black on black pot. 4" × 3". $250–$275.

Grace Chino. Acoma olla, 1989. $5^{3}/_{4}$" in diameter and 5" tall. $2,000–$2,250.

Maria Z. Chino. Polychrome vase with bird, feather, geometric and fine-line designs, ca. 1960s. Signed "Marie Z. Chino, Acoma, New Mexico." $14^{1}/_{4}$" high × 11" in diameter. $5,000–$5,250.

Carolyn Concho. Pot. Raised turtle seed pot. 1" high × 3" wide. $140–$160.

————. Hand-formed seed pot from the Acoma Pueblo in New Mexico. The seed pot has a three-dimensional ladybug on the top. The pot is signed. About $^{3}/_{4}$" tall and $1^{1}/_{2}$" in diameter at its widest point. $70–$90.

Tony Dallas. Hopi mudhead figure. $4^{2}/_{3}$" tall, 3" wide, and $4^{1}/_{4}$" deep. $280–$320.

————. Mudhead with five happy little mudheads features the artist's usual crisp colors and attention to detail. $6\frac{1}{4}$" high × 5" wide. $1,350–$1,400.

Virginia Ebelacker. Wedding vase. $6\frac{1}{4}$" diameter × $11\frac{1}{2}$" tall. $5,000–$5,250.

Grace Medicine Flower. Serpent vase, 1974. 2" diameter × $3\frac{1}{4}$" tall. $1,500–$1,750.

Juanita C. Fragua. Jemez wedding vase. Vase is designed with the artist's famous sculptural curves, or ribs, that go all around the bottom. Special designs on the front and is topped off by a rope, or twisted handle. $8\frac{1}{2}$" × $5\frac{1}{2}$". $385–$400.

Joanne Chino Garcia. Pot. 11" in diameter and 11" tall. $450–$500.

Barbara Gonzales. Plain black bowl. 6" diameter × $2\frac{1}{2}$" tall. $750–$900.

Lois Gutierrez de la Cruz. Pot. Decoration depicts two Yei dancers encircling the vase. $6\frac{1}{2}$" diameter × $5\frac{1}{2}$" high. $850–$900.

Rondina Huma. Pot in browns, reds, and blacks, very detailed design. $5\frac{7}{8}$" diameter × 5 $\frac{1}{2}$" high. $5,900–$6,300.

Marie Juanico. Miniature Trinity canteen stylized after the prehistoric Chaco canteen form. The design is an ancient Tularosa spiral with a fine line background. $6\frac{1}{4}$" long × 2" tall. $345–$360.

Joseph Lonewolf. Miniature pot, created in 1985. Features several incised Mimbres animals, including an elk with a large set of antlers, a white-tail deer, a rabbit, and two other animals. Each animal has stylized symbols incised on their bodies, and colored in various shades of green, white, and yellow. The entire upper half of the pot is incised, revealing the animals, while the lower half of the pot is highly polished. Between the animals are kiva steps and zigzag lines, with incised feathers in green. $1\frac{3}{4}$" tall and 2" in diameter. $2,550–$3,000.

Elizabeth Medina. Lidded jar. 13" tall and 8" in diameter (includes lid). $550–$600.

Teresita Naranjo. Traditional black jar. *Avanyu* (water serpent) encircles the mid-body, above and below, which are wide bands burnished in black. 7" tall × $7\frac{1}{4}$" diameter. Minor scratches and abrasions. $950–$1,000.

Virginia Naranjo. Black bear storyteller figurine with six cubs, ca. 1998. Handmade of natural clays and painted with natural pigments. $6\frac{3}{4}$" tall. $1,500–$1,750.

Joy Navasie. Vase, made in the early to mid-1980s. $8\frac{1}{2}$" in diameter and 12" tall. $6,000–$6,500.

Seferina Ortiz. Figurine, dated 2001. Female storyteller figurine wearing a traditional Pueblo dress draped over one shoulder and under the other, and wearing a flowered cape draped over her back. Her hair is tied in the Pueblo *chonga*, and she is wearing traditional Pueblo moccasins. Standing on her lap or seated on her legs are four children—two boys and two girls—one of whom is holding a ball. Overall height is 6½". $1,795–$1,900.

Gladys Paquin. Olla (a pre-1900 Laguna design). 10" in diameter and 10¼" tall. $1,050–$1,150.

Rose Pecos and Sun Rhodes. Navajo Mother Storyteller. $425–$500.

Russell Sanchez. Cliff jar. Polished red and green with turquoise inlay. 4½" high × 4½" diameter. $2,850–$3,100.

Eusebia Shije. Polychrome plate with roadrunner design. 1" high × 5" diameter. $75–$100.

Stella Shutiva. Olla with turtles, 1974. 10" diameter × 10" tall. $5,000–$5,250.

Jacquie Stevens. Bowl. White mica weave, earthenware, hand-coiled. 6½" × 13½" × 13½". $1,200–$1,400.

Camilio Tafoya. "Hummingbirds and Flowers," made in 1980. Miniature pot, highly polished red slip, sgraffito carved. 3½" × 2¼". $2,200–$2,500.

Margaret Tafoya. Jar. Incised *avanyu* storage jar. 9" tall × 8½" diameter × 4" opening. $11,995–$12,500.

CHAPTER 9

Sandpainting

Sandpaintings are a relatively new collectible Native American art, largely because sandpaintings have traditionally been done on a hogan's dirt floor and blown away when done. It was not until David Villasenor developed a "How to Sandpaint" kit in 1960 that the work was done in a permanent manner.

Originally, sandpaintings were produced to be a spiritual remedy to an acute problem. It is believed that the Pueblo Indian tribes taught the Navajos the art, yet the Navajos insist their art was taught to them by the "Holy Ones."

Sandpainting has traditionally been used by the tribe's medicine man in an effort to maintain the delicate balance of the world. That balance can only be upset by man when he "causes" a disaster or illness. The shaman comes to the offender's hogan, designs his sandpainting on clear white sand on the hogan's dirt floor, and incorporates an opening in the painting that faces east. This opening is intended to make it difficult for evil to enter.

Only five sacred sand colors are used in sandpainting, and each detail in the process of creating a sandpainting must be perfect. The slightest deviation in this ritual is believed to cause great trouble.

The medicine man, in a deep trance, takes the design for the sandpainting from his mind, never making two alike. Once the painting is finished, the patient is brought to the center of the work, and the medicine man performs his ceremony to drive the evil away. When the ceremony is finished, the sandpainting is swept into a blanket. Before sunset, the blanket is carried outside and the sand is blown into the wind—to be returned to Mother Earth so that the evil forces trapped by the sandpainting will not escape.

Historians and traders began reproducing sandpainting designs in the early 1900s, and today both natural and synthetic dyes are used to make sandpaintings. The sands are glued to a chipboard support so that they may be hung. Only hand-ground rocks, minerals, pollen, charcoal, or sandstone are used to craft a sandpainting. The work is a buildup of these materials, with the finest sands producing the highest-quality work. Though sandpaintings have only been commercially available for about 35 years, one can sometimes find earlier examples.

The Artists

DANNY AKEE

Navajo; Tuba City, Arizona
Sandpainter

ABOUT THE ARTIST: Akee's work is experimental both in color and in design. He has produced a technique called "split paintings" where one half of the painting is, for instance, a still life, and the other half is an abstract of a spirit. He has combined both traditional and nontraditional subject matters in this way.

HARRY A. BEGAY

Navajo; Sheep Springs, New Mexico
Sandpainter

ABOUT THE ARTIST: Begay's late 1970s sandpaintings were created with the tourist in mind. His Holy People are generalized figures, created without the specificity that they would have had if they been done by a medicine man using the sandpainting in its original form—as a healing tool to be blown away when finished.

HERMAN R. BEGAY
(a.k.a. War Eagle)

Navajo (1965–) Two Grey Hills, New Mexico
Sandpainting, painting

EDUCATION: Learned some of the arts of his people from his mother, Alice, a weaver, and from his brothers and sisters, also weavers. He got his name from his grandfather, a medicine man who used eagle feathers. Begay learned how to work with watercolors, oils, and acrylics when he studied art in school, but he followed his sister into sandpainting.

REPRESENTATION: Cristof's Art Gallery, Santa Fe, New Mexico.

ABOUT THE ARTIST: Begay has been a painter since 1972, Begay's sandpaintings show a wide artistic range of talent and subject matter, from human images to detailed landscapes. Some of his paintings are accented with acrylics. He usually signs his work "War Eagle."

JOE A. BEGAY

Navajo; Sheep Springs, New Mexico
Sandpainter

EDUCATION: Self-taught.

REPRESENTATION: Heard Museum, Phoenix, Arizona.

ABOUT THE ARTIST: Begay has done some full sandpainting reproductions, which are easily named and identified, though changes are made so that they don't offend the religious. Some of his work was adapted from Newcomb and Reichard's books of sandpaintings.

KEITH BEGAY

Navajo; Shiprock, New Mexico
Sandpainter

AWARDS: Begay has won awards for his work, including first prize at the New Mexico State Fair (1978).

JOE BEN, JR.

Navajo; Shiprock, New Mexico
Sandpainter

EDUCATION: University of New Mexico; teaches sandpainting at the School of Fine Arts in Paris and the School of Fine Arts in Grenoble.

AWARDS: One of five Americans invited to create a work in celebration of the 50th anniversary of the United Nations at the European headquarters in Geneva, Switzerland.

ABOUT THE ARTIST: Ben uses original ceremonial designs, but changes the colors since it is considered sacrilegious to use the original colors. To get the many different shades of colors used in his sandpaintings, he crushes lapis, azurite, coal, galena, gypsum, and malachite. His sandpaintings range from 7 by 7 inches to 48 by 14 inches to large ceremonial installations. He creates sandpaintings because people have been cured by them and because, as he puts it, "[t]his is my way of life."

WILSON BENALLY

Navajo; New Mexico
Sandpainter

ABOUT THE ARTIST: Benally has created some sandpaintings in which the four Cloud People have been moved from their original positions. Since sandpainting is considered a medicine man's art that has gone commercial, it is theorized that the reason why sandpainters make errors in their paintings is so the item becomes more secular and less a religious object.

NOTAH H. CHEE

Navajo; Newcomb, New Mexico
Sandpainter

ABOUT THE ARTIST: Chee is one of the sandpainters who will create a sacred sandpainting template, but will change something about it. For example, in a painting done in 1975, Chee eliminated the number of outlines that surround the sun's face and changed the number of feathers in each quadrant of the painting.

TIMOTHY HARVEY

Navajo; Lukachukai, Arizona
Sandpainter

ABOUT THE ARTIST: In the late 1970s Harvey was one of the sandpainters who created nontraditional works, such as his "Father Peyote" (1977), a sandpainting depicting that personage. He has attempted to bring his work to a higher level, using more details and employing all his skill so that his work will be called "fine art." He has also been one of the only sandpainters to create action shots and one of the few who signs and dates his work.

MARIAN HERRERA

Navajo; Torreon, New Mexico
Sandpainter

ABOUT THE ARTIST: In the late 1970s Herrera painted Pollen Boy in different colors and added the four sacred plants to her painting, as well as four rainbow bars, in order to make her work different enough from the original sacred sandpainting that the Holy People would be pacified.

EUGENE BAATSOSLANII JOE
(a.k.a. Baatsoslanii)

Navajo (1950–) Shiprock, New Mexico
Sandpainter

EDUCATION: Self-taught and learned the art of sandpainting from his father, James C. Joe, a medicine man. Took formal art classes from Don Esley, a Shiprock artist, in 1972.

AWARDS: Special award, San Antonio Arts and Crafts Show (1974); named among the "Best Artists of the Year," New Mexico State Fair (1974); and many others throughout his career.

REPRESENTATION: Cristof's Art Gallery, Santa Fe, New Mexico.

ABOUT THE ARTIST: As a child, Joe listened to Navajo elders telling tales of his culture and often translated those tales into sketches with pencil or crayon. As he grew into his art, Joe has attempted to move the art of sandpainting into the realm of fine arts. His still lifes are often drawn from the crafts of the Southwest (e.g., pottery, fetishes, baskets). His work has been collected by actors such as Robert Redford, Kris Kristofferson, and Ernest Borgnine.

JAMES C. JOE

Navajo; Shiprock, New Mexico
Sandpainter

EDUCATION: Self-taught as a medicine man.

REPRESENTATION: Heard Museum, Phoenix, Arizona.

ABOUT THE ARTIST: In 1965 Joe made the first nontraditional sandpainting. He is known for creating a sandpainting of Water Creature from Beautyway, a figure most Navajos won't re-create. He also teaches others the technique of sandpainting. His son, Eugene B. Joe, has brought the work of commercial-artistic sandpainting into the realm of fine arts.

GEORGE JOHNS

Navajo; Farmington, New Mexico
Sandpainter

ABOUT THE ARTIST: Johns is a master at working with sand and in 1977 was commissioned to do a portrait of Jesus Christ. He did this in great detail, laying some of the grains of sand individually to create contours on the face.

DAVID LEE

Navajo; Shiprock, Arizona
Sandpainter, jeweler, silversmith

EDUCATION: Self-taught.

REPRESENTATION: Heard Museum, Phoenix, Arizona.

ABOUT THE ARTIST: In the late 1970s, Lee created sandpaintings that had subsidiary themes in them, such as the four sacred domesticated plants (corn, beans, tobacco, and squash).

CHEE MCDONALD

Navajo; Sheep Springs, New Mexico
Sandpainter

EDUCATION: Taught by James Joe of Shiprock.

REPRESENTATION: Heard Museum, Phoenix, Arizona.

ABOUT THE ARTIST: McDonald either adds or subtracts details from his sandpaintings and also changes the color, so that the Holy People are placated.

FRANCIS MILLER

(a.k.a. Frances Miller)

Navajo; Sheep Springs, New Mexico
Sandpainter

EDUCATION: Fred Stevens, Jr., encouraged Francis and his wife, Patsy, to become sandpainters and to experiment with their styles.

ABOUT THE ARTIST: Miller's work is often large and complex, and his lines thin and clear, with every detail intricate and fine.

PATSY MILLER

Navajo; Sheep Springs, New Mexico
Sandpainter

EDUCATION: Inspired by the master sandpainter Fred Stevens, Jr. She was a member of the same clan as he, and he encouraged her and her husband, Francis, to experiment with their own style.

ABOUT THE ARTIST: Miller has created a sandpainting of Big Blue Thunder, a figure not often made, but she changed the headdress and markings on the body so that the Holy People would not be disturbed. Some women will not make this figure while pregnant because they believe it will damage the child they are carrying.

MARY LOU PESHLAKAI

Navajo; Sheep Springs, New Mexico
Sandpainter

ABOUT THE ARTIST: Her first attempt at portraiture, in 1977, was the "Indian Chief" a sandpainting of a chief holding a peace pipe. Because sandpainting mistakes are difficult to correct, she started the painting at the top and worked downward, creating a man whose legs were too short (simply because she'd run out of room).

WILSON PRICE

Navajo; Sheep Springs, New Mexico
Sandpainter

ABOUT THE ARTIST: When creating his sandpaintings, Price uses new color hues and new materials in order to counteract the power of the Holy People. He was one of the first sandpainters to create nontraditional sandpaintings, such as his 1977 work depicting the masked impersonator who dances in Big Godway and Nightway ceremonies.

WILBERT SLOAN

Navajo; Tohatchi, New Mexico
Sandpainter

ABOUT THE ARTIST: Sloan is one of the sandpainters who started painting rugs in 1977. His rug sandpaintings and still lifes have been made ever since.

FRED STEVENS, JR.

(a.k.a. Grey Squirrel)

Navajo (1922–) Sheep Springs, New Mexico
Sandpainter

EDUCATION: Self-taught. Medicine man.

ABOUT THE ARTIST: Stevens fell into sandpainting by a fluke of fate. An artist who'd been creating sandpaintings for the tourists at a private museum along Route 66 fell ill and Stevens took over for him. Through the years, Stevens became well-known as a sandpainting expert, demonstrating techniques at the Arizona State Museum, then all over the United States and Europe, Mexico, Japan, South America, and Canada. Stevens was also a Navajo singer, an expert at Blessingway Ceremony chants, as well as Nightway and Female Shootingway ceremonies. He decided to make permanent sandpaintings in 1946, but his early paintings were mediocre at best. Eventually, he mastered the art, leading the way for other Navajo sandpainters. He exhibited his work and did demonstrations during many Heard Museum festivals and special events.

JUANITA STEVENS

Navajo; Chinle, Arizona
Sandpainter

ABOUT THE ARTIST: Stevens often creates some of the good subjects who
help Earth people, such as Mother Earth and Father Sky. Like other sandpainters, she leaves out certain details or adds things to her paintings that
are not made in the original sandpainting created by the medicine man.

ALFREDO WATCHMAN

Navajo; Sheep Springs, New Mexico
Sandpainter

ABOUT THE ARTIST: Watchman worked with extensive color changes when
creating sandpaintings in the late 1970s. By doing so, he counteracted
any negative reactions that would have been caused by re-creating a holy
symbol.

ELSIE Y. WATCHMAN

Navajo; Sheep Springs, New Mexico
Sandpainter

ABOUT THE ARTIST: As with many other sandpainters, Watchman intentionally makes errors on her paintings, such as neglecting to put hands on
her figures, so that the religious intent of the work is negated. She usually
creates simple, single-figure Holy People because of economic, as well as
religious, considerations.

CORNELIA AKEE YAZZIE

Navajo; Tuba City, Arizona
Sandpainter

ABOUT THE ARTIST: Yazzie has created sandpaintings that are completely
enclosed in a border so that the power of the symbols will not escape. The
figures are also placed differently than they would be in a medicine man's
sandpainting.

JAMES WAYNE YAZZIE

Navajo (1943–69) Sheep Springs, New Mexico
Sandpainter

EDUCATION: Self-taught.

ABOUT THE ARTIST: One of the sandpainters who started creating works for tourists in the 1970s, Yazzie was encouraged to improve his craftsmanship so that retailers could better sell his work.

Prices

Joe Ben, Jr. "Night Chant." Image size 5" × 10", frame 13½" × 18½". $400–$450.

Eugene B. Joe. "Baatsoslanii." Examples of this artist's work range from $2,000–$6,000.

Francis Miller. "House of Many Paints." $150–$250.

James Wayne Yazzie. "Yei Ba Chai." 20" × 24". $2,500–$3,000.

CHAPTER 10

Sculpture

Native Americans have been sculpting since the point in time when they acquired the tools to do so. This chapter deals with all sculpture other than wood-carvings (see the "Carving" chapter) and incorporates so many different styles and artists that it's difficult to pinpoint one particular piece of information to deliver in this introduction.

As with other arts, the sculpture produced by these Native American artists has both a symbolic and artistic meaning to the creator. Some of the sculptors create works that are instantly recognizable as Indian, while others are more formal artists who might create abstract sculptures or work that has no Native American connection at all. Some sculptors work in alabaster, while others work in marble or another type of stone. Some use power tools, while others rely on hand tools. Some create only one type of sculpture (e.g., fetishes), while others might work both in miniatures and grand-scale sculptures.

Perhaps it's best to let the sculptors speak for themselves. . . .

The Artists

ANDY AND ROBERTA ABEITA

Andy: *Isleta Pueblo* (July 24, 1963–) Chicago, Illinois
Roberta: *Navajo* (August 13, 1951–) Rehobeth, New Mexico
Sculptors, jewelers

EDUCATION: Self-taught.

AWARDS: The Abeitas have won many awards at the shows and festivals they do around the country, including first place/Best of Show for sculpture at the 1996 Pasadena Indian Market; first and second place at the 1994 Gallup Intertribal Ceremonial.

REPRESENTATION: Silver Sun Traders, Santa Fe, New Mexico.

ABOUT THE ARTISTS: Andy began carving fetishes during his teenage years and continued improving upon his work. Roberta creates the medicine bundles that are tied to the backs of Andy's fetish carvings. This husband-and-wife team creates carved fetishes, both large and small. Their signature is a heart-line, and the fetishes are decorated with inlaid semiprecious stones and feathers. The couple travel all over the country educating others about their craft, their heritage, and their history.

ABRAHAM APAKARK ANGHIK
(a.k.a. Abe Ruben)

Eskimo (1951–) Paulatuk, Northwest Territories, Canada
Sculptor, silversmith, carver, printmaker

EDUCATION: University of Alaska.

ABOUT THE ARTIST: Anghik's work is both Eskimo and Inuit. He utilizes his educational background, as well as what he learned from an Inuit teacher, Ronald Sengungetuk.

ARNOLD D. ARAGON
(a.k.a. "Buck" Aragon)

Crow/Laguna (July 9, 1953–) Crow Agency, Montana
Sculptor—stone; artist—colored pencil

EDUCATION: A.A., three-dimensional arts, Institute of American Indian Arts; three years in economics and art at University of Nevada, Reno.

AWARDS: His awards include first place in sculpture, Fort Hall Art Show, Fort Hall, Idaho (1994); first place, Nevada Day Art Show (1989); first place/Best of Show, California Indian Market (1988); first and second place, California Indian Market/Nevada Museum of Art, "Native Visions Show" (1987); as well as others.

REPRESENTATION: Riata Gallery, Virginia City, Nevada; Vigil's Native American Gallery, Nevada City, California; Out West, Walker, California; Three Flags, Walker, California.

ABOUT THE ARTIST: Aragon's stone sculptures are owned by collectors such as Randy Travis and held in private collections in the United States, Canada, and France. His sculptures and art reflect the culture and heritage of both Plains and Pueblo peoples. He carves warrior figures, bear fetishes, and other stone pieces.

MARIE BITSUIE

Navajo (February 6, 1959–) White Rock, New Mexico
Sculptor, painter, weaver

EDUCATION: Self-taught and influenced by a family full of artists.

REPRESENTATION: Cristof's Art Gallery, Santa Fe, New Mexico.

ABOUT THE ARTIST: Bitsuie creates distinctive bear fetishes, usually working in alabaster. She is also a weaver, creating her rugs in the new Burnham regional style. She was influenced by Bobby Johnson, a Navajo artist with whom she lived and had children until his death in 1989. She now works and lives with his younger brother, Larry Johnson.

RANDALL CHITTO
(a.k.a. Randy Chitto)

Choctaw (August 9, 1961–) Philadelphia, Mississippi
Sculptor

EDUCATION: Institute of American Indian Arts of Santa Fe, New Mexico.

AWARDS: First place, Category 1608, storytellers, nontraditional, and third place, Category 1607, sets and scenes, SWAIA (1995); second place, Class II, Pottery Div. H., Category 1514, storytellers, nontraditional, SWAIA (1996); first place, Category 1509, single figures black, SWAIA (1998).

REPRESENTATION: Long Ago & Far Away, Manchester, Vermont; Heard Museum, Phoenix, Arizona; El Parian de Santa Fe, Santa Fe, New Mexico; Institute of American Indian Arts Museum, Santa Fe; Packard's Indian Trading Co., Inc., Santa Fe.

ABOUT THE ARTIST: Chitto's turtles represent storytellers, warriors, dancers, and musicians. His creations echo his Choctaw heritage; they believe the turtle is the keeper of their history. Each of the turtles Chitto carves has a specific identity and is garbed with traditional accoutrements that the artist makes from deer hide, buckskin, wood, bone, and other materials.

DENNIS R. CHRISTY

Saginaw Chippewa (July 14, 1955–) Mount Pleasant, Michigan
Sculptor—stone, wood, bronze

EDUCATION: A.F.A., Three-Dimensional Design and Sculpture, Institute of American Indian Arts, Santa Fe, New Mexico (1976).

AWARDS: Christy's many awards include first, second, and third places and honorable mentions, as well as special merit awards and best of class, from such places as the Annual Indian Market in Dayton, Ohio, the Michigan Indian Arts Show in Mount Pleasant, and the Eiteljorg Museum in Indianapolis, Indiana.

REPRESENTATION: Sunwest Silver, Albuquerque, New Mexico; Galeria

Capistrano, Santa Fe, New Mexico; Woodard's Native American Art Gallery, Santa Fe.

ABOUT THE ARTIST: A member of the Black River Swan Creek tribe of the Saginaw Chippewa, Christy began carving wood as a young boy. He often worked alongside his grandmother, a basketmaker. Now Christy's work has been shown in both solo and group shows throughout the country and owned by museums such as the Heard, Wheelwright, and Institute of American Indian Arts, as well as by private collectors.

JON DECELLES

Gros Ventre/Assiniboin Sioux (1958–) Tillamook, Oregon
Sculptor—stone

EDUCATION: Portland State University, Portland, Oregon (1977); A.F.A., Three-Dimensional Design, Institute of American Indian Arts, Santa Fe, New Mexico (1984).

AWARDS: DeCelles's many awards include Best of Show at the 1992 New Mexico State Fair and first prize for sculpture at the 1984 Big Lake Trading Post and Museum Indian Market, Page, Arizona.

REPRESENTATION: Sunwest Silver, Albuquerque, New Mexico.

ABOUT THE ARTIST: This artist became interested in art as a child, but it wasn't until he studied at the Institute of American Indian Arts that he found his real love in stone sculpture. He has studied both classical and modern sculpture, believing that "the fusion of these two styles allows me optimal expression." DeCelles exhibits in solo and group shows throughout the Southwest, and his work is held in private collections, as well as by the Institute of American Indian Arts.

ELK WOMAN

(a.k.a. Kathy Whitman, Kathy Elk Woman)

Mandan/Hidatsa/Arikara/Norwegian (August 12, 1952–) Bismarck, North Dakota
Sculptor, painter, jeweler, leatherworker

EDUCATION: Standing Rock Community College, North Dakota (1973–76); Sinte Gleska College, South Dakota (1976–77); University of South Dakota (1977–78).

AWARDS: Many, including Best of Show at the 1991 Pasadena Western Relic and Native American Show, first place at the 1990 Eight Northern Pueblos Arts and Show, and many first and second place prizes at the SWAIA Indian Market throughout the 1980s and 1990s.

REPRESENTATION: Silver Sun/Hardin Estate, Santa Fe, New Mexico; Attic-Hogan Gallery, Prescott, Arizona; Crazy Horse, Frandor, Illinois; Fred Harvey Enterprises, Grand Canyon, Arizona; Heard Museum Gift Shop, Phoenix, Arizona; Lovena Ohl Gallery, Scottsdale, Arizona; Moondancer Gallery, Redondo Beach, California; Morefields Gallery, Ruidoso, New Mexico; O B Enterprises, Denver, Colorado; Phoenix Gallery, Coeur d'Alene, Idaho; Santa Fe Connection, San Antonio, Texas; Sun Silver West Gallery, Sedona, Arizona; Tanner-Chaney Gallery, Albuquerque, New Mexico; Tribal Expressions Gallery, Arlington Heights, Illinois; Turquoise Tortoise, Sedona, Arizona; Vision Quest, Dallas, Texas; White Pelican, Dana Point, California; Wrights Gallery, Albuquerque, New Mexico; Yah-ta-hey Gallery, New London, Connecticut.

ABOUT THE ARTIST: Elk Woman experienced a transformation in her life when she attended a 1977 Sundance ceremony held in South Dakota—it was there that she received her new Indian name, Elk Woman. She started her artistic career as a painter but switched to sculpture in 1983. Four summers later, she had won several prizes for her art. She works in metal, stone, and alabaster to create works that are symbols of nature. Her strong belief in spiritual aspects of the world inspire her work and help her to "find" the subject and spirit of the art within.

UPTON ETHELBAH
(a.k.a. Greyshoes, "Uppie" Ethelbah)

Santa Clara/White Mountain Apache (1948–   )
Sculptor

EDUCATION: Self-taught.
REPRESENTATION: Jill Giller, Native American Collections, www. nativepots.com.
ABOUT THE ARTIST: Ethelbah was a longtime educator, working in Native American programs, and at 54 he turned his attention to sculpting. He gave his first piece, a drum fashioned from red and green Utah alabaster, to his mother so that it would remain in the family. After finishing that first piece, he created more sculptures, becoming an award-winning sculptor and at last finding his dream.

ANITA FIELDS

Osage/Creek (July 7, 1951–   ) Hominy, Oklahoma
Sculptor—clay; ribbonworker; clothing designer/decorator

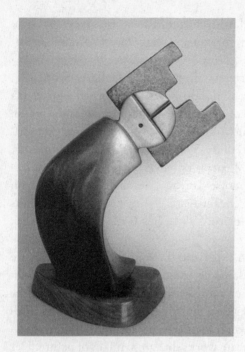

Bronze sculpture by Upton Ethelbah. "Song of the Corn Dance." Courtesy of Jill Giller, Native American Collections, www.nativepots.com. Photo by Bill Bonebrake.

Stone sculpture by Upton Ethelbach. Courtesy of Jill Giller, Native American Collections, www.nativepots.com. Photo by Bill Bonebrake.

EDUCATION: Northeastern Oklahoma State University (1980); B.F.A., Oklahoma State University (1991).

AWARDS: Best of Division/Diversified Art Forms, Red Earth Festival (1994); Best of Division, Class VI Pottery, nontraditional, Heard Museum Guild (1998); first place, Class II Pottery, nontraditional, SWAIA (1999); as well as others for sculpture and pottery.

REPRESENTATION: Artables Gallery, Houston, Texas; Heard Museum, Phoenix, Arizona; LewAllen Contemporary Arts, Santa Fe, New Mexico;

Tulsa Ceramic Arts Gallery, Tulsa, Oklahoma; Four Winds Gallery, Pittsburgh, Pennsylvania; Henry Roan Horse Gallery, Santa Fe; Galleria, Norman, Oklahoma.

ABOUT THE ARTIST: Fields considers her art "an expression of my spirit. It is about transforming my dreams, thoughts and inspirations into clay objects and forms." She has participated in group shows and museum exhibits throughout the United States and is highly recognized in her field. In addition to her art, Fields has taught elementary students how to create Osage ribbonwork, clay, pottery, and sculpture.

CLIFF FRAGUA
(a.k.a. Clifford Fragua)

Jemez (October 21, 1955–) Albuquerque, New Mexico
Sculptor

EDUCATION: Institute of American Indian Arts; San Francisco Art Institute. Studied under Allan Houser.

REPRESENTATION: Faust Gallery, Scottsdale, Arizona; Ray Tracey Gallery, Santa Fe, New Mexico; Galeria Capistrano, San Juan Capistrano, California; Wadle Galleries, Ltd., Santa Fe.

AWARDS: Third place, Class V Sculpture, alabaster, and second place, Cate-

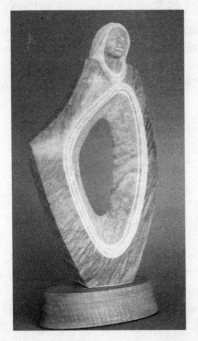

Stone sculpture by Cliff Fragua. Woman with cutout center. Courtesy of Jill Giller, Native American Collections, www.nativepots.com. Photo by Bill Bonebrake.

Bronze sculpture of woman with blanket and turquoise necklace by Cliff Fragua. Courtesy of Jill Giller, Native American Collections, www.nativepots.com. Photo by Bill Bonebrake.

gory 2706, SWAIA (1998); and many other awards at SWAIA, as well as other markets.

ABOUT THE ARTIST: Fragua uses Utah alabaster and other stones in his abstract, symbolic sculptures. He was influenced by the Art Deco style and the French artist Erté, but his works strongly reflect his own heritage. Fragua believes stones have their own personalities, some being hard to work with while others are soft. He lets the stone decide what image it will eventually present.

EVELYN FREDERICKS

Hopi; Kykotsmovi, Third Mesa, Arizona
Sculptor, carver, basketmaker, weaver

EDUCATION: B.A. and M.L.S., library science, University of Arizona. Learned the Native arts of basketry, carving, and textile weaving from family members when growing up.

AWARDS: Charles Loloma Award of Excellence (1997).

REPRESENTATION: Jill Giller, Native American Collections, www.nativepots.com; Turquoise Tortoise, Sedona, Arizona.

ABOUT THE ARTIST: Fredericks incorporates tribal and family mythology into the stone sculptures she creates. She learned most of her art from fam-

Alabaster sculpture by Evelyn Fredericks. Two women holding pots on their heads. Courtesy of Jill Giller, Native American Collections, www.nativepots.com. Photo by Bill Bonebrake.

"Sewa" by Evelyn Fredericks. (Sewa means Little Sister). Bronze sculpture. 21" high. $3400. Courtesy of Turquoise Tortoise, Sedona, AZ.

Sculpture by Evelyn Fredericks. Woman with hands in her pockets. Jacket is yellow and blue, dress is blue, face is bronze, and hair is brown and carved down her back. Courtesy of Jill Giller, Native American Collections, www.nativepots.com. Photo by Bill Bonebrake.

ily members as she was growing up, then continued to work on her skills until she perfected them.

RETHA WALDEN GAMBARO

Creek/Muscogee/Cherokee (1917–) Lenna, Oklahoma
Sculptor—bronze, wood, stone; weaver

EDUCATION: Corcoran School of Arts, Washington, D.C.; apprentice with Berthold Schmutzhart, Washington, D.C.; daily observation of spirituality in art forms since childhood.

AWARDS: Gambaro's main awards include Best in Sculpture, Mystic Harbor Invitational, Mystic, Connecticut (1985); Best in Show, Whirlwind Gallery, Florida (1989); and many others.

REPRESENTATION: Via Gambaro Studio-Gallery, Washington D.C.; Amerind Gallery, Daleville, Virginia; Buffalo Gallery, Alexandria, Virginia; Four Winds Gallery, Naples, Florida; Kline's Gallery, Boonesboro, Maryland; Western Heritage Art Gallery, Taos, New Mexico; Yah-Ta-Hey Gallery, New London, Connecticut; Buffalo Gallery, McLean, Virginia.

ABOUT THE ARTIST: A member of the Muscogee Indian Nation, Gambara started sculpting at the age of 52 and, since that time, has taught, held one-person shows all over the country, exhibited at many museums, festivals, and shows, and has been commissioned to produce her sculptures by such associations as the International Franchise Foundation, Hawaii, and Howard University. She states that "accomplishing a special communication among sculptor, sculpture and viewer is my aim and my reward." She often collaborates with her husband, Stephen, a world-known photographer.

TED GARNER
(a.k.a. Ted Sitting Crow Garner)

Sioux (February 10, 1957–) Seattle, Washington
Sculptor

EDUCATION: B.F.A., Kansas City Art Institute (1979–82). Assistant to sculptors Jerry Peart, John Henry, and Mark diSuvero (1974–78).

AWARDS: Garner has won numerous awards and honors, including the Sixth Martin and Doris Rosen Award from Appalachian State University, North Carolina, and the First Award of Excellence in the "New Horizons in Art—22nd Exhibit of Illinois Artists" (both in 1992).

REPRESENTATION: Jan Cicero Gallery, Chicago; Heard Museum, Phoenix, Arizona; Sacred Circle Gallery of American Indian Art, Seattle, Washington.

ABOUT THE ARTIST: Garner's work has been installed in dozens of major exhibits across the United States and has been included in four major touring exhibits (each of which printed catalogs), and he has also constructed major projects for internationally known artists and institutions. In addition, he was invited to give the 1993 inaugural lecture at the National Museum of Natural History in Washington, D.C.

JACK GLOVER

Cherokee; Texas
Sculptor—bronze

EDUCATION: Largely self-taught.

REPRESENTATION: Glover's Old West Museum and Trading Post, Bowie, Texas.

ABOUT THE ARTIST: Author of 14 books on Indian culture, collector of Indian artifacts, and owner of an Old West museum and trading post in Bowie, Texas, Glover sculpts investment-quality bronzes.

CRAIG GOSEYUN
(a.k.a. Craig Dan Goseyun)

San Carlos Apache (March 31, 1960–)
Sculptor

EDUCATION: Institute of American Indian Arts, Santa Fe, New Mexico. Influenced strongly by Allan Houser through six-year apprenticeship.

AWARDS: Grand Award, Red Earth Awards, Oklahoma (1992); second place, Category 2407, sculpture, and first place, Category 2408, sculpture, SWAIA (1992); Best of Show, SWAIA (1993); Best of Show, University of Kansas Sixth Annual Lawrence Tuskan Art Show; second place, Category 2802, and first place, Category 4102, SWAIA (1995); first place, Class XI Monumental Sculpture, SWAIA (1996).

REPRESENTATION: Joy Tash Gallery, Scottsdale, Arizona; Contemporary Southwest Galleries, Santa Fe, New Mexico; Plainsmen Gallery, Dunedin, Florida.

ABOUT THE ARTIST: Goseyun counts Mexican artist Zuniga, Japanese-American sculptor Noguchi, Michelangelo, and Brancusi among those artists that have had a strong influence on his work. He incorporates those influences with his own cultural background to create his works in stone and bronze. He works in fairly large formats and likes doing monuments.

ROLLIE A. GRANDBOIS
(a.k.a. Rollie Grandbois, Rollie Anthony Nichlaus Grandbois, Rollie A. Grandboise)

Chippewa/Cree/French (September 8, 1954–) Belcourt, North Dakota
Sculptor—stone, bronze, cast paper; jeweler

EDUCATION: Institute of American Indian Arts, Santa Fe, New Mexico (1983).

AWARDS: Sculptor of the Year, Grand National Art Show American Endangered Species Foundation (1990); Best of Show, Intertribal Arts Expo (1991); first place, sculpture, Santa Fe Indian Market (1992); second place, Category 2706, SWAIA (1994); second place, Category 2704, marble, SWAIA (1995); first place, monumental sculpture, SWAIA (1996); first place, Class V Sculpture, bronze, SWAIA (1997); third place, miniatures, SWAIA (1998).

REPRESENTATION: Sunset Silver, Albuquerque, New Mexico; Institute of American Indian Arts Museum, Santa Fe, New Mexico; Turquoise Tortoise Gallery, Sedona, Arizona; Eagle Mountain Fine Art, Jemez Springs, New Mexico.

ABOUT THE ARTIST: Grandbois served as a combat infantry tactics instructor for West Point before turning to sculpture. He works with life- and heroic-sized stone sculptures, an example being "Ancient Guardian," a 9-foot sculpture made of marble, neon, and steel. Grandbois believes that "the light represents the spirit, the marble is antiquity and the steel is strength." He was one of four Canadian artists chosen to sculpt a 10-foot-tall historical monument.

JUDITH GREENE

Seneca (1940–) Buffalo, New York
Sculptor—mixed media

EDUCATION: B.F.A., SUNY College of Ceramics, Alfred University (1984); M.F.A., University of Massachusetts, Dartmouth (1990).

ABOUT THE ARTIST: This sculptor, a member of the Deer clan, works in mixed media and is formally trained. She does shows throughout her area and represents her own work.

ROBERT HAOZOUS

Chiricahua Apache/Navajo/English/Spanish (April 1, 1943–) Los Angeles, California
Sculptor—stone, metals

EDUCATION: Utah State University, Logan; California College of Arts and Crafts, Oakland.

AWARDS: Many honors and awards, including Best of Show, SWAIA (1984); Best of Division, stone sculpture, and Special Award, sculpture, SWAIA (1975).

REPRESENTATION: David Rettig Fine Arts, Inc., Santa Fe, New Mexico; Wheelwright Museum of the American Indian, Santa Fe; Philbrook Museum of Art, Tulsa, Oklahoma; Shidoni Gallery, Tesuque, New Mexico.

ABOUT THE ARTIST: A son of Allan Houser, Haozous is the only one of his brothers to follow in their famous father's footsteps. Haozous humorously (bordering on the sarcastic) depicts the way the white man's civilization poses a threat to traditional Indian life. He often uses steel and stainless steel, as well as mahogany and stone, and frequently works with animal forms. In a June 1986 article in Southwest Airlines' *Spirit* magazine, Haozous is quoted as saying, "What I'm doing is taking the philosophy of the

Native American and pursuing it with honesty, as a direct reflection of my experience." He has exhibited throughout the United States since 1970.

JAMES PEPPER HENRY
Kanza (Kaw)/Creek (1966–) Portland, Oregon
Sculptor—bronze, terra-cotta

EDUCATION: B.A., fine arts, University of Oregon, Portland.
REPRESENTATION: Littman Gallery, Portland, Oregon.
ABOUT THE ARTIST: As guest curator for special exhibits at the Portland Art Museum, gallery coordinator of the Firehouse Cultural Center (in Portland), and a mask carver who also exhibits, Henry is a busy artist who is constantly spreading his knowledge and love of Native art. Henry, a descendant of the Chiricahua Apache leader Geronimo, learned about Northwest Coast art when his family moved to British Columbia. He utilizes what he has learned through his family and the courses he took in school to produce his own style of sculpture. He has sold to private collectors and does shows throughout the Northwest.

JOHN J. HOOVER
Aleut (October 13, 1919–) Cordova, Alaska
Sculptor—polychrome wood, bronze, aluminum; painter

EDUCATION: Leon Derbyshire School of the Fine Arts, Seattle, Washington; artist-in-residence, Institute of American Indian Arts, Santa Fe, New Mexico.
AWARDS: Hoover was asked to judge the sculpture at the Santa Fe Indian Market in 1990. He has received many awards for his sculptures, including first place at the 1978 Heard Museum show, a first award in sculpture at the 1974 Philbrook Art Center show, and many more.
REPRESENTATION: Glen Green Gallery, Santa Fe, New Mexico; Stonington Gallery, Anchorage, Alaska, and Seattle, Washington; Quintana Gallery, Portland, Oregon; Amy Burnett Gallery, Bremerton, Washington; Heard Museum, Phoenix, Arizona; Sacred Circle Gallery of American Indian Art, Seattle, Washington.
ABOUT THE ARTIST: Because Hoover grew up knowing little of his heritage, he soaked up the Northwest Coast's myths and legends when he became an adult. In fact, he still takes off in the spring to fish Alaskan waters until the end of September. He specializes in Indian myths, legends, and shamans

in his sculptured pieces and commonly uses raven and salmon motifs. He uses traditional colors and tools in his work and experiments with his own interpretations of the ancient arts. His wife, Barbara (born in Montana in 1926), is also a painter and recognized as an award-winning primitive artist. Hoover's sculpted pieces have been exhibited all over the world.

ALLAN C. HOUSER
(a.k.a. Haozous, "Pulling Roots")

Warm Springs Chiricahua Apache (1915–94) Apache, Oklahoma
Artist—painter, sculptor

EDUCATION: Studied with the muralist Olaf Nordmark and also worked with Dorothy Dunn in Santa Fe, New Mexico. Director of the sculpture division of the Institute of American Indian Arts, Santa Fe (1971–75).

AWARDS: Scholarship for sculpture and painting from John Simon Guggenheim; a Certificate of Appreciation by the IACB in 1967; three Grand Awards and a trophy for outstanding work in Indian art from the Santa Fe Indian School; as well as numerous other awards throughout the years.

REPRESENTATION: American Foundation Museum, Dragoon, Arizona; Philharmonic Galleries/Philharmonic Center for the Arts, Naples, Florida; Glen Green Galleries, Santa Fe, New Mexico; Wheelwright Museum of the American Indian, Santa Fe; Heard Museum, Phoenix, Arizona; Dewey Galleries, Ltd., Santa Fe.

ABOUT THE ARTIST: Houser painted murals in Indian schools, such as Fort Sill, Riverside, and Jicarilla, and he sculpted the marble war memorial entitled "Comrades in Mourning" at the Haskell Institute in 1948. Exhibitions include the "National Exhibition of Indian Art" in New York (1937), where he was the only American Indian represented; the "O'Hara Exhibition" in Maine (1937); the New York World's Fair (1939); and one-man shows at the Art Institute of Chicago, the Denver Art Museum, and others. His work is held in collections, such as the Fort Sill Indian School in Oklahoma, the Museum of New Mexico, the Philbrook Art Center, the Heard Museum, the Smithsonian Museum, and the Arizona State Capitol. Because of his connection with the Institute of American Indian Arts, Houser influenced the lives of many young artists with whom he worked. He is one of the most celebrated Native American artists in the world. A quote from Houser was etched in the base of his work "Sacred Rain Arrow," exhibited at the 2002 Winter Olympics: "I believe sculpture is the art that people respond to most naturally—they can take hold of it, they

Bronze frog by Stan Hunt.
Courtesy of Tribal Expressions,
Arlington Heights, IL.

can enjoy it with the sense of touch as well as the sense of sight, and they can enjoy it from all sides."

STAN HUNT

(*see* biography in the "Carving" chapter pp. 205–206)

DOUG HYDE

Nez Percé/Chippewa/Assiniboin (1946–) Hermiston, Oregon
Sculptor—stone, wood, bronze; painter

EDUCATION: Influenced by mentor Allan Houser. Institute of American Indian Arts in Santa Fe, New Mexico; San Francisco Art Institute; faculty member, Institute of American Indian Arts.

AWARDS: First prize, Scottsdale National Indian Art Exhibition (1966); First Award, Heard Museum (1972); Distinguished Artist Award, Santa Fe Rotary Foundation (1996); and many other awards, as well as commissions.

REPRESENTATION: Hahn Gallery, Philadelphia, Pennsylvania; Glen Green Galleries, Scottsdale, Arizona; Fenn Galleries, Santa Fe, New Mexico; Louis Newman Galleries, Beverly Hills, California; Nadler's Indian Arts, Scottsdale, Arizona; Nedra Matteucci Galleries, Santa Fe, New Mexico.

ABOUT THE ARTIST: Hyde does not have a particular idea what his subject is going to be when he begins a project; instead, he lets the material with which he's working suggest a design. Like other Native American artists,

Hyde depicts the legends and rituals of his people in his work. His work has been exhibited throughout the United States, such as with the U.S. Department of Interior, Washington, D.C.; the Museum of the Plains Indian and Crafts Center, Browning, Montana; the Institute of American Indian Arts; and many others.

JIM JACKSON
(a.k.a. James C. Jackson, James Conway Jackson)

Klamath/Modoc (June 18, 1963–) Klamath Falls, Oregon
Sculptor—clay, bronze

EDUCATION: Mostly self-taught; some classes at the Institute of American Indian Arts (1981–82) and Portland Community College (1983–84). Studied with Rollie Grandbois, Lillian Pitt, and Baje Whitethorne.

AWARDS: Jackson's awards are many, including first place, American Indian Invitational, Dallas, Texas (1986); Metropolitan Arts Commission one-man show, Portland, Oregon (1986); first place, ceramic sculpture, Colorado Indian Market (1987); first place, Native American Art Show, Great Falls, Montana (1987); first, second, and third place, honorable mention, and best craftsman awards from such places as the Lawrence (Kansas) Indian Art Show, SWAIA (Santa Fe), the Red Earth Art Show, and many others.

REPRESENTATION: Adobe East, Milburn, New Jersey; Attic Gallery, Portland, Oregon; Southwest Trading Company, St. Charles, Illinois.

ABOUT THE ARTIST: Jackson began sculpting and painting at a very young age, and by his early 20s had already established his career as a sculptor. He comes from an artistic family (his father also sculpts and has occasionally shown his work with Jim). Jackson's bronze and clay sculptures are in much demand by collectors throughout the United States. His work usually represents traditional tribal members in a lifelike stance. He creates all types of sculptures, from clay wall hangings to 8-foot-tall bronze monuments.

LAWRENCE JACQUEZ. (*see* Dolls and Kachinas, pp. 242–243).

ORELAND JOE
(a.k.a. Oreland C. Joe)

Ute/Navajo (1958–) Shiprock, New Mexico
Sculptor—stone, bronze; painter

EDUCATION: Self-taught.

REPRESENTATION: Pierce Fine Art, San Francisco, California, Horwitch Galleries, Scottsdale, Arizona, and Santa Fe, New Mexico; Wadle Galleries, Santa Fe.

ABOUT THE ARTIST: Joe was first inspired to carve when on a trip to Paris with an Indian dance troupe in 1968. They visited Versailles, and Joe was impressed by the statues in the gardens there. However, he didn't begin sculpting until 1980. He likes to work in alabaster, limestone, and marble, and inspiration for most of his pieces comes from his background as a Southern Ute. Joe formed a group of fledgling artists called Eagles in Flight, in Shiprock, New Mexico, and became a member of the prestigious Cowboy Artists of America in 1992.

PRESLEY LAFOUNTAIN
(a.k.a. Preslay LaFountain)

Turtle Mountain Band Chippewa (1956–) Lynwood, California
Sculptor, carver

EDUCATION: Mostly self-taught.

AWARDS: One of the first awards LaFountain won was the Purchase Award at the Institute of American Indian Arts in 1976. Since that time he has received many awards, including Most Promising Young Sculptor and Carver at the 65th Annual Indian Market/Wheelwright Museum Award (1986); third prize, bronze sculpture, SWAIA (1987); second prize, sculpture over 21 inches, SWAIA (1989); and second prize, sculpture, Northern Plains Tribal Arts, Sioux Falls, South Dakota (1989).

REPRESENTATION: Sunwest Silver, Albuquerque, New Mexico; Margaret Kilgore Gallery, Scottsdale, Arizona.

ABOUT THE ARTIST: LaFountain works with stone and is often amazed at how pieces come together naturally. He used black African wonderstone in his sculpture "Night Wind" and will also use Utah alabaster and other stones. He states, "I carve deliberately without detail; I carve shadows, using shadows as lines. I don't want to carve just beautiful objects . . . I want to carve a whole spectrum of emotions." His work is held in museums throughout the United States, such as the Heard, Phoenix; Institute of American Indian Arts, Santa Fe; and the Wheelwright, Santa Fe.

TRUMAN LOWE
(a.k.a. Truman T. Lowe)

Winnebago (January 19, 1944–) Black River Falls, Wisconsin
Sculptor

EDUCATION: B.S., art education, University of Wisconsin at LaCrosse (1969); M.F.A., University of Wisconsin at Madison (1973). Professor of art, University of Wisconsin at Madison (1975–).

AWARDS: Lowe's numerous awards include a Chancellor's Development Grant in 1991, many commissions, and honors.

REPRESENTATION: Jan Cicero Gallery, Chicago; Kathryn Sermas Gallery, New York City; Lazzaro Signature Gallery of Fine Art; Eiteljorg Museum of American Indian and Western Art, Indianapolis, Indiana.

ABOUT THE ARTIST: Lowe is interested in using natural forms in his sculptures, placing his materials in a contemporary context. His Winnebago culture is strongly represented in his work. His work has been exhibited in solo and group shows around the world. In a 1985 article in *Wisconsin Academy Review*, Lowe said, "My inspiration comes from tribal art and objects of the mid-states' Indians, but not from any one specific nation or tribe. None of my sculptures is religious, nor do I allow myself to be influenced by any sacred objects."

ALVIN MARSHALL
(a.k.a. Alvin K. Marshall)

Navajo (April 9, 1959–) Shiprock, New Mexico
Sculptor, painter

EDUCATION: Marshall started drawing at age three or four, after watching his father "draw on anything." Tutored by Oreland C. Joe.

REPRESENTATION: Heard Museum, Phoenix, Arizona; Artistic Galleries, Scottsdale, Arizona.

ABOUT THE ARTIST: Marshall did not begin working as a sculptor until he left the army and met Oreland Joe in 1981. Prior to that point, he'd been a painter, but two years later, he was awarded Best Sculptor of the Year by the Heard Museum—at only 24 years old. Since that time, he has been part of many shows and won many awards. Even fellow artist R. C. Gorman celebrates Marshall's talent by adding the sculptor's work to his own collection. Marshall uses alabaster, golden alabaster, and other materials to make his sculptures. His work makes a statement about Navajo ways of living in harmony with nature.

MICHAEL NARANJO
(a.k.a. Michael A. Naranjo)

Santa Clara (August 28, 1944–) Santa Fe, New Mexico
Sculptor

EDUCATION: Learned how to make traditional pottery from his mother, aunt, and grandmother.

AWARDS: Profiles in Courage Award, New Mexico Vietnam Veteran's Association (1982); New Mexico Veteran of the Year, New Mexico Chapter of the D.A.R. (1986); Distinguished Achievement Award, American Indian Resources Institute, National Press Club, Washington, D.C. (1990); recipient of the first Clinton King Purchase Award, Museum of Fine Arts, Santa Fe, New Mexico (1991); first prize, Southwest Art Exhibition, Del Rio Council of the Arts, Del Rio, Texas (1992); and many more.

REPRESENTATION: Michael A. Naranjo Gallery and Studio, Espanola, New Mexico; Heard Museum, Phoenix, Arizona.

ABOUT THE ARTIST: One of 10 children, Naranjo grew up in Santa Clara Pueblo with a Baptist minister father and potter mother. Blinded in Vietnam, Naranjo works with his hands, using his memory and imagination to create his pieces. He has full use of only one of his hands due to an ambush in Vietnam. In 1983 he had an audience with the Pope and was allowed to touch the Vatican's collection of sculptures, including some of Michelangelo's. Naranjo's human figures do not have eyes and are simple, flowing sculptures, void of extraneous detail. His work is held by many museums throughout the world, including collections of the Vatican, the Smithsonian, the Heard Museum, the White House, and many others.

TIM NICOLA

Penobscot (1949–) Indian Island, Maine
Sculptor

EDUCATION: Self-taught and Institute of American Indian Arts.

AWARDS: Best of Class, sculpture, and second place, Div. B Bronze and Other Metal, SWAIA (1995); first place, Class V Sculpture, Div. A Stone, Category 2703, SWAIA (1996); first place, Class V Sculpture, Div. A Stone, Category 2701, SWAIA (1997); first place, Div. A Stone, Category 2703, alabaster over 30 inches, SWAIA (1998); and many other awards.

REPRESENTATION: Squash Blossom Galleries, Inc., Palm Desert, California; Byrne-Getz Gallery, Aspen, Colorado; Frank Howell Gallery, Santa Fe, New Mexico; Dakota Gallery, Boca Raton, Florida; Adobe East, Melbourne, New Jersey; Canyon Road Gallery, Denver, Colorado; El Cerro Art, Los Lunas, New Mexico.

ABOUT THE ARTIST: Nicola is married to artist Mary Yazzie and did his first joint show with her—they both sold out, something of a phenomenon in the art world. He concentrates on Navajo themes, often inspired by photos friends send him of babies or family members. He sometimes uses Utah alabaster for his simple, elegant figures and prefers to sculpt women.

CHARLES PRATT
(a.k.a. Charlie Pratt)

Cheyenne/Arapaho/Sioux/French (1937–) Concho, Oklahoma
Sculptor/jeweler—various metals and semiprecious stones; painter; silverworker

EDUCATION: Self-taught artist; learned how to work with clay from grandfather.

AWARDS: Listed in *Who's Who in American Art* and has won approximately 400 awards for his work, including being named Indian Arts and Crafts Association Artist of the Year in 1985; first place, three-dimensional, Red Cloud Indian Art Show, Pine Ridge, South Dakota (1988).

REPRESENTATION: Silver Sun Traders, Albuquerque and Santa Fe, New Mexico; Heard Museum, Phoenix, Arizona; Cristof's, Santa Fe.

ABOUT THE ARTIST: Pratt was influenced by Allan Houser's 1960s welded sculptures. He creates large-scale as well as miniature creations, in cast-bronze, metal sculpture, and stone, and is an accomplished silversmith. He weaves colors and textures from his heritage into his signature works, which include "The Blue Corn People." He has had works commissioned by the Heard Museum, the Philbrook Art Center, the Oklahoma Science and Arts Foundation, and the Alfred P. Murrah Federal Building (Oklahoma City).

HARVEY RATTEY
(a.k.a. Harvey L. Rattey)

Pembina/Assiniboin (1938–) near Harlem, Montana
Sculptor—bronze

EDUCATION: Hines-Zemsky workshop with Robert Bateman, Zahourek Anatomiken workshop, Edward Fraughton workshop.

AWARDS: Blue Chip Award, U.S. Chamber of Commerce (1993); National Wild Turkey Federation Sculptor of the Year (1992); Best of Show, Western Artists of America, Reno, Nevada (1982); Bronze Medal, Western Artists of America (1981); Gold Medal, Western Artists of America (1979); and numerous others.

REPRESENTATION: Bridger Foundry & Gallery, Montana.

ABOUT THE ARTIST: Rattey portrays his ancestors, cowboys, and animals in a "wild and wooly" fashion. His sculptures have been collected by dignitaries, and his work has been exhibited in museums and shows all over the United States and Europe.

WILLARD STONE
(a.k.a. Jess Willard Stone, Ne-Ah-Yah, "Rock")

Cherokee (February 29, 1916–March 5, 1985) near Oktaha, Oklahoma
Sculptor—wood

EDUCATION: Bacone Junior College, Bacone, Oklahoma.

AWARDS: Artist-in-residence at the Thomas Gilcrease Museum, Arizona (1940–43); Grand Award winner of the Five Civilized Tribes Master's Show (1983).

REPRESENTATION: Gilcrease Museum, Tulsa, Oklahoma.

ABOUT THE ARTIST: Stone was considered by many to be the finest wood sculptor in America. He created many pieces, in spite of the fact that he lacked parts of two fingers and a thumb on his right hand due to a childhood accident. He worked in wood and particularly loved cherry, walnut, sassafras, and cedar. His works were commissioned for the Cherokee Cultural Center in Tahlequah, Oklahoma, as well as for many others. In his

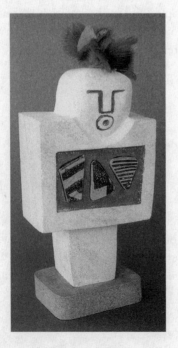

Sculpture called "Look at the Shard I Found #2!" by Mark Swazo-Hinds. It depicts a man, adorned with actual Anasazi shards, but adorned on the top with the "Swazo" parrot feathers. 8½" high by 4" wide. $400. Courtesy of Jill Giller, Native American Collections, www.nativepots.com. Photo by Bill Bonebrake.

Sculpted bear fetish by Mark Swazo-Hinds. He has used a veined New Mexico Alabaster from Clines Corner. It is dressed with parrot and turkey feathers, shards, and semiprecious stones. The bold blue and orange natural parrot feathers make a beautiful contrast to the quiet, muted alabaster. 12" high by 24" wide. $2400. Courtesy of Jill Giller, Native American Collections, www.nativepots.com. Photo by Bill Bonebrake.

Lucite prayer stick with jade bear and crystal figure by Mark Swazo-Hinds. $1000. Courtesy of Jill Giller, Native American Collections, www.nativepots.com. Photo by Bill Bonebrake.

"Chongo Love" by Roxanne Swentzell. Courtesy of Jill
Giller, Native American Collections, www.nativepots.com.
Photo by Bill Bonebrake.

work, he strived to reflect the suffering and survival of his people. His
style is recognized as original to the artists of Oklahoma.

MARK SWAZO-HINDS

Tesuque; Tesuque Pueblo, New Mexico
Painter, Ssculptor

EDUCATION: Learned some of his techniques from his father, Patrick
Swazo-Hinds.
AWARDS: Many awards throughout the years.
REPRESENTATION: Native American Collections, Inc., Denver, Colorado.
ABOUT THE ARTIST: Swazo-Hinds is known for his bear fetishes, but he has
done some more abstract sculptures and has also worked in watercolors on
paper. He comes from an artistic family. His father, Patrick, was a well-
known artist and mentor to many young artists.

ROXANNE SWENTZELL

Santa Clara/Anglo (December 9, 1962–) Taos, New Mexico
Sculptor—clay

EDUCATION: Institute of American Indian Arts, Santa Fe, New Mexico; Portland Museum Art School, Portland, Oregon. Studied as a child with Michael Naranjo and Rina Swentzell.

AWARDS: Swentzell's many awards include yearly awards at the Santa Fe Indian Market, as well as the Joy Levine Art Scholarship (1980).

REPRESENTATION: Four Winds Gallery, Pittsburgh, Pennsylvania; Studio 53, New York City; Heard Museum, Phoenix, Arizona; Denver Art Museum, Colorado; Smithsonian Museum, Washington, D.C.

ABOUT THE ARTIST: This sculptor comes from a family of potters, sculptors, educators, and architects. She is a fifth-generation artist (her aunt is potter Jody Falwell and her grandparents are Michael and Rose Naranjo). Swentzell's sculptures are actually figures, studies of the human body, as well as emotions. She builds her sculptors in the coiling style some potters use. All of her figures have gestures and humanistic expressions that appear to change as you study them.

DANIEL THOMPSON

Mohawk (1953–) Rooseveltown, New York
Illustrator, stone- and wood-carver, photographer

EDUCATION: Self-taught.

AWARDS: Thompson has won awards for his stone-carvings and has illustrated many books for presses throughout the country.

ABOUT THE ARTIST: Thompson not only does illustrating, but also writes poetry. A multitalented artist, he carves with soapstone and wood, making pipes, sculptures, and canes. He demonstrates and teaches his craft at culture centers.

GORDON VAN WERT
(a.k.a. Waboosa [rabbit], Benzoo [skeleton])

Red Lake Chippewa
Sculptor

EDUCATION: Institute of American Indian Arts, Santa Fe, New Mexico; worked with Allan Houser, Fritz Scholder, and Charles Loloma.

AWARDS: First prize, Heard Museum (1975, 1976); second prize, Phoenix, Arizona (1975–76); first prize, Scottsdale National (1976); first prize, Ojibwa Exposition (1977); and many others.

REPRESENTATION: Linda McAdoo Galleries, Santa Fe, New Mexico; Nadler's Indian Arts, Scottsdale, Arizona; Heard Museum, Phoenix, Arizona; Wheelwright Museum, Santa Fe; Moondancer Gallery, Palos

"Chief Crazy Horse" sculpture by Augie Velasquez. This sculpture is made of lapis and weighs 50 lbs. It measures 11" × 15" and is from the Sar-e-Sang mine in Afghanistan where the best lapis lazuli in the world has been mined for 6000 years. $180,000. Courtesy of White Buffalo Productions, www.whitebuffaloprod.com.

Verde, California; Squash Blossom, Aspen, Colorado; Museum of Northern Arizona, Flagstaff, Arizona.

ABOUT THE ARTIST: Van Wert grew up on the Chippewa Red Lake Indian reservation in Minnesota. He likes to carve animals and little children with chubby faces. He uses good, often translucent, alabaster or fine marble for his work.

"Geronimo" by Augie Velasquez. Courtesy of White Buffalo Productions, www.whitebuffaloprod.com.

"The Pathfinder" by James Vigil.
16½" × 5½". $900. Courtesy of Jill
Giller, Native American
Collections, www.native pots.com.
Photo by Bill Bonebrake.

"Celestial Bear" by James Vigil. 13"
× 6". $950. Courtesy of Jill Giller,
Native American Collections,
www.native pots.com. Photo by
Bill Bonebrake.

AUGIE VELASQUEZ

Yaqui; Northern California
Sculptor

EDUCATION: Self-taught.

AWARDS: Various awards at the following shows and festivals: South West Art Festival, Indio, California; Indian Art Northwest, Portland, Oregon; Hilton Indian Market, Santa Fe, New Mexico; Indian Ceremonial, Santa Monica, California; Las Vegas Museum of Art, Las Vegas, Nevada; San Juan Bautista Mission Days, San Juan Bautista, California.

REPRESENTATION: White Buffalo Productions, www.whitebuffaloprod.com.

ABOUT THE ARTIST: Velasquez chose the Yaqui Deer Dancer as his logo because he feels it represents his heritage and spirit. He was born and raised in California and worked there as a stonemason and brickmason. That background helped him understand the materials with which he currently sculpts. He believes that the stone has a spirit and he can feel that spirit when he's working. His work has been shown in galleries and exhibits all over the Southwest.

"Protecting the Generations" by Kathy Whitman/Elk Woman. Colorado white marble. $5800. Courtesy of Tribal Expressions, Arlington Heights, IL.

"Warrior's Way" by Kathy Whitman/Elk Woman.
Courtesy of Tribal Expressions, Arlington Heights, IL.

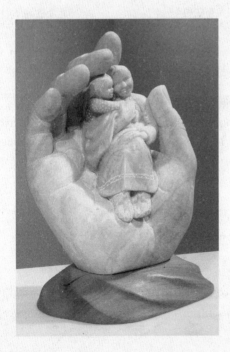

"Creator's Love" by Kathy
Whitman/Elk Woman. Courtesy of
Tribal Expressions, Arlington
Heights, IL.

JAMES VIGIL

Jemez (July 30, 1948–) Jemez Pueblo, New Mexico
Sculptor

EDUCATION: Learned from family members and from a stone apprentice-ship that began in 1987.

AWARDS: Many awards at markets and festivals like the Santa Fe Indian Market and other Native Arts competitions.

REPRESENTATION: Jill Giller, Native American Collections, Inc., www.na-tivepots.com.

ABOUT THE ARTIST: Vigil creates stone sculptures in his unique style, using his personal experiences of Tewa culture and history, as well as what he learned during his stone apprenticeship. His works often depict pueblo life and people in alabaster, steatite, marble, and other stones.

KATHY WHITMAN

(a.k.a. Elk Woman) (*See* biography under that name p. 412.)

JOHN JULIUS WILNOTY

(a.k.a. John Wilnoty)

Cherokee (1940–) Bigwitch, North Carolina
Sculptor—pipestone, catlinite, other stone

EDUCATION: Self-taught.

AWARDS: First and second place, Class IX Sculpture, stone under 12 inches, Intertribal Ceremonial (1988).

REPRESENTATION: Heard Museum, Phoenix, Arizona.

ABOUT THE ARTIST: Wilnoty concentrates on bringing the history of his people to life. His carvings are meticulous and often influenced by his study of pre-Columbian pipe bowls of the southeastern United States.

DUFFY WILSON

(a.k.a. Se-Gwai-Don-Kwe)

Tuscarora/Iroquois (1927–) Lewiston, New York
Sculptor—stone

EDUCATION: Self-taught.

AWARDS: Won his first award in 1973: first prize of specially designed gold medal and $2,500 at the Indian sculpture show at the Heard Museum, Phoenix, Arizona.

REPRESENTATION: Heard Museum, Phoenix, Arizona; Lovena Ohl Gallery, Scottsdale, Arizona.

ABOUT THE ARTIST: Wilson is often credited with bringing the Iroquois art of sculpting back to his people. His modern works reflect his heritage and traditions. He uses steatite stone from North Carolina to translate thousands of years of cultural imagery. At one point, Wilson was executive director of the Native American Center for the Living Arts in New York.

TEX WOUNDED FACE

Mandan/Hidatsa (May 9, 1955-) Watford City, North Dakota
Sculptor

EDUCATION: Studied sculpture under Allan Houser, Institute of American Indian Arts, Santa Fe, New Mexico (1971–72); Arizona State University, Tempe (1977–78); Boise State University, Boise, Idaho (1979–80); San Francisco Art Institute (1980–81); Arizona State University, Tempe (1983–85); Arts Administration Fellowship, National Endowment for the Arts, Washington, D.C. (1988); Arts Leadership Institute, Hubert H. Humphrey Institute for Public Affairs, University of Minnesota (1989).

AWARDS: Best of Show, American Indian Arts Collection Exhibit, Shawnee, Oklahoma (1979); Lawrence Indian Art Show, Museum of Anthropology, University of Kansas, Merit Award (1990); first place, Governor's State Craft Competition, Bismarck, North Dakota; first and third place awards, Indian Affairs Commission, North Dakota Regional Craft Competition, Bismarck; and many others.

REPRESENTATION: Americana West Gallery, Washington, D.C.; Quintana Gallery, Portland, Oregon; Heard Museum, Phoenix, Arizona; Indian Craft Shop, Washington, D.C., Museum of Northern Arizona, Flagstaff, Arizona; Mudhead Gallery, Denver, Colorado; Kiva Gallery, Estes Park, Colorado; Eagle Plume Gallery, Allenspark, Colorado; Eagles Roost Gallery, Colorado Springs, Colorado; Covered Wagon Gallery, Albuquerque, New Mexico.

ABOUT THE ARTIST: Wounded Face works in stone, porcelain, and other materials. His sculptures reflect the Native American experience. In an artist's statement he says, "My work is contemporary, yet has an individualistic appeal that moves from tradition and beyond ancient metaphor towards a contemporary sculptural expression of contemporary issues within the arts forum."

"Bear Fetish" by Lance Yazzie. Silver Cloud Alabaster. 19" × 13". $850. Turquoise Tortoise, Sedona, AZ.

"Cedar Woman" by Larry Yazzie. Bronze. 7" × 5". $23,000. Turquoise Tortoise, Sedona, AZ.

LANCE YAZZIE

Navajo (ca. 1974–) Tuba City, Arizona
Sculptor

EDUCATION: Self-taught while watching father, Larry Yazzie, sculpt.

REPRESENTATION: Turquoise Tortoise, Sedona, Arizona.

ABOUT THE ARTIST: Yazzie started learning how to sculpt by cleaning stones for his father, Larry Yazzie, who started teaching his son the basics of sculpting. Through the years, Lance moved from simply making allowance money to refining his art. By the age of 13, he had his own show. He strives to find new ways to express himself with his art.

LARRY YAZZIE

Navajo; Tuba City, Arizona
Sculptor

EDUCATION: Self-taught, one year at community college, and classes at the Institute at American Indian Arts, Santa Fe, New Mexico.

REPRESENTATION: Turquoise Tortoise, Sedona, Arizona; Lovena Ohl Gallery, Scottsdale, Arizona.

ABOUT THE ARTIST: Yazzie started his artistic career as a painter, then moved on to sculpting, where he discovered he excelled. He works with many different types of stone—including marble and soapstone—and, often, bronze. He sculpts women's faces more often than men's because (in his words), "I believe that the Great Spirit has blessed women in a special way. I know few men who can endure all that a woman must."

Prices

Andy and Roberta Abeita. Various size fetish sculptures, ranging from $25–$250 each.

Jon DeCelles. "Fleur," edition 9 of 15. 30" tall. (Won first place in the Bronze category at the 2000 Santa Fe Indian Market.) $4,500–$4,800.

Anita Fields. "Incident Southwest of Town" Series. 40½" high × 12¾" wide × 8¼" deep. $4,500–$5,000.

Craig Goseyun. Large pieces of public sculptures, ranging from $4,000–$40,000.

Allan Houser. Works range from $2,000–$500,000.

Presley La Fountain. "On a Yellow Moon," 2001. Alabaster. 27" × 13". $4,000–$5,000.

Michael Naranjo. Limited editions of this sculptor's work sell for approximately $400–$40,000.

Tim Nicola. "Moving Forward." Alabaster. 39" tall. $10,500.

Charlie Pratt. "Birdwoman." Portrait of Laura Birdwoman, a Cheyenne. Called Aunt Laura, this small-boned, hunched-over woman never married, but was known as a bighearted, giving person. The white feather down her back is a symbol of her virginity. 5' 4" high. $23,000–$25,000.

————. "Blue Sky," 1993. Turquoise nugget out of Senora mine in Mexico. Feathers are fabricated brass, and medallion is turquoise, coral, and Pacific clam. 17" × 10". $2,600–$2,750.

Willard Stone. "Something to Believe In." Pewter castings. $500–$600.

Roxanne Swentzell. "Window to the Past." Larger-than-life-size bronze, studio edition. $50,000.

————. "Somewhere in Here." Bronze. $1,000–$1,250.

————. "Framed." Bronze. $5,700–$6,000.

————. "Choices." Bronze, edition of 25. $5,300–$5,800.

Gordon Van Wert. "Spirit Seeker Apache." Alabaster. 22½" high. $4,650–$4,800.

Tex Wounded Face. "Americanization of the Native American." Alabaster. $2,500–$3,000.

CHAPTER 11

Textiles, Blankets, and Rugs

Rugs, blankets, and other textiles have been woven by Native Americans since ancient days, but many of the early pieces did not withstand the test of time, nor do we know the names of the weavers. Because of these reasons and because this volume concentrates on the artists themselves, we'll define the tribes, their blankets and rugs, and the periods by which they're defined, then simply introduce the makers we now know.

Hopi

Traditionally woven by men, Hopi blankets may be white or cream-colored wool with blue, brown, or black horizontal stripes, although the "Moki" blanket (one of the oldest Hopi styles) is woven with dark blue or black stripes. Shoulder blankets often have checkered or tartan patterns.

All blankets woven by the Hopi have a looser weave than those textiles woven by Navajos. Embroidery weaving is routinely used by the Pueblo weavers to decorate their textiles.

Navajo

The most prolific rug and blanket weavers in the Southwest, the Navajo have been weaving since the Pueblo dwellers sought refuge from the Spanish during the Pueblo Revolt of 1680. During the 200-year period from the late 1680s to the late 1880s, the Navajo people learned to weave and took advantage of the Santa Fe Trail's trade with its abundant supply of materials like cloth, yarn, and dye.

Navajo rug and blanket weaving is so distinctive that historians have separated the styles into named periods, defined as follows:

The Classic Period (1700–1850): Identified by the use of upright looms and simple patterns, rugs and blankets of this period primarily consist of narrow stripes and bands of white, gray, brown, tan, and black. The Spanish introduced indigo blue to the Navajo and it was widely used.

Late in this period the Mexican-Saltillo serapes that found their way into the upper Rio Grande area began to influence the Navajo weavers, and they adapted their designs to include diamonds and broad, wavy band motifs.

The Late Classic Period (1850–63): Pieces from these years are identified by the broad black, indigo, and white horizontal bands used to make chief's blankets. Later blankets would incorporate red *bayeta* threads, and designs would include diamonds, boxes, crosses, and stripes.

The serape and poncho serape were also popular during this period. Made to be worn over the head, they covered the weaver's body, both front and back.

As weavers became more highly skilled, they began to experiment and traded for the English material baize (*bayeta*). They unraveled the fabric so they could reweave it into their own designs.

This period of experimentation died when the Navajo people were captured and forced into reservation life.

The Transition Period (1863–90): These 27 years were a time when the Navajo people began to rebuild their flocks of sheep and started to use more commercial yarns; they used almost any color they could find. Germantown yarns were introduced in the early 1870s, and the height of Germantown rugs came in the 1890s when crazy designs and gaudy colors became the norm.

As the 20th century approached, two main changes helped the weaving industry regain its balance—the shift went from blanket to rug trading, and regional weaving styles were developed.

The Rug Period (1890–1930): This period marked the era when commercial dyes began to be commonly used among reservation weavers. They experimented with new styles, including a rug with a border.

By 1900 rug weaving was a highly successful trade, and markets, fairs, ceremonies, trading posts, railroads, and publications all helped the Navajo sell their work. Traders such as Juan Hubbell and John B. Moore helped the craft attain higher standards by demanding that the Native American weavers use better dyes and more tightly woven fabrics. Hubbell encouraged a return to the Late Classic Period designs, while Moore ordered rugs that were identified as the Two Gray Hills style, a bordered rug of natural wool tones of black, brown, and white, patterned with carded blends of beige, tan, and gray with commercially dyed blue and red.

The Revival Period (1930–40): This era is distinguished by the work of Inja and Leon H. McSparron of Chinle, Arizona, and Mary C. Wheelwright, a Navajo patron. They encouraged weavers in the area to experiment with old vegetal-dye methods. Ultimately they developed terraced and squash blossom patterns in pastel browns, golds, and greens in simple stripes and bands on a borderless fabric in what was called the Chinle regional style. This style eventually used dyes made by the DuPont Chemical Company and the Diamond Dye Company.

The Wide Ruins style was also the result of native plant dyes. The style was encouraged by Bill and Sallie Lippincott of Wide Ruins Trading Post in the 1930s. Gray and white were used sparingly, and combinations often resulted in soft pastels. The weaver used the Classic Period stripes and bands on a borderless background. Simplicity is a word often used when describing Wide Ruins rugs

After the Wide Ruins and Chinle styles were developed, experiments carried out by Nonabah G. Bryan and Stella Young over a period of six years developed 84 shades of color dyes. Their research contributed to one of the most important changes in Navajo weaving.

During the mid-1930s the U.S. government implemented a stock reduction program that virtually wiped out the smaller sheepherders of the Navajo Nation. Because herds were smaller, less mutton was produced for food, and fewer hides and less wool for rugs. The poverty this program imposed on the tribe was devastating.

The Regional Style Period (1940–present): The 1950s saw the beginning of six new styles of rugs: Shiprock, Lukachukai, Teec Nos Pas, the new Crystal, Two Gray Hills, and Ganado. Each is distinguished by style, color, dye, and design so that a collector can identify them at a glance.

The Shiprock rug, called a Yei, was developed from stylized sandpaintings and is often small to medium sized, with bright, slender, front-facing figures. The background color is usually white or light tan and is finely woven with commercial yarn.

The Lukachukai rug is a larger Yei rug of handspun wool and synthetic dyes of gray, red, black, or brown. Examples usually have a darker border, and the Yei figures tend to take on a more human appearance.

Teec Nos Pas rugs are tightly woven with a Persian flair; they are intricately designed with flamboyant colors of bright greens, oranges, reds, and blues. Typically they have a large border that incorporates a design, usually H, T, or L arrangements.

The Crystal rug pattern was designed by the owner of the trading post, J. B. Moore. It incorporates numerous crosses, diamonds, terraces, hook and fork patterns, swastikas, and arrows. The Crystal design is borderless and generously embellished with aniline red and outlines of blue.

Usually examples are composed of all-vegetal earth-toned colors such as brown, orange, beige, and gold, with subtle hints of green, blue, and maroon, in the basic classic pattern.

Two Gray Hills rugs are bordered (usually in black) and made with natural wool tones of black, brown, and white. Other than black, no dyes are used. These rugs are some of the most expensive contemporary Navajo rugs and are characterized by their light weight, careful carding and spinning, and high thread count, sometimes in excess of 120 wefts to the inch.

Ganado rugs are boldly designed, usually with a diamond or cross in the middle, sometimes outlined in another color. Deep red is the dominant color, although more contemporary designs have switched to a burgundy. They are larger than the other rugs, sometimes measuring as much as 24 by 36 feet.

Red Turkish woolen cloth called "balleta" (or bayeta) was first acquired by the Navajo from the Mexicans, and later from trading posts that sold it by the bolt. Indians would buy the cloth and unravel it, using the thread for their blankets.

From the time the Navajo first began making bayeta blankets, the blankets were noted for their durability, their warmth, and the quality of their weaving. Prices were high for a fine bayeta blanket ($200 in the early 1900s) and have risen. The work on these blankets takes a Navajo woman many months to complete; the weaving is so fine that these blankets can literally hold water.

Most of the early blankets were made to be worn on the chief's shoulders and might have had a slit in the center for the head, allowing the blanket to be worn as a poncho or serape. The finest examples of these blankets were worn only on festive occasions or at ceremonies.

The Navajo learned about dying wool from Mexicans and Pueblo Indians, whose skills were limited; thus the color selection seen in Navajo blankets of the time is limited as well. Blue was made from indigo; the bayeta wool was made in reds, blacks, blues, greens, pinks, oranges, and yellows.

One can tell a bayeta blanket by examining a single thread. Threads from bayeta blankets are single strand, while a triple strand indicates the yarn is Germantown. Other experts argue, though, that one can only tell a true bayeta when it's burned or by its distinctive rough and fuzzy texture.

Chief's blankets are woven crosswise instead of lengthwise. The Navajo term for these blankets is *Honal-Kladi* or *Honal-Chodi*. Chief's blankets were meant to be wrapped broadside around the body to better display the stripes.

Chief's blankets have gone through three phases. During the first phase these blankets were a favored trade item among the Ute and Sioux. This version had a black "streak" or belt in the center. Blankets of the second phase had small red rectangles woven into the ends and middles of the blue stripes. This created a 12-block pattern. In the 1860s the third-phase chief's blanket pattern emerged with a full diamond in the middle, quarter diamonds on each corner, and half diamonds in the center of each edge. During the 1880s weavers began incorporating pictorial elements and cross motifs into their textiles.

Though it was originally noted that chief's blankets were the property of men of high standing in the tribe, there is much documentation of women wearing the blankets (e.g., Brule Sioux women wore them on special occasions).

When it is almost impossible to stretch the stitches of the weft so that you can see the warp, the blanket will likely hold water. Blankets of this quality are the most collectible and are the ones that bring the highest auction prices. Such blankets are few and far between now, though the quality of today's Navajo blankets is of the highest order and unchallenged by blankets woven any other way. Perhaps that is the most amazing thing about Navajo weaving: the work is still woven by hand, and the products are far superior to anything that is machine-made.

Germantown yarns were introduced to the Navajo by 1850, and the Indians, not satisfied with the texture, twisted it to make it firmer and tighter. These yarns were dyed with vegetable dye, which made the colors reliable and resistant. Though some feel the introduction of Germantown yarns produced a deterioration in the Navajo blankets, certain weavers did their best work with these yarns and continued to produce weavings that could hold water.

Certain trading posts, such as Hubbell's in Ganado, Arizona, began to offer these blankets for sale. The first Navajo blankets Juan Hubbell put up for sale were marked to sell at $2 each. Little by little, Hubbell and his partner, C. N. Cotton, urged Navajo blanket weavers to produce more of their weavings. The Indians saw a growth in their income and were pleased. Hubbell and Cotton saw a way to make money, and they were pleased. A viable commercial industry was born. More trading posts got on the bandwagon. Soon, aniline dyes were introduced to the Navajo women who lived around Fort Defiance. Later, cotton warp was sold at low prices to Indian weavers, consequently creating a market for cheap blankets.

The Navajo women were urged to make more blankets in less time, and they began to take less care in cleaning their wool. The result was wool that did not take a proper dye and produced uneven colors. All these factors combined to make a blanket of lesser quality, looser weave, and harsher fabric. Ultimately this resulted in lower pay for the weaver. The art of weaving deteriorated quickly. Thankfully, there were those in the business determined to build weaving back into the art form it once was.

Dealers who understood what was happening (that poor quality articles could result in little or no sales) decided to refuse to trade any blanket that was not of the highest quality. J. B. Moore, whose trading post was near what is now Crystal, New Mexico, took it upon himself to take the raw wool the Navajos produced and ship it East for cleaning. After cleaning, the wool was shipped back to New Mexico and the Indians were free to card, spin, and dye the yarn in the manner they chose.

The weavers who had proven themselves proficient were given specific amounts of wool (enough for a particular size blanket) and only given more when the first supplies were returned as a finished work. As a result, Moore's mail-order business was successful, and the quality of the rugs produced by the people working for him was much higher, thanks to his innovative methods. Through Moore's efforts, the Navajo weavers improved their skills, and the quality of their work soon rose to a standard close to what it had been in years past.

As demand for blankets and rugs made from the wool of their sheep grew, the Navajo had to be taught more advanced methods of raising their sheep to maximize wool production. In 1911 the U.S. government put together a plan for Navajo sheep breeding and taught them what to do to increase the size of their animals and improve the quality of mutton and wool. These suggestions were carried out, and by 1912 blanket production quadrupled.

The Navajos have used colors as symbols in their weaving since the advent of the art. Green is the color that symbolizes youth, while yellow, blue, orange, and red represent maturity or harvest time. Brown and gray represent death and decay, and black is symbolic of mourning. Nature is the basis of Indian color symbolism. If one takes the time to research their history, the reasoning behind the symbolism is easy to understand. Red, for instance, the color associated with the life-giving sun, is the favorite of the Navajo weavers.

The dyes to make the colors for Navajo rugs were made from natural ingredients. Sumac, yellow, ocher, and pinon gum were boiled together to make black dye; yellow dye came from the flowering tops of *Bigelowia graveolens*; red from the bark of *Alnus incana va. virescens* (black alder) and juniper twigs mixed with a few other ingredients; and blue came from a native blue clay that was boiled with sumac leaves.

As there is symbolism connected with the colors that are used in Navajo blankets and rugs, so is there symbolism in the design elements incorporated into the weaving. Each weaver infuses some of her own thoughts and interpretations of designs into her weaving, but the origin of the designs reaches far back into Navajo history. Designs are borrowed from the Mexicans, the Pueblo tribes, the sacred sandpaintings of the medicine man, and nature itself. An escape hatch of sorts is built into each design—an exit for the weaver's spirit so it does not get trapped in her work. It is an intentional error to declare their knowledge of the small place a human holds in this universe.

Some of the designs medicine men used, which were later copied by weavers, featured the Navajo gods, the Yei. Divine characters, the Yei were both male and female and are shown in these depictions as extremely long and thin beings wearing masks. A male Yei wears a helmet-like mask and is known by the eagle plumes or owl feathers attached to the mask. He is also identified by the spruce twig he holds in his left hand and the gourd in his right. The female, usually dressed in white, is indicated by her rectangular mask, yellow arms, and chest (females were created of yellow corn, males of white), and the spruce wand held in each hand. Each Yei figure represents a different god. There are Ganaskidi, which are mountain sheep or bighorn gods; Hastseyalti, or the Talking God; and Hastsehogan. The Rainbow Goddess usually borders the description.

When weavers first began interpreting Yei figures or Kachina figures into their blankets and rugs, it upset the Indian population greatly, and a dealer who had such a piece for sale in his trading post considered his life in jeopardy. After the initial arguments, dissension was still strong and the tribe still believed the sacred Yei figure should not be represented on something more lasting than a sandpainting. However, the weavers continued to make a few here and there, and today the figures are commonly seen as part of rug and blanket designs. Older versions, however, are still rare and considered highly collectible.

Corn is one of the most important foods to the Navajo and represents a vital part of their ceremonies. Its symbol is used everywhere in paintings, on masks, and in the designs for rugs and blankets. Sunbeams are made of parallel straight lines in scarlet and are often depicted in sand-paintings or on masks and in designs on blankets and rugs. The queue symbol, representing the scalps of enemies, is painted on depictions of the god Tobadzistsini or Child of the Water. Lightning is represented by zigzag lines, which Navajo myths say gods use as ropes. When painted in white on a black background, they represent lightning on the face of a cloud. Geometric designs used by weavers incorporate parallel lines, zigzags, triangles, spurs, quadrilaterals, hourglass figures, rectangles, double triangles, terraced edges, S-forms, crooks, feathers, stars, key patterns, bird forms, mosaic patterns, and any combination of the above.

Trading post owner Juan Hubbell had a group of blanket designs painted in oil and hung them on his office walls. "Modern" Navajo blankets appeared with designs that had names such as Tsin alnazoid (Roman cross), Kos yischin (cloud image), Be 'ndastlago noltizh (cornered zigzag), and Nahokhos (swastika cross). They were used in conjunction with the old designs or on their own, according to the weaver's preference.

Northwest Coast

Though Chilkat women, like Navajo women, wove the blankets of the tribe, the blanket patterns were designed by the men, and deviations from those designs were forbidden. Aristocratic leaders wore the Chilkat robes displaying the animal totem of the clan in tribal ceremonies.

Chilkat blankets were made of mountain goat wool, which was tightly woven with yellow cedar bark. The Tlingit tribe (of which the Chilkat was a division) produced most of them, and they are considered the robes of Northwest Coast Indian nobility.

Their abstract representations of crest animals were woven into the fabric, and three edges of the blanket have thick fringe. Ravens, salmon, and whale heads are commonly depicted on these 19th-century blankets. The "diving whale" blankets are the most common and, at first glance, examples appear identical.

Actually, the fineness of yarn and quality of weave differ in each blanket. Early and mid-19th-century examples are finer than later ones. The blankets are woven on a bar loom, which resembles the letter H. The horizontal bar on this loom could be set at a level that was comfortable for the weaver. The warp was suspended from the loom in lengths that followed the form of the blanket, known as the "warp-weighted loom" technique.

The threads that were yet unwoven were kept wrapped in bags to protect them from soiling since it took six months to a year to make a blanket. The actual weaving was done in a tapestry-twined technique, and the long fringed sections were filled in with goat wool when the weaving was completed. Though these blankets could be as large as 72 by 38 inches, more commonly a dance apron was 18 by 38 inches.

Button blankets evolved when the Northwest Coast tribes began trading with the white Europeans and colonists who visited them during the latter part of the 18th century. These blankets were usually made from blue Hudson Bay Company blankets, which were bordered on three sides with red trade material. An appliqué crest would be sewn to the blanket and outlined with mother-of-pearl buttons.

Because mountain goat wool was highly prized, often the only blankets in a Nootka tribe belonged to the chiefs of the tribe, who wore them only on ceremonial occasions. The blankets were decorated with bold designs of the region.

Haida, Tlingit, and Kwakiutl tribes all made blankets in the late 19th and early 20th centuries.

Salish

Salish blankets were sometimes finger-woven, as the Tlingit blankets were, but often they were twill-plaited, and usually white. The materials used by the Salish included mountain goat wool, down, cattail fluff, and hair from white dogs.

The mountain goat wool was cleaned and the coarser outer hairs removed. The finer hairs were beaten to straighten them, and other fibers (e.g., bear, raccoon, or squirrel fur) may have been added to increase the thickness of the weave. The fibers were worked onto spindles with rods that were often 3 to 4 feet long.

Designs used in these early blankets were complicated and colorful. We do not know the actual colors the Salish used because no examples have survived. Sketches show us there were three types of blankets: a plain diagonal weave, a twined-weave "nobility blanket," and the decorative twined weave.

The white blankets were brightened with clay and were cleaned with beating. Many were used as shrouds and buried with the bodies of tribe members, leaving us few examples of this type of weaving.

In more modern times, the Salish used commercial yarns and a weaving frame, which produce finer, more decorative textiles.

Zuni

The Zuni style of weaving differs from the Navajo mainly in quality. The Navajo are the superior weavers. Zuni work is characteristically black or dark blue wool woven in a diagonal style.

Squaw dresses were basically blankets woven diagonally and worn wrapped around the wearer under the right arm and fastened over the left shoulder.

The Artists

BESSIE BARBER

Navajo (1955–) Aneth, Utah
Weaver

EDUCATION: Barber learned how to weave in her late teens from her mother, Anna Mae Barber.

AWARDS: First place, Navajo rugs, Intertribal Ceremonial (1988).

REPRESENTATION: Toh Atin Gallery, Durango, Colorado.

ABOUT THE ARTIST: Barber and several of the women in the Barber-Begay family developed a distinctive style by using only native, handspun sheep wool and small accents of bright dyes. This changed the Two Grey Hills style just enough to make it their own and it is now called the Burnham style.

The family of weavers includes Anna Mae Barber (Bessie's mother), Alice, Helen, and Sandy Begay (Anna Mae's sisters), Laverne, Lorene, and Bessie (Anna Mae's daughters), and Teresa and Julia (Anna Mae's young nieces), as well as a sister of a brother-in-law.

LORENE BARBER

Naakaii Dine' (Mexican) and Navajo/Many Hogans Clan (1957–) Burnham Area/Navajo Reservation
Weaver

EDUCATION: Learned to weave from her mother, Anna Mae Barber.

REPRESENTATION: Cristof's Art Gallery, Santa Fe, New Mexico.

ABOUT THE ARTIST: Barber learned to weave at the age of 15 and works in the new Burnham regional style. She uses very finely spun wool, working it into tapestry-quality weavings. Other family members who also weave include her aunt Marie Begay, her three sisters, Laverne, Bessie, and Bernice Barber, and her sisters-in-law Marie, Lorene, Linda, and Esther Bitsuie. Her cousin, Bobby Johnson, provided many of the patterns for Burnham-style weavings. Barber's work appears in a number of collections, including the Wheelwright in Santa Fe and the Cowboy Hall of Fame in Oklahoma City.

EMMA BEANS

Kwakiutl; Alert Bay, British Columbia, Canada
Blanket maker, clothing maker

ABOUT THE ARTIST: Beans designs blankets with buttons, abalone, and sequins. She uses the animal motifs of the Northwest Coast (e.g., eagle design).

ALICE N. BEGAY

Navajo (1940–) Pinon, Arizona
Weaver

EDUCATION: Learned from her grandmother in the early 1960s how to make the cross-shaped wall hangings, but learned how to make standard rectangular rugs from her mother.

AWARDS: Begay's unusually shaped rugs have won many prizes.

ABOUT THE ARTIST: A Mormon, Begay often makes rugs shaped like Latin crosses, but denies they have any symbolic Christian meanings. Most of her designs are based on Ganado Red patterns, though she also weaves in the Two Grey Hills style. Her weavings are from her imagination, and she intentionally stays away from photographs and others' weaving techniques.

AMY BEGAY

Navajo (1965–) Chinle, Arizona
Weaver, basketmaker

EDUCATION: Learned how to make tufted rugs from her mother, Elsie Nez. Degree in early childhood education and special education, Northern Arizona University.

AWARDS: Regularly wins prizes in the novelty weave category of the Museum of Northern Arizona's annual Navajo show.

ABOUT THE ARTIST: Begay uses fleece from large goats to create her tufted rugs that are normally single or double saddle blanket size (36 inches square or 30 by 60 inches). The mohair is washed and used for tufts; the sheep wool is carded and spun, then used for the wefts and warps.

GLORIA BEGAY

Navajo (1970–) Ganado, Arizona
Weaver

EDUCATION: Begay learned how to weave from her mother, Mary Lee Begay. A.A., computer science, Scottsdale Community College.

AWARDS: Miss Indian Scottsdale Community College (1991).

ABOUT THE ARTIST: Begay's whole family weaves, but she is considering a career that may take up most of her time, thus leaving her little for her weaving. In the meantime, however, it takes her approximately six months to finish a rug, and she uses the same designs her mother and grandmother have used.

MAMIE P. BEGAY

(a.k.a. Mammie P. Begay)

Navajo (ca. 1949–) Sweetwater, Teec Nos Pas, Arizona
Weaver

EDUCATION: Learned how to weave from her grandmother at the age of 12.

ABOUT THE ARTIST: Begay's serrated-outline rugs are large and in the Teec Nos Pas/Red Mesa style. She sells her rugs at the Crownpoint Rug Auction in New Mexico, trying to have a new rug ready every six weeks. She was married to Ernest Begay and has a daughter, Marlena.

MARIE BEGAY

Navajo (ca. 1942–) Burnham, New Mexico
Weaver

EDUCATION: Learned to weave from her mother and grandmother, as well as from adoptive mother, Anna Mae Barber.

REPRESENTATION: Cristof's Art Gallery, Santa Fe, New Mexico.

ABOUT THE ARTIST: Begay helped Anna Mae Barber establish the new Burnham regional style and is incredibly versatile in that she weaves classic Two Grey Hills designs, Teec Outline patterns, and Burnhams. She works with very finely spun yarn, utilizing the wool from a herd of crossbreed sheep who produce fine, shorter-length wool. Her well-known daughter, Theresa Begay, is making an impact on Navajo textile weaving.

MARY LEE BEGAY

Navajo (1941–) Ganado, Arizona
Weaver

EDUCATION: Begay learned how to weave from her mother, Grace Henderson Nez.

AWARDS: First place, Navajo rug, Gallup Intertribal (1983); first place, Navajo rugs over 25 square feet, Gallup Intertribal Ceremonial (1987).

REPRESENTATION: Hubbell Trading Post, Ganado, Arizona; Heard Museum, Phoenix, Arizona.

ABOUT THE ARTIST: Begay started weaving rugs for the Hubbell Trading Post in 1971 and is often commissioned to design particular patterns for customers such as the Denver Art Museum. She makes Burntwater, Two Grey Hills, Storm, Wide Ruins, Revival patterns, and other designs. She demonstrates weaving at the Hubbell Trading Post, and her work is often shown in urban art galleries.

NELLIE S. BEGAY

Navajo (June 24, 1957–) Lake Valley, New Mexico
Weaver

EDUCATION: Learned how to weave from family members.

AWARDS: Traditional Weaving Award for a Second Phase Chief's weaving, Santa Fe Indian Market (1995).

REPRESENTATION: Cristof's Art Gallery, Santa Fe, New Mexico.

ABOUT THE ARTIST: Begay weaves smooth, flat textiles with very fine thread. She creates Revival patterns based on 19th-century Navajo weavings and creates exceptional Chief Blanket designs in all three phases, though she prefers weaving Second Phase blankets. When she works on larger blankets, Begay always weaves smaller pieces (e.g., saddle blankets) as well so that her income is steady. She comes from a large family of weavers, is married to Bill Begay, Sr., and has three children.

VERA BEGAY

Navajo (1922–) New Mexico
Weaver

EDUCATION: Learned from her mother and other weavers and began making her own weavings at the age of 15.

ABOUT THE ARTIST: Begay's first weaving, a saddle blanket, is still in her possession—she refuses to sell it. She creates what the traders tell her people want and supports herself selling her weavings.

LAVENA TOM BENALLY

Navajo, Red House Clan, born for Mud Clan (ca. 1976–)
Teec Nos Pas, Arizona
Weaver

EDUCATION: Learned to weave from her mother, Nellie Tom, and influenced by maternal grandmother, Alice Thomas, and paternal grandmother, Mary Poyer.

REPRESENTATION: Cristof's Art Gallery, Santa Fe, New Mexico.

ABOUT THE ARTIST: Benally's whole family weaves, thus she is able to share their techniques, as well as her own. She weaves straight, tight pieces in the Teec Nos Pas style and specializes in incorporating colorful commercially dyed wool in her complicated abstract designs. She works in formats up to 5 by 7 feet.

HELEN BIA

Navajo (1945–) Three Turkey Ruins, Arizona
Weaver

EDUCATION: Helen's mother, Mary Bia, taught her the Three Turkey Ruins style, which is now shared by Helen, her sisters (Ruth Ann Tracey, Lucy Begay, and Alice B. Begay), her daughter (Gloria), and her niece (Irene).

AWARDS: Best of Show, Heard Museum's Indian arts and crafts exhibition (1974).

ABOUT THE ARTIST: Helen's Three Turkey Ruins rugs are different from Burntwaters as they have fewer colors and incorporate more symmetrical design components. She creates both small and large rugs, often shopping around for the best price for her work or taking commissions. She and her daughter, Gloria, often set their looms up side-by-side to work on their rugs.

LINDA BITSUIE

Navajo (April 17, 1963–) Whiterock, New Mexico
Weaver

EDUCATION: Learned how to weave from her mother, Ruth Bitsuie, and sisters, Lorene, Esther, and Marie.

REPRESENTATION: Cristof's, Santa Fe, New Mexico.

ABOUT THE ARTIST: Bitsuie's work has been published in quite a few sources. Her fine weavings are Navajo tapestries, and chances are good that she will end up specializing in ultrafine tapestry weaving. She weaves in the Burnham style.

LORENE BITSUIE

Navajo (March 18, 1961–) Whiterock, New Mexico
Weaver

EDUCATION: Learned how to weave from her mother, Ruth, and sisters, Linda, Esther, and Marie.

REPRESENTATION: Cristof's Art Gallery, Santa Fe, New Mexico.

ABOUT THE ARTIST: Bitsuie weaves in the Burnham regional style and uses mostly processed wool that has been respun. She weaves intricate designs, incorporating many different significant elements from her life. Some of those elements include the Kokopelli, bear fetishes, and pots. Lorene frequently signs her weavings by incorporating her initials into the border.

ANNIE BONNY

Navajo (1932–) Wide Ruins, Arizona
Weaver

EDUCATION: Self-taught, but inspired by her mother, Blanche Hale.

REPRESENTATION: Cristof's Art Gallery, Santa Fe, New Mexico.

ABOUT THE ARTIST: Bonny weaves in classic Wide Ruins regional style, using natural handspun wool and handmade vegetal dyes. She concentrates on the use of color and design in her weavings and makes fine quality Navajo textiles. She teaches her family, including son Eddie, to weave.

MARY BROWN

Navajo (1950–) Phoenix, Arizona
Weaver

EDUCATION: Learned how to weave from her mother, but gave it up for quite a while until challenged by a friend to make a seat cover for his pickup.

ABOUT THE ARTIST: The rug Brown made for her friend's pickup is a Stacked Boxes design, one of the patterns used for saddle blankets and

Portrait of Annie Bonny with one of her rugs.
Courtesy of Cristof's, Santa Fe, NM.

throw rugs. It is an optical illusion design, often used by Navajo weavers because of its figure/ground ambiguity. After weaving it, Brown kept on weaving, creating at least four more in the following year.

HELEN BURBANK

Navajo; near Ganado, Arizona
Weaver

EDUCATION: Learned to weave from her aunt and grandmother.

AWARDS: Honorable Mention, Class IV Textiles, Homespun, Traditional Design/Color, Scottsdale All Indian Days Fine Arts and Crafts Show (1988).

ABOUT THE ARTIST: Burbank sold her first weaving at the young age of eight. She does *yeibichai* rugs and is starting to incorporate features in her rugs that go beyond the traditional regional style.

NORMAN BUSHYHEAD

Cheyenne
Weaver

AWARDS: Best of Division, cultural items/textiles, Red Earth Awards Ceremony, Oklahoma, (1994).

IRENE CLARK

(a.k.a. Irene H. Clark, Dáa Naäze'bah, "One Who Protects")

Navajo (December 26, 1934–) Crystal, New Mexico
Weaver

EDUCATION: Clark began to weave after her children were grown and she was in her late 40s. She worked with her mother, Glenabah Hardy, to design a distinctive version of the Crystal style.

AWARDS: Best of Textiles and Best of Show, Museum of Northern Arizona Navajo Show (1990); first place, Museum of Northern Arizona Annual Navajo Show (1993); Best of Classification, Class II Fiber Art, Crystal Design Rug, Heard Museum Guild (1994); Honorable Mention, Class II Fiber Art, Heard Museum Guild (1995); and other awards.

ABOUT THE ARTIST: Clark's rugs are owned by private collectors as well as museums, such as the Denver Art Museum, Denver, Colorado. She is often commissioned by collectors to create a specific kind of rug. One such rug, titled "Rainbow," was made in 1990 for Gloria F. Ross Tapestries and features 10 stripes of different colors. Clark states, "[E]very strand of naturally dyed yarn interwoven is my family's clanship and the belonging to one another. All the colors of the rug symbolize the array of colors depicted in the rainbow." Clark has guided her daughter Teresa, daughters-in-law Evelyna and Julie, and sister-in-law Marjorie Hardy in weaving techniques.

MARITTA TOM CLYDE

Navajo (ca. 1956–) Farmington, New Mexico
Weaver

EDUCATION: Learned how to weave from family members.

REPRESENTATION: Cristof's Art Gallery, Santa Fe, New Mexico.

ABOUT THE ARTIST: One of the best Teec Nos Pas weavers, Clyde comes from a large group of weavers. She uses rich deep colors in her classic Teec Nos Pas patterns, and her work has been published in *Treasures of the Navajo* by Theda Bassman.

Portrait of Maritta Tom Clyde with one of her weavings. Courtesy of Cristof's, Santa Fe, NM.

BESSIE COGGASHELL

Navajo (ca. 1942–) Red Mesa, Arizona
Weaver

EDUCATION: Learned how to weave from her mother.
REPRESENTATION: Cristof's Art Gallery, Santa Fe, New Mexico.
ABOUT THE ARTIST: Coggashell has been weaving the Teec Nos Pas style since an early age and typically weaves small pieces, often respinning the wool to make it very fine. Her daughter, Ruby, also weaves, and they often collaborate at the loom.

SADIE CURTIS AND KURT BELONE

(Sadie a.k.a. Sadie Curtiss)

Navajo (1930–) Kinlichee, Arizona
Weavers

Portrait of Bessie & Ruby Coggashell with one of their weavings. Courtesy of Cristof's, Santa Fe, NM.

EDUCATION: Curtis learned how to weave from her mother, Elsie Jim Wilson, and often collaborates with her aunt, Alice Belone.

AWARDS: Curtis's American flag rug appeared on an *Arizona Highways* magazine cover in July 1976. Awards include first place, Class IV Textile, rugs, Heard Museum Guild (1979).

REPRESENTATION: Gallery 10, New York.

ABOUT THE ARTISTS: Considered a masterful weaver, Curtis once worked for the Hubbell Trading Post but is now retired. She likes to create chief blankets and revivals of early designs. She prefers to make small rugs because the large ones take up so much time. Her sisters, Elsie Wilson and Mae Jim, her daughter, two daughters-in-law, and her granddaughter are all weavers. Curtis's son, Earl, is a silversmith and leatherworker. When Curtis and Belone work together they have used dye artists from one area and weavers from another. The American flag rug that graced the 1976 cover of *Arizona Highways* magazine took Curtis three months to complete.

LENA BEGAY CURTISS

Navajo (August 25, 1964–) Sanders, Arizona
Weaver

EDUCATION: Learned to weave from her parents, Susie Begay and Keith Begay.

REPRESENTATION: Cristof's Art Gallery, Santa Fe, New Mexico.

ABOUT THE ARTIST: Curtiss comes from a large family of weavers and is teaching her older step-daughter, Michelle, how to weave. Curtiss and her half-brother, Larry Yazzie, began a new regional style in the early 1990s to honor their homeland, Blue Canyon. The entire family weaves in the Raised Outline technique; however, Yazzie still incorporates new designs and colors into his work, making the design and color easy to recognize.

SUSIE SHIRLEY DALE

Navajo (1931–) Kinlichee, Arizona
Weaver

EDUCATION: Dale learned basic and herringbone twill weaves by watching her mother, then taught herself two-faced rugs after watching her aunt, Edith James.

Portrait of Lena Begay Curtiss with one of her weavings. Courtesy of Cristof's, Santa Fe, NM.

REPRESENTATION: Hubbell's Trading Post, Ganado, Arizona; J. B. Tanner's, Ya-Ta-Hey, Arizona.

ABOUT THE ARTIST: Dale's rugs are pastoral scenes of Navajo life the way it used to be. She uses geometric designs in her rugs and likes to create the medium-sized pictorials because they usually bring in a little more money. She makes Yei pictorials as well. Three of Dale's four sisters weave, but only a few of the younger generation have learned the art.

VIRGINIA DEAL

Navajo (1929–) Toadlena, New Mexico
Weaver

EDUCATION: Learned how to weave by helping her mother, as did her sisters, Elizabeth Mute and Marie Lapahie.

ABOUT THE ARTIST: Deal sold her first rug at the age of 13 and is now passing her skills on to her daughter, Caralena.

MARGARET EMERY

Salish; Yale, British Columbia, Canada
Weaver

EDUCATION: Self-taught.

ABOUT THE ARTIST: Emery often finishes two rugs a year. She does everything, from start to finish, herself.

BESSIE GEORGE

Navajo (1932–) Wide Ruins, Arizona
Weaver

EDUCATION: Learned how to weave from her mother. One of her sisters also weaves.

ABOUT THE ARTIST: George has 15 children, but only one of them weaves. She supports her family with her efforts.

SADIE HARRIS

Kispiox; British Columbia, Canada
Blanket maker

ABOUT THE ARTIST: Sadie handsews blankets for 'Ksan ceremonial functions or dances. Blankets for her own family may be decorated with the Double Killer Whale design, which is the family crest of her husband, Walter.

JASON HARVEY

Navajo (February 24, 1974–) Shiprock, New Mexico
Weaver

EDUCATION: Learned how to weave from his grandmother Dorothy Harvey, and began weaving as a teenager. Has taken college courses in accounting.

AWARDS: Best of Show, Fiber Arts Festival, Museum of Indian Arts and Culture, Santa Fe, New Mexico (1999).

REPRESENTATION: Cristof's Art Gallery, Santa Fe, New Mexico.

ABOUT THE ARTIST: Harvey creates approximately three to four weavings a year, each usually 4 to 5 feet in size, though he has done some smaller pieces and some larger. His work is held in several private collections, and his shows include one at the National Cowboy Hall of Fame in Oklahoma City in 1997. At a very young age, he established himself as a weaver to watch, often combining an assortment of elements in his weavings. He has worked with a variety of regional designs and has created 19th-century blanket and serape patterns.

Portrait of Jason Harvey with one of his rugs. Courtesy of Cristof's, Santa Fe, NM.

Portrait of Irene Hollie with one of her rugs. Courtesy
of Cristof's, Santa Fe, NM.

IRENE HOLLIE

Navajo (April 24, 1959–) Flora Vista, New Mexico
Weaver

EDUCATION: Self-taught, but influenced by her mother, Nellie Tom, and
grandmothers, Alice Thomas (maternal) and Mary Poyer (paternal).

REPRESENTATION: Cristof's Art Gallery, Santa Fe, New Mexico.

ABOUT THE ARTIST: Hollie weaves the Teec Nos Pas style with an extraordinary sense of color and depth. She comes from a family of weavers and
is currently teaching her daughter, Raelene.

MARTHA JAMES

Salish; Skwaw Reserve, Chilliwack, British Columbia, Canada
Weaver

ABOUT THE ARTIST: James's rugs often have a narrative story woven into
them.

Rug by Irene Hollie. 24" × 27". Courtesy of Tribal Expressions, Arlington Heights, IL.

MARGARET JIMMIE

Salish; Squialla Reserve, British Columbia, Canada
Weaver

ABOUT THE ARTIST: Jimmie often weaves rugs with typical Northwest Coast designs, such as the eagle.

THERESA JIMMIE

Salish; Squialla Reserve, British Columbia, Canada
Weaver

ABOUT THE ARTIST: Jimmie has taught the art of spinning, knitting, and weaving to the Salish Weavers.

GRACE JOE

Navajo (1908–) Red Valley, Arizona
Weaver

EDUCATION: Learned how to weave from aunt Louise Chee, and Joe's mother taught her the finer points.

ABOUT THE ARTIST: Joe sold her first rug when she was 20 and has supported herself and her family by weaving ever since.

ISABELL JOHN
(a.k.a. Isabel John)

Navajo (1933–) Many Farms, Arizona
Weaver

EDUCATION: Learned how to weave when she was about eight years old.

AWARDS: First prize, Class I, Navajo rugs, pictorial rug, 25 square feet and over, Intertribal Ceremonial (1988).

REPRESENTATION: Coming Home, Dodgeville, Wisconsin; Toh Atin, Jackson David Co., Durango, Colorado.

ABOUT THE ARTIST: John creates pictorial rugs that often feature the *yeibichai* ceremonials. She hopes to keep the Navajo identity and traditions through her rugs, to show people what the Navajo people are all about. She was the first to put people, animals, and landscapes into her rugs (in the 1970s), but other weavers quickly imitated her. Sometimes her rugs are signed, but their large size and distinctive pictorials give her little need to do so.

JULIA JUMBO

Navajo (1929–) Newcomb, New Mexico
Weaver

EDUCATION: Learned how to weave from her mother.

AWARDS: First place, Two Grey Hills rug, 9 to 15 square feet, Gallup Intertribal Ceremonial (1982); first and second place, Category 2501, Pueblo and Navajo rugs, SWAIA (1992); first and third place, Pueblo and Navajo rugs, SWAIA (1994); first and second place and Class Award, Class VI Weaving, traditional weaving, SWAIA (1996); first place, Class VI Weaving and Baskets, traditional weaving, and Division Award, Pueblo and Navajo rugs up to 36 inches, SWAIA (August 1998).

ABOUT THE ARTIST: Jumbo sold her first rug at the age of 20 and has had continued success with her weavings ever since. She keeps her own herd of sheep, shears them, then prepares the wool to make her textiles. She specializes in smaller, super-fine weavings.

JOSEPHINE KELLY

Salish; Soowahlie Reserve, British Columbia, Canada
Weaver

EDUCATION: Learned the art of weaving from Oliver Wells, who researched the art and revived it by sharing what he'd learned with the local women.

ABOUT THE ARTIST: Kelly works with the Salish Weavers, often cooperating with the others by sharing dyes or other tools. She makes her own dyes and explains that it depends on the time of the year regarding what colors she'll get from particular plants.

DORAN KINSEL

Navajo (February 16, 1959–) Pine Springs, Arizona
Weaver

EDUCATION: Learned how to weave from her grandmother Irene Yazzie.

Portrait of Doran Kinsel with one of her rugs. Courtesy of Cristof's, Santa Fe, NM.

REPRESENTATION: Cristof's, Santa Fe, New Mexico.

ABOUT THE ARTIST: Kinsel weaves in the classic Burntwater design, usually working a number of elements toward the center of the piece. She buys her wool already vegetally dyed and is a fairly prolific weaver, keeping to smaller-sized pieces.

MARIE LAPAHIE

Navajo (1938–) Toadlena, New Mexico
Weaver

EDUCATION: Learned how to weave from Daisy Taugelchee, a well-known weaver. Lapahie's sisters, Virginia Deal and Elizabeth Mute, are also weavers.

ABOUT THE ARTIST: Lapahie started weaving at the age of 10 and sold her first rug at the age of 15. She often uses a light pink wool made from the belly of a newborn lamb.

CHARLENE LAUGHING

Navajo (January 13, 1969–) Fort Defiance, Arizona
Weaver

EDUCATION: Learned how to weave from her mother, Mona Lula Laughing.

REPRESENTATION: Cristof's Art Gallery, Santa Fe, New Mexico.

ABOUT THE ARTIST: Laughing comes from three generations of weavers, including her mother and grandmother. She weaves full-time and her sister, Michelle, and brother, Milton, weave actively. She uses Crystal design elements in her weavings; that fact combined with the wool produced by her family's herd and her knack with harmonious color make her textiles unique.

MICHELE LAUGHING

Navajo (July 4, 1971–) Fort Defiance, Arizona
Weaver

EDUCATION: Learned how to weave from her mother, Mona Lula Laughing, and her maternal grandmother, Elsie Mark. B.S. in biochemistry, University of New Mexico; currently in graduate program.

REPRESENTATION: Cristof's Art Gallery, Santa Fe, New Mexico.

ABOUT THE ARTIST: Born into a three-generation family of weavers, Laughing is the first to become cosmopolitan. She has traveled the world and uses the income from her weaving to finance her education. She likes to create other styles besides the Crystal regional design, such as Revival and Storm patterns, as well as multiple-patterned designs. She uses the soft fluffy wool produced by the sheep in her family's herd and uses strong colors.

MONA LULA LAUGHING

Navajo (June 16, 1946–) Fort Defiance, Arizona
Weaver

EDUCATION: Learned how to weave from her mother, Elsie Mark.

REPRESENTATION: Cristof's Art Gallery, Santa Fe, New Mexico.

ABOUT THE ARTIST: Laughing prefers to be known by Lula rather than her first name. She has been weaving most of her life and has put six children through college with the income from her art. She weaves the Crystal regional design with the soft fluffy wool from her flock of sheep and strong colors. An expert dye artist, she creates warm shades for her textiles. Two of her daughters and three of her sons are also weavers.

Portrait of Mona Laughing. Courtesy of Cristof's, Santa Fe, NM.

BESSIE LEE

Navajo (1921–) Red Mesa/Teec Nos Pas, Arizona
Weaver

EDUCATION: Lee learned how to weave from other family members.

ABOUT THE ARTIST: Lee weaves Teec Nos Pas rugs, avoiding bright colors that some other weavers choose to use. Her rugs usually have black backgrounds. She is one of the few weavers who sell to many dealers, negotiating until she gets the price she wants for her work.

KATHY LEE

Navajo
Weaver

AWARDS: Lee's work consistently wins awards.

ABOUT THE ARTIST: Lee uses vegetal-dyed wool. She began creating award-winning pieces when still in her 20s.

TERESA MARTINE

Navajo (1920–) Ramah, New Mexico
Weaver

EDUCATION: Martine was 12 when her mother taught her to weave. She studied imported and local dyestuffs in workshops taught by weaver D. Y. Begay.

AWARDS: Martine brings her work to the Indian Market in Santa Fe, New Mexico, and has won many awards for her weavings.

ABOUT THE ARTIST: Martine uses the wool of *churro* sheep, an old Navajo breed, to make her rugs, raising the sheep herself. She creates twill and two-faced rugs and sash belts, in addition to tapestry-weave rugs of old designs she finds in books and magazines.

DOROTHY MIKE

Navajo (1924–) Toadlena, New Mexico
Weaver

EDUCATION: Learned how to weave from her mother.

REPRESENTATION: Heard Museum, Phoenix, Arizona.

ABOUT THE ARTIST: Mike wove her first rug, in the Two Gray Hills style, at the age of 13. She stopped weaving in 1977 due to a back injury.

ROSE MIKE

Navajo; Toadlena, New Mexico
Weaver

AWARDS: First prize, Fifth Scottsdale National Indian Arts Exhibition (1966).

ABOUT THE ARTIST: Rose, a well-known tapestry maker, is Dorothy Mike's sister-in-law. She weaves in the Two Gray Hills style.

BRUCE AND NADINE NEZ

Navajo
Weavers

ABOUT THE ARTISTS: Nadine designs the patterns and Bruce weaves the rugs. They make pictorials, including rugs that are decorated with birds, flowers, and animals.

DESPAH NEZ

(a.k.a. Desbah Nez)

Navajo (1908–) Black Rock, New Mexico
Weaver—textiles; sandpainter

EDUCATION: Nez learned how to weave from her stepmother.

AWARDS: First prize, ceremonial and Yei rugs, 13th Annual Scottsdale National Indian Arts Exhibition (1975).

REPRESENTATION: Edith and Troy Kennedy.

ABOUT THE ARTIST: Nez left school in the ninth grade to stay at home and care for her father. Shortly after, she sold her first weaving, a Yei rug. Today she is considered an important weaver. Her two daughters also make rugs.

GRACE HENDERSON NEZ

Navajo (1913–) Ganado, Arizona
Weaver

EDUCATION: Taught how to weave by her mother.

AWARDS: Heard Museum's Timeless Impressions Award recipient (1995).

REPRESENTATION: Smithsonian Museum of the American Indian; Denver Art Museum; Heard Museum, Phoenix, Arizona.

ABOUT THE ARTIST: Nez began doing weaving demonstrations for tourists at the Hubbell Trading Post in Ganado, Arizona, in the 1970s. This weaver still lives in the traditional Navajo hogan, speaks no English, raises sheep, and wears the gathered skirts and jewelry as did her ancestors. She works on a heavy lumber loom built by her late husband. She creates bold designs that are easier for her to do because of her fading eyesight and limited dexterity. Her rugs are in the Ganado style.

IRENE JULIA NEZ

Navajo (1928–) Kinlichee, Arizona
Weaver

EDUCATION: Learned how to weave from her mother, Edith James.
AWARDS: Has won awards for her two-faced and twill weaves.
ABOUT THE ARTIST: Nez creates large twill-weave rugs and has become well-known for combining the two-faced technique with her diamond-twill weaves.

LINDA NEZ

Navajo (ca. 1956–) Bitter Springs, Arizona
Weaver

EDUCATION: Nez learned how to weave by herself, but was influenced by her mother, Frances Sampson, and aunt, Suzy Black.
REPRESENTATION: Cristof's Art Gallery, Santa Fe, New Mexico.
ABOUT THE ARTIST: Nez fills her pictorial rugs with animals, butterflies, birds, and fish, as did her aunt. She utilizes rounded shapes for added depth and gives the rugs a three-dimensional style. Other members of her extended family weave in a similar style. Her larger pieces often take four months to make. Nez's work has been featured in many publications.

BARBARA JEAN TELLER ORNELAS AND ROSE ANN TELLER LEE

(Barbara a.k.a. Barbara Ornelas, Barbara Teller, Barbara Teller Ornelas)

Navajo (November 26, 1954–) Montrose, Colorado
Weaver

EDUCATION: Learned how to weave from their mother, Ruth Teller, and grandmother Susie Tom.
AWARDS: Best of Show, 1987 Santa Fe Indian Market, for a rug made with sister, Rosann Teller Lee—the first time a Navajo rug had ever taken Best

of Show at the Market. Best of Show, Santa Fe Indian Market (1991); 1991 Award for Excellence in Navajo Weaving sponsored by Gloria Ross.

REPRESENTATION: Margaret Kilgore Gallery American Indian Art, Scottsdale, Arizona.

ABOUT THE ARTIST: These two sisters sell their rugs directly to clients at the Santa Fe Indian Market. Ornelas also demonstrates at museums and galleries. She creates intricate patterns in shades of white, purple, yellow, gray, pale pink, and blue. Her outspoken thoughts on the subject of weaving are effective in bringing ethnic artists together and convincing others that weaving is an art, not just a craft. Lee weaves only in the Two Gray Hills style, while Ornelas does Burntwater and Ganado. The rug that won Best of Show in 1987 made weaving history when it sold for $60,000. It took them and their sister Rosann four years to weave the rug.

ROSE OWENS

Navajo (1929–) Cross Canyon, Arizona
Weaver

EDUCATION: Self-taught.

ABOUT THE ARTIST: Owens had the idea to weave round rugs back in the 1950s. She said she was inspired to weave round rugs when her eye was caught one cold morning by a spider web. Today fewer than 24 weavers create round rugs. She mainly weaves in the Ganado Red design, but also uses twill and two-faced weaves. She is a versatile weaver who also makes full-scale chief blankets, rectangular Ganado Red rugs, experimental patterns, and twill saddle blankets. Her secret for weaving the round rugs is shared only with her daughters. In addition to round rugs, she also weaves special designs for customers all over the country. She credits weaving for keeping her healthy, sane, and strong. Owens is an herbalist and contributes that knowledge to others, to keep the Navajo ways alive.

ELLA ROSE PERRY

Navajo (1929–) St. Michaels, Arizona
Weaver

EDUCATION: Perry's mother taught her how to weave.

AWARDS: Main Trail Galleries Indian Room Grand Award, 13th Annual Scottsdale National Indian Arts Exhibition (1975).

REPRESENTATION: Cristof's Art Gallery, Santa Fe, New Mexico; Toh Atin Gallery, Durango, Colorado; Heard Museum, Phoenix, Arizona.

Portrait of Ella Rose Perry with one of her large rugs. Courtesy of Cristof's, Santa Fe, NM.

ABOUT THE ARTIST: The Crystal rugs that Perry weaves are recognizable for their soft colors and mohair-like texture. She uses her own handspun wool in natural and vegetal-dyed colors in her work. She takes pains to give her side selvages a near-perfect edge and is well respected for her talent. For 30 years she worked at the Bureau of Indian Affairs boarding school in Crystal, New Mexico, which is where she learned the Crystal style of weaving. She is now teaching her daughter, Marlene, the art.

JULIA PETE

Navajo (ca. 1970–) White Rock, New Mexico
Weaver

EDUCATION: Learned to weave from her mother, Bessie.
REPRESENTATION: Cristof's Art Gallery, Santa Fe, New Mexico.

ABOUT THE ARTIST: A young weaver, Pete is skilled and adept. She likes to weave in the Revival style, but she is able to weave anything. Her work has been featured in at least two publications.

MARY PETERS

Salish; Seabird Island Reserve, British Columbia, Canada
Weaver

EDUCATION: Peters learned the art of weaving from her family.
ABOUT THE ARTIST: This weaver was the last of the Salish Weavers until Oliver Wells started reviving the art. She has made blankets with the symbol of flying geese, which has become the trademark of Salish weaving.

NORA PETERS

Salish; Green Point, British Columbia, Canada
Weaver

EDUCATION: Peters learned about working with wool from her family.
ABOUT THE ARTIST: Peters has acted as the president of the Salish Weavers, spinning and dyeing their wool for them. Her whole family helps with the weaving, including her husband, daughters, sons, and other members.

MARY POYER

Navajo (ca. 1914–) Red Mesa, Arizona
Weaver

EDUCATION: Self-educated.
REPRESENTATION: Cristof's Art Gallery, Santa Fe, New Mexico.
ABOUT THE ARTIST: Poyer has taught two generations of weavers and has both children and grandchildren who weave, as well as in-laws (Hugh and Hazel Poyer's family). She is known for her vibrant colors in her Teec Nos Pas patterns and is known for packing the wool densely.

MAGGIE PRICE

Navajo (1934–) Sanders, Arizona
Weaver

EDUCATION: All of the women in Price's family weave. They learn from each other.
REPRESENTATION: Lovena Ohl Gallery, Scottsdale, Arizona; The Hand and the Spirit Crafts Gallery, Scottsdale, Arizona.

ABOUT THE ARTIST: Price sold her first rug when she was 19 and often turns out an average of three rugs a year. She weaves in the Burntwater pattern. Price's daughter is also an excellent weaver.

RAMONA SAKIESTEWA

Hopi/Anglo (ca. 1948/49–) Albuquerque, New Mexico
Weaver—tapestries; writer

EDUCATION: Self-taught. Sakiestewa has worked with Peruvian weavers to study their craft and native dyes.

AWARDS: First and second place, Category 2601 Rugs, SWAIA (1992); first and third prize, Category 3101 Rugs, SWAIA (1994); overall, first, second, and third prize, Category 2601, weaving, nontraditional, SWAIA; and many other awards.

REPRESENTATION: Horwitch LewAllen Gallery, Santa Fe, New Mexico; Wheelwright Museum of the American Indian, Santa Fe; Heard Museum, Phoenix, Arizona.

ABOUT THE ARTIST: Sakiestewa started weaving rugs in 1970 and takes her inspiration from the 1867–1900 period of weaving when Pueblo tribes and Navajos were wearing horizontally striped clothing. She studied the works of two anthropologists, then later worked directly with one of them, Kate Peck Kent, who wrote *Weaving of Cotton in the Prehistoric Southwestern United States*. A year after she began weaving full-time (1982), Sakiestewa founded her own company, Sakiestewa, Ltd., and began producing functional weavings. By the 1900s she had hired assistants and was creating more than 30 major pieces a year. Sakiestewa uses a European horizontal (or floor) loom instead of a traditional vertical loom. She only uses plant dyes. Her stepfather (an Anglo) made certain she was surrounded by items that reflect her Native American heritage. Sakiestewa became head interior designer for the Smithsonian National Museum of the American Indian in 1996.

GENEVA SCOTT SHABI

Navajo (October 23, 1957–) Chambers, Arizona
Weaver

EDUCATION: Learned how to weave from members of her family.

AWARDS: Best of Show, Gallup Intertribal Ceremonial (1995).

REPRESENTATION: Cristof's Art Gallery, Santa Fe, New Mexico.

Portrait of Geneva Shabi with one of her rugs. Courtesy of Cristof's, Santa Fe, NM.

ABOUT THE ARTIST: Shabi weaves in the Wide Ruins regional style with commercial, vegetally dyed wools. She started weaving at the age of 12 and has taught her children. Her mother, Marjorie Spencer, and her three sisters (Brenda, Vera, and Irma) are all weavers.

MARTHA SMITH
(a.k.a. Winnie James)

Navajo (ca. 1940–) Sanders, Arizona
Weaver

EDUCATION: Learned from members of her family.

AWARDS: Second prize at 1974 Gallup Intertribal Ceremonial, as well as other awards.

REPRESENTATION: Cristof's Art Gallery, Santa Fe, New Mexico.

ABOUT THE ARTIST: Smith's mother and aunt are both weavers, and Smith started weaving at the age of 12. During the 1960s–70s she began weaving Burntwater-style rugs, but she has also done rugs in Ganado, Klagetoh, and Two Grey Hills styles. Widely published, she has sent her four sons through school on her weaving income. In 1990 she changed her name to Martha Smith.

Portrait of Martha Smith with one of her rugs. Courtesy of Cristof's, Santa Fe, NM.

HARRIET SNYDER

Navajo (ca. 1952–) Church Rock, New Mexico
Weaver

EDUCATION: Self-taught.

REPRESENTATION: Cristof's Art Gallery, Santa Fe, New Mexico.

ABOUT THE ARTIST: Snyder creates the double-weave, or two-faced, textiles, a style of weaving that requires an intricate loom setup and excellent control of the warp combination. Usually, Snyder chooses a Ganado-style color scheme, but she has been known to weave twills, Yeis, and other designs.

LILY SPECK

Kwakiutl; Alert Bay, British Columbia, Canada
Blanket maker

ABOUT THE ARTIST: Speck does the sewing, using buttons and other materials, and sometimes her husband, Henry, creates the design.

MARJORIE SPENCER

Navajo (1936–) Wide Ruins, Arizona
Weaver

EDUCATION: Spencer learned to weave when she was 27. She was influenced by Bill Young, a Hubbell trader.
REPRESENTATION: Hubbell Trading Post, Ganado, Arizona.
ABOUT THE ARTIST: Originally, Spencer used the traditional colors of golds, yellows, browns, grays, and whites for her Wide Ruins rugs, but now she uses pinks and blues to satisfy customers' desires. Spencer has taught three of her daughters (Vera Spencer, Irma Spencer Owens, and Geneva Scott Shabie) the Wide Ruins style. Another daughter, Brenda, weaves Burnt-water patterns.

ANABEL STEWART

Salish (by marriage), *Skwaw Band;* Canada
Weaver

EDUCATION: Oliver Wells taught some of the Salish Weavers by taking Stewart's great-grandmother's rag rug apart and showing the weavers how it was done.
ABOUT THE ARTIST: Stewart is a prolific weaver.

PEARL SUNRISE

(a.k.a. Gleh-Dez-Bah, Pearl Pintohorse)

Navajo (1944–) Whitewater, New Mexico
Weaver, basketmaker, songstress, educator, consultant

EDUCATION: Learned how to weave and to make basketry, clothing, and jewelry from her parents and aunts. B.A. and M.A., art education, University of New Mexico. Professor of fiber arts, fashion design, and Navajo language classes at the Institute of American Indian Arts, Santa Fe, New Mexico. Taught Native arts at the University of New Mexico, Highlands University, Navajo College, the Institute of American Indian Arts in Santa Fe, CONVERGENCE '78, Colorado State University, the Haystack Mountain School for Crafts in Maine, the Appalachian Mountain Crafts Center in Tennessee, and Textile Workshop, Inc., Santa Fe.
AWARDS: Fulbright Scholarship (1986); Governor's Award for Outstanding New Mexico Woman (1988); Great Achievement Award, Indian Village, State Fair (1990). Numerous awards for art at New Mexico Arts and

Crafts Fairs, Gallup Intertribal Indian Ceremonial, Southwest Arts and Crafts Fair, New Mexico State Fair, Navajo Tribal Fair, All Pueblo Cultural Center, and "Shared Horizons," Santa Fe, New Mexico. New Mexico arts commissioner since 1993.

ABOUT THE ARTIST: A traditional third-generation Navajo weaver, Sunrise uses raw wool and natural dyes, as her ancestors did hundreds of years ago. She also follows the Native American's unwritten law to never take more than she needs from the earth. All of her designs are her own variations. Sunrise's baskets are used in Navajo healing ceremonies. She only uses one pattern, that which depicts the clouds, rainbow, and four sacred mountains. She also makes clothing and jewelry, though she prefers weaving above all. Sunrise has traveled throughout the world both to teach weaving and to research how other cultures, like New Zealand and South African, have woven textiles throughout the years.

ANNA MAE TANNER

Navajo/Hopi (1929–) Phoenix, Arizona
Weaver

EDUCATION: Learned how to weave from her mother, Despah Nez.

REPRESENTATION: Edith and Troy Kennedy.

ABOUT THE ARTIST: Tanner wove her first rug at the age of six, believing the task so impossible that she cried. Since that time she began weaving sandpainting rugs suggested by Edith and Troy Kennedy. She weaves pictorial rugs in the Red Rock designs. Weaving is her only source of income.

ESTHER TAUGELCHEE

Navajo
Weaver

AWARDS: First prize, Navajo rug, Intertribal Indian Ceremonial (1961); second prize, Arizona State Fair, Phoenix (1961).

REPRESENTATION: Heard Museum, Phoenix, Arizona.

ABOUT THE ARTIST: Thought to be related to Daisy Tauglechee.

PRISCILLA TAUGELCHEE
(a.k.a. Priscilla Tauglechee)

Navajo (1947–) near Tonalea, Arizona
Weaver

EDUCATION: Taugelchee learned how to weave from her mother, as well as her mother-in-law, Daisy Tauglechee.

AWARDS: Second Award, Classification IX, Textiles, traditional rugs, 14th Annual Scottsdale National Indian Arts Exhibition (1976).

ABOUT THE ARTIST: Priscilla and her mother-in-law are considered two of the finest Two Gray Hills weavers.

DAISY TAUGLECHEE

(a.k.a. Daisy Touglechee, Daisy Taugelchee, Daisy Taugleschee)

Navajo (1909–90) Two Grey Hills, New Mexico
Weaver

EDUCATION: Learned how to weave from family members.

AWARDS: First prize, Navajo rug, Intertribal Indian Ceremonial (1954); grand and first prize, Navajo rug, Intertribal Indian Ceremonial (1960); first place, Class XIII, textiles, Heard Museum Guild Indian Arts and Crafts (1973).

REPRESENTATION: Cristof's Art Gallery, Santa Fe, New Mexico.

ABOUT THE ARTIST: Tauglechee had the reputation of being a top weaver by the 1940s and was often called the "greatest living Navajo weaver." Her rugs were tightly woven, sometimes with 115 weft threads to the inch. She wove in the Two Gray Hills style, but brought that style to even greater heights with her own impeccable weaving skills. When her eyesight began to fail, Tauglechee worked with her daughter-in-law Priscilla.

ALBERTA THOMAS

Navajo (1927–) Oak Springs, Arizona
Weaver

EDUCATION: Learned how to weave from her mother, Despah Nez, and her sister, Anna Mae Tanner.

REPRESENTATION: Troy Kennedy.

ABOUT THE ARTIST: Thomas sold her first rug at the age of 10. She now weaves to help support the family.

JENNIE THOMAS

Navajo (1957–) St. Michaels, Arizona
Weaver

EDUCATION: Thomas and her three sisters learned how to weave from their mother, Betty B. Roan, and grandmother Blanche Hale.

AWARDS: Best of Show, First Award, Second Award, Intertribal Ceremo-
nial, Gallup, New Mexico (1987, 1994, 1994, 1982); Best of Class Division,
Northern Arizona Museum, Flagstaff (1989); Best of Class/Best of Show,
O'odham Tash, Casa Grande, Arizona (1988); third place, Category 3001,
Pueblo and Navajo rugs and blankets (vertical loom only) up to 36 inches,
SWAIA (1995).

REPRESENTATION: Garland's Rugs, Sedona, Arizona; Cristof's Art Gallery,
Santa Fe, New Mexico.

ABOUT THE ARTIST: Thomas comes from a large family of weavers, most of
whom have used the Wide Ruins style. She was introduced to weaving as
a young girl because her family were sheepherders. She completed her
first Wide Ruins–style rug at the age of 17 and now creates Burntwater-
bordered patterns that highlight small-scale details and a subtle change of
pastel colors. Though she is inspired by Two Grey Hills and Ganado
styles, she reworks the design to fit her own creative sense. Thomas has
passed on her knowledge to other women and her own daughter, Desiree.
She lives in Phoenix, Arizona.

NOWETAH TIMMERMAN
(a.k.a. Nowetah, Karen Timmerman)

Abenaki/Susquehanna-Cherokee (1947–) New Haven, Connecticut
Weaver, porcupine quillworker, glass beadworker, glassblower, leatherworker, teacher, writer

EDUCATION: Some college and glassblowing apprenticeship.

AWARDS: Received awards for educational programs on Indian history,
dancing, and crafts and blue ribbons at county, state, and local fairs for her
arts.

REPRESENTATION: Nowetah's American Indian Museum and Gift Store,
New Portland, Maine.

ABOUT THE ARTIST: Mother of seven daughters, Nowetah has brought at
least one of them into the Indian crafts business and owns a museum and
store in Maine where she showcases her own and her daughter's work. A
believer in keeping the earth free of garbage, Nowetah loans customers
the catalogs for items sold in her shop rather than sending them out in
mass mailings. She has received local recognition for her store as well as
the items she produces, and she works hard to keep the public informed
about New England Indian life and history.

484 NATIVE AMERICAN ART

WANDA TRACEY

Navajo
Weaver

AWARDS: Best of Division, Scottsdale Native American Indian Cultural Foundation Arts & Crafts Competition (1987).

SARAH VAN WINKLE

Navajo
Weaver

AWARDS: First place, Navajo rugs without border over 40 square feet, Intertribal Ceremonial, Gallup (1987).

ABOUT THE ARTIST: Van Winkle creates traditional designs such as Burntwater-style weavings.

LILLIE WALKER

Navajo (1929–) Coal Mine Mesa, Arizona
Weaver

EDUCATION: Learned how to weave from family members.

ABOUT THE ARTIST: Walker weaves side by side with her daughter, Cecilia Nez, at Nez's house in Tuba City. Walker's rugs are simple geometric designs with a limited color range and rough texture, resembling the rugs made in the 1930s. She uses processed yarn because she no longer keeps sheep.

MARIE WATSON

Navajo
Weaver

AWARDS: Second place, Intertribal Ceremonial Prize Winners Award, Class I, Navajo rugs, raised outline rugs under 15 square feet.

ABOUT THE ARTIST: Watson is known for her rug-within-a-rug or double rug designs. She creates Wide Ruins, Pine Springs, and Burntwater designs.

KATIE WAUNEKA

Navajo (1941–) near Fort Defiance, Arizona
Weaver

EDUCATION: Learned how to weave from mother, Nellie Williams.

ABOUT THE ARTIST: Wauneka, the sister of Daisy Redhorse and Betty Jumbo, wove her first rug at the age of seven and has been weaving ever since. She and her sisters gather the materials for their dyes themselves.

AUDREY SPENCER WILSON

Navajo (1920–) Indian Wells, Arizona
Weaver

EDUCATION: Learned how to weave from her mother.
REPRESENTATION: J. B. Tanner Trading Company, Ya-Ta-Hey, New Mexico.
ABOUT THE ARTIST: Wilson often makes large, ambitious projects. She uses the same kind of loom she learned on and often weaves sash belts and other items while also working on a large rug. Her designs reflect the Two Grey Hills rugs, though her weavings are often a little more innovative. Usually, she weaves complex two-faced and fancy weaves, as well as designs that incorporate Yei figures. Wilson cannot card and dye her own wool any longer because of painful arthritis.

ELSIE JIM WILSON
(a.k.a. Elsie Wilson)

Navajo (1924–) Kinlichee, Arizona
Weaver

EDUCATION: Learned how to weave at a young age.
AWARDS: One of four Native American artists to be awarded the 1990 Arizona Indian Living Treasure Award.
REPRESENTATION: Hubbell Trading Post, Arizona; Cristof's Art Gallery, Santa Fe, New Mexico.
ABOUT THE ARTIST: Wilson makes a version of the Ganado Red regional style (a style that is recognized by its central diamond and fancy borders and is predominantly red in color). She repeats finely stepped motifs in the center and border areas of her rugs and frequently utilizes hooked frets and small stepped triangles. Wilson works on an unusual welded steel loom. Her sisters (Sadie Curtis and Mae Jim) are also weavers, and Wilson has taught her own daughters to weave. As Wilson grew older, her youngest daughter, Ruby, began assisting her with the large rugs.

BETTY JOE YAZZIE

Navajo (1932–) Red Rock, Arizona
Weaver

EDUCATION: Grace Joe, Yazzie's mother, taught her how to weave.

AWARDS: First Award, Classification IX, textiles, traditional, aniline dyes, 13th Annual Scottsdale National Indian Arts Exhibition (1975).

ABOUT THE ARTIST: Yazzie has woven all her life, but did not become a regular weaver until the 1970s. She passes on her knowledge to the younger weavers and asks for input from the people who buy her rugs. She also weaves in the Teec Nos Pas style

ELLEN YAZZIE

Navajo
Weaver

ABOUT THE ARTIST: Yazzie does pictorial rugs, some with hundreds of figures, that depict daily Navajo life.

LARRY YAZZIE

Navajo (1955–December 1995) Coal Mine Mesa, Arizona
Weaver

EDUCATION: Yazzie learned how to weave from his mother and grandmother when he was very young. He had four years of art in school.

AWARDS: Best of Show, O'odham Tash Arts and Crafts (1987).

REPRESENTATION: Garland's Navajo Rugs, Sedona, Arizona; Cristof's Art Gallery, Santa Fe, New Mexico.

ABOUT THE ARTIST: Yazzie did not begin weaving until 1986, after a stint in the service. His whole family is involved with the art of weaving; both the males and females excel at the task. His sisters Wanda Begay and Lena Curtis are weavers. Larry taught the younger children how to weave. He elaborated on the old-style raised outline designs and used some of the figures from both Teec Nos Pas and Two Gray Hills styles in his own work. He also created pictorials and Blue Canyon–style rugs, incorporating a style of weaving known as Raised Outline. The Blue Canyon style is fairly new to Navajo weaving (begun in the 1950s) and incorporates lots of blues in the weaving, a color not typical to Navajo rugs. Yazzie enjoyed experimenting with color and size, often making hall runners. He named his particular style Blue Canyon Raised Outline. Yazzie worked in Tuba

City, Arizona, until he died of AIDS. His family members continue to produce his style of weaving.

MARGARET YAZZIE

Navajo (1929–) near Newcomb Trading Post, New Mexico
Weaver

EDUCATION: Learned how to weave by watching her foster grandmother, Adzani Baah.

AWARDS: Second place, Navajo rugs, tapestry 80 threads, Intertribal Ceremonial (1987); first place and Best in Category for hand-spun Native wool rug and winner of Don Watson Memorial Award, Intertribal Indian Ceremonial, Gallup (1988).

ABOUT THE ARTIST: Yazzie weaves rugs to support her family. She is regarded as one of the better weavers on the Navajo reservation.

PHILOMENA YAZZIE

Navajo (1927–) Querino, Arizona
Weaver

AWARDS: First prize in New Mexico and Arizona state fairs in 1971 and 1972.

ABOUT THE ARTIST: One of the creators of the style called Burntwater, Yazzie and her aunt, Mary Goldtooth Smith, and cousin, Maggie Price, are considered the premier weavers of the style that was first introduced in 1968. Yazzie uses as many as 12 colors in a single rug, and her designs have been copied by both Native Americans and Europeans. Because her eyesight is failing and she has arthritis, she tries to keep her designs simple and her colors bold.

ASON YELLOWHAIR

(a.k.a. Mrs. Yellowhair, Old Lady Yellowhair, Asan Yellowhair, Asun T. Yellowhair)

Navajo (September 15, 1930–) Smoke Signal, Arizona
Weaver

EDUCATION: Learned how to weave from family members.

REPRESENTATION: J. B. Tanner Trading Company, Yah-Ta-Hey, New Mexico.

ABOUT THE ARTIST: Yellowhair has passed on her skills to her nine daughters and two of her daughters-in-law, most of them learning how to weave before they were 10. She has begun to teach her grandchildren as well. She specializes in large rugs, often uses birds in her weavings, and gets her inspiration from her love of the outdoors.

Prices

Isabell John. Blue Ribbon rug serigraph (*not* a rug, but a limited edition print of a rug). $400–$500.

CHAPTER 12

Miscellaneous Media

Some artists we discovered simply do not fit into any of the categories in this book, and instead of leaving them out of this volume, we are inserting them here. Some of the media with which they work is not considered "traditional" Native American craft or art, but they are all artists just the same and should be included. It is important to note that Native American artists all over the country have learned different ways of making their natural surroundings into some kind of art, whether wearable or usable.

In the Southwest, they use the desert clay to make pottery. In the Southeast, they use trees and grasses to make baskets and cotton to make clothing. In the Northwest, they use trees for totem poles and animal fur for clothing. In the Plains, animal hides created shelter and clothing. When the first telegraph poles came across the United States, the Native Americans used the copper wiring for jewelry and other artistic items. Artistic designs were repeated on the sides of cave walls, on horse flanks, on tepee flaps, on the rims of baskets, on the sides of pots, on earrings and necklaces, and on clothing.

Suffice it to say that no single volume could ever contain all of the artistic impressions of the American Indian, thus this miscellaneous chapter is a very small nod to the multitude of arts not covered in this book.

The Artists

SARAH DUBUC
(a.k.a. Yeh Sah Gehs)

Tuscarora (1916–) Sanborn, New York
Wireworker, beadworker, dollmaker

EDUCATION: Learned from her mother and her sister.

ABOUT THE ARTIST: Dubuc has often sent her work to the New York State Fair. She has made beaded wirework (miniature) chairs, cups and saucers, turtles and baskets, cornhusk dolls, beaded velvet picture frames, cushions, boots and boxes, and beaded medallions and necklaces.

ELSIE TAYLOR GOINS
(see biography in the "Jewelry" chapter pg. 277)

MILLY GRAYSON
Glassworker

EDUCATION: Degrees in anthropology and Native American studies.

REPRESENTATION: White Buffalo Productions, www.whitebuffaloprod.com.

ABOUT THE ARTIST: A world traveler, Grayson did not start working in stained glass until her daughter bought her a glass grinder for Christmas. Because she'd always loved working with glass, she enrolled in a class and is now creating stained-glass pieces that reflect her Native American heritage. She uses the Kokopelli often in her work, creating windows, lamps, and other items in that image, and is starting to incorporate etched designs in her work.

Burned wood design on cross by Ambrose Begay, ca. 1995. Wood often serves as the media for Native artists. This cross depicts Navajo reservation life. The design was burned into the wood, then painted with muted water colors. Courtesy of Jay Sadow and The Eastern Cowboys, Scottsdale, AZ.

Totem Wall Hanging by Elsie
Taylor Goins. Cotton appliquéd.
45" × 36". 1982. Courtesy of
Eastern Cherokee, Southern
Iroquois and United Tribes of
South Carolina.

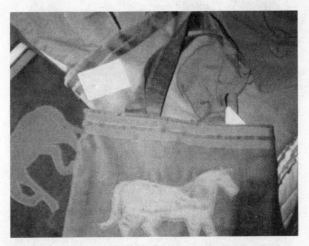

Corduroy Applique Tote Bags by Elsie Taylor Goins, ca.
1982. Cotton with ribbon. 20" × 18". Eastern Cherokee,
Southern Iroquois and United Tribes of South Carolina.

Stained glass Kokopelli Garden Stake by Milly Grayson. Kokopelli is approximately 7" tall and the stake is an additional 18" high. Shade of red glass will slightly vary. $28.00. Courtesy of White Buffalo Productions, www. whitebuffaloprod.com.

Stained glass hanging by Milly Grayson. Kokopelli with feathers and cactus. 15½" × 10½" wide. $175. Courtesy of White Buffalo Productions, www.whitebuffaloprod.com.

ARIEL HARRIS
(a.k.a. Ga Wen He Henz, "Holding Flower")

Onondaga (1929–) Ohsweken, Ontario, Canada
Wireworker, clothing designer, beadworker, crocheter

EDUCATION: Harris learned wireworking from a woman at Tuscarora, and learned some of her other skills on her own or from her mother.

ABOUT THE ARTIST: Harris displays her many craft items at fairs and pow-wows, making a living with her work since the age of 14. Her wirework items include chairs, bracelets, rings, baskets, turtle earrings, and Indian head earrings. She does beadwork jewelry, crocheted items, and novelty items, as well.

TONY JOJOLA
Isleta (early 1960s–)
Glassmaker

EDUCATION: Apprenticed under hot glass artist Dale Chihuly at the Pilchuk Glass School (1980–81).

REPRESENTATION: Jan Cicero Gallery, Chicago; Columbine Galleries, Santa Fe, New Mexico.

ABOUT THE ARTIST: Jojola began working with hot glass in the late 1970s and has continued to improve on what he learned in his apprenticeships with various glassmakers. He got his inspiration from his maternal grandfather, Patricio Olguin, a silversmith, carver, and beekeeper. Jojola's work reflects his knowledge of traditional Pueblo pottery, and his work has been exhibited throughout the country. He was one of the key figures in establishing the Hilltop Artists in Residence at Taos Pueblo, New Mexico.

JUDY KENNETH
Navajo; Crownpoint Reservation, New Mexico
Seamstress

EDUCATION: Learned how to sew with her mother and is essentially self-educated.

REPRESENTATION: Native Artists United, Thoreau, New Mexico.

ABOUT THE ARTIST: Kenneth makes a variety of items from Pendleton wool, including quilts, dolls, clothing, and various household items. She has been commissioned by the Smithsonian Museum, as well as the city of Washington, D.C., to create quilts.

MADELINE MODESTE

Cowichan; Koksilah Reserve, British Columbia, Canada
Knitter

EDUCATION: Learned from family members.

REPRESENTATION: Judy Hill Gallery, Duncan, British Columbia, Canada.

ABOUT THE ARTIST: Modeste, like other women in her business, dries, cleans, bleaches, cards, and spins her own wool.

LILLIAN PITT

Warm Springs Yakima/Wasco (1943–) Warm Springs, Oregon
Mask artist—ceramicist, mixed media

EDUCATION: A.A., Mount Hood Community College, Gresham, Oregon.

AWARDS: Governors Award for the Arts, Oregon (1990); City of Oguni, Niigata Prefecture, Japan, Gift to City; Purchase Award, Oregon Percent for Arts, Metropolitan Arts Commission; Purchase Award, Washington State Arts Commission.

REPRESENTATION: Adobe East, Summit, New Jersey; American Indian Contemporary Arts, San Francisco; Artique Gallery Ltd., Anchorage, Alaska; Bailey Nelson Gallery, Seattle, Washington; Buffalo Gallery, Alexandria, Virginia; Images of the North, San Francisco; Quintana Gallery, Portland, Oregon; Rattlesnake & Star, San Antonio, Texas; Scanlon Gallery, Ketchikan, Alaska; Sunbird Gallery, Bend, Oregon; Lillian Pitt Gallery, Portland, Oregon.

ABOUT THE ARTIST: Pitt was first inspired by the Northwest Coast masks she owned and decided to try to imitate their style. Though she usually embellishes her work with Plateau and Wasco decorations and patterns, she has also been influenced by those who use the Japanese ceramic firing method called Raku and the Anagama firing method. Her masks are both human and animal, images derived from the long history of those masks carved by Northwest Coast tribes. She shows all over the world, and her works are held by many museums and galleries and featured in many publications.

BRENT TAYLOR

EDUCATION: Self-taught.

REPRESENTATION: White Buffalo Productions, www.whitebuffaloprod.com.

Iron Kokopelli water fountain pot by Brent
Taylor. $130. Courtesy of White Buffalo
Productions, www.whitebuffaloprod.com.

ABOUT THE ARTIST: Taylor creates unusual Kokopelli-inspired pieces, like
iron and pottery water fountains.

SIMON TOOKOOME

Inuit (1934–   ) Baker Lake, Northwest Territories, Canada
Stone-printmaker

EDUCATION: Self-taught.

REPRESENTATION: University of Lethbridge Art Gallery, Alberta, Canada;
the Upstairs Gallery, Manitoba, Canada.

ABOUT THE ARTIST: Tookoome creates prints about the stories of his clan.
His narratives are always recognizable, though often abstract in style. He
is one of the last of the Inuit clan to live in the far North and speaks no English, just his native tongue.

RUSTY WILBER

Oneida
Ironworker

REPRESENTATION: Eastern Cowboys, Scottsdale, Arizona.

ABOUT THE ARTIST: Wilber sometimes creates artistic works out of iron.

Unusual hand cut wrought iron picture by Rusty Wilber. Courtesy of Jay Sadow and The Eastern Cowboys, Scottsdale, AZ.

Prices

Lillian Pitt. Pair of rings. Based on a pictograph in the Columbia River Gorge, the "Eternity Pairs" ring has a thunderbird, a rainbow, and a star that points to the four directions. Available in 18-karat gold ¼" wide. This ring is available in women's and men's sizes. Price varies depending on size. Typically the price for women's sizes is $920 and men's $960–$1,000.

———. Bronze mask. "She Who Watches is a pictograph found along the Columbia River. She overlooked the village where my great-grandmother lived. Because she wanted to watch over my people forever, Coyote changed her into a rock. Under her watchful gaze, my people remember her as the last woman chief of the Columbia River People." 9" long and 11" wide bronze limited edition of 35. Each $2,800.

Simon Tookoome. "Inuit Together." Linocut and stencil. 24½" × 34". $1,500–$1,800.

Galleries and Museums That Represent Native American Artists

Abeyta Studios, Venice, Italy and Sante Fe, New Mexico
Adobe Walls Antique Mall and Trading Post, Colorado Springs,
    Colorado
Agape Southwest Pueblo Pottery, Albuquerque, New Mexico
Alaska Museum Show, Juneau, Alaska
Alaska Native Heritage Center, Anchorage, Alaska
American Legacy Gallery, Kansas City, Kansas
Americana West Gallery, Washington, D.C.
Andrea Fisher Fine Pottery, Sante Fe, New Mexico
Antiques and Art, Seattle, Washington
Artistic Galleries, Scottsdale, Arizona
Arizona State Museum, Tucson, Arizona
Artables Gallery, Houston, Texas
Armadillo Trading Company, Albuquerque, New Mexico
The Art Shop Gallery, Homer, Alaska
ArtNatAm, www.arrtnatam.com
Attic-Hogan Gallery, Prescott, Arizona
Bahte Indian Arts, Salt Lake City, Utah
James Baird Gallery, St. Johns, Newfoundland, Canada
Bashas Art Gallery, Tucson, Arizona
Bead Fever, Ukiah, California
Bear Creek Gallery at River Crossing, Indianapolis, Indiana
Blair's Dinnebito Trading Post, Page, Arizona
Blackhawk Gallery, Saratoga, Wyoming
Blue Deer Gallery, Dallas, Texas
Blue Rain Gallery, Taos, New Mexico
Bjorges Gallery, Big Fork, Montana
Byrne-Getz Gallery, Aspen, Colorado
Canada House Gallery, Banff, Alberta, Canada
Canyon County Originals, Tuscon, Arizona

El Cerro Art, Los Lunas, New Mexico
Simon Charlie Consulting, British Columbia, Canada
Cincinnati Art Museum, Cincinnati, Ohio
Coastal Peoples Fine Arts Gallery, Vancouver, British Columbia, Canada
Coghlan Studio and Gallery, Aldergrove, British Columbia, Canada
Columbine Galleries, Santa Fe, New Mexico
Coming Home, Dodgeville, Wisconsin
Mittie Cooper Gallery, Oklahoma City, Oklahoma
Covered Wagon Gallery, Albuquerque, New Mexico
Dakota Gallery, Boca Raton, Florida
Daybreak Star Arts Center, Discovery Park, Seattle, Washington
Decker/Morris Gallery, Anchorage, Alaska
Deschutes Gallery, Bend, Oregon
Dusty's Gold Gallery, Nome, Alaska
E-pueblo, www.e-pueblo.com
Eagle Aerie Gallery, Vancouver, British Columbia, Canada
Eagle Mountain Fine Art, Jemez, Springs, New Mexico
Eiteljorg Museum of American Indian and Western Art, Indianapolis, Indiana
Elk Ridge Art Company, Golden, Colorado
eSouthwest, Albuquerque, New Mexico
Faru Gallery, St. Louis, Missouri
Faust Gallery, Scottsdale, Arizona
Fenn Galleries, Sante Fe, New Mexico
Firecloud Arts, Pacifica, California
Frye Backroads, Republic, Kansas
Gallup Intertribal Ceremonial State Art Show, Gallup, New Mexico
Gallery of Contemporary and Indigenous Art, Tucson, Arizona
Jill Giller's Native Pots Gallery
Garland's Rugs, Sedona, Arizona
Goldwater's, Scottsdale, Arizona
John Gonzales Pottery, Sante Fe, New Mexico
Grey Dog Trading Company, Tucson, Arizona
Grover/Thurston Gallery, Seattle, Washington
The Hand and the Spirit Crafts Gallery, Scottsdale, Arizona
The Heritage Center, Inc., Pine Ridge, South Dakota
Hoel's Indian Shop, Sedona, Arizona
Horniman Museum and Garden, London, United Kingdom

Frank Howell Gallery, Sante Fe, New Mexico
Hozhani, Naperville, Illinois
Indian Arts and Crafts Association, Albuquerque, New Mexico
Indian Jewelry Center, Sacremento, California
Indian Summer Native American Art, Salt Lake City, Utah
IroqArt, www.iroqart.com
Jamison/Thomas Gallery, Portland, Oregon
Jewels of Clay, Scottsdale, Arizona
Jackson David Co., Durango, Colorado
Fred Jones Jr. Museum of Art, University of Oklahoma, Norma,
    Oklahoma
Kamloops Art Gallery, Kamloops, British Columbia, Canada
Kennedy Indian Art, Bluff, Utah
Kiva Gallery, Gallup, New Mexico
Kleywood Southwest,, An Antonio, Texas
Koshari Gallery, Scottsdale, Arizona
The Legacy, Ltd., Seattle, Washington
Duane Maktima Studio/Gallery, Glorieta, New Mexico
MacLaren/Markowitz Gallery, Boulder, Colorado
Nedra Matteucci Galleries, Sante Fe, New Mexico
Meadowlark Gallery, Billings, Montana
Mesa Verde Pottery, Cortez, Colorado
Modo Gallery, Hudson, New York
Moorefields Gallery, Coeur d'Alene, Idaho
Morning Star Gallery, Sante Fe, New Mexico
Museum of Fine Arts, Boston, Massachusetts
Museum of Man, San Diego, California
Museum of New Mexico Shops, Sante Fe, New Mexico
Museum of Northern Arizona, Flagstaff, Arizona
Nadler's Indian Arts, Scottodale, Arizona
Michael A. Naranjo Gallery and Studio, Espanola, New Mexico
National Museum of the American Indian, New York, New York
Native American Traders, Decatur, Georgia
Native Artists Trading, Isle of Man, United Kingdom
Native Artists United, Thoreau, New Mexico
Native Hands, Sante Fe, New Mexico
Native Online, www.nativeonline.com
Native Pots, Denver, Colorado
Nofchiissey-McHorse Studio, Sante Fe, New Mexico

Nonart Gallery, Tahlequah, Oklahoma
Old Town Gallery, Flagstaff, Arizona
Oneida Nation Museum, Oneida, Wisconsin
Pacific Editions Ltd., Victoria, British Columbia
El Parian de Sante Fe, Sante Fe, New Mexico
PDX Contemporary Art, Portland, Oregon
Penfield Gallery of Indian Arts, Albuquerque, New Mexico
Perry House Galleries, Alexandria, Virginia
Lillian Pitt Gallery, Portland, Oregon
Plainsmen Gallery, Dunedin, Florida
Pueblo Arts, Scottsdale, Arizona
Pueblo Pottery Gallery, San Fidel, New Mexico
Rainmaker Gallery, Bristol, United Kingdom
Reflections of Culture, Fort Atkinson, Wisconsin
Douglas Reynolds Gallery, Vancouver, British Columbia, Canada
Sacred Hoop Trading, Minneapolis, Minnesota
Sante Fe Connections, San Antonio, Texas
Sante Fe Gallery, Madison, Wisconsin
Sante Fe Trails Gallery of Southwestern Art, Sarasota, Florida
Sedona Indian Jewelry, Sedona, California
Sedonawolf, Sedona, Arizona
Sherwoods, Beverly Hills, California
Shidoni Gallery, Tesuque, New Mexico
Silver Bear Jewelry, St. Louis Missouri
Soaring Eagle Gallery, Inc., Albuquerque, New Mexico
Southwest Art Collection, Wheatland, Oklahoma
Southwest and More, Laurence, Kansas
Stone Flower, Detroit, Michigan
Sunshine Studios, Sante Fe, New Mexico
Tanner's Indian Art, Wheatridge, Colorado
To'Baane Fine Art, Winslow, Arizona
Thunderbird Shop, Sante Fe and Tucson, Arizona
University of Alaska Museum Shop, Fairbanks, Alaska
University of Lethbridge Art Gallery, Lethbridge, Alberta, Canada
Twin Rocks Trading Post, Bluff, Utah
Roy Henry Vickers Gallery, Vancouver, British Columbia, Canada
Upstairs Gallery, Manitoba, Canada
Village Goldsmith, Estes Park, Colorado
Vision Quest, Dallas, Texas

White Hills Indian Arts, Camp Verde, Arizona
White Horse Gallery, Boulder, Colorado
White Pelican, Dana Point, California
Wright's Collection of Indian Art, Albuquerque, New Mexico
Zuni Fetishes Direct, Gallup, New Mexico

Index

HOUSE OF COLLECTIBLES
COMPLETE TITLE LIST

THE OFFICIAL PRICE GUIDES TO

American Arts and Crafts, 3rd ed.	0-609-80989-X	$21.95	David Rago
American Patriotic Memorabilia	0-609-81014-6	$16.95	Michael Polak
America's State Quarters	0-609-80770-6	$6.99	David L. Ganz
Collecting Books, 4th ed.	0-609-80769-2	$18.00	Marie Tedford
Collecting Clocks	0-609-80973-3	$19.95	Frederick W. Korz
Collector Knives, 13th ed.	0-676-60189-8	$17.95	C. Houston Price
Collector Plates	0-676-60154-5	$19.95	Harry L. Rinker
Costume Jewelry, 3rd ed.	0-609-80668-8	$17.95	Harrice Simmons Miller
Dinnerware of the 20th Century	0-676-60085-9	$29.95	Harry L. Rinker
Flea Market Prices	0-609-80772-2	$14.95	Harry L. Rinker
Glassware, 3rd ed.	0-676-60188-X	$17.00	Mark Pickvet
Hake's Character Toys, 4th ed.	0-609-80822-2	$35.00	Ted Hake
Hislop's International Guide to Fine Art	0-609-80874-5	$20.00	Duncan Hislop
Military Collectibles	0-676-60052-2	$20.00	Richard Austin
Mint Errors, 6th ed.	0-609-80855-9	$15.00	Alan Herbert
Native American Art	0-609-80966-0	$24.00	Dawn E. Reno
Overstreet Comic Book Grading	0-609-81052-9	$24.00	Robert M. Overstreet
Overstreet Comic Book Price Guide, 33rd ed.	1-4000-4668-8	$25.00	Robert M. Overstreet
Overstreet Indian Arrowheads Price Guide, 8th ed.	0-609-81053-7	$26.00	Robert M. Overstreet
Pottery and Porcelain	0-87637-893-9	$18.00	Harvey Duke
Records, 16th Edition	0-609-80908-3	$25.95	Jerry Osborne
Vintage Fashion and Fabrics	0-609-80813-3	$17.00	Pamela Smith

THE OFFICIAL GUIDES TO

How to Make Money in Coins Right Now	0-609-80746-3	$14.95	Scott A. Travers
The Official Directory to U.S. Flea Markets	0-609-80922-9	$14.00	Kitty Werner
The One-Minute Coin Expert, 4th ed.	0-609-80747-1	$7.99	Scott A. Travers
The Official Stamp Collector's Bible	0-609-80884-2	$22.00	Stephen Datz

THE OFFICIAL BECKETT SPORTS CARDS PRICE GUIDES TO

Baseball Cards 2003, 23rd ed.	0-609-81037-5	$7.99	Dr. James Beckett
Basketball Cards 2004, 13th ed.	1-4000-4863-X	$7.99	Dr. James Beckett
Football Cards 2004, 23rd ed.	1-4000-4864-8	$7.99	Dr. James Beckett

THE OFFICIAL BLACKBOOK PRICE GUIDES TO

U.S. Coins, 42nd ed.	1-4000-4805-2	$7.99	Marc & Tom Hudgeons
U.S. Paper Money, 36th ed.	1-4000-4806-0	$6.99	Marc & Tom Hudgeons
U.S. Postage Stamps, 26th ed.	1-4000-4807-9	$8.99	Marc & Tom Hudgeons
World Coins, 7th ed.	1-4000-4808-7	$7.99	Marc & Tom Hudgeons

AVAILABLE AT BOOKSTORES EVERYWHERE!